WHILE GOD IS MARCHING ON

WHILE GOD IS MARCHING ON
The Religious World of Civil War Soldiers

Steven E. Woodworth

UNIVERSITY PRESS OF KANSAS

© 2001 by the University Press of Kansas

Published by the University Press of Kansas (Lawrence, Kansas 66049), which was
organized by the Kansas Board of Regents and is operated and funded by Emporia
State University, Fort Hays State University, Kansas State University, Pittsburg State
University, the University of Kansas, and Wichita State University.

Library of Congress Cataloging-in-Publication Data

Woodworth, Steven E.
    While God is marching on : the religious world of Civil War soldiers /
Steven E. Woodworth.
        p. cm. — (Modern war studies)
    Includes bibliographical references and index.
    ISBN 0-7006-1099-5 (cloth: alk. paper) ISBN 0-7006-1297-1 (pbk: alk. paper)
        1. United States—History—Civil War, 1861–1865—Religious aspects.
    2. Soldiers—Religious life—United States—History—19th century.
    3. War—Religious aspects—Christianity—History—19th century.
    I. Title. II. Series.
    E635.W75 2001
    973.7'78—dc21   2001001123

British Library Cataloguing in Publication Data is available.

Printed in the United States of America
10 9 8 7 6 5 4

AGAIN, FOR LEAH
To God alone be the glory.

CONTENTS

PREFACE

In the immensely popular and successful 1990 PBS documentary series on the Civil War, the television audience frequently heard quotes by Civil War soldier Elisha Hunt Rhodes. None of those statements gave any hint that Rhodes was a devout man. Neither his religion nor that of the other soldiers seemed to matter in that series or in most other presentations of the war. The marginalized role to which religion has been relegated in modern America has made the vital faith of past generations almost invisible to students of history. Even in a field as widely studied as the Civil War, religion has been the subject of relatively few books.

This is a book about the religious world of Civil War soldiers. Readers should be advised what is meant by that description and intended in this book. First of all, this is not an encyclopedia of unusual religious groups or practices. Rather, this book is concerned with the mainstream religion of the overwhelming majority of Civil War soldiers who took any interest in religious matters. That religion happens to have been Protestant Christianity. There were, of course, a fair number of Catholics, some Jews, and even a few avowed atheists in the ranks, but their numbers together constituted a small minority of the soldiers, and their beliefs and practices play little role in these pages.

Second, this is a book about the religious world of *the soldiers*. That means several things. Although I did not exclude officers from consideration, I emphasized the writings of the common soldiers. Officers' comments, when used, count for no more than those of any other individual soldier. In short, in this study, rank did not matter.

This emphasis on the soldiers also means that I did not go out of my way to find the papers of chaplains or even particularly religious soldiers. Indeed, I tried to hold down the number of chaplains' comments in favor of the words of the common soldiers themselves. This is not because I think the chaplains were dishonest, but rather because their view of the religious state of the army would necessarily be skewed. Chaplains' views appear in this book, but only alongside larger numbers of ordinary soldiers' comments. I devoted one chapter specifically to the chaplains and their relationship with the soldiers but otherwise tried to keep the focus on the common soldiers. Besides, there is a good modern book on Union chaplains.[1]

Casting my research net for all soldiers, rather than only those that the various research indexes or card catalogs identified as particularly religious, made my job more difficult. For one thing, it meant reading the papers of a number of soldiers who had little if anything to say that shed any light on my subject. Still, I wanted to get an overall view of what the bulk of the soldiers were thinking and writing, and it was worth the extra work.

Civilians enter into this work tangentially, because they were part of the religious world the soldiers inhabited. The soldiers themselves, however, remain at center stage. This is a matter of expedience in two ways. First, a book about the religious world of everybody during the Civil War would simply be too big. Second, much more evidence exists on the soldiers' views than on those of the folks back home. This is because letters from the soldiers to their families and friends survived in vastly larger numbers than did letters traveling the other way.

The same principles apply even more strongly to the coverage of theologians, denominational leaders, and members of the civilian clergy generally. They make their appearances in these pages, but this book is not primarily about them. Readers can and should look elsewhere for a primary emphasis on such topics as the wartime teachings of the Northern Protestant clergy or their Southern counterparts.

My goal was to let the soldiers' own thoughts and beliefs, as expressed in their diaries, letters, and (occasionally) reminiscences, set the tone and agenda of this book. By this I do not mean to make any absurd claims about being unbiased. No one is. Rather, I mean that if the soldiers had much to say about a topic, then I included much about it in this book. If the soldiers did not address a topic, I did not either. I did my best to avoid the sort of distortion that would make the Civil War soldiers into late-twentieth-century or early-twenty-first-century postmodernists dressed up in blue and gray uniforms.

The purpose of this book is to help readers understand better the Civil War soldiers and their motivations, the sectional conflict, and the shape of American society and culture in the nineteenth century. Along with all this—and part of it—comes an understanding of the vital religious component of the American tradition, a component that was a constant of American life throughout most of the nation's first two centuries and is clearly revealed in the voluminous writings of the Civil War soldiers.

Although I used far less than half of the source material I gathered for this book, I am aware that I reproduced more examples, anecdotes, and quotations than many professional historians would have in writing a book of this sort. Without implying any criticism of those who would do things differently, I believe that the relatively large amount of concrete examples makes this book more vivid, colorful, interesting, and, I hope, persuasive.

I take pleasure in expressing my thanks to the many persons who helped me with this project. First of all, my friends and colleagues Profs. Mark Grimsley and Brooks D. Simpson, by whose suggestion I undertook the research and writing of this book. Brooks also read the manuscript and offered helpful advice, as did Prof. James M. McPherson. The final decisions, however, were my own, and they cannot be blamed for any problems that remain.

It was a pleasure to work with the always kind and helpful staff of the United States Army Military History Institute archives: Dr. Richard Sommers, David Keogh, Pamela Cheney, and James Baughman. Likewise, Nan Card of the Rutherford B. Hayes Center in Fremont, Ohio, went out of her way to help me. These people distinguished themselves

among the many friendly and helpful staff members of the various institutions at which I did research.

James Ogden, chief Park Service historian at the Chickamauga battlefield, drew my attention to the enormously useful Alfred Tyler Fielder
diary. David Slay was immensely helpful in finding all manner of valuable materials. Stewart Bennett generously shared with me his large trove
of Civil War soldier materials. Prof. Bertram Wyatt-Brown was kind
enough to provide me with a copy of a paper he had written for a conference session.

For hospitality when research travel took me to far-flung corners of
the country, I am deeply grateful to Mr. and Mrs. Stanley Bunke, Rev.
and Mrs. Patrick Davis, Mr. and Mrs. David Miller, Dr. and Mrs. Stephen
Miller, and Mr. and Mrs. Harold Lauer.

In addition, I owe a debt of gratitude to those who took a particular interest in the project and supported me from time to time during its completion with their encouragement and advice. They include John Conaway,
Thomas Duncan, Gene Hood, Ronald Johnson, Melvin Swanson, and
Roger Swanson.

And then there is Leah. Who can adequately praise a wife who, while
pregnant, lived whole weeks of the summer in a tent at campgrounds
conveniently located near various manuscript repositories and spent her
days entertaining five children on the playground, wading in the creek,
and the like while her husband disappeared into the archives every morning and reappeared in the evening, having spent the day reading dead
people's mail? For this alone she deserves the most effusive praise, and it
is but a small part, a single episode, in her constant and inestimable support and help. I am under renewed and happy obligation to express my
most profound gratitude. "Her price is far above rubies."

I

THE RELIGIOUS HERITAGE AND BELIEFS
OF THE CIVIL WAR SOLDIERS

1

"IN SUCH A COUNTRY AS THIS"
Christianity in America Before the Civil War

The sun shone pale through a thin layer of clouds on a mild fall day in the pretty little town of Holly Springs, Mississippi. From the dignified building of the town's Episcopal church came the sound of organ music and a choir singing hymns. It was Sunday morning, November 30, 1862, and many of Holly Springs' citizens were at worship, as was their custom. Not so customary this Sunday morning was the column of dark-clad figures that emerged from the haze at the far end of the high road that led through town, Union soldiers passing through this Confederate village as part of operations that neither they nor the townspeople understood.

They swung down the main street and past the Episcopal place of worship, colors flying, fifes and drums playing a rousing martial air to the beat of hundreds of boots thudding rhythmically onto the packed dirt of the street—a strange clash of musical messages as the jaunty notes of the fifes mixed with the stately tones of the organ and choir within the church. In his place at the head of his company in the column of marching men, Capt. Luther H. Cowan of the Forty-fifth Illinois was struck by the contrast. Far from resenting the interference with his unit's martial display, however, Cowan thought it "quite nice" to hear the sounds of worship. It reminded him of Sunday mornings in his own home in Warren, Illinois. The Americans, an overwhelmingly religious people, were at war with each other, but the religion they shared in common was still with them—still vital to them—a discordant note in the midst of civil strife.[1]

The contrast and seeming incongruity of religious pursuits amid the scenes of warfare struck Confederate staff officer Charles Minor Blackford as he attended a religious service in a church building near the camps of the Army of Northern Virginia on Sunday, June 14, 1863. The preacher of the hour was "the Rev. General Pendleton." William Nelson Pendleton had graduated from the United States Military Academy in 1830 and after three years' service left the army for a career as an Episcopal minister. Like a number of ministers both Northern and Southern, Pendleton joined the rush to arms in 1861, and by the time Blackford attended his preaching, he was a brigadier general and Robert E. Lee's chief of artillery. Blackford found that Pendleton's two callings were "curiously mixed in his apparel." As a good Episcopal high-church man, Pendleton wore a clerical robe over his Confederate general's uniform, and Blackford noticed that "the gown covered up his uniform entirely except for the wreath and stars of a general on his collar which peeped out to mildly protest against too much 'peace on earth' and the boots and spurs clanked around the chancel with but little sympathy with the doctrine of 'good will towards men.'" Blackford was not sure he approved of such a mixture, yet Pendleton's case personified, to some extent, the situation of a very devout nation at war.[2]

That situation, along with the perplexing fact that both warring sides held to the same religion, was illustrated even more starkly at about the same time and half a continent away from Blackford's Virginia worship service. On May 16, 1863, Ulysses S. Grant's Union army met John C. Pemberton's Confederates in the fierce battle of Champion's Hill, Mississippi. The fighting ended late in the day with the beaten Rebels in full retreat toward their fortress at Vicksburg, while the victorious Federals remained in control of the field. Some of the victors were famished, having scarcely eaten in two days of hard marching and fighting. Two years of war had left little squeamishness in these soldiers, and one of them, Ira Blanchard of the Twentieth Illinois, sat down beside the corpse of one of his fallen foes, an erstwhile Confederate soldier who would definitely have no further use for the corn bread and beef that filled his haversack. Blanchard helped himself and "made a sumptuous meal."

His hunger assuaged, he then became curious about the fallen Southerner who had become his unwitting benefactor. He poked around in the dead man's pockets and found a copy of the New Testament. Blanchard was not an exceptionally religious man, but like most Civil War soldiers, he had a strong interest in the Bible and a voracious appetite for whatever reading material he could lay his hands on. Still seated there beside the stiffening corpse, he began to devour the words of Scripture as he had the corn bread and beef. The irony that he and his now-dead foe read the same Bible and prayed to the same God was apparently lost on him until he came to a passage that said, "If thine enemy hunger, give him to eat," and he thought that the dead Confederate had now unwittingly done so, "if never before in all his life."[3]

Abraham Lincoln was not a typical American in his religious beliefs, but he perceived clearly the almost excruciating irony that the two contending sides slaughtering each other on the battlefields professed to have the same ultimate allegiance in adherence to the same God. "Each party claims to act in accordance with the will of God," he mused in September 1862. "Both may be, and one must be, wrong. God cannot be for and against the same thing at the same time. In the present civil war it is quite possible that God's purpose is something different from the purpose of either party." It was something to think about, and Lincoln did. He was not alone in his musing.[4]

A Union soldier, taken prisoner and then exchanged in the fall of 1862, admitted to being deeply disturbed by the fact that the Rebels, whom he had seen close up while a prisoner, appeared to be devout adherents of the same faith he held. How could they be that way and espouse the cause they did? Yet they seemed so sincere. To a fellow Northerner he explained that "he met with nothing so discouraging as the evident sincerity of those he was among in their prayers."[5]

About a year later, the fact of the joint religious interest pervading both sides was brought home forcibly for Lt. Chesley Mosman of the Fifty-ninth Illinois. On September 19 and 20, 1863, Union and Confederate forces fought the bloody battle of Chickamauga in northwestern Georgia, and the defeated Federals took refuge in fortified lines around the city of Chattanooga,

Tennessee. One evening a week after the battle, as the two armies faced each other in uneasy anticipation of a possible renewal of combat, Mosman noticed a curious fact. From a short distance away, inside the Union lines, he could hear a preacher addressing an eager congregation of Union soldiers. Yet at the same time, a distant voice reached his ears from the other direction. There was preaching in the Rebel lines as well, and for some time Mosman listened to two sermons, preached from the same Bible, in two hostile camps arrayed in arms against each other.[6]

It was far from the first time such a situation had occurred. There had been plenty of wars of religion in Europe over the centuries in which both sides claimed the religion of Jesus Christ, but few conflicts saw such religious similarity between the combatants as that which existed between North and South in this great fiery trial of the American Republic. The differences were few but ultimately profound, the common ground immense, and this pungent contrast struck the likes of Lincoln and Mosman. Meanwhile, the prevalence of religious concerns and, even more important, the predominance of a Christian worldview made such issues applicable to much of what was thought and said and done during the conflict. Understanding the war and its participants must include understanding the religious concerns that were central to so many of their lives.

Religion had always been important in the life of America. Pilgrims and Puritans had come to New England in the seventeenth century for overtly religious purposes, to create on those cold and rocky shores a "model of Christian charity" and a "city set upon a hill," as Massachusetts's first governor, John Winthrop, had put it. New England would be an example to the rest of the world of how a godly society should work and how God would bless a society that honored Him. The Puritan colonies did prosper, and though the fires of their religious fervor waned in the late seventeenth and early eighteenth centuries, they were rekindled in the wave of revivals known as the Great Awakening and were burning bright by the time of the American Revolution.

Pennsylvania had religious roots as well, in the offshoot Quaker sect, and, after a fashion, it had its own mission to fulfill, in William Penn's vision of the good society. Many others migrated to Pennsylvania from other parts of Europe; some of them were German Protestant refugees from religious persecution, a group also represented in several other colonies. Likewise there were Scots-Irish Presbyterians in various parts of North America.

Some colonies were born of primarily secular motives and generally fared less well. From the "mixed multitude" of colonial New York to the rough days in early Virginia, where life was "nasty, brutish, and short," the pursuit of purely secular happiness in colonial America proved a rough road to travel. James Oglethorpe's Enlightenment experiment in social engineering in Georgia became the most spectacular failure of all. Still, even these colonies had their nominal Anglican establishment, their smattering of German Protestant and French Huguenot immigrants, and, by the end of the colonial period, the beginnings of an evangelical movement, particularly Baptists, among their lower classes.

The Revolution and Founding Era would become known, in the twentieth century, as times of dominance of the Enlightenment, with its rationalism and Deism, but that myth was but weakly supported by historical fact. The Enlightenment never held the sway in America that it did in Europe, and the peak of its influence on this side of the Atlantic was still a decade away when the United States Constitution was written by a collection of fifty-five men, fifty-two of whom were members in good standing of orthodox Christian denominations. Of the three nominal Deists present, one, Benjamin Franklin, took the very un-Deistic step of recommending that the convention's sessions be opened with prayer.[7]

Christianity retained an even greater influence among the common people of America. The New England troops, who were first in the fight against British tyranny, sang,

> Let tyrants shake their iron rods
> And slavery clank its galling chains.
> We fear them not; we trust in God.
> New England's God forever reigns.

The song later became an anthem of the Continental army.[8]

The last decade of the eighteenth century and the first of the nineteenth brought the high tide of Deism's influence in the United States.

Such as it was, it was strong enough to lead some religious leaders to fear, and Thomas Jefferson to hope, that the passage of another generation would see Deism and Unitarianism overrun the land. Those who thought so, however, reckoned without the widespread series of revivals known to history as the Second Great Awakening. Beginning with the new century and continuing all the way to the Civil War and beyond, the great revivals restored the previously fading religious zeal of the northeastern states and spread Christianity to the previously indifferent South as well as to the new, all-but-heathen western states of Kentucky, Tennessee, Indiana, and Illinois. The forms, methods, assumptions, and terminology of the Second Great Awakening provided the framework and trappings for the religious beliefs and practices of the Civil War soldiers.

One of the more noticeable features of the great wave of revivals during the first half of the nineteenth century was the camp meeting. The form originated as a practical means by which isolated settlers in frontier Kentucky could assemble to attend weeklong series of religious meetings. With its multiple services each day, from predawn prayer meeting to evening preaching, the camp meeting was an intense religious experience that came to be widely used even in settled farming regions, particularly by the Methodists. Although the massive Cane Ridge camp meeting in 1801 was the most famous, its excesses of noise and frantic emotion were at best a caricature of the exuberant, heartfelt worship that characterized the great revivals, both in camp meetings and at more ordinary services.[9]

During the 1850s, future Confederate soldier David Holt attended camp meetings at "Bethel Campground" as a boy in his native Wilkinson County, Mississippi. By that time, camp meetings and their infrastructures had become established fixtures. "The buildings," Holt recalled years later, "though called tents, were in reality large and commodious houses." Everyone—slaves excluded, of course—was welcome to come and board there during the meetings, with neither invitation nor previous acquaintance being necessary. "One had only to be white and sober." The meeting lasted two weeks each summer. Food was bountiful and freely provided, in appropriate forms for both man and horse, by the generosity of local sponsors. "No charge was made for anything at these campgrounds." One large "tent" that Holt remembered had two stories, the upper providing Spartan bunk space for up to 100 men. The ladies lodged in more comfortable quarters below; they had mattresses.[10]

In towns and cities where large numbers of persons lived near enough to attend services and still sleep in their own homes at night—or in rural districts where it seemed inexpedient to mount a major logistical effort to host a camp meeting—an alternative was the "protracted meeting." This involved preaching services each evening for anywhere from one to six weeks or even longer. In rural districts, such meetings were generally limited to the relatively slack period in the agricultural work cycle between the time crops were "laid by" (no longer required cultivation) and the frantic rush of harvest.

A protracted meeting could be a purely local production, with preaching by an area minister, or it could feature a nationally known figure such as Charles Grandison Finney, the greatest preacher of the era. Conversions could be numerous and might significantly change the culture of a locality, as new converts forsook their previous sinful ways and the businesses, such as saloons, that had catered to them. Like camp meetings, protracted meetings were exuberant outlets for the religious expression of a highly emotional era. This was especially true in rural areas, where believers who were thrilled with the inward assurance of salvation and close personal communion with God might shout praises to Him in their ecstasy.

Civil War soldier Julius Birney Work noted in his diary a protracted meeting he attended in January and February 1863 while back home in Ohio recovering from an illness he had contracted in camp. Aside from a nightly commentary on who had been converted, his diary also included a similar notation about who had "shouted." "Mrs. Hines, Liza Kees, Harriet McCollough, Louisia McCollough, Henry Fisher all shouted Glory." Or "there was a general shout in camp"—the latter phrase being a figure of speech, since they were not in camp at all but in their ordinary place of worship. And the figurative reference was to the camp of the Israelites in the Old Testament, rather than to a camp meeting.

Work also mentioned other common aspects of the revivals of the early nineteenth century. "Mourners" were unconverted persons who began to feel sorrowful for their sins and to seek conversion. They might attend the meetings night after night with the openly professed purpose of seeking to become Christians, and they might sit at a special "mourners' bench," a pew reserved for such persons near the front of the building. There they could hear the sermon without distraction and could more easily receive whatever counseling or exhortation the ministers might be able to give them. Thus Work noted in his diary that "Dunlavey Long was down at the mourners bench." After several nights of this, a mourner might finally be converted, feeling the assurance that he was at last received into God's forgiveness. Thus Work made such notations as, "Harriet McCollough got through converted."[11]

Persons who mourned over their sin and were dramatically converted were common features of many revivals of the time, but not all religious meetings during that era were as noisy as the ones Work attended. Indeed, shouting may have been more the exception than the rule. Staid Presbyterians or Episcopalians would look with disdain upon the more vocal style of worship among their Methodist or Baptist neighbors, and even within a denomination such as the Methodists, differences might be equally pronounced. Illinois Methodist circuit rider (itinerant preacher) Peter Cartwright was dubious regarding the spiritual fervor of his coreligionists back east in Philadelphia, and they would have harbored similar doubts about the good sense of Cartwright and the rest of the more vocal Methodists of rural and western areas.

The majority of religious meetings attended by nineteenth-century Christians were neither camp meetings nor protracted meetings but simply the weekly services of their local churches. The most important of these by far was the Sunday morning service, common to Christian churches since apostolic times. Some churches also held a second preaching service or prayer meeting on Sunday evening, as well as a prayer meeting one evening per week. Additionally, many communities had Sunday schools for the religious instruction of children. A Sunday school might be set up as a cooperative venture by several local churches or might be the creature of a single church, especially that of the Methodists, who were particularly active in the Sunday school movement.[12]

Before he became old enough to enlist in the Union army, John T. McMahon wrote about his religious activities as a devout member of a Methodist church in upstate New York during 1861 and 1862. On one particular Sunday in October 1861, he attended morning worship at the church in the village, then an afternoon preaching service at a nearby Methodist college. "In the evening," he recorded, "we had a good prayer meeting at the church." McMahon also attended prayer meetings on Thursday evenings and, whenever possible, "class meetings" on Tuesdays. The class meeting was a Methodist institution, a closed meeting for members only in which a dozen or so regular participants both encouraged one another and held one another to strict accountability in their godly behavior and spiritual growth.[13]

Religious worship was by no means limited to the church or confined within the walls of houses of worship. "Family prayers," held each evening in each Christian home, were as important to nineteenth-century Christians as any of the corporate worship services of the church. The practice of family worship ran the gamut, from devout Methodists like McMahon to relatively permissive Episcopalians like Holt. Vermont soldier Wilbur Fisk noted that reading a chapter of the Bible and praying together had been his family's "custom from time immemorial." Deep in the South, not far from Atlanta, James A. Connolly and other Union officers found themselves quartered with a Southern family, in whose house the Army of the Cumberland's headquarters was located. That evening, Connolly and other staff officers joined the family in their regular evening prayers, including the singing of hymns.[14]

The growing breadth and intensity of Christian belief during the first half of the nineteenth century fueled powerful efforts to alleviate some of the ills of society and reform some of its abuses. Christian charitable organizations reached out to the urban poor, as well as to those (especially women) who had found America's growing cities not only centers of economic opportunity but also vortices of vice. Groups of Christians in large cities endeavored to extend to such persons not only an offer of escape from their deplorable conditions but also the good news of reconciliation to God through Jesus Christ.[15]

Christians also took an active role in such reforms as the temperance movement, and over the first half of the century, they succeeded by means of both "moral suasion" and government restriction in significantly reducing the nation's per capita consumption of hard liquor. Another target of Christian-sponsored reform movements was combating prostitution and the attendant newly sprung practice of abortion.[16]

Yet by far the most controversial reform movement driven by the intense Christianity of that half century was the antislavery movement, the most virulent form of which was abolitionism. Christians predominated among the rank and file of the abolitionist movement, and their ways of thinking prevailed to a certain extent even among those members of the movement who rejected orthodox Christianity. To Christian abolitionists, slavery was not just an abstract social problem; it was a sin. Unitarian and other non-Christian members of the movement, who, as a general rule, had little use for the concept of sin, were quick to seize upon it in this case. Sin was not a matter for compromise, and its guilt would logically attach to any who became complicit in slavery by consenting to laws that tolerated what laws ought not to tolerate: the wronging of one's fellow man.[17] Abraham Lincoln, himself no Christian, demonstrated the prevalence of the Christian abolitionist argument in applying the teaching of Christ directly to the issue of slavery: "As I would not be a slave," Lincoln said, "so I would not be a master."

Northern Christians in their thousands plunged zealously into the abolitionist movement, forming the American Anti-slavery Society in 1833. Charles Finney himself took a prominent part in supporting the cause. Theodore Dwight Weld, who was converted at one of Finney's revival meetings, became a firebrand leader in the movement and by the mid-1830s was preaching the immediate elimination of slavery. When nearly the entire student body of Cincinnati's Lane Theological Seminary embraced Weld's message, the administration expelled them all—institutional religious leaders were as averse to boat rocking then as they had been in Christ's own day. Undeterred, Weld led the dismissed students in creating a new institution, Oberlin College, where Finney was honored, abolitionism preached, and the Fugitive Slave Law flouted by men and women bound to obey God rather than man.[18]

Abolitionists, Christians and the rest, did not initially see government power as the answer to the slavery problem. Rather, they hoped to use moral suasion to convince slaveholders to turn from their sin, just as thousands of Americans were renouncing various vices under the influence of the revivals sweeping the nation. They would preach against the sin of slavery as they and others had been preaching against drunkenness, profanity, sexual immorality, and sabbath breaking, and sinners would either convert or at least be shamed into forsaking overtly public debaucheries.

It was not to be. Unlike most other sins, slavery had a coherent and influential constituency of persons who did not blush to own its cause. Well might the abolitionists lay aside all thought of using government to accomplish their good ends; the power of government was soon arrayed against them at the behest of the champions of slavery. Likewise against them was the wrath of racist mobs. Even in the North, an abolitionist speaker risked abuse ranging from pelting with rotten produce to arrest by the authorities. In 1835 Rev. George Storrs was arrested during a religious meeting in Northfield, New Hampshire, because he had preached against the sin of slavery. The following year the sheriff of Pittsfield, New Hampshire, dragged the same preacher out of the pulpit for the same offense. Meanwhile, any abolitionist preacher who went south with his message might as well hope to be arrested and shipped north by the authorities before he met a gruesome death at the hands of a mob. Calling slavery a sin was condemned as an infringement of slaveholders' right to their "property," and besides, the pro-slavery lobby complained, people who condemned slavery as wrong might thereby inspire others, in this case the slaves, to commit acts of violence against slaveholders.[19]

The slave power mobilized the U.S. government as well, and it responded by banning abolitionist literature from the mails. Congress announced that it would not even go through the motions of receiving petitions for the curtailment of slavery in such federally governed jurisdictions as the District of Columbia. Moral suasion failed, perhaps in part because it found no resonance in slaveholders and their allies, but also because pro-slavery forces ensured that it was given no chance to succeed. Not until long after the defenders of slavery had successfully marshaled the power of government against them did abolitionists begin to advocate that government's power be used to end slavery.

Through it all, Christian abolitionists carried on with the fortitude that Christians have often shown in the face of persecution. However, as Christians in previous centuries had often learned, those in the abolitionist movement soon discovered that danger lurked within as well as without. The desire for even the most righteous reforms could become a monster within that would devour the spiritual life of its adherent if allowed to usurp the heart's first allegiance due rightly to God alone.

Finney saw the danger and wrote to Weld about it in 1836. "Abolitionism has drunk up the spirit of some of the most efficient moral men and is fast doing so to the rest," Finney warned, "and many of our abolition brethren seem satisfied with nothing less than this. This I have been trying to resist from the beginning." Finney feared that such ruthless drive for abolition for its own sake rather than for the sake of God and His glory would result not in a happy ending for the slaves and the country but rather in a civil war "that will roll a wave of blood over the land." The only answer, he believed, was to emphasize salvation—the reconciling of an individual human being to God, with all that that entails—with abolition as one of the natural results to follow. Abolition, Finney insisted, should be "an appendage of a general revival of religion."[20]

Yet the problem was even more complicated than Finney perceived. He had been true to historic biblical Christianity in teaching that salvation was to be demonstrated in a changed life. The Christian must be not only pure in his personal life but also upright in his public positions. As Finney put it, "The church must take right ground in regards to politics. . . . Politics are a part of a religion in such a country as this, and Christians must do their duty to their country as a part of their duty to God."[21] In the 1830s that duty included taking a stand against slavery. Religious fervor, love for God, would initially provide a man or woman's antislavery zeal, but for some Christians, abolitionism had soon "drunk up the spirit," supplanting love of God as the soul's prime mover. Then, instead of antislavery being a part of one's Christian witness, Christianity became a useful (or perhaps not necessarily so useful) tool for antislavery agitation.

Finney perceived this and stressed that salvation must remain the central focus of Christianity, with antislavery, like all good works, being the fruit that sprang from the converted life. He urged abolitionists like Weld to back away from the issue, emphasizing salvation instead and realizing that Southerners could not be expected to practice righteousness in this area until their hearts were changed. He had an excellent point but overlooked two equally good ones: First, Southerners had by this time developed a domesticated version of Christianity that was tolerant if not approving of slavery, and that Southern brand of the faith served as an inoculant against the truth Finney preached. Second, despite the fact that Southerners were not likely to do right in the matter of slavery until their hearts were made right by God's grace, the duty of the Christian who *did* see the truth about slavery was still to give his voice and his influence— including his political power, if any—in the cause of righteousness, including abolitionism.

It was a narrow path that Christian abolitionists had to walk, with spiritual pitfalls on either side. Some strayed. By the early 1840s, Weld himself had come to the point of abandoning his faith in Christ. Then, ironically but perhaps not surprisingly, he abandoned abolitionism as well, along with all hope of reforming society. Meanwhile, the abolitionist movement itself had split into two wings. One, containing by one estimate about seven-eighths of the adherents of the movement, continued to hold to orthodox Christian doctrine.[22] The other faction, a small but noisy minority, abandoned Christianity and went off in the train of such leaders as the Unitarian William Lloyd Garrison, sounding a veritable cacophony of calls for every reform that struck their fancy, from abolitionism to pacifism to women's rights and anarchy.[23] And all the while, substantial portions of the professing church in the North either took no role in abolition or actively opposed it.

By contrast, the church in the South enjoyed great unanimity on the subjects of slavery and abolitionism: the former was ordained by God, and the latter was of the Devil. Up until the beginning of the nineteenth century, the South had been distinctly less Christian influenced than the North, but in the great revivals of that century it was rapidly catching up. As was the case north of the Mason-Dixon line, the Presbyterians formed the third largest denomination, the Baptists the second, and the Methodists the largest. However, the Baptists in the South ran a much closer second to the Methodists than was the case in the North. Part of the reason for this difference was Methodism's early opposition to slavery. Its founder, John Wesley, was steadfastly opposed to the practice, and his followers took their lead from him in this as in other matters, believing slavery to be contrary to Scripture. By the mid-1830s, their influence in Britain had helped to eliminate slavery within the British Empire. In the American South, however, antislavery views were not popular, and neither was a denomination that held to them. Not until Southern Methodist leaders consciously decided to lay aside the slavery issue did the denomination begin to experience the pattern of growth there that it was already enjoying in the North.

Other denominations in the South had scarcely raised a voice against slavery in the first place. Slavery had always been an important issue in the South, but as slave-grown cotton brought a river of gold flowing into the region and growing moral awareness elsewhere came increasingly to focus on the South as the last bastion of chattel slavery, vocal support of what John C. Calhoun called the "peculiar institution" became the shibboleth of acceptance in any Southern state.

Southern Christians had to find ways of dealing with the implied contradiction between the religion of Jesus Christ and the practice of doing to others what white Southerners claimed they would rather die than endure themselves. They started with an emphatic assertion that slavery was endorsed by the Bible. On this point, scholars have frequently asserted that the Southerners' problem was in taking the Bible literally, but that was beside the point.[24] The North, after all, contained at least as many people who took the Holy Scriptures at their word, among them the vast majority of abolitionists. The Southern defense of slavery depended not so much on a literal interpretation of Scripture as on a superficial one.[25] Southern Christians endeavored to claim a kinship between American chattel slavery and the very different bond service of the Old Testament, and they construed the New Testament's admonitions against slave revolt and resistance as endorsements of the institution. Finally, the Bible never actually forbade Christians to own slaves, at least not as Southerners read it.[26]

Even once that claim was made—and repeated frequently, loudly, and stridently—Southern Christians still had a problem. While they defended slavery on the basis that, as they argued, the Bible included no explicit prohibition of it, they were confronted on all sides with the reality that many practical aspects of slavery constituted blatant violations of the spirit and letter of Scripture. American slavery was blatantly racial, but the Bible gave no basis whatsoever for classifying mankind into separate "races."[27] Additionally, in day-to-day terms, slave marriages had no standing in law, and slave families could be broken up by being sold at the whim of their master or the requirements of his creditors. In most jurisdictions it was illegal to teach slaves to read. This was to prevent them from reading any abolitionist literature that might reach their hands, but it also prevented them from reading the Bible, which Protestant Christianity stressed that every believer should do. Then too, little spoken of but present nonetheless, there was the use wicked slaveholders could and sometimes did make of their power over slave women.

In the face of this clear moral and spiritual problem within their society, what were Southern Christians to do? In fact, they found two ways of attempting to cope with this difficulty. The first was a retreat into wholesale pietism. Many Southern Christians, led by Presbyterian minister James Henley Thornwell of South Carolina, asserted that such spiritual problems in society were none of the church's business. Thornwell became the author of what was known as "the doctrine of the spirituality of the church." According to his teaching, the church should have no interest at all in the affairs of this world but only in those of the next. The church's sole purpose was to present the way of salvation so that men and women who accepted it could be assured of a future in heaven when this life was over, but nothing that went on in the present world was an appropriate subject for its concern. In short, the church should have nothing to say about slavery or anything else in society.[28]

Yet this was so contrary to the whole spirit of Christianity that many Southerners found it hard to hew to this line on issues other than slavery. During the 1850s, Georgia clergyman Augustus Baldwin Longstreet denounced the short-lived American (or Know-Nothing) Party on the grounds that its platform was immoral and therefore a fit subject for a preacher's public condemnation—unlike slavery, of which Longstreet was a vigorous defender. Other Southern Christians took an opposite view of the matter and endorsed the party, also for avowedly religious reasons. Longstreet and others had to fend off charges that they were engaging in "political preaching"—a grave offense in Southern thinking, since if it were accepted that preachers should denounce sin in society, the obvious next question would be why Southern preachers did not denounce the sins involved in the slave system. Still, some Southern Christians did venture so far as to lend their support to the temperance movement. The church in the South was not as heavily engaged in reform as was the church in the rest of the country, but neither was it as committed to the concept of the "spirituality of the church," as it sometimes claimed.[29]

Alternatively, those Southern Christians who were unwilling to take such an ostrichlike approach to society or to concede that the Gospel of Jesus Christ had no implications at all for the present life or for current relations between human beings might take a different position. Equally unwilling to concede the possibility that slavery might be wrong, these Christians instead called for Southern society to repent not of the institution but of its abuse. They called on the South to reform the practices of slavery. Specifically, they wanted laws changed so as to give legal validity to slave marriages, to prohibit the separation of slave families, and perhaps even to forbid the sale of slaves. Most of all, they wanted the elimination of laws that forbade teaching a slave to read. One Mississippian pointed out in 1859 that if Protestant Southerners did not permit slaves to read the Bible, they would render themselves hypocritical in their frequent criticisms of Roman Catholicism for withholding the Scriptures from the common people.[30]

Yet the message of reformed slavery met with fierce opposition in the South, and for good reason. As seen by most other Southerners and even a few of those who espoused it, this message contained the death warrant of the peculiar institution. Southerners might justify slavery on the basis of the Old Testament's Mosaic law, yet applying the restrictions of the law of Moses to American slavery would have demonstrated that it was a far cry from anything God had allowed to the ancient Israelites. And although Southerners might take comfort in pointing out that Jesus Christ had never forbidden slavery by name, they would find far less comfort in discovering, as they would if they endeavored to bring slavery into conformity with His teachings, that the things He did forbid made the practice of chattel slavery impossible. A Northerner, pastor Rufus Clark of New Hampshire, observed as much when he said, "Were the Mosaic system to be applied to American slavery, it would be, by the operation of those laws, very soon abolished."[31]

Others closer to home recognized the same thing. In May 1840, George F. Simmons preached two sermons on slavery in the church he pastored in Mobile, Alabama. He called for far-reaching reform of slavery, pointing out that the Mosaic law made no allowance for the sale of bond servants and that such could "belong" to their masters only in the sense that members of a family might be said to belong to each other. American slavery, Simmons asserted, should be brought into conformity with this biblical pattern, a change that would transform its very nature. "Thus," Simmons concluded, "will Christianity eat the heart of Slavery even while slavery continues." But most Southerners were not eager to hear this truth, much less see the heart eaten out of their peculiar institution, and Simmons left town hurriedly just ahead of a lynch mob.[32]

His case was not an isolated one. Georgia Methodist minister James O. A. Clark warned that a man in his position must be "prudent & cautious" when preaching on the subject of slavery, lest "a single false step" should "greatly endanger" his "usefulness." When Methodist presiding elder Josiah Lewis, a Georgia native, preached against masters who failed to provide adequate clothing for their slaves, he received messages threatening more than just his "usefulness." Many ministers decided that prudence and caution dictated keeping entirely silent on the issue.[33]

Thus calls for the reform of slavery went unanswered in policy. To be sure, some slave owners flouted the law and taught their slaves to read so that the latter could study the Scriptures on their own, and quite a number of slaveholders were apparently moved by religious considerations to treat their bondmen more kindly. Also, Christian leaders of various denominations in the South were vocal and steadfast in denouncing the claims of secular slavery advocates that black people had a separate origin from whites and were a separate species—in fact, no more than animals. In contradiction of the so-called scientific racists, Southern religious leaders insisted that blacks and whites were fellow humans and that blacks might one day, somewhere in the distant, unforeseeable future, be suited for freedom. They were vague as to when that day might come, but the implication was that its distance from the present was not to be measured in years or even in generations but rather in centuries. Meanwhile, no legal changes reformed the system, and various appalling abuses continued on a wholesale basis.[34]

Whether they made ineffectual calls for slavery's reform or whether they simply maintained that reform of anything was none of their concern or anybody else's, Southern Christians clung above all to their claim that the Bible was, at worst, silent on American chattel slavery and therefore posed no barrier to their being slaveholders, or advocates of slavery, and good Christians too.

Once the slavery issue was dispatched from conscious consideration—and Southerners made every effort to see that it stayed that way—remarkably little difference remained between Northern and Southern Christians. Revivals, camp meetings, and protracted meetings were features of religion on both sides of the Ohio River or the Mason-Dixon line. Neither doctrines nor practices differed between sections. Yet as long as Northern Christians believed that slavery was a sin and Southern ones maintained that it was not, that single issue was bound to loom larger with every passing year until it swallowed up all the common ground of churches North and South into one great field of conflict. Southern Christians, believing themselves to be as good as those in the North, would demand that Northerners give at least implied consent to that proposition, while Northerners, convinced that Southerners were in sin on this issue, could not give that implied consent without implicating themselves in the same sin. Under these circumstances, schism was a matter of time.

It came first in the Methodist Church. Abolitionists within the denomination became frustrated not only with the organization's Southern-dictated tolerance of the institution but also with the efforts of Methodism's bishops (its highest officials) to squelch antislavery concerns in the name of unity. Consulting their Bibles, the dissidents found as little justification for the traditional authority of bishops as for the acceptance of slavery. Rejecting both, twenty-two antislavery ministers and 6,000 members seceded from the Methodist Episcopal Church to form the Wesleyan Methodist Connection, which tolerated neither bishops nor slaveholders. Within two years their numbers had risen to about 15,000.[35]

Southern Methodists rejoiced at what they considered a backdoor revival, but the following year it was they who headed for the exits. The difficulty started when Bishop James O. Andrew of Georgia married a widow who owned slaves. Slaveholding had generally been considered a disqualification for episcopal office within Methodism, but Andrew pled in his defense that Georgia law forbade masters to free their slaves. Besides, he maintained, they were not his slaves but his wife's. Northern Methodists were having none of it, however, and at the Methodist general conference that year in New York, they called for his resignation.

Andrew considered resigning in order to prevent schism, but the Southern delegates to the conference urged—indeed, demanded—that he persevere. For him to have resigned would have been to concede that there was something wrong with slaveholding, that a man who owned slaves was, at the very least, unfit for spiritual leadership. That was exactly the point that Southern Christians were bent on denying, and it was on that point that the Methodist movement, the largest religious organization in the United States, split into the Methodist Episcopal Church and the Methodist Episcopal Church, South.[36]

The other large nationwide denominations were not far behind. The following year the Baptists also broke along North-South lines, with Southerners forming the Southern Baptist Convention. Presbyterianism was already divided between New School and Old School adherents. Although that schism did not spring from the issue of slavery, the question of the peculiar institution, like a great polarizing magnet, soon drew the separate factions into line with its own stresses. Old School Presbyterians such as James Henley Thornwell rejected revivals, reform, and rocking of the boat generally; therefore, their beliefs were more congenial to Southerners who were sensitive about slavery. By the late 1850s, large numbers of New Schoolers who happened to live in the South had switched to the Old School faction, showing that they ranked slavery a more important issue than all the rest of their theological differences. The rending of the nation's three largest religious denominations along North-South lines was a first harbinger that the issues dividing Americans were becoming more important than those that bound them together.

While the rival churches, North and South, may have been all but identical in every area of doctrine and practice other than slavery, the same could not be said of the societies to which they ministered and that they endeavored to reach with the Gospel of Jesus Christ. Societal features related to the sectional crisis made the South in some ways an easier field for Christian work, provided that a preacher did not feel led by God to address the sin of slavery. As the antislavery movement grew in the North during the early nineteenth century and the South turned more consciously and vigorously to the defense of slavery, the people of the Southern states developed a sort of regional bunker mentality. By the 1840s and 1850s, this way of thinking was intense and widespread.

It posited that the South was the last bastion of decency, honor, Christianity, and freedom—by which, of course, was meant slavery. The whole world was arrayed against this Southern citadel of civilization, and Southerners must therefore guard against any infiltration of outside thought.

This fear of and hostility toward any new ideas insulated the South against innovations of almost any sort, good or bad. As Southern journalist Walter Hines Page pointed out in 1902, slavery "pickled" Southern life, keeping it just what it was. There was, of course, considerable good in early-nineteenth-century society that the South perpetuated, but there was also bad. Yet the fear that any change of the status quo would endanger slavery kept both as they were.[37]

This bore on the religious world of the pre–Civil War South, in that Southern Christianity did not have to struggle against new winds of doctrine and strange fermentations of belief. Orthodox Protestantism, purged of most social concern, existed in comfortable exclusion of most other belief systems. A sizable proportion of the Southern population, like that of the North, continued to live outside the bounds of Christian faith, but their position was one of irreligion rather than rival religion. Southern Christians still had to do spiritual battle with the world, the flesh, and the Devil, but they did not have to contend in the marketplace of ideas against competing philosophies.

Such was not the case in the North, and especially in the Northeast, where systems such as Unitarianism, Universalism, Mormonism, and Transcendentalism made their rival claims against Christianity. In the 1850s another contending system emerged in the North in the form of the spiritist, or spiritualist, movement. Although it was to prove a mere passing fad, lasting scarcely more than a generation as a mass movement, the spiritist movement, with its séances, mediums, and professed concourse with the dead, came to fascinate an amazing number of Americans during the 1850s. Such prominent figures as John Greenleaf Whittier and Henry Wadsworth Longfellow attended séances regularly; Horace Greeley, Ralph Waldo Emerson, William Lloyd Garrison, and Charles Sumner also visited such events. Perhaps as many as 2 million Americans at least dabbled in spiritism, and some of the spiritists claimed to have even more adherents.

The teachings of the spiritist movement were contrary to those of the Bible, sometimes in matters of belief about future states—spiritists sang that "the resurrection trumpet shall not wake us from the sod," denying a future resurrection and judgment by God—and sometimes in matters of practical living. Spiritists claimed that mere bonds of marriage need not restrain their activities, and they claimed the "right" to have a physical relationship with anyone for whom they conceived a "spiritual affinity." Not surprisingly, they had a great many "spiritual affinities." Indeed, the movement's whole spirit, with its claim of personal independence from any divine law, was contrary to that of Christianity, and its practices were viewed by orthodox Christians as nothing short of satanic. Confined almost entirely to the North, it posed another competing belief system against which Northern Christians had to contend.[38]

Interestingly, in this context, Northern preachers during the Civil War era, unlike their Southern counterparts, turned fairly frequently to Jeremiah 6:16 as a sermon text—"Stand ye in the ways, and see, and ask for the old paths, where is the good way, and walk therein, and ye shall find rest for your souls"—as they strove to combat the creeping infiltration of anti-Christian ideas. Civil War soldier Gideon W. Burtch summarized in his diary one such sermon. The preacher, "Brother Yokum," had "stated that in this age of improvements & inventions people are constantly looking for something new & hence the old paths have been forgotten to an alarming extent."[39] John T. McMahon, another Civil War soldier, wrote with remarkable prescience in his diary, "I think that if the masses were educated more that Christianity would be far ahead of what it is now. I think this time will come, for schools are becoming more numerous every day, but if, in these schools, no attention is given to the training of the morals then but little good will come of them. We should be overrun with a lot of learned knaves."[40] In 1860, however, one had to be farsighted indeed to perceive a danger of Christianity being "overrun" in the United States.

Another rival religion with which Northern Christians had to contend was out-and-out atheism, called in those days "infidelity." It had appeared the century before when the wave of European "Enlightenment" thought broke just short of American shores and slid hissing back into the sea of foreign ideas. In the nineteenth century, infidelity was relatively rare in

America, but it was just common enough by midcentury to draw some return fire from Christian apologists. Union soldier David H. Blair spent some of his off-duty hours in 1864 reading an account of "a debate between a minister and an infidel lawyer." To his relatives back home Blair wrote, "It floors infidelity in every point. . . . It gives some of the most striking proofs of the existence of an Almighty power that I ever read. It appears to me that infidelity and all irreligion is the most unreasonable ideas in existence, putting man on a level with brute creation." But then Blair mused that perhaps infidels really were at that level, since they were "heirs of an eternal punishment."[41]

The book Blair read may very well have been James Smith's 650-page *The Christian's Defense, Containing a Fair Statement, and Impartial Examination of the Leading Objections Urged by Infidels Against the Antiquity, Genuineness, Credibility, and Inspiration of the Holy Scriptures.* Published in 1843, the book was the complete text of Smith's 1841 debate against prominent lawyer and critic of the Bible Charles G. Olmsted. Smith himself was pastor of First Presbyterian Church in Springfield, Illinois, of which Mary Todd Lincoln was a member and which her husband also frequently attended. He argued vigorously in his famous debate and book, as elsewhere, that men and women had before them good, adequate, and sufficient evidence to know, with their understanding, that the Bible is true and reliable. The nineteenth century may have been an era of emotions—and the great revivals certainly reflected that—but Smith challenged his readers with the assertion that Christianity could be successfully defended on the basis of reason and the same "arguments which are held decisive in other historical questions."[42]

Smith's arguments were indeed powerful. Though it is unclear whether Lincoln ever actually accepted Christianity for himself, he had to admit that Smith's case "in favor of the divine authority and inspiration of the Scriptures was unanswerable." Lincoln commented to an associate that "in view of the Order and harmony of all nature which we behold, it would have been More miraculous to have Come about by chance than to have been created and arranged by some great thinking power."[43]

Despite the loss of national unity within religious organizations and, in the North, the competition of non-Christian and anti-Christian philosophies such as Transcendentalism, spiritism, and infidelity, Christianity continued to thrive throughout the 1850s. Church growth went on apace in the various denominations, North and South, at as great a rate as ever. The revivals were quieter now, with little shouting. Reverent quietness was more likely to be the indication of intense fervor.

A renewed wave of revivals swept the country in 1857 and 1858, originating (for a change) in the towns and cities of the Northeast but taken up almost simultaneously elsewhere. The revivals began from daily noontime prayer meetings held by merchants or clerks in the financial districts of New York City. The meetings began in 1857 and were led and organized by laymen, without regard to denominational distinctions. Any man in attendance was free to pray, exhort, or lead in the singing of a hymn, provided he stayed within a five-minute limit and avoided controversial issues. The men came together for spiritual edification rather than theological argument. A "still, solemn, and tender" atmosphere prevailed at such gatherings, causing one observer to think that they seemed "more like a communion than a prayer meeting."[44]

The steady growth of these meetings gained extensive coverage in the press and eventually spread into a full-fledged religious awakening known as the "Businessman's Revival." Christians started similar meetings in many other cities, with great success. The movement expanded nationwide, affecting small towns and farm communities as much as it did large cities. It might take the form of the protracted meeting of previous revivals or that of the New York–style "union prayer meeting." The revival was strong enough in the South that the Georgia Methodist conference, for example, added more than 10,000 new members in 1858, while in Maine, protracted meetings went on for weeks, with one observer counting over 600 persons in the "inquiry room," seeking the way of salvation, at a single meeting on a single night.[45]

The 1858 revival included the cooperation of every major Protestant denomination. The clergy followed the laity's lead in laying aside sectarian controversy and, in the words of one Methodist minister, urged that God would bless His people if they would continue to "fix their minds upon the mark . . . of holiness of heart, of life, of conversation." The revival continued in numerous locations right up to the beginning of the Civil War.[46]

On the eve of the Civil War, Christianity suffused American society and culture. The United States had always had a strong Christian witness, and that influence was as strong as ever in 1860. Perhaps as many as 4 million of the nation's 27 million persons were members of Protestant churches. Since church membership was entered into primarily by adults, the relative number of adherents becomes even larger in view of the country's youthful population in the nineteenth century. Add to that the fact that persons usually joined churches only after prolonged periods of intense religious seeking and that many others continued to attend churches without ever becoming members, and the size of the churchgoing population appears enormous. Had all the Protestant church buildings in America been filled on any given Sunday morning in 1860, more than two-thirds of the nation's population would have been in attendance.[47]

It was therefore a nation strongly influenced by Christianity that faced the secession crisis of late 1860 and early 1861, following the election of Abraham Lincoln on a platform calling for no further spread of slavery. In April 1861 the new Confederate government opened fire on Fort Sumter in Charleston Harbor, South Carolina, initiating America's bloodiest war. Lincoln responded with a call for 75,000 volunteer soldiers to put down the rebellion, and Confederate president Jefferson Davis answered with a call of his own for 100,000. These calls were the first of many on both sides, followed eventually by conscription. The young men of America, in their millions, marched off to a war that for many would be the greatest test of their faith or of their religious training. For all of them it would be a time to try the soul and turn the thoughts to serious themes.

2

"A MERCIFUL PROVIDENCE"
The Actions of a Sovereign God

"Went to church this morning," wrote John T. McMahon in his diary on November 3, 1861. "The Rev. C. Glease preached from Matt[hew] tenth chapter and thirtieth verse, 'But the very hairs of your head are all numbered.' The subject was the providence of God." The teenaged McMahon, less than a year away from his enlistment in the 136th New York the following fall, went on to describe Glease's sermon. "Anyone that admits there is a God must admit He has a providence, for the great God that created all things would not leave them to take care of themselves." The preacher had gone on to point out that there were some who claimed "that God made all things and made laws by which they are ruled and then left them." This, however, made no sense, and Glease illustrated the fact with an analogy to a man-made piece of machinery. "If you look at an engine, we may admire its workmanship and its laws but this will not move without some help. . . . So it is in nature," Glease concluded. God was the one who moved the world and its parts. "And we may say that God rules the universe."[1]

This was the doctrine of divine providence. God is sovereign. He not only made the world but is presently, positively active in it, producing the good and permitting the evil, all for the accomplishment of His own purposes and the ultimate good of His people. The fervent belief in this doctrine on the part of nineteenth-century Christians was a direct denial of the Deism of the previous century's so-called Enlightenment movement—the view of those who claimed "that God made all things and made laws by which they are ruled and then left them." That philosophy posited that God was like a master clock maker who might make a fine timepiece, wind it up, and then let it run, never intervening in its subsequent workings. The Bible leaves no room for such ideas, and so the nineteenth century's resurgence of Christianity brought their downfall—they had never been very strong on these shores, anyway—and the reaffirmation of the same doctrine of providence that had been held by previous Americans from William Bradford and John Winthrop to Samuel Adams and George Washington.

This belief stood on the basis of God's ongoing involvement in what He had created. And Christians of that era had no uncertainty whatsoever that God had indeed created the universe. In July 1863 Alfred Tyler Fielder of the Twelfth Tennessee was moved to thought as he surveyed the view from the summit of Lookout Mountain. The spot was, he believed, "one of the best places for reflection and meditation upon nature and natures God." The words might have been those of Thomas Jefferson's semi-Deistic phraseology in the Declaration of Independence, but the concept in Fielder's mind was thoroughly biblical, for he went on, "My mind was actively engaged almost all the time I was there in thinking of the great power and wisdom of him that spoke all things into existance and upholds all things by the word of his power and in Comparison of which how weak, feeble and insignificant [is] the Creature man." Echoing this time the words of the Bible itself, Fielder made it clear that he believed that the God who "spoke all things into existance" was the same one who, day by day and moment by moment, upheld and ordered all things "by the word of his power."[2]

Agreement with that premise would have been virtually unanimous among American Christians in the Civil War era. Thomas F. Boatright of the Forty-fourth Virginia explained to his wife in a February 1863 letter that he had recently been reading a book that had been a great comfort to him. "Its title is The Providential Care of God to his creatures coming down to the most minute things on earth," Boatright explained.

"Though we are afflicted or troubled or separated or deprived it all will work out for our good if we are his by adoption."[3] From the Second North Carolina Hospital in Petersburg, Virginia, Levi Y. Lockhart wrote his sister in June 1863, "Give my love to Mother, and tell her not to be uneasy about me for all things work together for good to them that are called the Children of God."[4]

No other aspect of the Civil War soldiers' thought about God is more frequently repeated in their writings than this belief in God's superintending care of His creation. Often, out of reverence, they simply referred to God as "Providence" when referring specifically to His activity in the world. Sometimes the references became mixed, even within a single letter, with the word "providence" being used to signify a specific intervention by God, God's general oversight, or God Himself.

It was providence that preserved a soldier's life through the dangers of camp and battlefield. A Union staff officer wrote in September 1863 of the "Providence that has protected me in my rough pathway."[5] After the battle of Gettysburg, a soldier of the hard-hit Sixth Wisconsin wrote to his parents, "A merciful Providence has again taken me through the ordeal of battle unscathed," just as he had attributed to "an overruling Providence" his good health in winter camp the preceding February.[6] "I did not receive a scratch," wrote an officer of the Seventh Vermont, regarding a recent combat. "My escape was providential & I have reason to return thanks to Him who rules the destinies of battle."[7]

Likewise, the Thirty-fifth North Carolina's William H. S. Burgwyn wrote, "God in His merciful providence has preserved me unhurt and untouched through the five days and nights and a half of the dreadful carnage" of the battle of Fredericksburg.[8] On the outskirts of Atlanta after the three major battles of July 1864, James G. Theaker saw divine intervention on behalf of his company F of the Fiftieth Ohio, which throughout the bloody campaign up to that point had lost only one man wounded and none killed. "I sometimes think that I can plainly see a Providential hand connected with our co. so far. I do not put my trust in any arm of flesh nor in heavy battalions of men, but in Him who rules the armies & holds the destiny of the nation in His hands."[9]

In the same way, soldiers looked to providence for protection in battles to come. "May he be my shield and protection when the storm of the conflict rages around me," wrote Hoosier Maj. James M. Shanklin to his wife in May 1862.[10] From the camp of the Second Connecticut Heavy Artillery near the Weldon Railroad about ten miles from Petersburg, Virginia, in June 1864, Henry Hoyt expressed to the "dear ones home" his "trust that Providence will lead me safely through."[11]

It was providence that called out of the world those whose lives came to an end. In the camp of the Sixty-seventh Indiana near Young's Point, Louisiana, in February 1863, saddle maker-turned-soldier William Winters was profoundly saddened to learn of the death of his young son back home in Hope, Indiana. He wished that he might have been able to "see his little face once more or hear his inocent pratle again," but "an alwise providence has ruled otherwise."[12] James Theaker wrote to his family in May 1864 concerning the death of a nephew back home in Belmont County, Ohio, "I sometimes think Providence is very kind in calling away so soon the innocent before they become acquainted with the temptations, trials, and sorrows of this sinful, wicked world."[13]

It was providence that directed and controlled the circumstances of great battles. George Rogers of the Twentieth Ohio wrote to a friend after the battle of Shiloh that on the evening of the first day's fight, "Thanks to Providence, night came on just when our safety lay in darkness."[14]

Meanwhile, on the other side of the lines at that same battlefield, Company B of the Twelfth Tennessee had just twelve men left to stack arms for the night. Before seeking sleep, the men listened to one of their comrades read a psalm and then sang a Charles Wesley hymn, one of whose verses ran:

> In all my ways thy hand I own,
> Thy ruling providence I see;
> Assist me still my course to run,
> And still direct my paths to thee.[15]

It was providence that permitted or prevented the movements of armies and other developments in the war. A Confederate soldier wrote to his wife from Okolona, Mississippi, in February 1863, mentioning that the army had not marched away from that place several days earlier because "such were the designs of Providence, and our God overrules all things for the best."[16] From Fredericksburg, Virginia, in March 1863, Tally N. Simpson of the Third South Carolina noted that a snowstorm had made military operations temporarily impossible. "Providence has again," he concluded, "by this natural occurrence, forced upon the several armies in the field an armistice of several days."[17] Similarly, Confederate soldier Reuben Allen Pierson wrote, "It seems as if the divine Ruler of the Universe was procrastinating the great battle which appears to be so imminent."[18]

And it was God in His providence who would one day bring the war to a close when His purposes in it had been accomplished. "When that glad day comes," wrote the 142nd New York's William H. Walling, "the interposition of Providence will stay the flow of blood. There will be war no longer. There will be no North, no South—but one country. God hasten and bless the day."[19]

Providence could be hard to understand. God sees what man cannot, knows the end from the beginning, and His actions on behalf of His children may be hard for them to understand. Walling spoke of "the ways of a mysterious Providence."[20] When Ulysses S. Grant was injured in a fall by his horse in September 1863, Aurelius Lyman Voorhis of the Forty-sixth Indiana wrote in his diary, "The ways of Providence are past finding out."[21] When a much-hoped-for chance of getting out of the Confederate army proved illusory, a Mississippi soldier wrote, "God does all things right, and there is some hidden Providence in it. It may be a sorrowful one. It may be a more pleasant one. 'My times, my times are in thy hand, Oh Lord.'" Yet when one of his children died of disease back home, the same soldier wrote, "Truly the ways of Providence are inscrutable and past finding out."[22]

For this reason, it was important that Christians trust God's providential dealings in their lives, and many of the Civil War soldiers expressed that trust. Pennsylvanian Alfred Hough exhorted his wife to "continue the trust in Providence you always have had," and Henry Kauffman of the 110th Ohio reminded his wife that "we must trust to providence."[23] Col. William H. L. Wallace of the Eleventh Illinois told his wife Ann that he would do his best to do his duty, whatever might come, "with a firm reliance of God's all wise providence that it will result in good, in carrying out His Sovereign will."[24]

Yet trusting in God's providence did not mean having confidence that He would preserve His servants from sickness, sorrow, or death. Rather, it was an assurance that He would allow such painful providences to enter a Christian's life only when in His perfect wisdom He knew that those circumstances were necessary in order to make the believer's character more like that of Jesus Christ.[25]

The awareness that a wise and loving providence might permit what to man's reckoning seemed negative or even tragic was also reflected in the writings of numerous Civil War soldiers. This was true in small things as well as large. In the spring of 1862, while still on the farm in upstate New York, John McMahon noted that his father's red heifer had died and added, echoing the words of Scripture, "of a truth, God's ways are not our ways.[26]

Naturally, the same applied with even more force in matters of great moment. In writing about the deaths of several soldiers in his regiment, Chaplain Justine E. Twitchell of the 131st Ohio used the same words: "God ways are not our ways."[27] Similarly, in mentioning his gratitude to "a kind Providence" for having protected him thus far, Alfred Hough also expressed "an abiding faith that his will with me is right."[28] Speaking of several civilians back home who had recently lost loved ones due to natural causes, William Walling wrote, "I hope they will acknowledge the hand of God in their affliction and that he will sanctify this dispensation of his Providence to theirs and our eternal well being."[29] A captain in the Army of Tennessee, upon going into battle, was heard to say, "I believe God will take care of me; but should he see fit to take me, I am prepared."[30]

Hoosier Aurelius Voorhis expressed the same confidence when he wrote in his diary that even if the war lasted long enough that he had to serve out his whole three-year enlistment, "I reckon it is all right." The war did indeed last that long, though most soldiers hoped and expected that it would not. Voorhis, however, was at peace with the prospect. "God knows what is for our good," he wrote. Then, in what was an almost constant refrain of those soldiers who were Christians, he added, "I believe He will do all things well although at times it appears as though He was working against us, but it is for our good."[31] In similar vein, John Blair of Muncie, Indiana, wrote to his brother David in the Forty-fifth Ohio, "God in his wisdom directs all things well."[32] South Carolinian Tally Simpson thought in the same terms. "He doeth all things well," Simpson wrote in close paraphrase of the Bible, "to his will we humbly bow."[33] Levi Lock-hart told his sister, "God will do all things well," and N. H. R. Dawson of the Fourth Alabama assured his fiancée, "I am in the keeping of an all wise Creator, and an all wise God, who doeth all things well."[34] The Fiftieth Ohio's James Theaker wrote, "We are in the hands of mysterious Providence, but 'He doeth all things well.'"[35] When Marquis Townsend of the Thirteenth Iowa reflected on how much he wanted to see his wife and daughter, he nevertheless reminded himself of his trust in God, "for he doeth all things well." Months later in a letter to his sister, he remarked that God had thus far protected him from harm, adding, "I feel to trust all to him for he doeth all things well."[36]

The Forty-fifth Ohio's David Humphrey Blair got at the heart of the matter. He had had a close call, with an object in his breast pocket barely stopping a bullet that would otherwise have killed him. To his sister he wrote, "I am glad that you believe there is a being that doeth all things well. Lizzie if that ball had went through that hit me on the breast could you have still said he doeth all things well[?] I hope you would for I have reason to hope that I would now have been better off and been free from the troubles of war of camp life and of temptation"—that is, he would have been in heaven.[37]

Of even greater emotional impact is a final letter from John W. Mosely of the Fourth Alabama to his mother. Badly wounded on the second day of fighting at Gettysburg, Mosely was taken prisoner but treated kindly and was allowed to write a letter to his mother. Aware that he was dying, he wrote, "My Dear Mother, . . . Do not mourn my loss. I had hopes to have been spared, but a righteous God has ordered it otherwise and I feel prepared to trust my case in his hands."[38]

In a May 1864 letter to his mother, written from his regiment's camp near Decatur, Alabama, Richard R. Crowe of the Thirty-second Wisconsin stated this trust and its basis as clearly as any soldier ever did. "Now Mother, I tell you honest what it is," wrote Crowe. "You must not worry at all about your boys, for if there is a Supreme protecting power over us, it can certainly protect us as well here as in Wisconsin, and if," he continued, paraphrasing the words of Christ from the Sermon on the Mount, "the hair of our heads are all numbered and not a sparrow falls to the ground without the knowledge and will of this overruling power, why it is certainly wrong to think Providence will ordain any thing but what is right and just; then why complain or worry for fear something will happen to our friends when even if our worst fears were realized it might be the best thing that could happen after all."[39] Crowe's faith was firmly based in the teachings of the Bible.

So was Sidney A. Bean's. Bean had been a brilliant student at the University of Michigan and had graduated in 1855. He became a professor of mathematics at Carroll College in Waukesha, Wisconsin, and also lectured on languages at the University of Wisconsin. Bean was in poor health when the war broke out, but he enlisted and soon became lieutenant colonel of the Fourth Wisconsin. In a letter that began with the words, "This letter will be sent to you only in case I am killed or taken," Bean told his mother, "Keep a good heart. God is good & he is our all in all & will suffer no evil thing to befall us—none that will not be finally for our good—Goodbye. God bless you my dearest Mother." Bean was killed by a sharpshooter on May 29, 1863.[40]

The confidence in divine providence held by many Civil War soldiers could allow them to perceive God's goodness and to feel their hearts filled with trust and praise for Him, even in circumstances that made such responses seem incomprehensible to those of their comrades—probably about equally numerous—who did not share such an implicit confidence. One who did not was Maj. Abner R. Small of the Sixteenth Maine. One day during the brutal Overland Campaign in the spring of 1864, Small watched darkness creep over the bloody field of that day's fighting. Then, to his amazement, he heard rising from the lines where the sweaty and powder-grimed Union soldiers rested on their arms the sound of the hymn known as the Doxology:

> Praise God from Whom all blessings flow.
> Praise Him all creatures here below.
> Praise Him above ye heavenly host.
> Praise Father, Son, and Holy Ghost.

As Small listened in perplexity to thousands upon thousands of soldier voices taking up the song, he reflected that these men "didn't bother to think how many voices the war had stopped from praising God." He assumed that the soldiers must be singing this way simply because they liked the tune.[41] Yet his more devout comrades would have reminded him that God was still in control of all the vicissitudes of war and working them together for the good of those who belonged to Him.

The doctrine of providence was a pleasant and comforting one for those who held it, even if, like Pvt. Hiram M. Hunger of the Fifth Vermont, they could express it only in the simplest terms. "Be of good chear," he wrote to his sister back home, "for gods will must be done not ourn."[42] Theirs was not a belief in a distant, austere, impersonal, or inexorable force that disposed of man according to its own capricious whim. Rather, it was a confident trust in a warm, loving, heavenly Father whose actions, while sometimes difficult for His children to understand, were nevertheless all perfectly ordered and directed for their eternal good. A devotional book found in the possession of Confederate Maj. John Stewart Walker after his death at the first battle of Bull Run alluded to this: "Let the world imagine to itself a magnificent Deity, whose government is only general; the Christian rejoices in his providential superintendance of the smallest matters."[43]

Other soldiers also expressed this confidence. Confederate soldier James W. Bacon wrote of "the kind hand of Providence."[44] Thomas Boatright wrote that the book he had read on "The Providential Care of God" had sometimes moved him to tears in deep gratitude. "To think that the Lord has been so good to me such an unworthy creature to have spared my life while I have been so much exposed to things that were well calculated to take from me this fleeting breath and cause me to stand before his bar to give an account of the deeds of my life."[45]

This acceptance of God's will was true even in the most difficult dispensations of providence, as long as the believer kept clearly in mind that important as the affairs of this life might be, those of the next were more so. William Burgwyn wrote to his mother in August 1863 about the death of his brother, Henry, at Gettysburg the month before. Henry's death might, William suggested, be the occasion of turning their brother George to a greater interest in the things of God. "It is a severe way of accomplishing his good," William wrote, "but God in His great wisdom may have ordained that Harry should be killed to make a change in George and improve his character." Henry had "died willingly and resigned and

I know if you were certain all of us could be required to die and with a full belief we would go to heaven you would be contented if we were to be killed for what is a few days spent here compared with eternity in heaven."[46] Likewise, Tally Simpson, writing home regarding the death of two young friends, noted that it was "very sad and melancholy indeed. But," he added, "God who doeth all things well is the author of all good. And tho His designs may now be veiled from our sight, yet in the future we may see how beautifully He works for the best. It may be that the death of these noble boys may be the cause of softening the hearts of their hardhearted parents and awakening them to a full sense of their present perilous condition."[47]

This sort of trust did not necessarily come easily in the midst of difficult circumstances. Christians believed that they needed God's enabling help, grace, in order to exercise a proper trust in God and His dealings with them. J. Trooper Armstrong wrote to console his cousin on the death of her young son. "Of course we know this is all for the best, but it requires a great deal of Christian grace to feel and acknowledge it."[48]

Many of the Civil War soldiers' references to God in His providential role expressed the same concept without actually using the terms "providence" or "providential." Their letters are replete with references such as "the God of battles," "he who holds the destinies of nations," "him that governs all things," "Him who knows the end of events from the beginning," and "*Him* who 'knoweth all things.'"[49]

When the doctrine of providence was properly understood, it differed markedly from fatalism. God, unlike the concept of fate, is personal. God also responds to human action, prayer, though only according to His will, and He requires certain behavior of human beings, with rewards or consequences based on obedience or the lack of it. Tally Simpson showed an awareness of this when he wrote to his sister, "Let us act in such a manner that whatsoever cometh we may be able to say, it is the work of the Lord."[50] Only when living in conformity to God's will could a man be assured that God would order events for that man's eternal good. Yet all this had to be carefully tempered by the counterbalancing truth that God knew from eternity past what human actions would be taken and what prayers would be offered, and He planned and arranged to use all such things for His own purposes.

With a doctrine of such subtlety, some people, not surprisingly, got things a little bit wrong and ended up with a jumbled philosophy of providence that shaded over a good deal into the realm of fatalism. Peter Welsh, devout Catholic and color-bearer of the Twenty-eighth Massachusetts Regiment in the Army of the Potomac's famous Irish Brigade, expressed his faith in Christian terms, but with a content distinctly fatalistic. He assured his wife that neither his going off to war nor his service in the especially dangerous role of color-bearer made his death any more probable. "Our days are numbered," he wrote, "and we must fill them. That is an unalterable decree which no power on earth can change." A man could "as easily create himself as destroy his own life if his time is not full."[51] The fatalism came in with Welsh's assertion that his own actions had no bearing on his continued survival.

Others used more straightforward terminology to express a concept that was foreign to Christianity. "Only fate knows what is in store for a soldier," wrote William Winters.[52] Still others mixed both terms and concepts. A Virginia soldier wrote home lamenting the death of two comrades but in resignation stated, "We must submit cheerfully to these things. It is the fate of war. It is God's decree."[53] Confederate soldier Edwin Fay, who dabbled with both Christianity and other philosophies, was more explicit. "If it is my kismet (destiny) to come back to you, I shall do it," he wrote to his wife back in Louisiana. "If not, why who can change the decrees of God. This is Turkish doctrine but some philosophy after all."[54] The Twenty-eighth Alabama's Joshua K. Callaway also mixed concepts, though in a somewhat different way. "Let it be your constant prayer to God to spare me and no man shall hurt me," he wrote to his wife. "Yet pray God, that, if it is the fiat of fate that I must die in this war, that I may be ready and resigned."[55] His first statement, that God might see fit to protect him in answer to his wife's prayers, was consistent with orthodox Christianity. The idea of "the fiat of fate" was not. But this statement came early in the war and early in Callaway's own personal spiritual pilgrimage. His understanding deepened over the next couple of years. It was soldiers who knew a little of Christianity—and there were many such—who tended to confuse its teachings with fatalism.

Some higher-ranking individuals articulated a more thoroughgoing fatalism. Lincoln himself had, back in 1846, confessed that "in early life" he had been a believer in what he called "the Doctrine of Necessity." As Lincoln explained it, this doctrine held that "the human mind is impelled to action, or held in rest by some power, over which the mind itself has no control." In Lincoln's case, this belief was the mutant offspring of the rigorous Calvinism of his "hard-shell Baptist" upbringing crossed with the faith in human reason he embraced as a young man.[56] With its emphasis that man's actions counted for nothing, Calvinism tended toward fatalism, a point not lost on all Civil War soldiers. Sgt. Samuel McIlvaine of the Tenth Indiana found himself in a Presbyterian church whose obviously Calvinist minister, as McIlvaine put it, "preaches strong fatality."[57]

Of a somewhat lower rank but equally thoroughgoing fatalism (equal, at least, with the views of the youthful Lincoln), mixed nonetheless with some Christian ideas, was the outlook of Union Maj. Gen. John Gibbon. To two of his soldiers seeking shelter during the great Confederate artillery bombardment of the third day at Gettysburg he said, "All these matters are in the hands of God, and nothing that you can do will make you safer in one place than in another." A few moments later, with shells still raining down around them, he said to staff officer Frank Haskell, "I am not a member of any church, but I have always had a strong religious feeling, and so in all these battles I have always believed that I was in the hands of God; and that I should be unharmed or not, according to his will. For this reason, I think it is, I am always ready to go where duty calls, no matter how great the danger."[58] But what if taking shelter was equally consistent with the call of duty? Would Gibbon, or any other soldier, be equally protected if he then opted not to take shelter? Fatalism would say yes; Christianity, no.

This was illustrated in a story that made the rounds during the war. For several months during 1862, Rev. Robert L. Dabney, a Presbyterian minister, served on Stonewall Jackson's staff. One Sunday, so the story goes, Dabney preached a sermon at Jackson's headquarters on the subject of God's providence. "Every shot and shell and bullet was directed by the God of battles," Dabney was supposed to have said. Not long after, at the battle of Malvern Hill, Jackson's staff found itself under heavy fire, and the general ordered them to dismount and take cover. Looking over and seeing Dabney sheltering behind a large gatepost, another staff officer chided him, "Why Dr. Dabney, if the God of battles directs every shot, why do you want to put a gate-post between you and a special providence?" To which Dabney replied, "Why just here the gate-post is the special providence."[59] Whether true or not, the story illustrated the more orthodox Christian view of providence that Dabney and thousands of other soldiers held, even while, at the same time, many others held varying degrees of fatalism.[60]

The doctrine of providence, correctly understood, was central to the religious faith of a vast number of Civil War soldiers. Their views of themselves and the world were profoundly shaped by the realization that the sovereign God was actively at work within His creation, accomplishing His own good purposes through all the various circumstances He caused or allowed. The soldiers' ideas about God and His ways extended well beyond the doctrine of providence, whether correctly or incorrectly understood, but all of it stood on the foundation of the knowledge that God was there and that He was neither silent nor idle.

3

"IN THE LIGHT OF GOD'S THRONE AND THE PRESENCE OF JESUS"
The Life to Come

It was January 1863, but the night breeze was mild and balmy near Beaufort, on the South Carolina coast, where Col. Thomas Wentworth Higginson sat writing in his tent. He paused now and then to glance out at the constellation Orion hanging above his tent door and to listen to the singing of his soldiers, black soldiers of the Union First South Carolina. The song they sang this night, and many others, expressed in simple but forceful terms—and their own colorful manner of expression—a belief held by many Civil War soldiers.

> I know moon rise, I know star rise
> > Lay dis body down;
> I walk in de moonlight, I walk in de starlight,
> > To lay dis body down;
> I'll walk in de grave yard, I'll walk thro' the grave yard
> > To lay dis body down;
> I go to de judgment in de evening of de day
> > When I lay dis body down;
> And my soul & your soul will meet in de day
> > When I lay dis body down.[1]

The brevity of life and the certainty and universality of death and of judgment afterward were concepts familiar to most nineteenth-century Americans. Many a Civil War soldier, white or black, blue coat, gray, or butternut, would think often of the day when he would come to lay his mortal body down.

The faith of Christian soldiers in the Civil War encompassed many facets of life, and they also believed that this present life was not the conclusion of their existence. The hundreds of thousands of soldiers who believed the Bible also believed that there was a heaven to gain and a hell to shun. The two were opposite poles of the same truth—human beings will exist somewhere forever—but for obvious reasons, the soldiers spent far more time talking about the former than the latter.

From his regiment's camp near Slidell, Arkansas, on March 26, 1862, Texas cavalryman James C. Bates wrote sadly of the first death to occur in his company. "He was a good soldier—a brave man, a true christian, and he will be missed and his death lamented by all the company." Then he added, "It will be better for him *where he is now*."[2] The following year, Hamlin Coe of the Nineteenth Michigan wrote on the occasion of a comrade's death, "Poor fellow, he departed this life without a struggle and, I hope, has gone to a better world."[3] Similarly, Seymour Dexter of the Twenty-third New York wrote, "The spirit of Lucius Bacon at a quarter past six last Friday morning quit its tenement of clay and so we firmly believe winged its way to a land of eternal rest."[4] So believed many hundreds of thousands in the armies of both North and South, for the doctrine of eternal bliss in heaven for those who died in Christ was as widely accepted among Civil War soldiers as that of divine providence. As the Fourteenth South Carolina's Andrew B. Wardlaw wrote to his wife, "God may have in store for us as much of happiness yet on earth, & if we are but His children we can look forward to perfect happiness & unending companionship beyond the grave."[5]

Multitudes of soldiers enjoyed dwelling on such thoughts. They sang about it. As the Third Ohio stood halted on the march for hours in a steady, cold rain, their colonel was surprised to hear them singing "with great unction,"

> There is a land of pure delight,
> Where saints immortal reign;
> Infinite day excludes the night,
> And pleasures banish pain.
> There everlasting spring abides,
> And never withering flowers;
> Death, like a narrow sea, divides
> This heavenly land from ours.[6]

They meditated on it and searched the Scriptures for references to it. George S. Marks of the Ninety-ninth Illinois wrote down a list of "Bible Referances of Scripture of Paradise" in his diary. It included such verses as Luke 23:43, in which Christ assured the repentant thief on the cross next to His, "Verily, I say unto thee, To day shalt thou be with me in paradise." At the conclusion of the list, Marks added his own commentary: "This is the Paradise spoken of by the Saviour of the World as the home of the Children of God after they have finneshed thare work in Earth. Amen."[7]

And many of them wrote of it with intense feeling in their letters home. From his regiment's camp in Virginia, Reuben Pierson wrote to his father in June 1863, assuring him that if he fell in the coming campaign he would "die a Christian, as all the wealth of earth is not worth one moments time in heaven."[8] From the camp of the Forty-fourth Virginia, Thomas F. Boatright wrote in even more intense terms in a letter to his wife the preceding March. If he fell in battle, Boatright wrote, "this poor frail body may be left for devouring worms but He will take care of this soul. It will be housed in eternal mansions of glory. O what a pleasant thought to think and know after we have passed through all the afflictions of the body and troubles of the mind to go to that world where death cannot come nor trouble. Yes, where we have parents, sisters, brothers, and where all of the redeemed have gone through all ages of the world, yes, there to be with our Savior who has suffered so much for us, to enjoy his smiles through all eternity."[9]

"In the light of God's throne and the presence of *Jesus—Oh what must it be to be there?*" wrote Mattie B. Spafford to a friend whose soldier-brother died during the war.[10] It was a question to which many of the

Civil War soldiers and their civilian friends and relatives turned their minds repeatedly. In echo of scriptural promises, one of the themes that turned up most frequently when the soldiers wrote of heaven was their reflection on all the things that would be "no more." Near the end of the war, Aurelius Voorhis of the Forty-sixth Indiana was especially impressed by a sermon on the subject and recorded his thoughts in his diary. "Heard an unusually good sermon this morning," Voorhis wrote, "from the text viz. 'There remaineth therefore a rest for the people of God.' The minister touched feelingly on the joys of Christianity and what the Christian would feel when safe in heaven. No more trials, no more temptations, safe from all dangers." Voorhis reflected that the feelings of the Christian upon reaching heaven might be in some way similar to those the soldiers would experience when the war ended. "How truly thankful we will be to think that our hardships and dangers are all over."[11]

The list of things that would be "no more" was long indeed, and soldiers or their friends and relatives often alluded to them in letters of condolence. Chief among the things that would be no more was war itself. Nancy Richardson of Mississippi rejoiced that in heaven "there will be no more fighting," while Union soldier Joseph Whitney thought in similar terms of "Heaven where there will be no more war nor fighting; all is peace" and "where there will be no more war nor suffering."[12] "Where wars and rumors of wars are not heard," wrote Hamlin Coe of the Nineteenth Michigan.[13] "Where wars are not practiced and where there are pleasures evermore," wrote David Blair in 1864 from the fighting front outside Atlanta to his parents back home in Indiana.[14]

Also conspicuous by their absence in heaven would be all the sad conditions of human existence that war greatly intensified. To J. Miles Pickens, it was a "happy world where sorrow and pain is not known."[15] Confederate soldier Henry T. Morgan comforted his wife Ellen with reflections on "Heaven whare parting will be no more."[16] And so the list went on: "where pain and parting will be known no more," "where suffering and sighing never come," "where sorrow and where trouble never comes," "where there is no death, or war, or trouble," "whare wars and parting ar know more," "where pain and death are felt and heard no more," "where no sickness comes," "where parting and sorrow is not known."[17]

Again and again these same themes are repeated when the soldiers speak of what lies in store for the Christian after death.[18]

The Twelfth Tennessee's Alfred Fielder summed it up as he penned his reflections on what lay "beyond the vail that skirts time from eternity where there will be no wars, no sickness, no pain, no death ... no intervening enemy to sepperate between husband and wife, fathers, mothers and children brothers and sisters who have worshiped God acceptably, but heaven shall resound with praises to him that hath loved us and gave his son to redeem us from this world of sin and destress."[19]

Others reflected on additional aspects of life on earth that would no longer exist in heaven. One example: time. Back home in Wooster, Ohio, recent bride and still more recent widow Emily Elliot reflected on the lot of her late husband, Denton, a lieutenant colonel of the 103rd Ohio who had died several days earlier as a result of wounds received in combat. "Another day has been added to those my darling has spent in Heaven," Emily mused. "What have they been to him? A thousand years are to God as one day. Do our loved ones count the years and months as they pass? No, I think not. For they have done with time. Eternity is all they know now."[20]

If all these things would be no more, what sorts of things did the soldiers believe *would* be in heaven? Many mentioned it as a place of rest, not the rest of death in the grave, but a living rest of eternal life. "There remaineth therefore a rest unto the people of God" had been the text of the impressive sermon Aurelius Voorhis noted on the subject of heaven. Others thought the same. "What consolation to know," wrote Miles Pickens, "That the dear friends are now enjoying the rest prepared for the righteous beyond the grave."[21] "I am tired to death of the war," wrote Joshua K. Callaway of the Twenty-eighth Alabama, adding that he looked forward eagerly to the day "when we shall all sit down in his Kingdom."[22]

They also spoke feelingly of heaven as home. In a Confederate army hospital near Richmond during the Seven Days fighting of 1862, a young woman sat by the side of her dying soldier-brother. "Sister," he said, "I am going home to heaven. I am so glad it is such a good home."[23] And hundreds of miles away in Ohio, Emily Elliott took comfort in reflecting on this thought. "I feel assured, do I not, that my darling is at home, that he has reached that desired haven."[24]

Even more frequently they wrote of heaven as a place of happy meeting. The living looked forward to meeting those who had gone before. Capt. J. Trooper Armstrong of the Ninth Arkansas consoled his wife on the death of their young son, noting that the boy and another child of the Armstrongs who had died several years before "are with each other in a better world."[25] The Twenty-fourth Wisconsin's George A. Cooley reflected on his two-years-dead wife and hoped that they would "meet again in a better and happier world."[26] Isaac Jackson of the Eighty-third Ohio wrote to his brother Ethan about the recent death of their mother from typhoid fever. "We have one great consolation in knowing that she has gone to that better land," Isaac wrote, "and if we do our duty while here we will meet her there in happiness. I intend to try to meet her there, and hope and pray that all my Brothers and Sisters may try and do so too." He exhorted his brother to pray for their father, who was not a believer and thus had no such hope.[27]

While those who were living looked forward to heaven as a place for meeting their loved ones who had gone on before, those who were dying or who anticipated the possibility of impending death took comfort in the thought that their loved ones would follow them to heaven. Samuel P. Lockhart wrote to his sister from the camp of the Twenty-seventh North Carolina near Goldsboro, North Carolina, "if I never see you no more on earth, I hope we will meet on Canaan's Shore."[28] Hoosier officer James Shanklin expressed in a letter to his wife his hope that "we may spend the Eternal future together a united family in heaven."[29] Joseph Whitney wrote to his wife, "Tell Mother to be of good cheer and trust all to the Lord. Tell her I am striving to serve the Lord and if I never meet her on earth, I hope by the assisting Grace of God to meet her in Heaven," and a dying sergeant of the Eighth Illinois Cavalry told his fiancée, "We'll meet in Heaven. I'll wait for you there."[30] Similarly, as Horace Ashkettle of the Fifteenth Illinois lay dying at Pittsburg Landing, his last words were, "Tell my sister I will meet her in heaven."[31]

But happy meetings in heaven meant more than simply reunions with friends and loved ones. Emily Elliott sadly missed her dead husband. "Beautiful thought. I'll see him in heaven," she wrote in her diary several weeks after his death, "but Christ will occupy my thoughts there."[32] There were many for whom the hope of meeting "in a better world" after death was only a vague concept, the expected thing to say to the bereaved or prospective bereaved. For serious Christians, however, it was a definite and specific expectation. As part of that expectation, and towering in significance above all other hoped-for meetings with those who had gone before, was the anticipation of entering the immediate, visible presence of God and meeting Jesus Christ face-to-face. North Carolina soldier Robert Y. Walker wrote from his camp near Stoney Creek, Virginia, to console his cousin on the death of her brother, "I believe he has gone to live with Jesus."[33] Mattie Spafford, writing to a friend who had lost a brother, spoke of her meditation on "the joys of heaven," especially "the light of God's throne and the presence of Jesus. . . . Your Brother *now* knows *all* the height and breadth and depth of God's love."[34]

The concepts of being with Christ and being with loved ones naturally dovetailed, as expressed by Joshua Callaway. "May you, my dearest love, and I," he wrote in an 1863 letter to his wife, "go hand in hand through a long and peaceful life, stand together acquitted at the bar [i.e., place of judgment] of God and then on the wings of angels fly away [to] heaven to cast our crowns at the feet of Jesus and spend eternity in singing his praises, followed by our dear little children."[35]

"This," Callaway added, "is a delightful thought," and so it was. It was an enormous comfort to soldiers and their families alike. "This world is but a short period of our existence," wrote a Union soldier, and that awareness made it possible for society North and South to face the enormous sacrifices that the Civil War demanded.[36] In reflection on it, Emily Elliott was so much helped in her sorrow that she was able to write, "Sweet peace. The Lord is near me and that to comfort me." Then, in echo of the words of Scripture, "Oh Death, where is thy sting?"[37]

But the knowledge that "this world is but a short period of our existence" was a two-edged sword, for the writings of the Civil War soldiers reveal a realization that not everyone would be going to heaven. Another possibility existed after death, and it was not a pleasant one at all. The reality of hell as a place of eternal punishment for sin was something of which the soldiers spoke far less than they did of the comforting hope of heaven. They generally alluded to it only in oblique and indirect terms, such as Robert Walker's exhortation, "Let us so live that when time is no more with us in this world, we may be with Him in heaven." The implication was that it was possible to live otherwise and come to a very different end. Likewise, in a letter to his sister, Samuel P. Lockhart mentioned that he was sorry to hear of the deaths of two men back home. "I do not reckon they were prepared to die, but I do not like to judge," Lockhart noted gravely. "I hope they were prepared to meet their God in peace."[38]

Preachers seemed to mention hell more frequently and directly. Daniel Crotty of the Third Michigan referred to a combat scene in the fierce battle of the Wilderness as being "like the boiling cauldron of hell, as it is represented to us by our good Chaplains."[39] Hamlin Coe mentioned hearing a sermon in camp from a minister who "preached the principle of hell fire and damnation in the true Methodist style." Regarding the sermon's effect, Coe noted, "It did very well."[40]

As for the soldiers themselves, so grim was that prospect that those who took it most seriously mentioned it very rarely in their letters. When it was mentioned more or less directly, it was often by those alluding to it in slightly flippant terms. William Henry Walling wrote to his sisters from the camp of the 142nd New York near Franklin, Virginia, on January 17, 1862, "I am considerably out of humor this evening. . . . Capt. Parker [his cabin mate] has built up such a hot fire I am most roasted. You need not tell me I must govern myself or I shall find in the end a hotter place than this—I admit all that. But who likes to be too hot?"[41] From Port Royal, South Carolina, black soldier James H. Gooding of the Fifty-fourth Massachusetts wrote home to complain of "heat enough to make a fellow contemplate the place prepared for the ungodly."[42] The rarity of such mentions seems to indicate that most Civil War soldiers thought of hell as something that, if mentioned at all, was no joking matter.

The Civil War soldiers and their civilian friends and relatives, as well as most other Americans of that era, reflected a good bit on the fact that "this world is but a short period of our existence." That concept was kept vivid in their minds by that era's acute awareness of the reality of death. Nineteenth-century people stood no greater chance of dying than the people of the twenty-first or any other century—the odds for any given person in any given century being precisely 100 percent—but they showed far less propensity for evading thoughts about that unavoidable occurrence. "In the midst of life we are in death," the Episcopal liturgy reminded them, and the phrase became another of the stock expressions by which Americans of the Civil War generation acknowledged the fact that man's tenure in this life is brief and uncertain.[43]

"Life is uncertain," wrote Aurelius Voorhis in his diary, "in the midst of life we are in death. How careful then ought we to live so that when Death comes, we may be ready."[44] When a sick comrade in the Tenth Massachusetts unexpectedly and suddenly worsened and died, Berea Willsey wrote in his diary, "Surely, in the midst of life, we are in death."[45] Louisa D. Miller of Pennsylvania wrote to her soldier-husband in March 1865, "We are assured that life is uncertain for 'in the midst of life we are in death' therefore we should be prepared for that solemn change. Let us remember that it is our duty as well as our privilege to live in the service of him who has done so much for us, so that when life is ended we may be so unspeakably happy as to meet in that pure home where parting is unknown."[46]

It behooved a man, and a woman too, to be ready for death at all times. "All must die," wrote a soldier of the Ninety-third New York. "Let us bee prepared."[47] Wilbur Fisk found the funeral of a comrade to be a thought-provoking occasion. "As we fired the salute over his grave," Fisk wrote, "we felt that life is held by a very frail tenure indeed."[48] John W. Compton of the Seventy-fourth Pennsylvania assured his wife that the members of his mess were all good Methodists and that they regularly had evening prayer together. "We feel determent to pray & live right," he wrote, "so as if we should be cald off that we may be prepared to go."[49] Joseph Whitney noted in a letter to his wife the death of a comrade due to sunstroke. "Every such case," he added, "Shows me the shortness of life and the certainty of death, and how important it is to live faithfully. God has promised to give me Grace sufficient to withstand all temptations and He has not failed me in one single instance."[50]

The 158th Pennsylvania's Samuel E. Piper addressed the subject at greater length: "These are trying times," he told his wife, "and we should all humble ourselves and try to live as we should live and as we will wish we should have done when we come to die. We should live always with God before our eyes and endeavor to serve him continually. At best our days are few and evil, and we should live agreeable together in this world so that we may be better prepared to enjoy our heavenly home above; a few days, weeks, months or years at farthest we will be called upon to leave our earthly home and if we live right the days allotted to us here below the change will be a good one. If not it will certainly be a very bad one."[51]

It behooved preachers, as well, to warn their hearers of the need to be ready for death, and by all accounts, great numbers of them faithfully did just that. At Second Presbyterian Church in Nashville one Sunday in February 1864, a Union officer's wife in the congregation recorded, "The text was 'it is appointed to all men once to die and after that the Judgment.' It was an exhortation to be ready when Death comes."[52]

Soldiers might be expected to reflect on their mortality because of their frequent exposure to death in battle or by camp diseases. From the camp of the 129th Illinois "within two miles of Atlanta," on July 28, 1864, LaForest Dunham wrote to his sister, Hercy Dunham, back in Illinois. "If thare is any place that a person ought to lade a criston life," LaForest mused, "heare is the place, for a person dont know what time he will be cald up for to leave this world of trouble. Iff it should be my lot to fall, I hope and trust that we will all meat in a better world whare wore and troubles are know more."[53] The somewhat better educated William H. Walling of the 142nd New York expressed the same thoughts that same summer in a letter to his sister from the fighting front near Gaines's Mill, Virginia. Speaking of the constant danger from Rebel sharpshooters when his regiment was manning the picket lines, Walling wrote, "Everytime out we lose some. God only knows who will be 'next.' Now ought all to be ready to obey the summons of our Heavenly Master. Surely we know not the day nor the hour when He will call for us." Walling had already made his own peace with God. "I feel that he who cares for the sparrows in their fall will care for me," he wrote. "My mind is at rest and the issue of life and death I will leave with Him who has them in His hand."[54]

Confederate officer Thomas Boatright had similar thoughts but saw in the issue a significance beyond the risks he had to take as a soldier. "Oh how often do I think of this," he wrote, "that if I were killed in battle instantly while in excitement and my soul rushed in the presence of my final judge would I be prepared? This I hope and pray may never be, but one situated as I am [is] bound to think of these things at times." Then he added significantly, "Nor do I long to shun such thoughts, for I know the time will come for me to die, how soon I know not."[55] Death would come to all, sooner or later, in battle or in peace and old age at home. The important thing was to be prepared.

Awareness of the uncertainty of life was not limited to the soldiers themselves, any more than death was confined to the camp or the battlefield. Sgt. Tom Benton wrote from the camp of the Nineteenth Indiana, "Today we are well and life is no more uncertain here than at the home fireside."[56] The people at home knew it too. "I am aware that life is short, and that our days are all numbered," wrote Lucina Pettit from her home in rural Wilson, New York. Her brother Ira was a soldier in the Eleventh U.S. Infantry, and Lucina told him of several people in the neighborhood—young, old, and in between—who had died of natural causes within the past several weeks. "May we be prepared for death," she admonished, "so that we may meet in Heaven to part no more."[57] Ira Pettit died in Andersonville prison the following year.

Concern with the need to be prepared for death might be seen by some modern observers as evidence of a morbid frame of mind, but mid-nineteenth-century Americans would more likely have suggested that it was simply an acceptance of the fact that life on this earth is a terminal condition. The certainty of death made preparation for it the only sensible course.

And those Civil War soldiers who were ready for death, in Christian terms, found that their preparation stood them in good stead when the hour came for them to die. Among the sick in a Confederate army hospital, Sumner A. Cunningham of the Forty-first Tennessee remembered, "One old man talked of heaven and how bright was all before him whose soul left his body before the morrow."[58] Outside Atlanta in the bloody summer of 1864, the Second Iowa's John J. McKee was visiting a Union army hospital when a hideously wounded soldier was brought in. Asbury Tate of the 111th Illinois had been struck in the shoulder by a large cannonball, tearing off the shoulder and part of the neck, so that his windpipe was torn and he breathed through the hole. He was, as McKee wrote in his diary, "the worst wounded man I ever saw to live as long as he did." Yet "he appeared perfectly willing to die and seemed happy. He was biding all his friends farewell and indicated by signs (he could not talk) that he was going home, pointing upward. His eyes were bright and natural. He appeared to be smiling."[59]

In another military hospital, this one Confederate, a chaplain was making the rounds of the many desperately wounded, counseling and praying with them. Coming to one who obviously did not have long to live, he stooped over him and asked him how he was. "I know in whom I have believed, and am persuaded that he is able to keep that which I have committed unto him," the soldier replied, quoting the Bible. The chaplain continued his rounds and, on passing the dying soldier's place again, noticed that he still lived. Again, he inquired of the young man if all was still well with his soul. The dying soldier could not speak above a whisper, but leaning close to his face, the chaplain heard him say, again in the words of Scripture, "I had rather depart and be with Christ, which is far better." The soldier died peacefully.[60] Ignatius Brock was impressed with the peace in which his own brother spent his dying moments. "His end was peaceful in the full assurance of eternal rest," Ignatius wrote to his sister afterward. "It was a beautiful example of the power of our holy religion. May we all enjoy its full power and like him die in peace!"[61]

Death held few terrors for those who were prepared to meet it. In June 1863 a dying Confederate cavalryman said to his comrades, "I know that my wound is mortal, and that in a very short time I shall be in eternity; but I die as has been my aim for years—prepared to meet my God." He urged his fellow soldiers to become followers of Christ. Then he said, "Tell my wife to educate my two children and train them up to such a way as to meet me in a better world. Before she hears of my death I shall be with our little Mary in heaven."[62]

4

"PEACE WITH GOD"
The Way of Salvation

Writing from the camp of the Forty-fifth Ohio outside Atlanta, David H. Blair consoled his parents on the death of his brother, Morrow, in a military hospital in Jeffersonville, Indiana. "We are . . . not called to mourn as those that have no hope. . . . We have reason to hope that Morrow is now in a better mansion than a military hospital. . . . Could we wish for him to return from happiness to this sinful vale of tears? Perhaps, Dear Parents I may never be allowed the privilege of meeting you again on earth but if not I hope & pray that we may meet where wars are not practiced and where there are pleasures evermore. Then let us live according to our best knowledge of the will of Him who died that we might have life. Then let us obey His will and then trust for all we need to His grace and mercy."[1]

In writing of "Him who died that we might have life," Blair was obviously not referring to his recently deceased brother but rather to Jesus Christ, whose death by Roman crucifixion eighteen centuries earlier had satisfied the demands of God's justice for all the sins of mankind and made a way by which people like David and Morrow Blair and their parents, or anyone else, could be reconciled to God and assured of eternal life in heaven after this life on earth is over. Therein lies the very heart of Christianity. Everything related to it hangs on this point. It was Christ's sacrifice, the innocent Son of God suffering for guilty mankind, that made possible a future in heaven, peace when dying or at any other time, and confidence in the all-wise providence of a God who, though holy and utterly uncompromising in His hatred of sin, could nevertheless become, to the believer, a loving heavenly Father.

And therein lay a second key concept. Though Christ's death made Him, in the words of the Bible, "the propitiation for . . . the sins of the whole world," only believers, those who are "in Christ," could enjoy the benefits of Christ's sacrifice. To put it another way, Christ's death was sufficient to atone for all the sins that might ever be committed, but God, in keeping with His eternal plan, applies its merits only on behalf of those who come to Christ in repentance (turning from their sins) and faith (believing that Christ is the Son of God and will forgive them).

These twin pillars of Christianity—Christ's sacrifice and man's faith— fit into a basic view of the world that explains their necessity and must be examined here if the religion of the Civil War soldiers is to be understood at all. God created man to enjoy fellowship with Him forever. He also has a just claim to man's obedience. Because of the rebellion of the first man, Adam, all humans since have been, by nature and practice, sinners. That is, they are in a state of rebellion against God and are constantly transgressing His laws. Because of this, they are alienated from God, who is holy by nature and cannot tolerate sin. As sinners, humans cannot enjoy the fellowship with God for which they were designed. They are alienated from each other and from nature and suffer in various other ways, being without purpose in this life or hope for the next. Moreover, they are slaves of the very sin that separates them from God, utterly unable to stop sinning or to help themselves in any other way. When death overtakes them in this state, they at last and unavoidably come face-to-face with the full force of God's abhorrence of sin—the sin in which they are steeped—and suffer an eternity of torment finally and irrevocably separated from God.

God foresaw this lamentable state of affairs before ever creating the world or man, and He planned a remedy at infinite cost to Himself. One Person of the three-person unity that is God would humble Himself to the point of taking on the form of man—becoming genuinely human while remaining fully God. This Person, the Son of God, would be born as a baby to a virgin mother, He would live a perfect life completely free of sin, and then He would suffer a death in which God (the Father) would place on Him (the Son) all the guilt of all the sins of the whole guilty human race. Three days dead, He would rise and come bodily out of His tomb, appear to His followers for some days, and ascend into heaven, there by virtue of His perfect atonement to intercede with God the Father on behalf of every man, woman, or child who seeks Him in repentance and faith. He secures to them forgiveness, reconciliation with God, freedom from the bondage of sin, and the assurance of eternal life beyond the grave, where they will enjoy the complete fellowship with God for which they were designed. This Son of God and mediator between God and man is Jesus Christ.

This was the core and foundation of the faith of Christians in the Civil War era, as it had been for Christians since the first century and, on these shores, the faith of such men as John Winthrop, Samuel Adams, Patrick Henry, James Madison, and George Washington, to name only a few of the most prominent. Although it is always deceptive, if not downright delusional, to begin quantifying such things, it is probably safe to say that a large majority of the Civil War generation in America accepted this faith as true—that is, they believed that the view set forth in the preceding two paragraphs was correct. However, a far smaller number, probably fewer than half, would have claimed to be "in Christ" and the beneficiaries of His sacrifice.

Once again, the soldiers' diaries and letters reveal the beliefs and attitudes of Christians and almost-Christians during this era. Many soldiers commented on God's plan of salvation, revealing its importance to them and their outlook on it. This was often reflected in their reactions to sermons they had heard. A religiously inclined soldier would often record in his diary or report in a letter to the home folks the text and gist of such a sermon, especially if he thought it an unusually good or helpful one. He might also record his own thoughts on the subject.

John T. McMahon noted such a sermon in 1862, recording in his diary that the preacher "remarked that whatever God had made was glorious and the psalms described the glorious works of God, when he spake of the heavens as the handiwork of God. But his glory was seen most in the scheme of salvation." The minister had gone on to show how God's prophets had foreshadowed this plan, in general terms, repeatedly since earliest times. "It was the gospel of Jesus," McMahon recorded, "because he made it. It is the power of God unto the salvation of men."[2] On the other side of the lines, Reuben A. Pierson described in a letter to his aunt a sermon he had heard preached by "a man on Gen. Jackson's Staff," possibly Robert L. Dabney. Its text was "How shall we escape if we neglect so great salvation," and Pierson thought it first rate.[3]

Joshua K. Callaway described another sermon in a letter to his wife. The preacher took his text from 1 Peter 4:18: "If the righteous scarcely be saved, where shall the ungodly and the sinner appear?" He then proceeded to show, on the basis of the Bible, the answer to that question. The ungodly and sinners, those who were without Christ, would appear "first at the death scene, secondly at the judgment, and finally in hell." Callaway found this a harrowing thought. But the preacher had then gone on. According to Callaway, "He dwelled upon the great plan of the atonement. Showed how the plan was concealed"—in its details—"in the secret counsels of God for four thousand years, and how even the angels looked down with pity on mankind, wondering how their salvation was to be effected, till all hope had well nigh expired and the darkness of despair was fast settling on the forlorn scene. Then drew a very vivid picture of the wonder, astonishment of the angels when at last the fact was revealed to them—when they saw the second person of the 'adorable Trinity' descend to earth and take our nature and assume our sins! Wonderful condescension!" The preacher next described, in the flowery language that was then popular, how the angels must have sung the praises of God. Callaway found it a compelling theme, concluding, "Now, my Dear, let us join the chorus and keep it up till old Earth shall resound with the soul thrilling song of redeeming grace and dying love.... Let us praise God always for this great salvation. I do now feel, thank the Lord, that I have an interest in it."[4]

What Callaway meant by the last statement, "I have an interest in it," was that he felt the inward assurance that, by God's grace and his repentance and faith, God had forgiven his sins and accepted him as a son. This is one of several terms the soldiers and their contemporaries used to refer to that assurance, a spiritual "inward witness" that they held to be of great importance.

They also believed that salvation was an individual thing, but not in the sense that the plan of salvation could vary from one person to another, like some modern existentialist idea of self-actualization. Rather, they stressed that each person had to avail himself individually of God's plan of salvation, which was fixed by God and eternal. The Second Rhode Island's Elisha Hunt Rhodes reported in his diary hearing a Virginia slave preacher address the subject in very homey terms. "He tried to prove from the Bible that truth that every man must seek his own salvation," Rhodes wrote. "He said: 'Brethren, the Scripture says, "Every man for himself. Every tub on its own Bottom."' Not exactly Scripture," Rhodes commented, "but it came near the truth."[5]

Soldiers who took advantage of the free stationery provided by the U.S. Christian Commission (a charitable and evangelistic organization aimed at helping Union soldiers) sometimes got an additional reminder of God's plan of salvation. Some of the stationery was headed with the Bible verse: "This is a faithful saying, and worthy of all acceptation, that Christ Jesus came into the world to save sinners; of whom I am chief."[6]

They also had frequent reminders of the importance of making sure of their salvation, and many of them reflected earnestly on this. Here it was important that a man get to the substance of the matter rather than merely go through religious motions or mouth pious mumbo jumbo. There was very little about Civil War–era religion that was of a mechanical or automatic nature, as if observance of a mere form would produce a given result, regardless of the seeker's state of mind. Rather, chaplains and other preachers in their sermons, and individual soldiers in their written meditations, placed enormous emphasis on the need for a genuinely and profoundly felt religion of the heart.

Union soldier Gideon W. Burtch took notes on a sermon he heard during the war. The text came from 2 Timothy 3:5, in which a passage about particularly depraved individuals describes them as "having a form of Godliness, but denying the power thereof." The chaplain first applied this to the Roman Catholic Church, long seen by Protestants as a conglomeration of "papist, Romish, mummery." "But," he went on, "the Romish church does not contain all the formalism there is. Every church is in danger from this source." He went on to show his listeners that they too needed to guard against the danger of going through religious motions without genuine religious fervor—faith, repentance, love for God—in their hearts. "Formalism," he stressed, "consists in clinging to the form & trusting to the form after the life has departed."[7] In like manner, the Ninth Louisiana's Reuben A. Pierson lamented that in the several Christian denominations with which he was familiar, "mere formalities are too often substituted in place of real heartfelt repentance for sins."[8]

This was not a matter of trivial importance. One's eternal destiny might hang in the balance, and numbers of the soldiers left record of having taken the question very seriously. The inward struggles of Confederate Lt. Thomas F. Boatright provide an example of how earnestly men sought an answer for it. Boatright must have heard a similar sermon from a chaplain one evening in 1863. He described it as "an exhortation stating . . . what constitutes Christianity," and it left him feeling "sad" and fearing that he had "got hold of the shaddow and not the substance." He shuddered at the thought of finally being lost, eternally separated from God, after the many religious observances he had performed and his public identification with Christianity—that he should "then prove to be [a] hypocrit amidst all the instruction that I have had . . . and so many sermons I have heard."

He took stock of his life and the degree of inward spiritual assurance he felt. "Then I often think of the realities of eternity, and the certainty of death rushes upon my mind. Am I prepared to meet God if I were called this moment from this world, and, Oh, am I prepared—this great question." To find the answer, "I will go to the word of God," the Bible. There he found the old truths he had long known: God is holy and must punish sin; he, Boatright, had sinned and deserved that punishment. "But here is a promiss: we have an advocate with the Father, Jesus the righteous, who is able to forgive sinners." Then, however, his mind snapped back to the same frightening question: did he truly have saving faith in Christ? Was he seeking God out of love, or merely because he feared punishment? Of course, he *did* fear punishment. Did he also love God? Or was he merely fooling himself?

No wonder he felt sad and fearful, but all the teaching he had received had not been entirely in vain, as evidenced by his conclusion. "One thing

I am determined," he wrote, "though I feel like I do this morning: that while I am permitted to live, to try and live in such a manner that the Lord will open my eyes if they are shut and that I may see wherein I am wrong." This proved the right course. Two months later, Boatright was joyously writing to his wife of the religious revival taking place in the army and proclaiming his assurance of acceptance in Christ. "My heart has been filled to overflowing this night," he wrote.[9]

The issues of repentance and faith with which Boatright struggled were fundamental and universal for anyone who sought forgiveness and peace with God through Jesus Christ, and naturally, other Civil War soldiers wrote of them. Most frequently mentioned was the subject of faith, which in this context meant an active belief that Christ could and would save the individual in question from sin and its penalty.

Reuben Pierson expressed his faith in an 1864 letter to his father. "I have a hope that my sins have been forgiven through the mediation of . . . Him who was crucified that poor wretched, sinful mortals might find acceptance to a throne of grace."[10] Union soldier David H. Blair, for his part, spoke of the necessity of faith. In a letter to his sister that same year, he wrote, "Don't forget to commit me to the kind care of kind Providence for it is only by His protecting power that we are saved from these leaden missels or if they should take effect it is by the same power we will have to be saved from eternal punishment, and," he added, "we have to trust the work to him or he will not do it."[11]

Like Thomas Boatright, many soldiers, as well as others of that era, had difficulty with this requirement. Joshua Callaway struggled for weeks during 1863 seeking an assurance that he truly had saving faith. In mid-September, with the army of which he was a part maneuvering toward a showdown battle with Union forces in northwestern Georgia, Callaway wrote to his wife regarding the progress he was making in his personal spiritual battle. "I can now go into the fight without that great dread which has hitherto haunted me," he wrote. "I have a good mind to say that I believe that God is reconciled to me through the blood of Christ which interceedeth for me. But I am afraid to say it! Oh, for a little more faith!"[12] Callaway survived the subsequent battle of Chickamauga and so had more time to deal with his doubts.

The lack of faith that he perceived, and with which other Civil War soldiers struggled, was not an inability to believe that God existed. They believed very much in His existence, and they believed He would send them to hell if they could not somehow muster an inward sense of assurance that Christ would save them. They feared hell and feared that they could not summon the feeling of belief that would keep them out of it. In part it was a residue of previous Calvinist teaching that had once pervaded American religion. Though rejected by a large majority of American Christians by this time, its vestiges still influenced many to act and think as if the decision of belief or unbelief lay with someone other than themselves. In part, too, it was the spirit of the age. In an era that focused strongly on emotions, people were substituting the emotional feeling of inner assurance for the action of believing.

David Holt of the Sixteenth Mississippi heard a preacher try to combat this problem in a sermon preached in April 1864. "Belief," the preacher said, "is in your own control. When you make up your mind to believe, why you believe. And when you make up your mind not to believe, why you do not believe, and that is all there is to it." He went on to explain that although the matter was that simple, it had momentous results. "You either [have] on the one hand Salvation for your believing, or Damnation for your unbelief.... If you are lost you cannot blame our Lord. He has done everything consistent with our own manhood to influence our choice for the good and the rejection of the bad." Holt liked that preaching, and others did too. He noted that "about a hundred" had professed faith in Christ that day in response to the sermon.[13] But preachers did not always succeed in making the matter so plain, nor could the hearers always succeed in putting aside their doubts and fears. Many continued to struggle with them for months or years.

The other fundamental requirement for salvation—repentance—could also be a matter of personal struggle for members of the Civil War generation, though perhaps in a more straightforward way. Repentance is closely related to faith. As Union officer's wife Emily Elliott recorded in her diary her own strivings to be a better Christian, she wrote, "May my faith be shown by my works."[14] In this she was simply applying to herself the exact words of the Bible. Faith, if genuine, would always be reflected in good works. If Emily truly believed that Jesus was the Son of God and had forgiven her sins, then she would naturally show this in a changed manner of life, avoiding sin and trying to please God.

This change of heart that leads to a change of life is the essence of repentance. If a Civil War soldier, or anybody else, was going to find salvation in Jesus Christ, he would need not only faith but also its inevitable companion: repentance, or a turning away from sin. Some might balk at this requirement, being unwilling to give up their sinning ways, and the result would be another spiritual struggle. Samuel P. Lockhart wrote to his sister, "I would give any thing in this world to be a good Christian." That this was not quite true he revealed in the next sentence, when he admitted, "Still it looks like a hard matter for me to give up."[15]

For those who became Christians, the struggle to "give up," whether long or short, ended in a happy surrender and yielding to God's grace. Lt. Chesley Mosman of the Fifty-ninth Illinois recorded in his diary how several soldiers at an 1864 preaching service had risen to ask for prayer, confessing that they were "tired of rebellion and want to serve their God."[16]

Misconceptions about the doctrines of repentance and faith were as rife during the Civil War era as in any other, and as likely to produce confusion, frustration, and despair. Just as some made the mistake of thinking that emotional assurance preceded (rather than followed) the exercise of faith, so others became confused about the doctrine of repentance and tended to act and talk as if they hoped that a change of life (refraining from sin) would result in their acceptance with God. "Being a Christian," in their parlance, meant living according to certain standards, and, not surprisingly, one reads in their letters and diaries frequent laments that they were unable to do so, along with abundant excuses. "I cannot help thinking myself," William T. Stewart wrote to his wife, "why I cannot be a true christian. I wish to be but I have so many around me that are hard hearted."[17] If he just tried a bit harder, one presumes, or if he got more encouragement from those around him, perhaps he could make himself "a true christian." Similarly, an Alabama officer wrote to his fiancée, "I will try to be a better man, to be a Christian."[18]

Moses A. Parker of the Third Vermont, despite an abundance of good advice, seemed to think that becoming a Christian was a process akin to mucking out a barn. To "Friend Eliza" he wrote, "I have thought of your advice in the last letter you wrote to me a great many times since I read it warning me to put my trust in Him whose arm is ever able and willing to save those who will seek him. I have a good mother and two sisters at home who are continualy writing me such advices and it has been a subject on my mind for the past 4 months. . . . I have tried to pray, have had others pray for me . . . but still I feel myself a sinner but there is one thing that I have broke myself of and that is swearing."[19]

The idea that one had to—or could—earn one's way into God's favor, though quite foreign to the Bible, was reflected in some Civil War soldiers' attitudes toward the possibility of coming to Christ and finding forgiveness during the final hours of one's life. Edwin H. Fay, who mixed Christian ideas with his "Turkish doctrines," found the idea offensive. In a letter to his wife he mentioned a young man who had been shot in a drunken brawl. The youth "lived nearly a week and gave evidence as far as human judgment goes of a sincere repentance." That was not good enough for Fay, however. "I don't believe in, or at least, I think a death bed repentance in very bad taste to say the least," he opined. "To cheat ones Creator out of all the service due him to the last moment and then claim the advantages of a crucified Redeemer, God must be more tender than I am accustomed to regard him if he often makes a practice of accepting such a magnanimous offering." Still, Fay had to admit that Christ had forgiven a repentant thief who was crucified on the cross next to His own. In the end, Fay did not know what to think.[20]

An opinion similar to Fay's can be seen in even more stark form in the tale of Maj. James Doherty of the Fifty-seventh Massachusetts. Gravely wounded in the heavy fighting in Virginia during the summer of 1864, Doherty was carried to the division field hospital, but the surgeons could do nothing for him. The regiment's chaplain, the Reverend Mr. Dashiell, "pressed upon him the gracious offer of salvation through Christ," but the major, knowing he was dying, nevertheless replied that he "could not insult the savior by offering him the dregs of my life. God bless you, Chaplain," he said, and was gone.[21]

Christians often tried to help seekers find the way and avoid the pitfall of thinking that they could earn their way into acceptance with God. One Sunday afternoon, Union soldier Joseph Whitney heard a group of men from his regiment gathered for worship singing the hymn "Come Ye Sinners, Poor and Needy," a song that aimed at countering just this error.[22] The hymn writer, and those who sang his composition, strove to convince the wavering that if they were but willing, God would supply all that was needed:

Come, ye sinners, poor and needy, Weak and wounded, sick and sore;
Jesus ready stands to save you, Full of pity, love and power.
He is able, He is willing: doubt no more.

Now, ye needy, come and welcome; God's free bounty glorify;
True belief and true repentance, Every grace that brings you nigh;
Without money, Come to Jesus Christ and buy.

Let not conscience make you linger, Nor of fitness fondly dream;
All the fitness he requireth Is to feel your need of him:
This he gives you; 'Tis the Spirit's glimmering beam.

Come, ye weary, heavy-laden, Broken, ruined by the Fall;
If you tarry till you're better, You will never come at all;
Not the righteous—Sinners Jesus came to call.[23]

Some understood; some did not.

Some were hindered by the teachings of Calvinism, still held by such groups as the "Hard-shell" Baptists and the Old School Presbyterians. In Libby Prison, Richmond, Virginia, in October 1864, Abner Small, who had wondered at the soldiers singing the Doxology on the battlefield earlier that year, wondered again at the beliefs of a fellow prisoner. After a lengthy discussion with a Captain Stewart, Small wrote in his diary, "Capt. is a firm Calvinist and predestinarian . . . but fails to convince me in his theory. Seems as though I should be very unhappy did I believe it." Small wrote that he had "a strong desire to be a consistent Christian" but felt "chilled when Capt. Stewart tells me that God fore-ordained individuals to salvation before they were born."[24]

Levi Lockhart also found such doctrines repugnant. In an 1862 letter he told his sister, "There is preaching here today, but this is a hard-shell church. I would like to hear some good preaching."[25]

As they did with the misconception of earning God's favor, most Christians of the era tried hard to combat ideas such as those of Captain Stewart. Union soldier Gideon Burtch, for example, took notes on a March 1864 sermon on the Bible text "Whosoever will, let him come and partake of the water of life freely."[26]

Among his odd collection of beliefs, Edwin Fay included another feature of Calvinism and, unlike Small, found it much to his liking. From Okolona, Mississippi, in 1863 he wrote, "In an argument the other day with Jon & Capt. Webb, I had occasion to refer to my testament and I found there the doctrine of the final perseverance of the Saints so fully expressed that I am really encouraged to believe that I once had well grounded hope of Salvation through the atoning blood of a sacrificed Redeemer and that I shall be spared to come back into the Fold."[27] Since he had, as he supposed, truly come to Christ in repentance and faith at some earlier date, he imagined that his final salvation was guaranteed, notwithstanding his more recent dalliance with "Turkish doctrine" or his frequently and openly expressed bitterness against God for various wrongs he thought the Almighty had done him.

Not all Christians of that or other eras would have agreed. Thomas Boatright, speaking of the good things God had done for him and others in making the way of salvation possible, wrote, "If we who are so much blessed should live out of Christ and die out of him what ought to be our condition? Distruction. Distruction."[28]

Despite various pitfalls and the prevalence of some misconceptions, many during the Civil War did find repentance and faith and strongly expressed their satisfaction and comfort in being reconciled to God. The Twelfth Tennessee's Alfred Fielder had been a Christian before enlisting in the army and continued steadfast in the faith. After being wounded at the battle of Atlanta in July 1864, Fielder lay in the hospital, "quite feeble" in body, "but my faith and trust is strong in God through the merits of Christs death and passion [suffering] on the cross for me—and live or die I am his." He lived.[29]

Although repentance and faith are personal choices, those choices are made possible by the intervention of God's Holy Spirit, the Third Person of the Trinity. The Holy Spirit's role is to help believers and to draw unbelievers toward repentance and faith in Christ. The Christians in the Civil War armies sometimes spoke of this. Elisha Hunt Rhodes recorded in his diary, "We have Christian men in the Regiment, but there are many who take no interest in religious matters. I trust that God's spirit will move upon their hearts and turn them to repentance."[30] Ignatius Brock urged his sister to turn to Christ for salvation and not to reject the workings of the Holy Spirit in her heart. "You treat no other friend as you treat the Holy Spirit sent by our blessed Savior. He woos you to turn from your sins and be happy. You reject his entreaties; still He strives with you. He pleads with you by the love He has shown us but you say, Go thy way for this time, when I have a more convenient season I will call for thee. Do not thus grieve Him, he may depart never to return."[31]

Of course, many of the soldiers and their contemporaries did indeed reject God's offer of forgiveness. S. A. Cunningham noted after the series of battles for Atlanta that of all the soldiers in his Forty-first Tennessee who had died in those struggles, not "one was prepared to die. How strange," Cunningham wrote, "that men will go blindly into eternity, when a light is offered that will show them the way."[32] Lying badly wounded on the battlefield of Ball's Bluff, young Lt. Oliver Wendell Holmes, Jr., of the Twentieth Massachusetts thought that he was probably dying. Holmes was in a minority among Civil War soldiers, in that he openly denied the truth of Christianity. He now reflected "that the majority vote of the civilized world declared that with my opinions I was en route for Hell." It was, Holmes added, a thought of "painful distinctness." Changing his mind now, however, would involve humiliation, and "besides, thought I, can I recant if I want to, has the approach of death changed my beliefs much? & to this I answered—No." Holmes tried to apply his philosophy to the matter. "I am to take a leap in the dark," he thought, as he mused about what might be in store for him after death, but he decided that was all right. To a friend who found him lying there, Holmes said, "Well Harry I'm dying but I'll be G. d'd if I know where I'm going."[33] As it turned out, Holmes recovered from that wound and several others sustained during the war, and his leap into darkness was postponed several decades.

When, by the help of the Holy Spirit, an individual settled the issues of faith and repentance, the result was conversion, or what was often referred to, in words Christ used on one occasion, being "born again." Assured inwardly by the Holy Spirit of their acceptance by God, people in the highly emotional nineteenth century sometimes reacted in very emotional ways, with tears or even shouts of joy. Sometimes it was more quiet and restrained. Frequently their joy came through in the letters in which they informed the folks came home of their decision.

Ignatius Brock, taking stock of his life thus far on his twenty-first birthday, wrote to his sister, "I regard giving myself to God as the wisest step I ever took."[34] James C. Bates wrote home to his mother and sister in Texas from his regiment's camp near Atlanta in July 1864. "I have something else to tell you," wrote Bates, "which I believe will give you more pleasure than anything I have written. When I bid you good bye on leaving home & received the parting injunction to meet you in heaven if we should not meet again on earth—I resolved *that I would try,* and now through the mercy of the great & good God I feel that *my sins are forgiven me,* and that although we may never meet here again, I will meet you in Heaven where partings are not known. Oh I would not exchange the *peace & happiness* that this 'blessed hope' gives me, for the wealth of all the world."[35]

Twenty-six-year-old Lt. Nesbit Baugher of the Forty-fifth Illinois lived six weeks after receiving his death wound at the battle of Shiloh, but unlike Doherty and Holmes, Baugher during that time "proposed his whole dependence and earnest trust in Jesus Christ for salvation. His hope in the merits of the cross," a friend wrote, "was precious to himself and is to his friends," who could look forward to meeting him again in heaven one day.[36] Likewise, in a makeshift Confederate army hospital in Orange Court House, Virginia, Confederate soldier Thomas C. Render lay dying of typhoid fever one day in August 1861. Asked by fellow members of the Eighth Georgia if he was ready to meet God, he had to reply that he was not. His comrades prayed for him and returned later in the day. This time, Render accepted their urging that he seek God and could then assure his comrades that he was "willing to meet his Savior." Several hours later he died.[37] Nurse Mary Livermore told of a Union soldier who lay dying in the hospital ward where she worked. He was not prepared to die and knew it. "I have lived an awful life, and I'm afraid to die. I shall go to hell." Livermore told him to be quiet. Later a Methodist minister came to the

ward. He talked to the soldiers, urging them to trust Christ for their salvation, and he also sang hymns. After a time, the dying soldier said, "It's
all right with me chaplain! I will trust in Christ! God will forgive me! I
can die now!" Standing nearby, Nurse Livermore was impressed. "I looked
at the dying man beside me," she wrote, "and saw, underneath the deep-
ening pallor of death, an almost radiant gleam."[38]

B. F. Leitner of the Second South Carolina received a mortal wound
in the Seven Days battles. Asked what final message he wanted sent to
his family, he said, "Write, I die happy. My confidence in God and our
Savior is unshaken. I am going to heaven." In like manner, when T. S.
Chandler of the Sixth South Carolina lay dying after the battle of Murfreesboro, he wanted word sent to his mother: "My hope is in Christ, for
whose sake I hope to be saved. Tell her that she and my brother cannot
see me again on earth, but they can meet me in heaven." When a chaplain came to see Virginia Capt. James K. Lee, after Lee had suffered a
mortal wound during a skirmish in 1861, the minister spoke sympatheti-
cally of Lee's "intense sufferings." "Oh," replied the captain emphatically,
"They are nothing to the sufferings which Jesus bore for me!"[39]

Personal salvation by grace through faith in the merits of Jesus Christ
is the heart and soul of Christianity. As such, it was central to the religion of large numbers of Civil War soldiers, as well as their friends and
relatives back home. Vast additional numbers during that era essentially
believed the truth of this doctrine (at least in whatever form they understood it) without embracing it, or feeling able to embrace it, themselves.
To begin to understand the thoughts and motives—the worldview—of
the generation that fought the Civil War, it is necessary to understand
the assurance that led Gideon Burtch to write ecstatically in his diary, "I
have peace with God. I feel that I am rooted and grounded in Christ. [My]
Tabernacle is builded upon the rock of Ages which the crash of worlds
can not shake & which the combined powers of hell can never move. He
sent from above, He took me, He drew me out of many waters. The Lord
liveth & blessed be my rock & let the God of my salvation be exalted."[40]

5

"HIS GRACE IS EVER SUFFICIENT FOR ME"
The Christian Life

In the autumn of 1862, Confederate troops gathered at a large open-air meeting and began with the singing of a favorite hymn, a standby of camp meetings and Sunday services for longer than any of these young men—or their parents, for that matter—could remember:

> How firm a foundation, ye saints of the Lord,
> Is laid for your faith in His excellent word!
> What more can He say than to you He hath said,
> To you who for refuge to Jesus have fled?

The scene might have been in the Army of Northern Virginia or the Army of Tennessee or any of the other Confederate forces. It was repeated often in all of them.[1] Had the uniforms been different, it could have been in the Northern armies equally well. "How Firm a Foundation" was a favorite hymn of soldiers and civilians on both sides. Its author unknown, the hymn had first been published in London in 1787, and on these shores it was usually sung to a traditional American tune. It spoke of God's many precious promises to the believer, but most of all it emphasized that these were to be found in the Bible, "His excellent word," and that in that book

Christians had a "firm foundation" for their faith and all that they needed for the living of a godly life. The hymn itself and its great popularity emphasized the fact that Christianity in the nineteenth century—or any other, for that matter—was a religion based on one book, and that book was the Bible. It was of great importance to soldiers and their contemporaries who wanted to live the kind of life that was proper for a Christian. Many Civil War soldiers, North and South, would have agreed with the sentiment expressed by a black Union soldier: "Let me lib wid de musket in one hand and de Bible in de oder."[2]

What the Bible said was taken by all Christians and a great many others as undeniable truth. A soldier of the Sixth Wisconsin spoke of new recruits falling for the veterans' "big bear and bull stories" and believing them "as implicitly as if they read them out of the Bible."[3] The statement was indicative of the respect the book received, for most Americans in the nineteenth century believed it to be nothing less than the inspired Word of God.

The Bible consists of two parts, the Old Testament and the New Testament. The Old, written between the fifteenth and fifth centuries before Christ, is foundational to all of Christianity. It is about four times longer than the New Testament. The latter, written entirely in the first century A.D., contains more direct and open statements of such doctrines as salvation through Christ. For these reasons, many soldiers, eager to minimize the loads in their packs, pockets, or blanket rolls, chose to carry only the New Testament in a small pocket-size volume. If a soldier carried a complete Bible, he would want it to be an especially compact edition, but for a great many soldiers, any Bible was better than none.

The particular translation used by the vast majority of American Christians during the Civil War was the 1767 revision of the old 1611 "Authorized" or "King James" translation. Sometimes described as the only literary masterpiece ever produced by a committee—in this case, a team of English scholars of the Greek and Hebrew languages—the King James translation featured the melodic tones of Shakespearean English and the stately cadences that underlay the soaring public prose of Abraham Lincoln, who was steeped in its words from early childhood. Its stilted expressions and archaic verb forms, especially the "-th" endings in the third-person singular, found their way into the language of the Civil War soldiers when they wrote about religious topics. Ideas, word pictures, and examples from the pages of the Bible—things that belonged more to the Greek and Hebrew original texts than to any one translation—were the common coin of myriad discussions by all classes of people on all topics during the nineteenth century.

Reading the Bible, in language ever so archaic and a volume of whatever size, was a welcome encouragement to many amid the trying scenes of war. Samuel E. Piper of the 158th Pennsylvania wrote to his wife in April 1863, "My Testament is a great comfort to me . . . when I get a chance to read."[4] Aurelius Voorhis of the Forty-sixth Indiana wrote in his diary, "My Testament is my only companion."[5] Indiana soldier James Shanklin wrote, "The blessed promises of the Bible, when a man feels depressed and weary, are like a refreshing cordial."[6] Numberless times the soldiers told their correspondents as well as their diaries of reading the Bible on a regular basis. Phrases such as "Read the scriptures," "I finished reading the book of John," "I read the testament," "I have read five chapters in the Testament today," "I must now read some in the Testament," "I shall endeavor to obey your wishes in reading my Bible every night," appear again and again in their writings.[7]

In many cases, when a regiment or company was first being organized and preparing to march off to war, local citizens would provide New Testaments for distribution to all the departing soldiers. In 1861 the Atlanta Grays, soon to become Company F, Eighth Georgia, were typical. At a solemn ceremony before boarding the train for Virginia, the company paraded in the streets of Atlanta. A delegation of local ladies presented a fine silk flag, and then prominent Atlantan Mark A. Cooper delivered a farewell address. At the conclusion of the speech, Cooper walked down the line of new soldiers, handing a New Testament to each. More oratory and much shouting followed, and then the Grays went on their way to Virginia and to writing their own small piece of Civil War history.[8] Similarly, when the Tioga Mountaineers prepared to go off to become Company B of the 101st Pennsylvania, each man received a New Testament inscribed on its flyleaf with the words "Presented by the Ladies of Richmond," meaning Richmond Township, Pennsylvania.[9] The ladies of Monroe, Michigan, presented not only Bibles but also Episcopal prayer books to the soldiers of the Seventh Michigan as the regiment prepared to leave the city.[10]

This scene was repeated so often that it comes as a surprise to find that large numbers of Civil War soldiers lacked copies of any part of the Bible and were extremely eager to acquire them. This was especially true of soldiers from the South, which lacked major printing and book-binding facilities. Part of this desire for Bibles can be explained by an increased religious interest among the soldiers, and part of it undoubtedly stems from the fact that soldiers frequently lost their baggage. For example, a regiment would usually receive orders to remove and stack knapsacks before going into battle, and whether they ever saw those knapsacks or their contents again depended on the course of the fighting and perhaps other vicissitudes of war. No doubt many men lost their Bibles or Testaments in this way. After the September 1862 battle of South Mountain, a Union soldier found "a large pile of knapsacks belonging to the enemy & found in the knapsacks all Kinds of Little articles, such as razors, photegrafs, Bibles, with some very fine mottoes on the margins of them."[11]

It is also possible that men threw away Bibles or Testaments, as they did many other, sometimes valuable, personal possessions when on long, hot marches they became monomaniacs on the subject of traveling light, or they may have abandoned their Bibles in other circumstances. When Union troops in March 1862 took over the Centreville, Virginia, quarters previously occupied by the Confederates, the Yankees noticed that "there were quite a number of Bibles and tracts left in their cabins."[12] Finally, there were many regiments in which no initial distribution of testaments took place and in which the soldiers marched off wishing they had Bibles.

At any rate, Civil War soldiers were frequently extremely eager to receive copies of the Bible or portions thereof. John Stuckenberg, chaplain of the 145th Pennsylvania, noted in his diary in October 1862 that he had received a shipment of Testaments from the regiment's hometown of Erie, Pennsylvania, and distributed them to the men. "All seem to be glad at receiving the Word of Life," Stuckenberg wrote, "even those who are positively wicked."[13] Earlier in 1862, Rev. J. T. C. Collins visited Confederate camps and hospitals near Okolona, Mississippi, for the purpose of distributing Bibles and other religious literature. "The soldiers received the books with great eagerness," Collins reported, "I never in all my life saw such a desire to get Bibles. Every [hospital] ward I went into they would beg me for *Bibles and Testaments*. While they gladly received the other books, they wanted *Bibles*."[14]

Few aspects of Christian doctrine were immune to distortion by those who had not been well instructed or who were looking for ways, as they supposed, to use spiritual powers for their own ends. Respect for the Bible could sometimes be distorted into a strange and almost talismanic belief that the book itself had mystical properties. Instead of taking the Bible at its own claim—that its words were "able to make thee wise unto salvation"—some soldiers and their relatives got the idea that the very paper and leather of the book would be a shield in the day of battle—literally. Various stories were current at that time regarding Bibles or Testaments actually stopping what would otherwise have been fatal bullets. Some of these stories may indeed have been true. For example, oral legend in the family of David H. Blair, as told by his grandson, was that "he was shot by a sharpshooter while preparing supper, but the bullet hit a Bible that he was carrying in his shirt pocket and failed to completely penetrate the Bible. The impact knocked the breath out of him but no injury." Regarding the incident, on June 18, 1864, Blair himself wrote only, "I came near being shot by sharpshooter while getting dinner."[15] Confederate soldier Philip D. Stephenson knew of a "Lieutenant Jewell" in his regiment who at the 1863 battle of Ringgold Gap "was struck square in the heart by a bullet! Or rather, he would have been, had not a little testament stopped it. The testament saved his life." Jewell was later killed in action at another battle, and Stephenson speculated that perhaps God had sent the first bullet to warn him of the brevity of life and the need to prepare for death.[16]

With so many bullets striking so many soldiers—the Civil War saw 620,000 dead of all causes, and hundreds of thousands more wounded—it would not be too far-fetched to suppose that some providentially favored soldier did get struck in his Bible pocket, an event that would have made quite an impression on him. As the various stories made the rounds, it was also natural that many soldiers got the wrong idea. William A. Moore of the Third New York Independent Battery wrote in his memoirs, "I know of cases when card players, on going into battle, would throw away their cards and place their testament in their breast pocket over the heart."[17] Card playing was frowned on by most Protestant denominations at that time, so Moore's implication is that these men had not hitherto been taking their religion very seriously.

Those more familiar with Christianity seemed less likely to fall into this way of thinking. Virginia artillery officer John Hampden Chamberlayne chided his mother good-naturedly about a request she had sent him. "Since you desire it," Chamberlayne wrote, "I will certainly wear the testament over my heart, but if you mean it as a shield it is somewhat late seeing the campaign [Antietam] is over." Besides, he pointed out, the pit of the stomach was just as vital a part, so why not wear something to protect that? In any case, he sensibly reminded her, he did have the consolation of his faith in God, whatever the results of future battle might be. "Did I tell you," he asked in a final jibe, "of the man whose life was saved by a pack of cards in his breast pocket?"[18]

Oddly enough, Confederate soldier David Holt had another story of a man being saved by his deck of cards. A comrade of Holt's named Bill went into battle in May 1864 with a pack of cards in his breast pocket. "Bill," called another comrade as they marched into the fight, "ain't you going to throw away that new deck of cards you have got in your pocket?" Bill replied that he would not. His mother had taught him to play cards, and she was a good member of the Episcopal Church. Besides, he never gambled with that deck, and that was what mattered. Sure enough, not long after that, a bullet struck him, and down he went. Moments later he was up and fighting again. "When he got his jacket open, back there in the pasture," Holt recalled, "he found the ball that had penetrated the deck of cards, flattening out when it reached the ace of spades. Upon discovering this, Bill claimed the ace of spades to be his lucky card."[19]

Most Civil War soldiers would sensibly have concluded that neither a Bible nor a pack of cards was of primary use as body armor, but a large proportion of them would have accepted the proposition that the Bible was God's Word, conveying information that was vital to man's salvation and to living the kind of life that would be pleasing to God.

While God spoke to believers through the Bible, they spoke to Him in prayer. Chaplains and other ministers, both in and out of the army, taught about prayer. In a December 1861 sermon, one preacher took as his text Luke 18:1, "Men ought always to pray" and expounded on what prayer is and how the intercession of Jesus Christ assures that God hears prayers.[20] Chaplain E. E. Helsey of the Seventh Ohio wrote a brief note to the parents of John H. Burton, a wounded soldier from Cleveland. Helsey reported on their son's condition and the encouraging indications for his recovery and praised his fortitude. Then he wrote, "I hope your most earnest prayers will go up not only for his speedy recovery but also for his soul's salvation. The promise," he added, quoting the Bible, "is 'Ask and ye shall receive, seek and ye shall find.'"[21]

Nor were chaplains the only ones who valued the privilege of prayer. "I feel assured that I have your prayers," Thomas F. Boatright wrote to his wife. "Pray and the Lord will hear and answer them in his own good time."[22] Marcus A. Stults wrote from the camp of the Third New Jersey militia to his minister back home, thanking him for his prayers and confessing that since joining the army he had gained a whole new outlook on the subject. "I must say," Stults wrote, "I have never [before] truly appreciated the true benefit of prayer."[23] The Twenty-eighth Alabama's Joshua K. Callaway wrote to his wife, "I hope you will continue to do as you have been doing, pray for the preservation of my health and moral character. I am a believer in the power of prayer."[24]

Christians could, of course, pray at any time, but the privilege was valued most when they could not do anything else to influence the situation. Levi Lockhart wrote to his sister in 1863, warning that mail service between them might well be interrupted for a time, "but we can remember each other in our prayers to our Heavenly Father."[25] Distraught at news that her husband lay at death's door as a result of a wound, Emily Elliott fretted at the train delays that prevented her from rushing to his side. "I can pray for him," she wrote in her diary.[26]

Christians among the soldiers, as well as their friends and relatives back home, prayed for a variety of things and often saw the answers they had sought actually become reality. Not surprisingly, one of the things for which the soldiers and their families prayed was God's protection in battle. Henry Hoyt was a member of the Second Connecticut Heavy Artillery when he wrote in a letter to his family in May 1864, "This morning we got orders to prepare to take the field by tomorrow at daylight. . . . May your prayers go with us as I know they will & we will offer ours to the same being who watches over us in war as well as in peace."[27]

The first battle of Bull Run, in 1861, was fought on a Sunday, and the early stages of the fighting occurred during the very hours when Christians all over the nation were customarily worshipping God. Capt. N. H. R. Dawson of the hard-hit Fourth Alabama thought of this in the midst of the fighting, thought of how his fiancée back in Selma was probably even then praying for his safety, "and I was nerved and strengthened to do my duty."[28] Nearby, the Eighth Georgia was taking a terrific pounding, losing almost half its men in less than half an hour. Of its ten companies, only K, the Oglethorpe Rifles, came through the battle without a single fatality. Only a number of days later did the soldiers learn that, at the very day and hour when the Eighth was being shot to pieces in a nameless pine thicket on the slopes of Matthews Hill, the people back home in Oglethorpe County, Georgia, were holding a special prayer meeting at Atkinson's Church to pray for the safety of their boys in the Oglethorpe Rifles.[29]

At the December 1863 battle of Fredericksburg, the Twenty-third New York suffered severely. Afterward, Seymour Dexter of that regiment wrote to a friend at home to say that none of the boys from his particular locality in Elmira, New York, had been hit, despite 15 percent casualties in their company. They attributed their deliverance to "a prayer of faith that has ascended to the throne of mercy, from friends at home."[30]

Similarly, Reuben A. Pierson in 1863 attributed the relatively light losses of his company to divine intervention in answer to prayer. "I feel that the petitions of our pious old fathers and mothers, brother and sisters are often heard in heaven and blessings are showered upon our heads for the sake of those Christian friends who so often plead our cause before a throne of Grace."[31] Likewise, after the battles for Atlanta, James Theaker wrote that his Company F of the Fiftieth Ohio "has in all this campaign lost but one man wounded, & he is getting well." He attributed this to God's protection, writing to his sister, "I know that there do many prayers go up for me at the family altar [i.e., a time of family worship to God, usually held each evening in the home], and I hope & trust they may be answered, and my desire is that you will continue to pray for me, the success of our arms, the country, and peace."[32]

Peace was another earnestly desired subject of prayer, and, as in Theaker's mention, it was usually at least implicitly linked with "the success of our arms." A Mississippi soldier wrote of his hopes that the Yankees would give up the fight, adding, "God rules over nations as well as individuals, and if Christians would pray more sincerely I think an end would sometime come."[33] In soon-to-be-besieged Vicksburg, the Thirty-first Louisiana's Henry T. Morgan wrote to his wife in April 1863, mentioning how glad he was that "you all meet and helt prayer for the soldiers and fore pease. It is a good thing no dot. You may help end the war by so doing."[34]

Soldiers also prayed for their immediate needs, and perhaps none more earnestly than those who found themselves inside the Confederate prison camp at Andersonville, Georgia. Horrible conditions were created when Confederate authorities jammed tens of thousands of Union enlisted prisoners into a stockade enclosure and provided them with no order, no shelter, and little food. Any prisoner who ventured over a "dead-line" a few feet from the stockade fence was shot dead. In this unnatural state of nature, thousands of prisoners died. The chief cause of many of the deaths was the foul water supply. A sluggish creek ran through the camp of the Confederate guard detachment and then into and through the prison stockade. None too clean even when it entered the stockade, this creek was all the water the prisoners had for drinking, cooking, washing, or bathing, and lying in the lowest part of the enclosed area, it was also a natural sink for all the corruption of the prison. Andersonville prisoner William N. Tyler recalled the situation:

We had some praying men at Andersonville. They held nightly prayer meetings, and they prayed for water. They prayed like men that meant business, for we were all dying for the want of it. One day after one of these meetings there occurred one of the most fearful rains I ever saw. It washed out the stockade as clean as a hound's tooth. Right between the dead-line and the stockade it washed a ditch about two feet deep and a spring of cold water broke out in a stream large enough to fill a four-inch pipe. The spring is there yet, I am told, and to this day is called Providence spring. It broke out in the very best place it could for our benefit. The stockade protected it on one side from the Rebels, and the dead-line on the other side protected it from the prisoners. The fountain head was thus protected. We had good water from then on.[35]

Besides praying for protection, for peace, and for the supplying of their physical needs, Christians and those who inclined toward Christianity among the Civil War soldiers also prayed for their spiritual well-being and wanted the folks back home to pray to that end as well. "Pray for me," wrote a Union officer, "that I may do my duty to God and man."[36] In an October 1863 letter to his wife in which he spoke of his newfound faith in Christ, Joshua Callaway wrote gratefully about the prayers of many of his relatives for his salvation. "I know that the Lord has heard and is answering the prayers that have gone up to Heaven for me and my Soul thrills with joy at the thought of meeting all those dear relatives in heaven."[37] Albert M. Childs of the Thirtieth Wisconsin wrote to his brother, "Were it not for the fact that God is ever willing to listen to our prayers, wherever we may be placed, if they come from a contrite heart, and answer as well as listen to them, it would be vain for me to strive to be a Christian. But his grace is ever sufficient for me, and I am determined to strive on, til the end."[38] Similarly, near the end of the war, Louisianan Henry T. Morgan assured his wife, "My hopes is as strong and as good fore heaven as they was ever." Then he urged, "Ellen I earnestly ask your prayer in my behalf and you may rest assured the I will not forgit you and the children. This should be a time of prayer. Wee have prayer meetings hear every night at our tent."[39]

Prayer could be a confusing topic, if one thought deeply about it. What if one prayed for something that was not truly for the best? Would God grant such a prayer? And how did a belief in prayer square with a simultaneous belief in God's sovereignty? In fact, not all prayers appeared to be answered, at least not in the way conceived of by those who offered them. Clearly the sovereign God was not a menial servant at the beck and call of mere humans. Those who reflected on the matter at any length had to come to the conclusion that a prayer was just that, a request, and God in His wisdom and love might choose to grant it, deny it, or modify its fulfillment. But many still struggled with the concept.

Joshua Callaway, at a time when he understood relatively little of Christianity, wrote to his wife Dulcinea, "Let it be your constant prayer, faithful & fervent, that I return, and all the yankees in yankeedom can not hurt me, & I shall live to be blessed by you."[40] Yet eighteen months after Callaway penned those lines, an unknown Yankee did get him at the battle of Missionary Ridge. Did Dulcinea flag in the faithfulness and fervor of her prayers? Or did a sovereign God simply rule otherwise?

John McMahon mused on the subject while still living at home in upstate New York late in 1861. A man in his church "asked us to pray for his brother," who was a captain in the Seventy-eighth New York and had recently embarked on an amphibious expedition against the Southern coast. The man requested prayer that his brother's "life be preserved." "The thought came into my mind," McMahon reflected, "whether it was best to pray that the lives of our friends should be spared. We have been told that whatsoever we asked of God in the name of Christ believing, we should receive. If they die now, they may go to heaven but if they live they may go to hell. And there has been cases of the lives of persons being spared by praying earnestly when it was not for the best."[41] But then how could McMahon truly be sure that such had been the case? It was all very difficult for a mere mortal to sort out.

David Holt of the Sixteenth Mississippi came close to untangling it when he reminisced about his state of mind on the eve of the battle of Fredericksburg. "The greatest comfort was in prayer," Holt wrote, "that sort of prayer which may be called communion with God. One recognized the perfect Almighty all-loving Father on one hand, and the weak, erring child on the other, a child who is in a very tight place. The will of the Father seemed to me to be the one thing that I longed to see done, and yet I hoped that it was His will to spare me. You cannot keep out the personal feelings for self at such times, because you know how painful it is to get your own hide punctured."[42]

Holt had caught the essence of the issue. God's children might not always understand His ways or know what was best, and they might find it hard to sort out their own fears and desires when seeking His will, but nevertheless they felt assured that a loving heavenly Father was ready at all times to hear and, if consistent with their own best interests, to grant their prayers. "Prayer," as James Shanklin summed up the matter, "is a great thing, which can and ought to be indulged in all the time."[43]

Sunday, December 21, 1862, was a briskly cool day in the camps of the Army of Northern Virginia just back of Fredericksburg, but not too cold for divine service. The men of George T. "Tige" Anderson's Georgia brigade turned out to hear a visiting preacher from their home state, a Reverend Mr. Potter. The army was fresh from its overwhelming victory at Fredericksburg, and the men of Anderson's brigade remembered how just one week before they had lain in line of battle under intermittent artillery and sniper fire. Those present now were thankful to have come unscathed through the battle and were enjoying this day as the kind of Sunday they liked, one of rest and worship. That made it particularly meaningful to them when Potter recited the words of a John Newton hymn:[44]

> Safely through another week
> God has brought us on our way;
> Let us now a blessing seek,
> Waiting in his courts today:
> Day of all the week the best,
> Emblem of eternal rest.

It went on through several stanzas, finally ending with a line to which vast numbers of Civil War soldiers could and no doubt often did say "Amen":

> Thus may all our Sabbaths prove,
> Till we join the church above.[45]

Of all the issues that were involved in living a Christian life, none was more written about by the soldiers than the importance of keeping the Sabbath day holy. The word *Sabbath* came from a Hebrew word meaning "rest." According to the Old Testament book of Genesis, God created the world in six days, rested on the seventh day, and hallowed that day. Subsequently, in the book of Exodus, Sabbath observance was enjoined as part of the Ten Commandments. During the first century A.D., the church began observing the first rather than the seventh day of the week, in honor of Christ's resurrection from the dead on that day. By the time of the Civil War, Christians had for many centuries been observing the first day of the week as the Lord's day or the Christian Sabbath. No other religious topic was more likely to draw comment in soldiers' diaries and letters.

There were several reasons for this. Sabbath observance was widespread in nineteenth-century America and was often required to some extent by civil laws that forbade ordinary business dealings on that day. Nearly all the Civil War soldiers had experienced a thousand or more Sabbaths according to a certain pattern, and any deviation from that pattern was bound to be noticed and commented on. It was, if nothing else, a disruption of the very rhythms of which time seemed to be made, almost as shocking a departure from the proper order of things as if the sun and moon randomly exchanged their allotted roles and times. From the camp of the 145th Pennsylvania, Chaplain Stuckenberg wrote of a Sunday in October 1862, "It did not seem like Sunday and many thought it was Saturday."[46]

A second reason why the Sabbath got so much ink in the soldiers' letters was that Sunday in a wartime army was nothing like the pattern they had come to expect. As John McMahon explained, "Sunday is not observed in the army. Each Sunday we have Inspection in the morning, and Dress Parade in the afternoon."[47] Charles B. Haydon, a rather irreligious Michigan officer, wrote in similar terms. "The business of Sunday is about this: inspection, guard mounting, diner, reading newspapers, letters writing, euchre playing &c."[48] At least as pertained to activities such as inspection, dress parade, and guard mounting, this was the pattern for Sundays throughout both armies, and it meant that there would almost always be far more nonreligious activity on Sundays than most of the soldiers were accustomed to.

Besides the routine of Sunday duties set forth by army regulations, there was often additional labor on Sunday: marches, fatigue work, and even battles. On a Sunday in May 1864, Gideon W. Burtch wrote, "Notwithstanding this is the Lords day we have marched 18 miles. . . . Have endeavored to keep my mind stayed upon God & thus to keep his holy day in spirit if not in deed."[49] "It seems now that every Sunday we have some extra work or a long march to make," agreed R. M. Campbell of the Fourth Georgia.[50] Texas cavalryman James C. Bates wrote in his diary in March 1862, "Sunday morning yet we are again on the march—I wonder if the Sabbath is as little respected by the northern as the southern army."[51]

It was. "The day of rest for man to praise the name of God for his mercy the previous week in a time of Peace," wrote William Homan of the 125th Pennsylvania in his diary one Sunday in 1862, "but in the army all days are alike. Soldiers in the regiments are on their respective duty."[52] "It seems that the Sabbath is not respected very well here in the army," wrote Aurelius Voorhis of the Forty-sixth Indiana, "for some are chopping wood, others hauling, while some are out shooting at little birds."[53] Seymour Dexter of the Twenty-third New York complained of having to drill on Sunday, and Chesley Mosman of the Fifty-ninth Illinois quipped that the opposing armies were so active on Sunday that the commanding generals must "believe in the saying, 'The better the day, the better the deed.'"[54] The Twenty-fifth Indiana's Daniel Hughes was even more succinct: "This Sabbath passed away without the day being kept Holy."[55]

This was serious business, for how could the soldiers hope that God would bless their army with victory in battle if they profaned His Sabbath? As an example, some pointed to Pittsburg Landing, or Shiloh. There on Sunday, April 6, 1862, Confederate forces had attacked on Sabbath morning, and many Union soldiers believed that the subsequent defeat of the Rebels had been God's punishment for that sin. Cyrus Boyd of the Fifteenth Iowa wrote in May 1862, "I hope our Army will not attack the enemy tomorrow as it is Sunday and our men seem to have a dread of going into battle on that day unless in defence. The terrible Sunday at Pittsburgh [Landing] is pointed to and the reason given that the enemy was defeated because they commenced the fight on the day."[56] When their own side found it expedient to operate aggressively on Sunday, soldiers hoped God would understand. Tennesseean Alfred Fielder wrote in his diary on August 17, 1862, "This Sabbath day has been spent in hard marching in order to get in the rear of the enemy. I trust God will forgive what of sin there has been committed by us in order to achieve our independence & liberty."[57]

What, then, did the soldiers think the Sabbath day ought to be? A picture can be gained both from their criticisms of things that occurred on that day and from their comments about the rare wartime Sundays that actually seemed to be as they ought.

The soldiers expected the Sabbath to be a quiet day, without the bustle of weekdays. George M. Lanpher of the Fifth Vermont wrote to his family from Alexandria, Virginia, in 1862, "It is Sunday, but it hardly seems like the holy Sabbath. The streets are full of soldiers of all brigades and all sorts of uniforms."[58] In nineteenth-century America, streets should be quiet, still, and almost empty on the Sabbath, except for people going to and from church. James Bates wrote happily of another Sunday in 1862 that was "such a Sabbath as we have not had for a long while. A holy calm & quiet pervades today so unusual for a camp that it seems peace had begun her reign once more."[59] That day was more like the Sundays the soldiers had known before the war.

Another, and obvious, characteristic of the soldiers' expectations for the Sabbath was that it should be a day of rest. Charles Wills of the 103rd Illinois wrote of a Sunday in February 1864. "This has indeed been a day of rest," Wills wrote, "more like a home Sabbath, than the Lord's day often seems, here in the [army]."[60] In 1861 William H. Walling of the Sixteenth New York noted, "Thus far [in the army] Sundays have not been very scrupulously set apart for the sacred purposes for which they were divinely appointed, days of rest."[61] Likewise, the following year Allen Geer of the Twentieth Illinois noted an exceptional Sunday simply: "Spent the Sabbath properly, all business suspended."[62]

Another common expectation for Sunday was that it be a day of spiritual uplift. Back home, Sunday had been the primary day of church attendance, with virtually every Christian denomination holding services. When other activities foreclosed such observance in the army, soldiers missed it. When James Bates noted a Sabbath properly spent, he added, "In the afternoon listened to an excellent sermon by our chaplain."[63] William H. Walling wrote to his family, "Our Chaplain has given us a first rate sermon, so . . . it begins to seem like the Sabbath."[64] Gideon W. Burtch felt much the same way. "This is the first Sunday I have spent in camp that has seemed like the Holy Sabbath," he wrote. "The Lord has been very precious to me today & I still feel Him near. At 2 P.M. I listened to a sermon by the Chaplain."[65]

It felt especially like a Sunday at home if the soldier could manage to attend worship services in an actual church building, something that was not a common occurrence for the men in the armies. Aurelius Voorhis wrote of a Sunday in 1863, "This has been a very nice day and has been really a Sabbath. I attended church at the Methodist Church" in a nearby town.[66]

Yet another soldier expectation for the Sabbath was related, in an indirect way, to the custom of Sunday worship, for a part of that custom included apparel. People generally wore their "Sunday best" when attending worship. So although it was not specified anywhere in the Bible, for the generation of young Americans who were called off to war in 1861, seeing folks all dressed up on Sundays was a part of their mental picture of how the world ought to be—even in the army. Writing to the home folks one Sunday in February 1863 from his "Camp in Front of Vicksburg," the Eighty-third Ohio's Isaac Jackson seemed at first not to understand what was making the day seem unusually proper. "This morning seems very much like Sunday, which is seldom the case," Jackson began. "The men are all preparing for inspection of arms," he continued, in a description that certainly did not portray Sundays back in Harrison, Ohio. "Some are putting on their new clothes, others are cleaning their guns for inspection. I only wish I was home getting ready for Sunday school." Finally, after touching on some other matters, he added, "We drew new clothes [i.e., uniforms] last week. . . . the boys putting on their new clothes makes it seem more like Sunday."[67] This was true even for a man with as little religious interest as Charles Haydon, who wrote one Sunday in 1861, "Sunday really seemed considerable like home. I suppose it was because I washed & put on a clean shirt."[68]

Finally, a large number of Americans in the mid–nineteenth century, those of religious bent, expected that certain types of sin that might be tolerated, if frowned upon, in their irreligious compatriots the other six days of the week were not to be tolerated at all on Sundays. Obviously, not all—perhaps not quite a majority—of the soldiers were from rigorously Christian backgrounds, and while the more religious were deploring the irreligion evident in the army most glaringly on Sundays, others were grumbling about being obligated to observe any religious restraints whatsoever. One disgruntled soldier wrote home in 1863 complaining of restraints on the steamboat on which his regiment was being transported. "The boat has peculiar rules. . . . Today, it forbids card playing because it's Sunday," he wrote. "That doesn't break me up because I never play, but today I would really like to. If a person goes to hell at an early time for that reason, that is my look out. . . . What business is it if I want to go to hell, it's a free Count[r]y."[69]

Berea M. Willsey of the Tenth Massachusetts summed up the several ways in which Sundays in the army fell short of many soldiers' peacetime expectations in this 1862 lament: "How different the Sundays are spent in the army, to what they are at home. Here we have no preaching, no meetings of any kind, & everything & everybody is full of wickedness."[70]

Many soldiers blamed their commanders for this state of affairs. "Most of our sabbaths have been our busy days," wrote N. H. R. Dawson. "I think our authorities should regard the sabbath with more consideration."[71] Likewise, the Fifty-ninth Illinois's Chesley Mosman recorded in his diary one Sunday in 1863: "It is hardly an orthodox way to spend Sunday, on picket line, loaded musket in hand. But these general officers need a little brushing up in the Commandments. They really seem to favor Sunday for a battle."[72]

It might have surprised many soldiers on both sides to learn that at least some of the higher authorities did attempt to show respect for the Sabbath. Robert E. Lee issued orders calling for "a proper observance of the Sabbath . . . not only as a moral and religious duty, but as contributing to the personal health and well-being of the troops," and he specified that military duties on Sundays should be limited to what was "essential to the safety, health, or comfort of the army."[73] Lincoln also issued a proclamation enjoining proper observance of the Sabbath in the United States forces, and George B. McClellan issued a similar order for his own Army of the Potomac. These proclamations and orders were generally welcomed by the soldiers who heard about them. William McCarter of the 116th Pennsylvania noted of Lincoln's proclamation that "the news was hailed with no small delight by the troops." However, McCarter also recorded what came of it all: "I am sorry to say that for a variety of reasons, probably none of them good and sufficient, the proclamation did not receive the consideration and obedience to which it was so justly entitled."[74] And so it went with the others. Partially it was a matter of numerous midranking officers who cared little if anything for Christianity or its Sabbath, and partially it was a factor of necessity. The Bible clearly allows for necessary labor on the Sabbath, but for an army in wartime, that could be a fairly broad loophole. Even the sincerely pious Thomas J. "Stonewall" Jackson sometimes felt that it was necessary, as, for example, at the battle of Kernstown in 1862, to attack the enemy on Sunday.

Besides the obligation of keeping the Sabbath day holy, mid-nineteenth-century America felt a general consensus that certain other things were required by God and therefore ought to be observed—perhaps by any-one, perhaps only by Christians. Some of these standards of conduct were drawn more or less directly from the Bible. Others were indirect, as more devout Christians wished to be as careful and scrupulous as possible in avoiding anything that might be compromising, questionable, or spiri-tually distracting. As Thomas Boatright wrote when setting down the principles upon which he wanted to conduct his life, "I will try and never do anything that I cannot ask the blessings of God upon it."[75]

It was generally these indirect issues that were discussed in the sol-diers' letters and diaries. When it came to gross transgressions, people were often ashamed not only to do them but even to talk of them. Cen-tral to all this was the idea that a Christian ought to order his life dili-gently so as to bring the most possible service and glory to God. This idea was set forth in an August 1863 sermon by the chaplain of the Sixth Vermont. As Wilbur Fisk remembered it, the chaplain put the question rhetorically to the men: "Was it best to swear? Could any one say it was?" If not, then they should consistently refrain from it. "Was it best to play cards and gamble?" Fisk continued his summary of the sermon, "If it was, then on every opportunity, make it a business, and take the consequences. If it was not, then make a law to leave off at once."[76]

In fact, the issues mentioned by Fisk and the chaplain—cursing, card playing, and gambling—were among the most commonly named moral problems within the army. "Mr. Robb preached a very pointed sermon this evening," wrote Aurelius Voorhis, "denouncing swearing and card playing in very plain terms, those two evils are very much used in our regiment."[77] It was much the same on both sides of the front lines. The Twelfth Tennessee's Alfred Fielder wrote in August 1862 of a sermon by the regimental chaplain. "The sermon was lengthy and pretty severe upon the pernitious practice of profane swearing not more so than he ought to have been for it is a profitless disgusting practice."[78] Likewise, the Eighty-third Ohio's Isaac Jackson reported, "There is not a day passes but gam-bling, card-playing, swearing and every other kind of vice is in full progress."[79] Card games were generally frowned on because of their asso-ciation with gambling, which in turn was condemned as a manifestation of greed, an attempt to gain money without honest labor, and a guilty squandering of the money God had already given a man. Jerusha H. Hubbard of Whiting, Vermont, summed up Christian ideas about gambling when she wrote to her son Franklin in the Second Vermont Light Artillery, urging him not to keep company with men of bad habits, a "gambler, or any other immoral person."[80]

Cursing had long been forbidden to Christians by the Bible itself, and likewise the use of God's name as a byword. Such offenses were seen as particularly direct acts of dishonor and disrespect toward God. David Coon, working in an army hospital in 1864, was appalled that such language should be used there. "It is shaking," he wrote in a letter to his son, "to see men lieing at the point of death and hear them curse and blaspheme and to hear nurses taking care of the sick curse and swear but so it is, but I am thankful that it is not so with all."[81] In this area, many high-ranking generals set a poor example. Gens. Joseph Hooker and Philip Kearny were known as very profane men, but by all accounts, Gen. Winfield Scott Hancock surpassed them. "In giving orders to his men on the march, drill, parade, or even the battlefield," a soldier recalled, "he seldom did so without an oath of the most unpardonable nature. Indeed, he seemed to have got into such a habit of indulging in profane language that he could never address the troops without taking God's name in vain."[82]

Another deplored but sadly pervasive vice was the consumption of alcohol. The Bible forbade drunkenness and taught that alcohol is deceptive. Most Christians therefore judged that it was best to avoid the possibility of being betrayed into drunkenness by avoiding alcoholic beverages altogether. The matter was complicated somewhat by the fact that in those days alcohol was thought to have medicinal value. Indeed, the army issued whiskey to the troops, in relatively small amounts, in times of extreme stress or exposure to the elements on the theory that it would prevent illness. Christians differed in their views toward that practice but were definitely of one mind in condemning recreational intoxication.

Drunkenness, cursing, and gambling were thus to be combated, along with cards for gambling's sake. A minister visiting the Confederate army in Mississippi in 1862 to distribute religious literature was delighted to see some of the soldiers throwing away their packs of cards because they preferred to read the religious tracts instead, explaining that "they played only because they had nothing to read."[83] Similarly, Aurelius Voorhis of the Forty-sixth Indiana took up card playing to alleviate boredom while in the barracks. His conscience soon smote him, however, and he wrote in his diary, "I . . . am firmly resolved, the Lord being my help, to practice it no longer. I don't think the mere form is any great harm but it is a sure step downward. . . . I pray God to give me grace to resist every temptation."[84]

Sometimes other factors influenced men to get rid of their cards. Johnny Green of the Confederate Ninth Kentucky told of the effect in his regiment when Union forces in northwestern Georgia interrupted a winter lull in campaigning by pushing forward to probe Confederate lines around Dalton. "The cannonading was first heard out front," Green recalled. "It grew more vigorous & I observed several squads of card players who were proverbial gamblers soon lose their interest in the game. The firing came nearer. The games entirely stopped, the decks of cards were thrown upon the ground & soon these gamblers were discovered in their cabins or behind a big tree reading their testament."[85] The case was not an isolated one, for it was not unusual to see soldiers on their way to battle throwing away decks of cards or other gambling paraphernalia. Theodore Upson of the 100th Indiana remembered that "cards were lying all over the ground" and remarked, "It is curious how many of the boys will throw away their cards when going into a fight."[86] However, the long-lasting effects of such halfhearted repentance were usually not particularly noticeable.[87] As Green observed, no sooner was the scare over than "the gamblers had hunted up their various decks of cards."[88]

An additional, and presumably more effective, influence on the soldiers against vice of various sorts was their families back home. Mothers like Jerusha Hubbard, as well as fathers, brothers, and sisters, urged those away in the army to remain faithful to Christian standards of behavior. Maria H. Berry wrote to her son Abram H. Berry of the Eighth Massachusetts, reminding him, "you have promised me never to smoke or touch or taste ardent spirits of any kind and if you forget me you forget your God."[89]

When Caleb Blanchard's wife discovered that her husband, a soldier in the Eighteenth Connecticut, had taken up card playing while in the army, she was almost beside herself. "You cannot tell nor immagine how I felt about it," she wrote to him. "It come upon me so sudden. I was not thinking of such a thing, did not know as you used cards at all and was thinking of the same man that went away and hoping he would return the same and I still hope so. . . . cards can do you no good and pray dont use them any more for the sake of yourself and for your friends. There has been many a young man ruined by beginning to play for amusement. They are very enticeing, I know that, and when a man is alone he gets lonesome and does that which he ought not to do."[90]

Soldiers frequently wrote to reassure their relatives that they were still maintaining their moral purity. Albert M. Childs of the Thirtieth Wisconsin wrote that sort of letter to his brother. "I have a better disposition today than when we parted 18 months ago. I am quite as free from bad habits of every description now, as then. I have not commenced using tobacco in any form, and detest it as bad as ever. The only time any thing which could be called intoxicating liquor has passed my lips since I enlisted was once last summer I drank one glass of lager beer. I am as pure & as virtuous now, as then, am not in the habit of using any byword whatever."[91] Similarly, Justus Gale of the Eighth Vermont wrote to his sister, "I have now been enlisted 17 months and during all this time have been cirrounded by many temptations hearing the most vile oaths—having many invitations to play cards—take a drink of whiskey &c! but I have yet to play my first game of cards and to take my first drink of liquor"— except for some taken for medicinal purposes during a hard march the preceding summer.[92]

Not all Christian denominations took the same stands on these various issues. Episcopalians were the most lax. David Holt recalled that his father, a devout Episcopalian, saw nothing at all wrong in playing cards, so long as one did not gamble.[93] Episcopalians might also tolerate such practices as dancing and possibly taking a social drink or two. Lincoln once joked that "he preferred the Episcopalians to every other sect, because they are equally indifferent to a man's religion and his politics," but that was an exaggeration.[94] Presbyterians, Baptists, and Methodists were generally more conservative, with Methodists being the most zealous and careful in ordering their private lives. Discussions sometimes resulted, as when soldiers in the Twentieth Illinois's debating society hashed out the issue of dancing.[95] Good Episcopalian William H. S. Burgwyn occasionally complained to his diary of going to very boring parties, ruined by the fact that "all the ladies were Methodist and did not dance."[96] In the black First South Carolina (Union), a particularly devout soldier told Col. Thomas Wentworth Higginson that he had once been quite a sinful man. Pressed to reveal the lurid particulars, the soldier confessed, "Used to dance."[97]

Some issues were uncertain even within denominational boundaries, being truly matters of private conscience toward God. In answer to his sister's question about whether it was right for her to attend a play in a theater, William H. Walling wrote that he could give no simple answer, but he gave a wise one, and in doing so, he got very near the gist of the entire question of what Christians ought or ought not to do. "In regard to your going to the theatre," he wrote, "I cannot see any impropriety under the circumstances of which you speak. I admit there are nice points to be looked after. The pleasures of the world are given us for use and not for abuse. The dangers in the pursuit of them is manifest from the Scripture which says it is better to go to the house of mourning than to the house of feasting. Though the latter is not forbidden as sinful. Do you get my idea?"[98]

The idea was that the Christian life was not to be a fearful attempt to avoid the condemnation of a fierce and angry judge, but rather an earnest, careful, and happy process of drawing ever closer to a loving God. The Christians among the Civil War soldiers, along with their contemporary fellow believers, held that various practices were to be avoided— drunkenness, gambling, and swearing among them. They believed that the Bible was God's Word and that the Sabbath day should be kept holy. Such practices might seem burdensome to many modern readers, and they seemed so to many in the nineteenth century, but only to those who dabbled about the fringes of Christianity. Those who pursued Christianity earnestly did not find these practices burdensome at all. The many Civil War soldiers who wrote of their careful abstention from camp vices and other sins did not consider themselves to be in bondage to a harsh system, nor did they imagine that their debauched fellow soldiers were enjoying life more than they were.

But they could not always make their contemporaries understand that. John T. McMahon, in his diary for October 27, 1861, recorded some thoughts triggered by a sermon he had heard that day:

Heard a sermon from Rev. Mr. Knowles: The text Col 3:17. "And what-soever you do in word or deed, do all in the name of the Lord Jesus." There are two ideas which are wrong in respect to our religion. But if we take the middle ground we are safe. The first [wrong] doctrine says that we may do or say whatsoever we choose. The other, that the religion of Christ is a yoke of bitterness. And this reminded me of a conversation I had with a young man about religion. He would make a profession of faith if he could still enjoy himself but he thought this was impossible and I could not get his mind clear on this point.[99]

II

THE CIVIL WAR SOLDIERS,
THEIR RELIGION, AND THE CONFLICT

6

"WE ARE THE SWORD IN THE HAND OF GOD"
Northern Christians View the Early Stages of the War

It was Sunday evening, April 21, 1861—one week to the day after the surrender of Fort Sumter—and the Baptist church in Madison, Wisconsin, was filled to overflowing. The crowd also presented an unusual appearance in more ways than just its size. One large section of the congregation looked like a solid block of dark blue; there, all together in neat rows, sat "the volunteers," recently enlisted soldiers now temporarily quartered at nearby Camp Randall. The service began with a strong patriotic emphasis, as the choir sang "The Star-Spangled Banner." Then, instead of a sermon by the regular pastor, Dr. Brisbane, the congregants heard one by his adult son, who had enlisted that week and preached in his new uniform as an army officer. Young Brisbane had preached in that garb in the same pulpit that morning, but the solid block of soldier listeners had been elsewhere, at Madison's Episcopal church, hearing a "very appropriate and impressive" sermon by its pastor, Mr. Britton. Just as the evening service at the Baptist church was about to be dismissed that night, someone handed Dr. Brisbane a note with a false report that the Rebels had attacked Fort Pickens, Florida, and been decisively repulsed. He announced it to the crowd, and they responded with three cheers. Then, after this somewhat unorthodox closing to the service, the volunteers marched out of the church "and down the street to the sound of muffled drums."[1]

Similar scenes were enacted in many Northern communities during the early months of the war as the departing troops received the formal blessing of organized religion in their region. War rallies and recruitment meetings took place in church buildings throughout the North. The message was plain to even the least perceptive of potential recruits: the Christian church heartily endorsed the nation's preparations to defend itself against Southern aggression and put down the rebellion that threatened to sweep a third of the stars from the flag.

The impression thus created was literally true. In the days and weeks following Fort Sumter, church leaders and representative assemblies throughout the North sent a swarm of letters, memorials, resolutions, and the like to President Lincoln, assuring him of their support for him and a vigorous defense of the Constitution and the Union. Assurance of sympathy and prayer came from the Welsh Congregational Church of New York City. Resolutions of support came from the Philadelphia Presbytery of the Reformed Presbyterian Church in North America. Similar resolutions came from the ministerial association of Rushville, Iowa; from the New York East Conference of the Methodist Episcopal Church; and from the pastor of First Congregational Church of Exeter, New Hampshire. From Salem, Massachusetts, Rev. Alexander J. Sessions urged Lincoln to "call out half a million troops" at a time when the president was asking for a mere 75,000.[2] Going a step further, a number of pastors and other religious leaders enlisted and went off to war themselves. It was not unusual for the parents of a young man under age twenty-one to feel more inclined to give their consent to their son's enlistment when they considered that his company commander was his peacetime Sunday school superintendent. The Seventy-third Illinois, organized by Methodist minister James Jaquess, numbered so many ministers in its ranks that it came to be nicknamed "the Preacher Regiment."[3]

On what basis, then, did religious leaders and many thousands of Christian laymen throughout the North accord this sort of spiritual sanction to the outset of the North's war effort? The biggest part of the initial reaction seems to have been simple, almost instinctive patriotism. Americans had long considered their country a Christian nation, peculiarly loyal to God's ways. Love of country, like filial devotion, was seen as a characteristic of the godly Christian man. When country called, therefore, the moral, upstanding citizens ought to answer with alacrity—and with the hearty encouragement of their church affiliations. The decision to support the war effort, in this case, was really no decision at all. Church halls could be made available for rallies, patriotic services held, and young men encouraged to enlist simply because the country was going to war and all good men should come to its aid.

Some Christians were more explicit in thinking and writing about the cause they embraced, even during the early months of the conflict. Many looked to the biblical basis for the power of civil governments. The thirteenth chapter of the Epistle to the Romans begins, "Let every soul be subject unto the higher powers. For there is no power but of God: the powers that be are ordained of God. Whosoever therefore resisteth the power, resisteth the ordinance of God: and they that resist shall receive to themselves damnation." Clearly the Southerners were in violation of this command, for they had rebelled against a duly constituted, legally operating civil government, and they could not possibly point to any biblical injunction that required them in this case to disobey man in obedience to God. They were, in short, rebels and therefore condemned by God.

Thinking along these lines in the fall of 1861, a Reverend Mr. Hilton, Methodist minister from Janesville, Wisconsin, preached at the Methodist conference meeting in Madison, taking the passage from Romans 13 as his text and applying it to "the State of affairs in the Country."[4] Similarly, volunteer general Robert McAllister wrote home of the need to "put down this wicked rebellion and teach the Southerners with force what they would not learn in time of peace—that governments are not so easily broken up, and that God requires obedience to law and order." The victorious United States would, McAllister believed, teach "rebellious spirits in all nations that governments and their power come from God."[5]

This was consistent with Americans' long-standing belief in a balance of liberty and government power. In defiance of all the bitter taunts and smug predictions of monarchists and aristocrats overseas, America was to be a society of liberty without chaos and order without tyranny, founded on a bedrock consensus in Americans' fundamentally biblical way of this looking at the world. In time past, the threat to America's ordered liberty had been perceived as coming chiefly from the likes of George III, with his claims of unjustified authority and his redcoats to enforce them. Now the Rebels, by claiming slavery's exemption from moral absolutes and their own exemption from proper obedience to lawful authority, threatened the very moral consensus on which rested the delicate balance of liberty and order. Well might thoughtful Americans like Hilton and McAllister feel anxious that "God requires obedience to law and order."[6] Nor need one be able to articulate such concerns in order to feel them in a vague but urgent way. Union soldier Philip A. Lantzy wrote to his parents in the simplest terms, "I think it is gods will that the Rebels Should be made to come under our Stars and stripes."[7]

Some religious leaders saw even more in the conflict that burst upon the country in 1861. Chief among these was Connecticut Congregationalist minister Horace Bushnell. Bushnell saw in the war God's providential hand making something more out of America than it had ever been before. Previous crises, he believed, had begun and furthered the process of molding the American people according to God's will, and this final and greatest crisis would complete the process of making them into "a nation—God's own nation." The thought of this culmination so thrilled him that he exclaimed, upon the outbreak of hostilities, "I thank God that I have been allowed to see this day."[8]

The disastrous defeat of Union forces at Bull Run in July 1861 seemed not to shake Bushnell in the least. In response to it, he preached a sermon entitled "Reverses Needed." They were needed, he maintained, in order to teach the American people that God and God alone set up governments and upheld them. He directed the nation's destiny, not the people themselves—at least, not in the final analysis. "Reverses" like Bull Run would convince Americans of their dependence on God as nothing else could, and the blood shed in war would atone for the guilty national pride and self-will of the previous decades.[9]

A few others across the North shared Bushnell's exuberant vision, or at least parts of it. A number of Christian groups held to a doctrine that claimed that God would set up His kingdom on earth, through His people, for a thousand years of peace—the millennium—before Christ's actual prophesied return to earth. Some people thought that they saw the dawning of this epoch in the opening stages of the Civil War. A citizen of Urbana, Illinois, wrote to his brother in the first year of the war, expressing his hopeful expectations of what the conflict might accomplish. "For some few years," he explained, "I have thought the signs of the times indicate the approach of the great millenial day. The hand of providence has been overruling & moulding all the affairs of nations to introduce this glorious event, but one obstacle stared me in the face. How the dark blot of human bondage was to be wiped off this christian nation." The outbreak of civil war had taken care of that, however. "Now the mystery is solved," he continued, "for tho this dreadful rebellion springs out of the corruption of the human heart, God is directing the storm to wipe out the blot & before 1865 we shall be reinstated as a nation on a firmer basis of christian & republican principles than before."[10]

A bit later, Indiana officer James M. Shanklin expressed another variant of Bushnell's kind of thought. Shanklin was neither so optimistic nor so ready to prognosticate, but he too saw the war as something that would make the nation better by purifying it, though in a somewhat different way. "There must be a new era in the manners and morals of this Country," he wrote to his wife in the second spring of the war. "Our national misfortunes will humble all of us, and if they will only have the effect of destroying the Young America spirit which has been so universal over the land, they will have accomplished at least one great good." "Young America" was a name taken by an 1850s political movement that advocated aggressive, expansionist policies. Shanklin continued, "The arrogance and vain boasting with which we as a people have always been in the habit of treating other nations, has gradually led us to be arrogant and vain boasting in private life—and now that we can no longer be so arrogant towards nations, it may be that we will become less so among ourselves."[11] In these thoughts, however, Shanklin was well ahead of most others.

The vast majority of Northern soldiers during the first year of the war devoted little thought—or at least little space in their letters—to questions of which side God favored in the conflict or what His purposes in all this might be. For them, the rightness of their cause was an article of faith, not to be questioned. God's purposes were their purposes, and they were sure that He would support them. Shanklin, too, though thoughtful and reflective about the matter, was still convinced that the Union cause was right. "If I did not know that our cause is just and righteous," he told his wife, "I could not stand the life of a soldier."[12]

If many others omitted this sort of written soul-searching, they certainly did not lack the assurance of the rightness of their cause. A popular rhyme, oft quoted in soldiers' letters and occasionally printed at the top of patriotic-theme stationery used by them, summed up this way of thinking:

> For right is right, as God is God
> And right will surely win;
> To doubt would be disloyalty—
> To falter would be sin.[13]

Another bit of early-war stationery verse proclaimed:

> One last great battle for the right—
> One short, sharp struggle to be free!
> To do is to succeed—our fight
> Is waged in Heave's approving sight—
> The smile of God is victory![14]

And civilians at the Northwestern Sanitary Fair—a fund-raising event with the goal of providing better food and medicines for the soldiers—sang an "Anthem of Liberty":

> Onward, still onward, flag of our might!
> Onward, victorious, God for the right![15]

The theme had many expressions and variations from the less facile, or at least less rhyming, pens of soldiers and citizens. Civilian Lester A. Miller wrote to Lincoln in April 1861, likening the Union to the Kingdom of Israel (God's people) and Jefferson Davis to the wicked King Ben-Hadad of neighboring Syria.[16] In November of that year, Col. Napoleon Buford led his Twenty-seventh Illinois into battle at Belmont, Missouri, shouting "The Lord of Hosts is our leader and guide."[17]

Yet the vicissitudes of war were simultaneously prompting men to reflect. In September 1861, Ohioan John Beatty, no doubt thinking of the previous summer's Union debacle at Bull Run, wrote of a day of fasting and prayer proclaimed by President Lincoln. "I trust the supplications of the church and the people may have effect," Beatty wrote, "and bring that Higher Power to our assistance which hitherto has apparently not been with our arms especially."[18]

The spring of 1862 saw the beginning of heavy fighting, with blood-letting on a scale hitherto undreamed of in American history. Among the Union soldiers, this fiery trial prompted more thought but no change in conclusions. From Ship Point, Virginia, on April 30, 1862, William Henry Walling wrote to his sisters back home, "My prayer is that God will not forsake us in this hour of need—that with our eyes fixed upon his holy temple he will enable us to triumph over our enemies. One of the best evidences in my mind why we can claim the divine blessing is, there is a manifest desire on the part of the Government to do what is right for the sake of right." As an example of this, Walling held up a recent act of Congress abolishing slavery in the District of Columbia. This was evidence that the Union was on God's side and would finally win the day.[19]

By late autumn of that year, many soldiers continued to express faith in the rightness of their cause but varying degrees of confidence as to whether God would defend it. Watching the buildup of armies on either side of the Rappahannock River Valley, which within a few weeks would lead to the battle of Fredericksburg, the 116th Pennsylvania's William McCarter felt "more convinced than ever that the cause for which I fought was truly the cause of God and humanity. I felt confident that in endeavoring to perform my duty faithfully, God would give me the necessary strength and courage and enable me to meet every danger and trial."[20]

For obvious reasons, military authorities were eager to promote the idea that God would favor the Union cause. For this reason, along with sincere piety on the part of many leaders, formal religious observances were sometimes held in the army. Observance of the first Independence Day of the war in the Rhode Island brigade included not only the reading of the Declaration of Independence but also prayer by the chaplain of the Second Rhode Island and a sermon by the chaplain of the First Rhode Island.[21] A third of a continent away, the troops of the Twentieth

Illinois, camped near the Mississippi River town of Alton, celebrated the same day in like manner with a sermon from their chaplain.[22] Similar observances were held in numerous regiments at various times and occasions—dress parades and the like—whenever the chaplain and the commanding officer felt the situation warranted a sermon, a prayer, or the singing of a hymn.[23]

Such observances occurred throughout the Federal armies when President Lincoln proclaimed days of prayer or thanksgiving. One such day that was particularly widely observed was Sunday, April 13, 1862. On the Virginia peninsula, where fighting clearly loomed in the coming weeks, soldiers of the Tenth Massachusetts formed a hollow square that morning and heard their chaplain give his first sermon since the regiment had disembarked.[24] At Pittsburg Landing on the Tennessee River, where one week before the battle of Shiloh had been fought, soldiers of the Eleventh Illinois assembled for dress parade as usual that morning and listened to their regimental adjutant read an address from their division commander, Illinois politician Maj. Gen. John A. McClernand, and then heard a prayer by the regimental chaplain.[25] Allen M. Geer of the Twentieth Illinois was rather matter-of-fact in recording his regiment's observance in his diary. "Complied with orders from the war department by offering up prayers to the Almighty for success to our arms and right at five p.m."[26]

In other regiments, the observances on that day were less perfunctory and more pointed. In the Fifty-ninth Illinois, "prayer and thanksgiving were offered for the success of our army, in compliance with orders from the War Department," but then the chaplain got up and preached a sermon from Daniel 11:40—"And at the time of the end shall the king of the south push at him: and the king of the north shall come against him like a whirlwind, with chariots, and with horsemen, and with many ships; and he shall enter into the countries, and shall overflow and pass over."[27] One suspects that the burden of that sermon had little to do with the actual meaning of that Scripture in its context. Meanwhile, in the Fourth Iowa, Henry G. Ankeny, in a letter to his wife, expressed his pride that the chaplain was from his very own Company H and summarized the good parson's remarks: "He was very much rejoiced that the Lord was on our side and knew he always would be, but he was inclined to think we could fight better on full rations." Ankeny added, "It is supposed that the Lord will take the hint—I hope so."[28]

While the great majority of Northern soldiers might confide that their cause was just, hope that God would favor them, and rejoice to hear preachers proclaim as much, a small but steady undercurrent continued throughout the war from both soldiers and civilians to the effect that God might not be for the Union or that if He was, preachers ought not to speak of it. William H. Walling believed strongly in the rightness of the Union cause, but he wrote to his sisters back home a veritable diatribe against ministers "preaching on political subjects." Southern preachers, he believed, had played a key role in stirring up the rebellion, and now he was down on all "political preachers." With startling illogic he argued, "The question naturally suggests itself that if the southern political preachers turn out to be such vile characters would not those of the North reveal themselves equally infamous under like circumstances." Instead of proclaiming God's truth about human relations, preachers should "keep within their legitimate field of operations. Their commission reads thus, 'Go ye into all the world and preach the gospel to every creature.'"[29]

On the occasion from which Walling's quotation was drawn, Christ had added, "Teaching them to observe all things whatsoever I have commanded you."[30] Yet there were others who chose to see Christianity as having no legitimate business telling people how God expected them to live. George M. Turner of Battery A, Third Rhode Island Artillery, complained in June 1862 that "the [worship] services were conducted by some abolitionists who came from the state of Massachusetts and there was so much talk about the confounded niggers that I came out disgusted."[31] Edward Watson of the Ninth Michigan Cavalry made a similar complaint: "Tomorrow will be Sunday.... The program for the day will be inspection of arms and equipment at nine.... After inspection, divine service when our fat Chaplain will deal out politics to us."[32]

The same sentiments could be found on the home front as well. Before enlisting in the army, Pennsylvanian Wesley W. Bierly noted in his diary that a nearby camp meeting had been relatively sparsely attended. Many who would ordinarily have been there stayed away "because some of the preachers are too hard Republicans or Politicians"—and thus could be expected to say something against slavery. Bierly noted that it was a good camp meeting anyway.[33]

A substantial number of soldiers and civilians took a somewhat different approach to the question of why the war was happening to them and what it all meant. Like those who claimed that the North was wrong, or at least not particularly godly in its cause, these men and women believed that the North had indeed committed sins and that God was therefore justly displeased with it. These people believed passionately that the North's cause was God's own, and they would have been among the most approving of "political preachers" who applied God's commandments to human relations. In short, they believed that the North, or the nation as a whole, had sinned and that God was punishing or chastening the nation by means of a civil war. When God in His mercy saw that the nation had suffered enough and had learned the lessons of that suffering, He would bring about the Northern triumph that had always been His plan. The exact nature of the sin or sins that had provoked God's wrath varied in different assessments by different individuals, but the theme of the war as divine punishment for national sin was repeated again and again throughout the entire course of the conflict from Sumter to Appomattox.

Among the first to sound this note were the representatives of the United Presbyterian Church of North America meeting at the General Assembly in Monmouth, Illinois, in June 1861. They drew up a petition and sent it to Lincoln, calling on him to proclaim a day of "fasting, humiliation and prayer." They assured the president that they were "calm anti-slavery men," but they added, "We do not think all the sin which has involved us, as a nation, in this terrible calamity has been committed by the South. Far from it. We would see the hand of God in our troubles. He alone can deliver us out of them, and he will, if we repent of our sins & humble ourselves before him in the name, and in humble dependence on the merit of our Lord Jesus Christ. This is our duty as individuals, and, surely, it is so as a nation." Among the greatest of the national sins for which the Presbyterian leadership believed the country needed to repent was "forgetfulness of God, and deep ingratitude for all his goodness to our fathers and to ourselves."[34]

Of course, Lincoln proclaimed a number of national fast days, as well as days of thanksgiving, during the course of the war. For one such day in October 1861, Lincoln attended a Presbyterian church in Washington with his youngest son, Tad, and heard a sermon by the Reverend Dr. Gurley, who identified some half a dozen national sins.[35]

Many nonclerics thought in more or less similar terms, and the themes of national pride and forgetfulness of God and His blessings are common in their writings. "May God speed the right," wrote Joseph Ankeny from his home in Millersburg, Ohio, to his soldier-son Henry, "and that He will, I have no doubt, [and] eventually preserve this union. He may scourge us first severely. We as a nation have all greatly sinned and abused our high privileges. It may be for our benefit to be thus scourged, to teach all how to use our great and glorious privileges bequeathed to us by our fathers."[36]

The always thoughtful James M. Shanklin wrote in a similar vein, "The fact is we were a selfish, grasping people, who had forgotten what a good Country we had, and all this is a visitation of Providence on us." That is, the war was God's punishment. Yet Shanklin did not believe the Northern cause was wrong. "I tell you what I think," he wrote two days later, "I believe God is on our side, but I believe also it is His design to humble us first before allowing us the victory. If that is so, our humility should be speedy and deep."[37] Union soldier John S. Copley felt the same way. Before peace could be restored, he believed, there would have to be "an acknowledgment of Gods dealings with us because of our great national and individual sins. . . . [U]ntil we as a nation and as individuals acknowledge this and repent of our sins and turn to God and respect his laws I cannot expect this strife to cease." Likewise, Burage Rice believed that although Union victory was assured, God would prolong the conflict as long as necessary "to punish us as a wicked nation for our sins."[38]

Continued military setbacks in the eastern theater of the war during late 1862 and early 1863 prompted restatements of this same theme. One such occasion was the disappointing defeat of a magnificent Union army under Maj. Gen. Joseph Hooker at Chancellorsville, Virginia, in May 1863. After that debacle, a Massachusetts soldier wrote, "It was God's will. . . . Our national pride is not yet sufficiently humbled."[39] Richard S. Thompson of the Twelfth New Jersey believed that the Confederates had actually been as good as beaten in that battle, "but God did not intend us to succeed. As a nation we put too much trust in our own power, too much confidence in human skill. Had we been entirely successful, we would have called it Hooker's Victory, and forgot God." The solution to this, as Thompson saw it, was simple but difficult: "Let those at home pray that the nation and army may trust in God."[40]

It has been said that the prospect of imminent death concentrates the thoughts wonderfully. It can certainly be said, and accurately, that the imminence of death and maiming, suffering, and hardship concentrated the religious thinking of the Civil War soldiers and, to a degree, that of their friends and family back home. In the spring of 1862, the pace of the war changed from what had been a period of skirmishing and preparation to one of furious fighting on a massive scale. A series of appallingly bloody battles followed throughout that year and continued until the end of the war. The frightful casualties entailed by all this fighting would eventually lead those who went on living to think anew, more deeply and more searchingly, about what it all meant and where God was in the midst of all the horror. And even prior to the emergence of this thoughtful re-evaluation, it produced a more strident insistence on the rightness of the Union cause and the evil of the Rebels.

Berea M. Willsey of the Tenth Massachusetts spoke of "this unholy rebellion."[41] James Magill of the 128th Pennsylvania wrote to his Quaker mother back home, expressing his determination to see "this wicked rebelion" put down.[42] "Wicked" and "unholy" are terms with religious significance. The Rebels, these soldiers implied, were enemies of God. Luther Cowan was saying much the same when he wrote that the men of his Forty-fifth Illinois were "anxious to walk into the sacreligious rebels."[43]

Others would do more than imply this. From Libby Prison in Richmond, wounded Union prisoner of war Andrew Roy mused on the rights and wrongs of the sectional conflict. "I would question with myself," he later recalled, "whether or not the Southern people, who are hopelessly in the wrong, will succeed in breaking up the Union." He had to admit that they were "terribly earnest," but then he asked himself, "Will a just God hearken to the prayers of the people fighting to establish a government, the corner stone of which is founded on human slavery?"[44] Joseph Whitney heard his chaplain preach a sermon in which he "compared the sesesh to the Devil" and thought it "the best sermon I ever heard in my life."[45]

The Second Vermont's Wilbur Fisk was even more explicit as he reflected in April 1863 on all the Northern widows and orphans who had been made such by the war over the past year. "What a fearful load of guilt," he mused, "the band of traitors who caused this calamity have to meet at the bar of justice, when the Father of the fatherless, and the Judge of the widow calls them to their final account. If there is pit in hell deep enough to receive them it must be a very deep one indeed."[46]

Combating such wicked rebels in a cause that was favored by God was a holy duty, and the men and their families soon had a good deal more to say about that. George W. Crosley wrote that during the battle of Shiloh he had been comforted by the thought that, in fighting the Rebels, "I was in the performance of the noblest duty—except the worship of God that a man is ever permitted to perform here upon earth."[47] Expressing a similar religious zeal for their cause, black soldiers of the Union First South Carolina had as their "favorite idea" that of being "a religious army," a "gospel army."[48]

Some even began to take that idea a bit further. In January 1863, R. W. Lloyd of the Eighty-third Indiana wrote of those who had done their duty under fire at the recent battle of Chickasaw Bayou as having proved themselves faithful to their country, "as did the Martyrs of old prove themselves true to their God."[49] Similarly, William McCarter of the 116th Pennsylvania had referred to a fallen comrade the preceding autumn as "a martyr to the cause of liberty and humanity."[50] About the same time, Seymour Dexter referred to the dead of Antietam as "martyrs to the cause of freedom, justice and our union."[51]

These may have been mere flights of rhetorical excess in praise of fallen comrades, but rhetoric has meaning, and such flights can land in unexpected places. Within the Christian tradition, martyrs were those who gave witness to their faith in Christ at the cost of their lives. Thus, this term was as loaded with religious meaning—though in an opposite sense—as was "unholy," "wicked," or "sacrilegious."

Meanwhile, other soldiers were already putting the matter in even stronger terms. When a comrade died early in 1862, George H. Allen of the Fourth Rhode Island wrote, "He gave up his young life a sacrifice upon the altar of his country."[52] Here was another statement full of religious imagery, and "sacrifice," when used in this sort of heavily religious context, was a term of even greater significance than "martyr."

The word *sacrifice* could, of course, be used in varying ways. Victory in the war would obviously entail great sacrifices of human life as well as material wealth. In that sense, the word simply meant something given up to obtain something else. However, when used in connection with the concept of an "altar," the word had a much stronger religious connotation. Things sacrificed on an altar were offered directly to the deity whose altar that was, for the purpose of propitiating that god or atoning for wrongdoing. The Old Testament Scriptures spoke of sacrificing animals to the God of Israel as a token of the final sacrifice that God would provide Himself. It also spoke of heathens sacrificing animals and sometimes even their own children to their various false gods. The ultimate sacrifice in the Bible had been Christ, who offered Himself to God the Father on the cross in order to atone once and for all for the sins of mankind. The animal sacrifices described in the Old Testament had been representations—foreshadowings—of that ultimate sacrifice. Thus, for people in the Civil War era, most of whom were familiar with at least the terminology of Christianity, to say that a soldier was "a sacrifice upon the altar of his country" was to give that soldier a special place in a new theology in which country, not God, occupied the position of deity.

That the resulting theology was not that of Christianity becomes readily apparent in further statements of some of the soldiers. Allen himself, several months later, carried the matter further in speaking of a comrade killed at Antietam. "We trust," Allen wrote, "that his noble and heroic sacrifice in giving his young life to his country has gained for him a crown of glory in that better land beyond the skies."[53] In short, Allen was suggesting that his comrade's death for the noble Union cause had gained the deceased admission into heaven. Orthodox Christian teaching, as per the Bible, had always been emphatic about the one and only way of gaining admission to heaven, and this was not it.

Yet Allen was not alone in his misconception. Michigan soldier Charles B. Haydon, not a particularly religious man at the best of times, wrote that God would have a "kind reward at last" for all those who gave "their all to a sacred cause" and vouchsafed that if he should fall in battle, he had "little doubt that there is some reward in store for the soldier who does his best in his country's cause."[54] Maj. John H. Halderman of the First Kansas assured his men that any of them killed in the line of duty were sure to go to heaven.[55] So august a personage as Massachusetts governor John A. Andrew proclaimed to black soldiers of the Fifty-fourth Massachusetts, upon presenting to them their regimental flag, that should they fall in battle, "your spirit will soar to that home in store for those who faithfully do their duty here to Humanity, their Country and their God!"[56]

The Christian view, of course, is that doing one's duty is all very well, but heaven is in store for those who put their faith in Christ. What was happening was that the pressure, pain, and enthusiasm of war were leading some Northerners to create a form of civil religion, a twisted version of Christianity in which the nation was god and rewarded those who sacrificed themselves in its cause. Significantly, however, it was a concept that seemed to have most resonance with persons who had only a passing acquaintance with the concepts and terminology of Christianity. A number of Northerners did begin to talk in such terms, but it is important to remember that they remained a minority and that the teachings of orthodox Christianity remained predominant.

Nonetheless, those who blurred the terminology of Christianity into the substance of civil religion were numerous and vocal enough to make its ideas heard frequently. The most famous and by all odds the most elusive enunciation of such ideas came from the pen of Julia Ward Howe. Her "Battle Hymn of the Republic" invoked the image of the second coming of Christ to picture the nation's current upheaval. The Lord, in His truth, had unsheathed His sword and pressed the "grapes of wrath" for the great judgment of sin that was to take place as a result of the war. His approach was to be seen in the "hundred circling camps" of the armies, whose evening campfires constituted altars of worship. His gospel was a fiery one, "writ in burnished rows of steel." The "hero born of woman," who was to "crush the serpent with his heel," was an unmistakable biblical allusion to Christ but, just as unmistakably, in Howe's song referred to the Union soldier. "As He [Christ] died to make men holy," she concluded, "Let us [Northerners] die to make men free." Thus Howe likened

the Union soldier who died to end slavery to Christ Himself in His atoning death on the cross.

It was, or at least could be taken to be, as one modern historian judged,
"almost blasphemous."[57] Or it could be taken in a more restrained sense
that signified, for all its overwrought language, only the orthodox thought
that God was working providentially through the war to accomplish His
purposes in ending slavery, chastising sin, and preserving and cleansing
the American experiment in self-government. The only obvious things
about "The Battle Hymn of the Republic" were that it was poetry and
that it was figurative, and a great many people were going to take it to
mean what they wanted it to mean. God was marching on, and so were
the armies, but for what purpose and whether for the same purposes were
not as clear.

Whether in terms of a heretical civil religion or more orthodox Christianity, Northerners were coming increasingly, during the second half
of 1862, to see the conflict as one between good and evil, between the
people of God and people who were God's enemies. As Richard E. Blair
of the Eighty-third Indiana wrote early in 1863, "I think that now is the
time to find out who are truly God's people."[58] The clear implication was
that they were the ones who supported the Union.

That being the case, what were Northerners to think of Southerners
and their religion? As Union armies moved into the South and Southern
churches came within Federal lines, how were the authorities to view
their clergy and people? Were the pro-Confederate prayers or sermons
of Southern parsons purely religious statements or political ones? The
fact was, of course, that like any statements of religious teaching about
human relations, they were both, but that did nothing to simplify the task
of Union authorities who moved into Southern locales for the purpose
of returning them to their proper relation to the nation.

One of the first places where the issue arose was Nashville. When
Federal forces captured the city in February 1862, they found that religious
conflict had long preceded them. When the war had begun, pro-secession
Tennesseeans had seized control of the city's Second Presbyterian Church,
ousting the Unionist pastor. Now, with blue-clad troops in town, the
Unionist faction appealed to the post commander and got their wish. U.S.
authorities seized the keys, records, and funds of the church and turned

them over to the Union faction, which remained in control, backed up by Federal troops, as long as the war lasted.[59]

Thus the first intervention was at the request of one of two contending factions of Southerners, but matters did not stop there. With the growing intensity of the war during the latter half of 1862 and the growing intensity of Northern religious fervor for its prosecution, Union officers took additional steps. In July 1862, Gen. Lovell H. Rousseau, to the immense satisfaction of his troops, had a "Reverend Mr. Ross" of Tennessee hauled off to jail "for preaching a secession sermon last Sunday."[60] It was a striking reversal of the situation in which antislavery preachers during prewar years had been arrested in the North and mobbed and lynched in the South.

And more was to come. During the winter of 1862–1863, several Southern ministers felt the disapproval of occupying Union authorities. A Southerner complained that "many were ejected from their pulpits, hurried away to the north, and, in some instances, confined in prison like common felons." It was not, of course, the first instance of Southern preachers being "hurried away to the north," but that treatment had hitherto been reserved for those who questioned the rightness of slavery.[61]

The problem of politics and religion was especially difficult to avoid in Episcopal churches. The Episcopal liturgy for the Sunday morning service included a prayer for the president. When the Southern states declared themselves out of the Union, pro-secession clergymen had simply made this prayer on behalf of the president of the Confederate—rather than the United—States. Because services were conducted according to the set pattern of the liturgy, there was no way to dodge the issue when the Yankees came to town. The parson could pray for either the U.S. president or his Confederate rival; his only other alternative would be a jarring and noticeable omission of part of the service. The religious similarity of the two regions of the country exacerbated matters, for Union troops stationed nearby would often jump at the chance to attend regular church services, and those in attendance were shocked to hear the prayer for the president omitted or even to hear a petition raised on behalf of his excellency Jefferson Davis. On rare occasions the flabbergasted bluecoats even responded by interrupting the service and demanding that the minister conduct it "correctly."

As the intensity of Northern war feeling increased, and with it the conviction of the rightness of the Union cause, many soldiers were led to think again and far more deeply about the reasons for the war, the cause for which they were fighting, and the purposes of God in the conflict. As they did so, two major themes emerged in their letters and diaries. The first was a belief that the great evil the Rebels were committing lay in their attempt "to destroy this 'Model Republic.'"[62] Since the days when John Winthrop had proclaimed the Massachusetts Bay Colony to be "a model of Christian charity" and "a city upon a hill," many Americans had considered their country to be an example to the world of the blessings that could be enjoyed in a godly society. Now the rebellion threatened all that; therefore, fighting to put down the rebellion was a sacred duty to God.

A Pennsylvania officer wrote to his wife of his determination to see the war out, hard as it was for him to be away from home and family. "Every day," he explained, "I have a more religious feeling, that this war is a crusade for the good of mankind. . . . I [cannot] bear to think of what my children would be if we were to permit this hell-begotten conspiracy to destroy this country."[63] For New Yorker John T. McMahon, even the issue of whether to enlist was an intensely spiritual one. He believed that God wanted him to be a preacher, yet, after much soul-searching, he came to believe that it was God's will for him to enlist in the army first and then, if he should come home alive, become a preacher after the war. "If the country is not saved," McMahon explained to his diary, "then all is lost. There will be no need of a preacher, for the people would not hear."[64]

This intense faith may be difficult to understand, but other Civil War soldiers spelled out the intermediate steps in McMahon's logic. Sgt. Samuel McIlvaine of the Tenth Indiana tried to explain it in a letter to his mother:

> Oh! That I had words to infuse this faith into your mind. It is true I feel an anxiety to live yet a little longer in this word, . . . but I fear not to die. . . . Did I not fully believe the work I am engaged in a justifiable one, and one of imperative duty, to all the lovers of liberty and light in the world, one that must not be shrunk from, then would I abandon it. But 'tis useless to argue this mater. Suffice it to say that to abandon

the cause I am now engaged in, and acknowledge the right of a portion of the people of the United States to sever, or rive in twain, and destroy this Government, which stands out to the rest of the world as the polestar, the beacon light of liberty & freedom to the human race, would be to undo all that I have ever learned, all that I have ever been taught in regard to the rights and privileges of the human race. Therefore I believe our cause to be the cause of liberty and light, to the masses of mankind, the cause of God, and holy and justifiable in his sight, and for this reason, I fear not to die in it if need be.[65]

This was not the same outlook held by those who believed that dying in the cause would guarantee a man a place in heaven. Rather, McIlvaine was asserting that because the cause was "the cause of God," he could fight for it with a clear conscience, without fear that if he died in the endeavor and thus was called to answer before God's judgment he would feel ashamed of having fought in an evil cause. Unlike the others, McIlvaine was not asserting that death in the cause was any substitute for faith in Christ.

Further explanation of the religious significance that many Union soldiers attached to the preservation of the United States comes from an Irish immigrant and devout Roman Catholic, Peter Welsh of the Twenty-eighth Massachusetts. In a letter to his wife, who was far from enthusiastic about the Union cause or her husband's participation in it, Welsh pointed out the general scriptural condemnation of rebellion and then stated the basic argument for saving the Republic. "All men who love free government and equal laws are watching this crisis to see if a republic can sustain itself in such a case. If it fails then the hopes of millions fall and the designs and wishes of all tyrants will suceed the old cry will be sent forth from the aristocrats of europe that such is the comon end of all republics. The blatent croakers of the devine right of kings will shout forth their joy." Then he pointed out the direct religious significance of all this. "Religeous as well as political liberty" was at stake. "One of the most important, yes, the most important of all rights enjoyed by the citezen of a free nation is the libety of concience. Free alters is an invaluable boon, and where on earth except in that fountain of religion Rome can any one point out to me a spot where the Church enjoys such fredom as in the

United States."[66] Except for the bit about "that fountain of religion," his Protestant fellow soldiers would have agreed with him entirely.

One of them, New York soldier William H. Walling, looked at the matter in terms of what he believed was America's God-ordained religious purpose and the threat posed to that by the rebellion:

> Previous to this dire necessity [he wrote to his sisters in October 1862], I have always felt that the American people had a greater mission among the nations of the earth than to show the old crumbling despotisms of the old world how to depopulate whole communities and to shed seas of blood. . . . We have held up our institutions, and extended a call to the oppressed and downtrodden of all nations to take refuge under them. . . . [T]he real mission of our government was to be instrumental in the spread of the Gospel, in the publication of salvation to a world lying in sin and wickedness and in gathering in the heathen whom God has declared he would have for an inheritance.

Now, however, the picture was sadly changed. The country was "divided, rent asunder, our divine mission apparently thwarted, our national existence even threatened." Defending the American system of government was for Walling something "sacred."[67]

This was the sort of motivation that could propel men into the ghastly killing fields of the war's great battles, solid ranks of soldiers advancing into enemy fire that buzzed so thickly around their ears that they instinctively hunched their shoulders as if walking into a hard, wind-driven rain. Thousands fell between sunrise and sunset at places such as Antietam and Fredericksburg. But Walling, writing between those two great bloodbaths, told his sisters, "I believe we have too much at stake in crushing out this rebellion to become disheartened though every household in the land is thrown into mourning for the slain in battle. And in this if it be necessary I would not make an exception even of the representative you have in this war."[68]

Alongside this powerfully motivating religious faith in the cause of the Union, a second religious explanation for the cause and purpose of the war began to appear in soldiers' letters and diaries during 1862. On leave back home in Keokuk, Iowa, Cyrus F. Boyd heard a local minister preach "that human slavery was the Cause and we should have no lasting peace until the Curse was wiped out." Boyd considered it "a good sermon."[69] Not long afterward, a Union naval officer wrote that "slavery is such a horrible blot on civilization, that I am convinced that the war will exterminate it and its supporters, and that it was brought about for that purpose by God."[70] Andrew Sproul opined that God "will carry on the war untill that he will make all flesh free."[71]

This growing conviction among both soldiers and civilians found expression in a sense of guilt for the entire nation's complicity in slavery and a belief that the chastening of God the country was now experiencing came exactly for that cause. New England Methodist minister Gilbert Haven preached as much, claiming that Union soldiers were now paying with their blood for the churches' failure to give a clear witness against slavery.[72] Similarly, Vermont soldier Wilbur Fisk wrote of the devastation the war was bringing to Virginia and of the price all the Southern states would pay for their rebellion. And yet they would not be paying the whole price, Fisk believed. "The whole Nation is involved, and deep grief and poignant sorrow must be borne by the North, to expiate the crimes of the South."[73]

The North, after all, had been for some "four score and seven years" part of a nation in which slavery was tolerated and even protected. "We as a nation have committed a great sin in cultivating and propping this institution up untill it has become so powerful that it has almost over thrown the Government," wrote Orra B. Bailey.[74] Capt. Jefferson Newman wrote to his sister explaining that his views on slavery had changed during his time as a soldier. Slavery, he now believed, "is one of the greatest sins that man ever committed—hold another being in bondage . . . and until this is ended there never can be any peace in the United States. We are a nation that has boasted our freedom and at the same time have been holding millions of human beings at the South in bondage and now if God ever punished a nation for anything He is punishing the whole United States for doing and allowing such things to be done. Slavery and freedom cannot exist together and one or the other must go down and it is for us to say which it will be."[75]

In similar terms, Robert H. Kellogg of the Sixteenth Connecticut wrote to his parents in September 1862. "We *must* free the blacks or perish as a nation," Kellogg wrote one week before the battle of Antietam. "I have long held this view and have been sneered at & called an abolitionist, but I am content to wait. I think I'm *right*." A few months earlier, it had appeared that the North was about to win the war. Now a series of reverses had changed all that, and the Federal forces were compelled to fight off Confederate offensives. "I honestly think it is because the nation has disregarded God's voice," wrote Kellogg. "We've not let the enslaved blacks go free when we had the power. Many if not most of our Gens are profane, wicked men—and as a nation we have been proud and corrupt. Are we not now receiving a just rebuke?"[76]

To those who felt this way, Lincoln's September 1862 preliminary Emancipation Proclamation came as a welcome step. A lieutenant in the Fifty-ninth Illinois wrote, "It allwais has been plane to me that this rase [i.e., the blacks] must be freed before god would recognise us. . . . We bost of liberty and we should try to impart it to others. . . . [T]hank god the chanes will soon be bursted . . . now I believe we are on gods side . . . now I can fight with a good heart."[77] Charles W. Reed wrote, "the prospect of our ultimate success seems better than ever. We now know what we are fighting for."[78]

Some believed that emancipation should have come sooner and that Union setbacks during the first half of the war were God's punishment for the delay. Lt. George W. Johnson of the Forty-ninth New York was in Washington, D.C., in February 1863 and went to hear a sermon in the Senate chamber delivered by the Reverend Dr. Cheever of New York. Cheever said that had the Union embraced the cause of emancipation from the outset, the war would have been short. Because it had not done so, God had allowed the loss of 200,000 Union lives to no purpose. "God was conducting this war for the emancipation of the negro from slavery," Johnson summarized Cheever's argument, "and until that was accomplished the war would not end."[79]

As growing numbers of Northern Christians came to see slavery as the cause of the war and the eradication of it as God's purpose in allowing the conflict, this too became a powerful motivation to see the war through, no matter how appalling the losses. "As the soldiers see more fully the depths of principle involved in this controversy, and the wisdom of the policy the Government is adopting to bring it to an issue that God must forever approve," wrote the Second Vermont's Wilbur Fisk, "the more determined and anxious are they to carry the war out successfully."[80]

This increased sense of religious motivation was reflected in more frequent, strong, and direct statements by the soldiers of their assurance that they were on God's side. An anonymous soldier of the Eighty-seventh Indiana wrote to a newspaper back home, calling on Southern sympathizers in Indiana to "forsake their treasonable purposes and come out on the Lord's side."[81] Speaking of his comrades, a soldier of the Nineteenth Indiana wrote, "They feel that God has committed a trust to their keeping."[82] "I believe we are doing God's service in fighting for our country," Union soldier Joseph Whitney told his wife.[83] Another Northern soldier, Jefferson Newman, put it as forcefully and directly as any: "We are the sword in the hand of God to put the rebellion down."[84]

Beginning in the fall of 1862, large numbers of Union soldiers began referring to the North as "God's country." On several occasions, soldiers returning from Confederate imprisonment wrote statements such as, "We felt we were now again in God's Country."[85] In September 1862, as soldiers of the Army of the Potomac in pursuit of Lee found themselves marching through pro-Union western Maryland and receiving the cheers of the populace, one soldier called out, "Colonel, we're in God's country again!"[86] Hoosier troops of the Eighty-third Indiana, pushing deep into the land of cotton in the state of Mississippi, met wide-eyed slaves who asked where they came from. "From God's country," was their reply.[87]

This corresponded naturally with a growing willingness to take a hard line with "the sacreligious rebels." Southerners were no longer to be viewed as misguided fellow countrymen but as evil foes of all that was good in America. "The more we learn of the despicable social condition of the South," wrote one Union soldier, "the stronger appears the need of the purification which, in the Providence of God, comes of the fire and the sword."[88]

Having begun the conflict with a facile assurance of their rightness and of God's favor, Northern Christians and the many others influenced by Christianity had found themselves tested by the unimagined bloodshed of the war, forced to think anew about what they were doing. For the great majority of them, that reconsideration did not lead to abandonment of the cause but rather to a rededication to that cause as one far more profound and sacred than they had originally imagined. As the Civil War approached its midpoint in the spring of 1863, they gathered a renewed and deepened sense of assurance that God favored their undertaking and that in fighting to save the Union and to end slavery as well, they were accomplishing God's purposes on earth. Yet at the same time, they bore an awareness, sharpened by experience, of just what sort of price God might call upon them to pay in the accomplishment of His ends and their own purification.

As for the soldiers, they hoped devoutly that the war might end soon and that they might be spared to see their loved ones again. They also knew that it might go on for a very long time and consume as yet unimagined numbers of lives. "We must keep up as good courage as possible," wrote the Second Connecticut Artillery's Sgt. Josiah B. Corban to his wife and children in June 1863, "and trust the all wise ruler of the universe to bring about peace when he shall see it is best with all his future designs and plans."[89]

7

"GOD HAS FAVORED OUR CAUSE"
Southern Christians View the Early Stages of the War

It was Sunday, May 26, 1861, and the large Presbyterian church in Rome, Georgia, was crowded. Taking up a large section of the pews near the front of the church were the newly minted soldiers of two of the four Floyd County companies then preparing for service. The Rome Light Guards, composed of the city's social elite, were dapper as usual in their natty, tailor-made gray uniforms, while the somewhat more plebeian Miller Rifles were less resplendent but still impressive in simpler suits of gray. Shortly before the service began, they had filed silently into the building and marched with military solemnity to the seats reserved for them. The service began with several pieces by the choir, all dealing with the theme of parting. Then Pastor John A. Jones rose to preach the farewell sermon to the troops, who were scheduled to board the train for Richmond the next morning.

The war had provided the subject matter for Jones's messages of the previous two weeks. He had expounded what he considered to be the reasons for the beginning of hostilities, the rightness of the Southern position, and, finally, "the evidences of God's favor to the South as manifested during the Revolution to the present." Now the Presbyterian minister addressed the large crowd of nearly 200 soldiers and over 800 civilians from the sixteenth chapter of the First Epistle to the Corinthians with the words, "quit you like men, be strong." The soldiers, he said, must face hardship with a proper manly fortitude, and they must be prepared for the fact that some of them would not be coming back. At this, one observer noted, "there was just one convulsive sob from one end of the church to the other, for the congregation was composed of the mothers and wives and sisters and daughters of the soldiers who were marching away." Jones was not indifferent to such feelings. His own nineteen-year-old son, Pvt. James Dunwoody Jones, sat among the ranks of his comrades of the Light Guards, "looking very solemn and attentive."[1]

Just as their brethren in the North rallied to the Union, so the vast majority of Southern Christians enthusiastically supported the Confederacy and its war, proclaimed the righteous cause of the South, and blessed the gray-clad soldiers on their way to fight against the hated forces of abolitionism. Rev. Benjamin M. Palmer of First Presbyterian Church of New Orleans had already declared himself on the subject. In a series of sermons beginning in November 1860, Palmer had trumpeted the divine ordination of slavery and the need for the South to separate from the North. Over 30,000 printed copies of these sermons were eventually distributed.[2] Georgia politician and pious Presbyterian Thomas R. R. Cobb, a fiery advocate of secession, was elated when the Southern states declared themselves out of the Union. "This revolution," he crowed, "has been accomplished mainly by the Churches." Charles A. McDaniel, president of Bowdon College, a small Methodist institution in Georgia, not only favored the Southern cause but also led most of the student body into the Confederate army, where they became a company and he their captain.[3] A Texas soldier remembered the first months after secession for the many war meetings held in church buildings in his state. "Instead of sending forth the voice of prayer or song of thanksgiving," as they usually did, these buildings "were filled with shouts of excited men as they were harangued by some friend to revolution."[4] By December 1861, the Georgia Conference of the Methodist Episcopal Church, South, was prepared to announce that no "Union party" existed among its clergymen.[5]

Yet this statement and Cobb's boast that the churches had brought about secession were not entirely true. Or at least they were not the whole truth. Some Southern Christians, particularly those of the older generation, were far from enthusiastic about secession. Methodist bishop James O. Andrew, whose ownership of slaves had split the nation's largest denomination back in 1844, wrote in January 1861, "the state of the country grieves me . . . because I fear it will seriously affect the spirituality and holiness of the church. May God help us." A few months later he wrote, "Confederate flags are flying everywhere; may God have mercy on us, and save us from war and bloodshed." A number of other Southern Methodist pastors, though a minority of the group's overall numbers, opposed secession openly in the political arena.[6]

Many others Southern religious leaders favored secession with the same enthusiasm as Cobb or McDaniel, but they had qualms about saying so openly and at once. For decades, a large segment of the Southern church had answered Northern condemnations of slavery by declaring the doctrine of the "spiritual church" and the claim that the affairs of this life should be of no concern to Christians. That argument now proved to be a two-edged sword. If, on this basis, Christians should take no interest in combating slavery, then by all rights they should take no interest in defending it either. A few of the most die-hard "spiritual church" men tried to maintain a semblance of consistency in this area. The inventor and chief advocate of the concept, South Carolina Presbyterian James Henley Thornwell, was one of them, reminding fellow Southerners that it was none of the church's concern what sort of government prevailed.

Yet even the doctrinaire Thornwell fudged on this point. He too enthusiastically approved of slavery and the Confederacy. "The parties to this conflict," wrote Thornwell, "are not merely abolitionists and slaveholders—they are atheists, socialists, communists, red republicans, jacobins on the one side, and the friends of order and regulated freedom on the other. In one word, the world is the battleground—Christianity and atheism the combatants; and the progress of humanity the stake."[7] Here was the guru of the "spiritual" church summoning Southerners to a North American Armageddon. With even an ideologue like Thornwell trimming his sails to the winds of expediency, other Southern religious leaders eventually had relatively little difficulty changing the tack they had previously taken regarding God and government. Methodist bishop George F. Pierce might indeed claim that no church in the South would tolerate "a political preacher," but he frequently preached political sermons in favor of the Confederacy, urging Southern Christians to fight against the evil Northerners. The Confederacy, he claimed, was "the last hope of Freedom and the last home of a pure Gospel," while the North was a corrupt society that now strove to make the Southern people the "victims . . . of this ungodly traffic in vice, of unscriptural theories of government, of fiendish schemes of power."[8]

Similarly, Episcopal bishop Stephen Elliot was not a step behind his Methodist colleague in denouncing the evil North. That region, he claimed, had undergone "moral deterioration" in recent decades, degenerating "in philosophy, in letters, in ethics, in religion . . . in politics . . . commerce and trade, and finance and social life." All this proved that "man is not capable of self government," Elliot maintained. What the South needed was a new government, purified of corrupt Northern ideas about the competence of the common man to govern himself. In other words, it should be a government that was properly aristocratic in nature.[9] The South was fighting for "the whole framework of our social life," asserted the bishop in an oblique reference to slavery; therefore, victory was imperative.[10] Elliot lost no time putting his ideas into religious practice. Immediately upon secession, he ordered Episcopal clergy within his diocese, Georgia, to delete from their liturgy the prayer for the president of the United States and substitute one for the governor of Georgia.[11]

Elliot's fellow Episcopal bishop, Leonidas Polk of Louisiana, went him one better. Polk was an 1827 graduate of the U.S. Military Academy, but he had resigned upon graduation, never held a commission in the U.S. Army, and, so far as any of his friends could say, had not so much as read a book on military affairs in all the intervening years. Nevertheless, Polk offered his military services to his old West Point crony, now Confederate president Jefferson Davis. Davis made Polk a major general directly from civilian life, partially because the Confederate president lacked insight into the shortcomings of his friends, and partially because he hoped that Polk's stature as a popular religious leader in the lower Mississippi Valley region would cement the people's allegiance to the Confederacy. In justification of his course, Polk said that he was "supported by the conviction that 'resistance to tyrants is duty to God,'" quoting (or rather misquoting) not the Bible but the Deist Thomas Jefferson. "The cause,"

Polk told his friend President Davis, was "equally that of our altars and our firesides."[12]

Upon assuming his new command, Polk issued to the people of the Mississippi Valley a florid, almost frenzied manifesto. "Numbers may be against us," the bishop-general wrote, "but the battle is not always to the strong. Justice will triumph; and an earnest of this triumph is already beheld in the mighty uprising of the whole Southern heart." The people of the South were unified, Polk claimed, in their determination "to perish rather than yield to the oppressor, who, in the name of freedom, yet under the prime inspiration of an infidel horde, seeks to reduce eight millions of freemen to abject bondage and subjugation." Just who those "eight millions" were is not clear. The free population of the South was about 5.5 million, with another 3.5 million slaves. At any rate, Polk wrote, all "eight millions" of them were bent on "rolling back the desolating tide of invasion, and . . . restoring to the people of the South that peace, independence, and right of self-government to which they are by nature and nature's God as justly entitled as those who seek thus ruthlessly to enslave them." The cause, Polk added in closing, included "the preservation of the purity of religious truth" and was therefore "the cause of Heaven, and may well challenge the homage and service of the patriot and Christian."[13]

Davis's political-religious appointment seems to have paid the desired dividends, linking the cause of the Confederacy with that of God in the minds of many Southerners, though they probably would have made the connection anyway. It apparently made a good impression. An officer in the Fourth Alabama wrote, "Bishop Polk has set an example worthy of all praise," and added, "I would like to see the church take a very decided stand upon the political questions of the day."[14] Some of its representatives certainly did. Pvt. Benjamin Barrett of the Second South Carolina Rifles wrote that his chaplain was "a Seceder. He preaches for the South and Prays for the South and dont mention the North any at all."[15]

The obvious question, of course, is how all this could be consistent with abstaining from "political preaching," to say nothing of political actions. The key, as far as Bishop Pierce was concerned, was that in this case the North was the aggressor, and the South was merely defending itself. That made Pierce's political preaching, and presumably Polk's and others' political actions, nonpolitical.[16] It seems that God was not indifferent to human government after all, but rather indifferent, if not downright hostile, only to antislavery ideas about human government. This was borne out in Southern attitudes toward the church in the North. The Southern religious press decried the "prostitution of the Northern pulpit" in support of the Union cause.[17]

Similarly, Southerners before the war had expressed shock, horror, and outrage at the claims of Northerners, such as New York senator William H. Seward, that there was "a higher law than the Constitution" when confronted with that document's compromises on the slavery issue. Now, however, with the South abandoning the old U.S. Constitution, along with the Union that had created it, Southern Methodist minister James W. Hinton inveighed against Northern Christians, accusing them of holding the Constitution "as sacred as the law of God deposited in the ark of the covenant."[18] In short, with the formation of the Confederacy and the initiation of war against the Union, the great majority of Southern religious leaders found it expedient to change their approach to church-state issues. While maintaining much of their previous rhetoric decrying "political preachers" and "religious fanaticism" in the North, they did their best to present the cause of the Confederacy as nothing short of a religious crusade, favored by God and claiming the zealous commitment of every godly Southerner.[19]

The Southern church's advocacy of the cause of the Confederacy began early. In his invocation at the February 1861 convention in Montgomery, Alabama, that called the Confederacy into existence, the Reverend Mr. Manly prayed, "Oh, Thou heart-searching God, we trust that Thou seest we are pursuing those rights which were guaranteed to us by the solemn covenants of our fathers, and which were cemented by their blood."[20] The Alabama Methodist Conference went on record as praying for "brilliant victories" for the Confederacy. Virginia Methodist Rev. R. N. Sledd claimed that the South was fighting for the "cause of Christ, the interests of religion." Church of Christ minister Rev. J. S. Lamar asserted fiercely that North and South differed "as radically and as rigidly as Puritanism differs from Christianity or as Abolitionism differs from the Bible."[21] In November 1861, Dr. George R. C. Todd, brother-in-law to Abraham Lincoln but, like many of the president's in-laws, an ardent

Southerner, stated in a lecture that the war was between the "children of the devil" and the "children of the Lord," leaving no doubt as to which side was which.[22]

Very early in the war, some 100 prominent Southern ministers of various denominations joined in issuing an "Address to Christians Throughout the World." In it, they characterized the South as peace loving and aggrieved, wantonly attacked by the North. They admitted that slavery was the cause of the conflict, but they defended the peculiar institution, claiming to know and understand it better than any critics outside the South possibly could. Slavery was a benevolent institution, they claimed, and the best possible situation for the blacks. Besides, because of slavery the blacks were in America, where they could hear the gospel, rather than in Africa, where perhaps they would not. Of course, Northern Christians would have agreed that hearing the gospel was a good thing but would have maintained that it did not justify the wrong of slavery.[23]

Churches and pastors all across the South sent their local soldiers off to war as the Reverend Mr. Jones of Rome did, with elaborate and detailed assurances of the rightness of the Confederate cause. In LaGrange, Georgia, Rev. C. W. Key exhorted the young men of his congregation to enlist to fight against the "fanatical enemy."[24] In Hancock County, Georgia, Bishop Pierce and other Methodist clergy formally blessed a company of soldiers setting off for the front.[25] In Marshall, Texas, Rev. T. B. Wilson passionately exhorted his young male parishioners to enlist. "In the name of God," intoned Wilson, "I say fight for such sacred rights. Fight for the principles and institutions bequeathed to you by the blood of revolutionary sires."[26]

In case some soldiers missed the point at these local events, the Southern religious press devoted prodigal amounts of ink to such topics as the defense of slavery and the claim that the war had been forced on the South by an aggressive North. The *Religious Herald,* a Richmond, Virginia–based Baptist publication that was the leading religious periodical distributed to the soldiers, was especially vociferous in such claims.[27]

Confederate soldiers could also look to the example of various clergymen in uniform around them. Besides the Right Reverend Major General Polk, there was Stonewall Jackson's chief of staff during three months of 1862, Robert L. Dabney, a Presbyterian minister. There was also Episcopal minister William N. Pendleton, serving as an artillery officer and rising eventually to be Lee's chief of artillery. Pendleton gained a bit of fame by naming the four guns of his first command "Matthew," "Mark," "Luke," and "John" and shouting during his first battle, "May the Lord have mercy on their poor souls—Fire!"[28]

There were also dozens of other ministers who, like Polk and Pendleton, joined the army not as chaplains but as combat soldiers or officers. Many a Methodist or Baptist minister became captain of a company of local boys going off to the war, and some simply signed on as private soldiers. James Iredell Hall wrote that his Company C, Ninth Tennessee, had "two ministers of the gospel and at least one theological student," and it was by no means a uniquely clerical outfit.[29]

Mark P. Lowrey was a Baptist minister in northern Mississippi. Though he had had a bit of military experience as a youth in the Mexican War, Lowrey had thought to sit out the conflict with the North. Early Confederate reverses, however, helped convince him that he must fight or else have "the enemy overrun my home and family." His parishioners also urged him to take up arms. "Churches felt that they had no use for pastors then—fighting men were in demand," Lowrey later explained. So in the spring of 1862 he raised the Thirty-second Mississippi "in a little less time than any other regiment was ever raised and organized in North Mississippi" and was unanimously elected its colonel.[30]

So many Methodist clergymen enlisted in the Confederate army that by the spring of 1862, Bishop Andrew and even Bishop Pierce were concerned. They complained of "the too extensive influence of the war spirit among our preachers," which was leaving Methodist pulpits empty back home. Besides, the bishops had begun to have qualms about merging "the preacher in the warrior" and urged Methodist preachers to go to war as chaplains, if they would, but not as combat soldiers.[31] Of course, ministers in the North joined the Federal armies just as readily—for example, the Seventy-third Illinois, or "Preacher Regiment"—but then Northern ministers had not been proclaiming any doctrines about a "spiritual church" that was blithely unconcerned with the affairs of this life.

The church in the South found other ways of showing its support for the Confederacy. In the spring of 1862, Gen. Pierre G. T. Beauregard put out a call for Southern churches and plantations to donate their bells to the Confederacy so that they could be melted down and cast into cannon. It was a silly idea on Beauregard's part, since his army already had as many cannon as it could profitably use, but the churches did not know that and responded enthusiastically. The Methodist church in LaGrange, Georgia, and both the Methodist and Episcopal churches of Rome were among many to offer bells to the Confederate government for military purposes.[32]

By October 1862, Georgia Methodists had so far departed from previous notions of a "spiritual church" that they were ready to endorse a position that would have warmed the heart of any old-time New England Puritan. "The Church," their statement read,

> has a right to be heard in all legislative questions, to have a voice in all the deliberations of cabinets and councils, to exercise its influence in all the great movements of the race, to dictate from her code to the legislators of the country, to demand that her severe rule of action should regulate the public conscience, to reign over the nation as well as the individual, in a word, that the Church should give laws to the world.[33]

The wording was strident and overstated, for the delegates did not really mean to claim for the institutional church an actual role in civil government. But the basic claim that Christian principles should prevail in the public square was neither novel nor radical; it was the belief of a majority of pre–Civil War Americans. Southern Christians within the Confederacy, relieved for the moment of the need to hide their peculiar institution from the scrutiny of God's law, were, like a newly bent sapling suddenly released, merely snapping back into what had been the common American position, with various nuances, since John Winthrop. The concept of the "spiritual church" had been an aberration within American religious thought, as it was within the entire Christian tradition, and even its inventors found little use for it beyond the initial expedience for which it was coined.

With the Southern church solidly committed to the cause of the Confederacy, the South's Christians were also concerned that God should take that side as well. At one point during the war, a North Carolina soldier prayed, "Lord, we have a mighty big fight down here, and a sight of trouble; and we hope, Lord, that you will take the proper view of the matter, and give us the victory."[34] Suggestions, during the early days of the war, that God might not "take a proper view of the matter" were rare but not unheard of. Mississippian Albert H. Clark, on his way to the fighting front in Virginia, wrote, "Well, Bill, we can never be conquered only by the ruling power of God but alas! if God is against us, we are ruined forever."[35]

This might seem a superfluous consideration, since God might be assumed to be on the side of whoever was right, which the Confederates had already decided themselves to be. However, that assumption was not necessarily a safe one. True, the Confederate cause might be a righteous one, and the Yankees might be unspeakably vile, but some Confederates believed that God might allow Southerners to be defeated if they proved to be unworthy of the righteous cause they espoused. Few Southerners gave the concept much thought during the first half of the war, but setbacks to the Confederate forces and the failure to win the expected quick and easy victory during the first year of fighting turned a few minds to the subject of whether God would support them.

The *Rome (Georgia) Courier,* published a series of articles in the spring of 1862 entitled "God in War." At considerable length the author demonstrated from the Bible that God is sovereign and can give the victory in war to whomever He will—as the author termed it, "the futility of superior numbers and munitions of war, when opposed to God and truth." The obvious significance of that consideration for the numerically and industrially outclassed Confederacy led the author to his next point: "Can we have the help of this great God . . . and how?" The answer to the first of these questions was easy. "Emphatically, we can," the author asserted. God was ready and willing "to display His power, and augment His glory in our salvation from our enemies, but this He can only do, when compatible with the principles of His righteous government."

There was the rub, however. "How may we secure His Providence in our behalf?" The author's answer was twofold: "Humility and submission to God." That was a prerequisite of any request to God, for the Almighty clearly would not countenance haughty or arrogant demands from His creatures. Of this, the author believed, Southerners had been guilty:

Pride has been the sin of our people from the first. Assuming that our cause is just, that our institutions are based on God's own word, that constitutional and religious liberty for the world, that the purity of religion and the Scriptures depend on our success, that the interests of humanity depend on the culture of cotton, and we seemed to suppose that all these interests, having in themselves an inherent moral power, and interwoven with God's own benevolent purposes, constituted a cause of such sublimely grand moral proportions, as would perforce command the blessing of God upon us, and thus He would be committed to prosper us.

God's actions are not at the "command" of any human, and so, the writer concluded, "We sinned in the manner of our appeal." It was not the rightness of its cause that could guarantee the Confederacy's success, but only God's favor, and that would be vouchsafed to the humble. "In contemplating the magnitude of the sins of the North," the author continued, "the South may forget her own.... God can save just principles and institutions, and destroy the wicked and unworthy advocates of them. The tongue that cries 'cotton is king' in a spirit of self-sufficient, impious infidelity, shall yet proclaim 'the Lord He is God,' though it be necessary for Him to desolate the whole cotton area of the South, or change the laws of nature itself." In short, God knew how to humble the proud, and the Southern people had best humble themselves before God before He humbled them at the hands of the Yankees.[36]

Needless to say, readers of the *Rome Courier* constituted only a tiny fraction of the overall Southern population, and in any case, some would little heed its editor's warnings. Some Southerners still displayed exactly the sort of attitude the author of "God in War" deplored. That same spring, James Iredell Hall wrote home asserting, "I believe in the justice of our cause and that we will soon regain all that we have lost. I have no fear of the final result of this war, if the people of the south will only do their duty. We have the men and the arms to drive every scoundrel of the Yankees off southern soil."[37] All that was necessary was for the Southern people to use their ability, and the war would be won.

Far more common were the expressions of other Southern soldiers who eschewed Hall's self-sufficient pride and expressed dependence on God,

as well as supreme faith that He would, in fact, grant victory and independence to the Confederacy. The Eighth Georgia's Melvin Dwinell
wrote in April 1862 that the coming battle around Richmond would be "a
most desperate and bloody one, but we are full of hope that victory will
finally perch upon the righteous standards of our glorious cause. We shall
go into the conflict, not with boasting, but" with trust in God.[38] In June
1862, in the midst of those same "desperate and bloody" battles, R. M.
Campbell of the Fourth Georgia wrote in his diary addressing an imagi-
nary Yankee: "By the help of the God of Battles we expect to defeat you
here & drive your army to the walls of fortress Monroe."[39]

Similar feelings prevailed in the Confederacy's western armies. In May
1862, New Orleans minister and rabid secessionist Rev. Benjamin M.
Palmer addressed Confederate soldiers in the lines around Corinth,
Mississippi, speaking on several occasions to various segments of the army
there. When he addressed men of Polk's corps, the bishop-general intro-
duced him personally. After hearing Palmer, the Twelfth Tennessee's
Alfred Fielder was deeply moved. He wrote in his diary that they were
expecting a battle in the next few days. "If so," he wrote, "may God who
has said the race is not to the swift nor the battle to the strong give us the
victory. We are fighting for our homes, our wives, and our families and
all that is sacred, and all we want [is] to be let alone. Our enemies are
fighting for conquest and plunder." The battle did not come off as anticipated, but two days later Fielder wrote in his diary, "I still put my trust
in God and try to feel resigned to his will feeling that our Cause is Just
and that God is Just and we shall finally be successful whether I live to
see the time or not."[40]

A summer's ferocious fighting did not change these attitudes. In September 1862, William Ross Stillwell of the Fifty-third Georgia wrote to
his wife, Molly, from near Frederick, Maryland, where Lee's army was
on the offensive. Stillwell told his wife that there might be bloody fighting if Lee led them to attack Washington or Baltimore, but echoing the
phraseology of the Bible, he added, "Be of good cheer for I believe God
will deliver them into our hands. Molly, I think God is going to stop this
unholy war before long," by which Stillwell obviously meant that the
Almighty would secure a Confederate victory.[41] In the event, none of
Stillwell's expectations were fulfilled.

The spring of 1863 saw no change in the Confederate soldiers' expressions that their cause was not only just but also virtually assured of victory through providential intervention. "God being on our side," wrote Flavel C. Barber of the Third Tennessee, "we will assuredly gain the victory."[42] Reuben A. Pierson voiced his confidence in May of that year, coupled with his disdain for Northerners. "Our enemies can never accomplish the unwholy design which they have formed for our subjugation. If we are only true to ourselves and God be for us the time will surly soon come when we shall be redeemed from the miseries of this horrid war and restored to our homes in peace and our enemies will then return to their idols and continue to worship their almighty dollar as has been their former custom."[43] Even with the Vicksburg garrison besieged and apparently in very dire condition, South Carolinian Tally N. Simpson, with Lee's army in Virginia, wrote, "God certainly is on our side, and we should trust in Him to deliver us from the hands of our enemies."[44]

Along with expressions of confidence that God would eventually give them victory over the Yankees, Southern soldiers occasionally wrote down in diaries or letters their reasons for believing that God was on their side. Sometimes these justifications took the same tack as Bishop-General Polk's pronouncements, claiming that the Confederacy was fighting for liberty and that liberty in itself was holy and favored by God. One soldier wrote to the *Richmond Examiner* that he and his comrades were "armed in the holy cause of liberty."[45] This, however, was not a common expression among the common soldiers. It was more the style of those who were self-consciously striving for eloquence and the Jeffersonian sound. Indeed, it was more than somewhat Jeffersonian in concept as well, with its not quite biblical system of values. Thus it should not be surprising that Polk, in advancing it, resorted to quoting Thomas Jefferson.

Often, Confederate soldiers' justifications of the rightness of their cause were bald assertions without any explanation to back up their claims. In setting forth his reason for enlisting, a Mississippi soldier claimed, "I viewed the contest as one of unparalleled wrong and oppression against truth and the right. I was persuaded that not only civil liberty but evangelical religion had a large stake at issue in the struggle." How civil liberty, much less evangelical religion, was threatened by the Republican Party's program of admitting no new slave states to the Union is puzzling indeed, and the soldier left no clue as to his train of thought in the matter. Nor did he give any indication as to what might qualify as the "unparalleled wrong and oppression" he had signed up to fight against. Perhaps he was not quite clear on that himself, for he not only failed to specify his meaning but also felt it necessary to insist, as did many other Confederate soldiers, "My conscience, therefore, was clear."[46]

More often, soldiers recorded in their writings more mundane justifications for the Southern cause. The most frequent of these down-to-earth reasons was that the Union army was invading the South, and Southern men were therefore obligated to fight for the Confederacy in order to defend their families and homes. A prominent Southern preacher asserted that what was going on was "a war of invasion" on the part of the United States, "and the determination to resist was deep and almost universal" among Southerners. "The strong feelings of religion and patriotism were evoked at the same moment, and by the same act, and men entered the ranks under the conviction that in so doing they were faithful alike to God and their country."[47] In the fall of 1862, T. J. Koger, a minister who had become a Confederate officer, explained his decision to enter the army in even more down-to-earth terms: "I could not be a soldier unless conscience approved. It is only when my own land is invaded, my wife and children endangered, that I dare bear arms."[48]

Southern religious newspapers were vociferous and voluminous in making similar claims. One of them announced in 1861 that Southerners had been "forced to defend ourselves." Another was much more explicit and high-flown: "In this unhappy war we find, on our side, no compromise of Christian principle," the editor wrote. "The South has accepted it as a last necessity—an alternative in which there was no choice but submission to a dynasty considered oppressive, and in its very principles antagonistic to her rights and subversive to her existence. Hence her sons, who are true Christians, have no compunctions of conscience when they go forth in her armies. They find, on the contrary, an approbation of conscience in their decision to fight for their homes and altars. 'In the name of our God we set up our banners.' We go to meet the invader 'In the name of the Lord of hosts.'"

Yet all this should do more than simply give Confederate soldiers clear consciences about serving in the Rebel armies; it should also assure God's favor to the Confederacy. "We are willing for Him to decide this contest on its merits," the same editor continued. "We protest, in the face of Heaven, we want nothing but our rights, we demand nothing but our rights."[49] A fairly large range of ideas might be included between the concept of "we demand nothing but our rights" and "my own land is invaded," but it all lies within the general claim that, in effect, Southerners had been peacefully going about their business when the North had launched an unprovoked and aggressive attack against them. They were merely defending themselves, which was their right, and defending their families, which was noble. Confederate soldier Ignatius W. Brock wrote to his sister in 1863, "From the time I entered into service I have felt that I owed it to my country my friends and my God to do all in my power to preserve my home from the touch of the despot's heel."[50]

Other Confederates based their belief in the rightness of their cause on such factors as the presence of well-known Christians Robert E. Lee and Stonewall Jackson in the Confederate army.[51] The Southern clergymen's "Address to Christians Throughout the World" announced triumphantly, "Our President, some of our most influential statesmen, our Commanding General, and an unusual proportion of the principal Generals, as well as scores of other officers, are prominent, and we believe consistent members of the Church. Thousands of our soldiers are men of prayer."[52]

Taking another tack, Rev. W. M. Crumley, chaplain to the Georgia hospital in Richmond, Virginia, even claimed that the South was right because it was fighting to keep the black race in its proper place. "One of the principal benefits to us, which this revolution will work out," Crumley wrote in a February 1862 letter to the *Savannah Southern Confederacy*, "is the true relation of the races to each other—making the Caucasian the Lord of Creation, and the negro his inferior and servant." However, relatively few Southerners had the nerve to make such blatantly racist arguments in the name of Christianity.[53]

More common than any reasoned explanations of the justness of the Confederate cause were simple assertions that God favored the South and that the proof of this was to be seen in His previous miraculous interventions on behalf of Confederate arms. This practice of claiming that the Confederate cause was just because God had shown favor to it in battle began remarkably early. In May 1861, when hardly any fighting had taken place, Lt. N. H. R. Dawson of the Fourth Alabama wrote to his fiancée back in Selma, "I have great confidence in the justice of our cause, and have an abiding faith that fewer of our men will be killed, [than] the circumstances would indicate. You will notice that in all of our battles so far, we have escaped almost miraculously, while the enemy have suffered greatly in comparison."[54] Of course, by the standards that would soon apply, nothing that had happened up to that time in the conflict could remotely be considered a battle. Nonetheless, Dawson saw in the few skirmishes and desultory picket firings the proof of God's intervention for the Confederacy.

In this opinion, Dawson was far from alone. Col. Daniel Harvey Hill saw in one of the first skirmishes, a minor but much-heralded Confederate success at Big Bethel, Virginia, on June 10, 1861, God's "wonderful interposition in our favor."[55]

The great Confederate victory at Bull Run (or Manassas, as they called it) in July 1861 brought an outpouring of such expressions. Stonewall Jackson won his nickname at this battle and asserted in his report that success had come "through the blessing of God, who gave us the victory." Gens. Joseph E. Johnston and Pierre G. T. Beauregard, in their joint congratulatory proclamation to their troops, expressed their "gratitude to an overruling God, whose hand is manifest in protecting our homes and our liberties." Even Col. Micah Jenkins of the Fifth South Carolina referred in his official report to "the providence of a merciful God," who had given the Confederates victory over what he imagined was a superior force and had also caused the Southerners to sustain only a "comparatively small loss under so heavy a fire."[56]

The Southern religious press was not slow to take up the refrain. "God has favored our cause," announced a religious paper in North Carolina.[57] The Confederate Congress followed suit, with a South Carolina representative offering a resolution: "That we recognize the hand of the Most High God, the King of kings, and Lord of lords, in the glorious victory with which he hath crowned our arms at Manassas."[58]

Lieutenant Dawson thought the message so clear after Bull Run that he wondered why the enemy themselves could not see it. "Would that . . . this glorious victory . . . would satisfy our Enemies and woo gentle peace to diffuse her gentle smiles again over our beloved Country," he wrote. "Will they longer continue this terrible War . . . even when they and we must believe God is on our side fighting for us, against their wicked schemes and devices?"[59]

That November, another Confederate success—this time, a relatively minor one on the shores of the Mississippi River at Belmont, Missouri—prompted similar statements. Brig. Gen. Gideon J. Pillow attributed the "glorious results" of the battle "to the overruling providence of a merciful God."[60] Of course, at face value, that was a statement to which almost any Northern soldier would agree. God providentially directs battles to accomplish His purposes. However, the subtext of such declarations on the part of Southerners was that God's miraculous intervention on their behalf proved that He favored their cause and would finally give them victory in the war. Even Jefferson Davis himself, in his February 1862 inaugural address as regular Confederate president (his previous status had been provisional), spoke of "acknowledging the Providence which has so visibly protected the Confederacy during its brief but eventful career."[61]

The problem with staking one's claim to divine favor on victories believed to have been given by God was that one had to account for the victories won by the enemy. That would not become a significant problem until the enemy actually began winning a number of significant victories. For the Confederacy, the need to come to terms with the reality of enemy successes began with the year 1862. In January, Confederate forces suffered defeat at Mill Springs, Kentucky. In February came disastrous twin defeats at Forts Henry and Donelson, opening Middle and West Tennessee to Union control, as well as the Confederate heartland beyond. March saw Confederate armies defeated at Pea Ridge, Arkansas, and at Glorietta Pass, out in the New Mexico Territory, jointly dashing Confederate hopes west of the Mississippi. April brought Confederate defeat at Shiloh, on the Tennessee River, along with the death of prominent Confederate general Albert Sidney Johnston, and May brought Union troops to the outskirts of Richmond. The South's most important cities had fallen one after another—Nashville in February, New Orleans in April, Memphis in early June. Where, a Confederate might have asked, was God in all of this?

Remarkably few framed that question in any form at all. A few days after Union troops arrived in her hometown of Murfreesboro, Tennessee, Alice Ready wrote, "I am a greater rebel than ever before. . . . I cannot feel yet . . . that God has forsaken us. I do not believe it; he will yet smile upon [us]."[62] Other Southern Christians also reacted with increased defiance. Georgia Methodist Gertrude Thomas called for war to the knife and "the knife to the hilt."[63]

Most, however, if they spoke of God's providence at all in connection with the disastrous string of Confederate defeats, simply took these events as mysterious dealings by an inscrutable but ultimately wise and benevolent God who would still give final victory to the Confederacy. "Our only trust is in God," wrote South Carolinian Tally Simpson. "May He give us victory—& liberty in the end."[64] Confederate defeats represented only God's testing and purifying and were not significant of any lack of divine favor toward the South.

Was victory or defeat then of no use in discerning God's position on the war? By no means. The return of Confederate victories later that spring and throughout the summer was once again hailed by Southern Christians as proof positive that God was on their side. When Stonewall Jackson won dramatic victories in the Shenandoah Valley that spring, a minister in Georgia proclaimed, "We have cause of gratitude to God for the manifest indications of his returning favor."[65] Sometimes it seemed almost as if the litany of Confederate defeats in the first half of the year had never happened at all. When Robert E. Lee induced Union general George B. McClellan to withdraw from the outskirts of Richmond, Tennessee, soldier George Phifer Erwin wrote, "we have every reason to thank the Supreme Ruler of events for the great victory given to our arms there. It really seems as if everything under the guidance of a kind Providence worked for our good. During the whole war, every battle, that exerted much influence upon the result of this contest has been decided in our favor."[66]

The more victories, the more certain many Confederates became of divine favor. By early September, with Lee's army ranging north of the Potomac in Maryland, William Ross Stillwell could write to his wife, "Molly, it looks strange that ten months ago the whole Yankee army lay in front of Richmond and now they have been driven back to defend

Washington. God is surely with us, [or] we never could have whipped them so bad."[67] At about the same time, Mayor Thomas J. Wood of Rome, Georgia, issued a proclamation calling for a day of public thanksgiving, pointing to "the multiplied evidences of the Divine approval and aid in our national struggle, in the long series of brilliant and signal victories, which He has vouchsafed to our arms."[68]

By year's end, the matter once again seemed to be so thunderously obvious that even the most thick-skulled of whining, canting Yankees could hardly be expected to miss its import. "How strange that enemies should force us to fight them," wrote the Eighth Georgia's Melvin Dwinell while the opposing armies prepared for what would be the battle of Fredericksburg, "while the voice of Providence is everywhere and at all times heard denouncing their unholy cause. They seem to be blinded by their folly, and maddened by their own wickedness." Dwinell concluded that the Yankees were indeed utterly and miserably blind to spiritual things. "Is it not remarkable," he continued, "that they should recognize in their numerous defeats—wherein, to all mere human appearances, they had greatly the advantage at the beginning of the battle—no higher agency than that of their Generals. . . . It may be heaven's decree that they shall perish by their own blind folly."[69]

As the war went on, that idea became popular in the South. God was confusing the minds of the Northern leaders so that they would continue the hopeless war and thus bring about the divinely ordained and richly deserved ruin of their section of the country. That punishment was merited, of course, because the Yankees had espoused and were fighting for such an "unholy cause," as Dwinell put it.

In November 1861, Reuben Pierson heard an incorrect report of a Confederate victory at Fort Pickens, Florida, and wrote to his father, "I hope it may prove true and that many other victories of the same kind may follow till Old Abe and all his cabinet become convinced that a supreme being is sending a just punishment upon them for their wickedness in waging war upon an unoffending country who plead for justice and right."[70] Hearing the following month of a possible break between the United States and Britain over the case of the Confederate diplomats James M. Mason and John Slidell, N. H. R. Dawson wrote, "Mr. Lincoln and his Cabinet are certainly infatuated. They are instrumentalities in the hands of God, to punish a vain-glorious and sinful people. The end draweth near, and soon the spectacle of a humiliated nation will be presented to the world."[71] From his regiment's camp near Jackson, Mississippi, another Confederate wrote to his family back in Anderson, South Carolina, in full agreement with Pierson's diagnosis of the North's spiritual fault. "I think peace will come," he wrote to his family, reproducing the phraseology if not the spelling of the Bible, "for pride goith before distruction."[72]

When by the following summer England and France still had not come to the Confederacy's aid, Tally Simpson added those nations to his list of those needing punishment. Simpson assumed, as many Southerners did, that the European nations' entire economies depended on a steady supply of Southern-grown cotton. Unlike most Southerners, however, he had a more thought-out reason for believing that God was on the South's side, and he also thought it possible that some of the punishment God was meting out might be intended for the South's own edification. "It may be that God intends to punish some wicked nations," he wrote in a letter to his aunt back in South Carolina. "The struggle may continue some time yet. England and France, I believe, are suffering more than our own country. The North I know is. I believe God is with us because our people are more conscientious and religious than our enemies or even the nations depending upon us for support across the water. He has inflicted this war as an evil upon the wicked ones, and until he has sufficiently punished them, and perhaps us for our sins, the war may be continued to carry out his divine purpose."[73]

The North, then, deserved great punishment for its pride and for attacking the unoffending Confederacy. Britain and France had also earned some chastisement by failing to come to the South's aid. A few Southerners also felt that their own section could be coming in for a very small dose of divine correction. One such was Flavel C. Barber of the Third Tennessee, who noted in March 1863 that his regiment's chaplain had recently preached a fine sermon "and among other excellent things gave it as his opinion that the war would never terminate until we as a nation acknowledged our sins and humbled ourselves in the dust before our Creator." Barber believed that the war was accomplishing this. "I think our national character will be much improved by this war. Our pride has already been humbled by sufferings and reverses and much of our wealth has been destroyed. God send us a speedy peace."[74]

Aside from pride and aggression, the supposed Northern sin most commonly mentioned by Southerners at the outset of the conflict was religious fanaticism. It might seem odd for men to march off with religious zeal in their hearts and weapons in their hands to defend the true faith while at the same time decrying religious fanaticism, but so it was. Fire-eating Presbyterian minister Benjamin M. Palmer of New Orleans had as good a claim to the title of zealot as the most dedicated New England abolitionist. In blessing Confederate troops bound for the front at the beginning of the war, he told them that they were going to fight in a holy cause, "a war of civilization against a ruthless barbarism which would dishonor the dark ages, a war of religion against a blind and bloody fanaticism."[75] The "Address to Christians Throughout the World" declared, "We regard abolitionism as an interference with the plans of Divine Providence. It has not the sign of the Lord's blessing. It is a fanaticism which puts forth no good fruit; instead of blessing, it has brought forth cursing; instead of love, hatred; instead of life, death—bitterness and sorrow and pain and infidelity and moral degeneracy follow its labors."[76] Other Southerners were more succinct. As Union prisoners of war were being marched through Richmond in 1862, an important-looking citizen called out to them, "Boys, charge all this up to religious fanaticism."[77]

The "fanaticism" of which such Southerners complained could actually be defined very neatly: it consisted of claiming that slavery was morally wrong. Leroy Pope Walker, the Confederacy's first secretary of war, complained that "for many years past" Northern missionaries to the Five Civilized Tribes of the Indian Territory had been "preaching up abolition sentiments under the disguise of the holy religion of Christ, and denouncing slaveholders as abandoned by God and unfit associates for humanity on earth."[78] Ultimately, for many Southern Christians, and no doubt for a great many other Southerners as well, the war was about punishing Northerners for having the temerity to label slavery a sin.

The all but inevitable coarsening influences of war combined all too readily with the increasing willingness to see the foe not as political enemies but as religious infidels, unspeakably vile. The two tendencies fed on each other and grew steadily. A Virginia woman described Union soldiers as "the most horrible set of creatures I ever saw." One, she claimed, "had the face of a fiend incarnate. . . . Certainly there was never such an army of demons collected before, outside of the infernal regions." Tennessee preacher Jesse Cox thought he saw in the war the fulfillment of biblical prophecy, in which he thought the Union army might be playing a particularly satanic role: they were "anti-christ, the Beast that [is to] assend from the bottomless pits."[79]

Attitudes influenced actions. When in May 1861 N. H. R. Dawson heard that Union Col. Elmer Ellsworth had been murdered by an Alexandria, Virginia, hotel keeper, he was exultant. "Providence seems to have cut him off, as soon as he touched our soil," Dawson reveled, speculating that the whole Union army might meet a similar fate. This was deserved, Dawson maintained, because Ellsworth's slogan in invading the South had been "Beauty and booty." This claim, of course, was utterly without foundation in fact, but it was a fiction often repeated by Southern leaders to fire the zeal of their soldiers. "There is great bitterness felt on our side," Dawson concluded, "and we will kill all that we can lay our hands on. . . . We are in the right, and this nerves me for the contest." The next day he wrote, "I think it will be a pleasure to meet our enemies in mortal combat. . . . We will now have a bloody war, and we intend to make it as destructive as possible. . . . Let us have trust and confidence in God."[80] Dawson, it should be noted, was interested in Christianity and, like the great majority of Americans of that era, believed in the truth of the Christian system, but he did not consider himself to *be* a Christian.

But others felt the same way. In January 1862, Reuben Pierson wrote to his father, vilifying the enemy in terms that included strong religious meaning. "Let the unholy and base legions of Lincolndom pour forth their fury and rage in all its power—we will meet them. We will defeat them or perish upon the soil of our loved and cherished southern republic."[81] Southerners frequently used the term *unholy* to describe Lincoln, the North, or the Union armies, indicating that Northerners were not just wrong in their desire to preserve the Union and end slavery but downright evil as well. In May 1863 a Tennessee lieutenant on the eve of the battle of Champion's Hill wrote of the fighting spirit of his own men, stating that they were "unconquarable with too much hatred to even wish for peace. . . . Ah, will the GOD of battles give this splendid army to

Lincolns hords who have robbed the defenseless women and children of the staff of life . . . No the God of Battles has given us Victory."[82] As it turned out, the God of Battles had done nothing of the sort, and the next day the lieutenant and his army were soundly thrashed by the Union army of Ulysses S. Grant.

The harboring of attitudes usually frowned on by Christianity became more acceptable in the light of such feelings. Mary Callaway of Alabama wrote to her cousin, "It seems to me revenge cannot be a sin in this war."[83] Speaking of Northerners, a Southern soldier wrote, "If it is a sin to hate them, then I am guilty of the unpardonable one."[84] After the Union retreat from the Virginia peninsula in July 1862, a large number of wounded Union soldiers were left behind and fell into Rebel hands. Evan M. Woodward of the Second Pennsylvania Reserves was among them and remembered a crowd of Confederate civilians who came out to gawk at the wounded Yankees while offering no aid of any sort. Most noticeable in the crowd was a preacher who, "in his bitter hatred of Union soldiers, . . . commenced upbraiding [them] as 'mercenaries' and 'hirelings,' the poor wounded sufferers, some of whom had lost their limbs, and others, from whose wounds maggots were crawling." The ill feeling in this case was definitely mutual, for Woodward later described the preacher as a "paroled prisoner of hell, clothed in the sacred garb of religion."[85]

Not all Southern Christians took such attitudes. Many bore in mind the biblical injunction to love one's enemies and struggled to maintain the proper attitude in the midst of many and powerful natural temptations to entertain bitter and hateful thoughts. In 1861 a Southern religious newspaper admonished, "Love is the royal law, and its dues are not intermitted even in war. It is never superseded by martial law, or any other law. Always difficult of exercise, 'Love your enemies, bless them that curse you,' is now the severe test of Christian character on a national scale." The editor conceded that in this case it was completely impossible to have peace with the Yankees "unless we sacrifice right, in the defence and preservation of which the highest duties to God and man are involved." Still, if there was to be war, and righteous war at that, he maintained, "We must, and by grace we can, keep the heart free from malice, hatred, revenge."[86]

Another Christian journalist wrote in similar vein, "Men's heads may be wrong when their hearts are right. This we must bear in mind; for it will not do to discredit the whole Christianity of the North." The Northern Christians were under the influence of the overwhelming political views—not to say, ignorance—of the surrounding society, and to some extent, they could not help themselves. Such facts "must be taken into the account in our moral estimate of many of our enemies, even those proposing, for their good and our own, to subjugate or exterminate us. And we must consider these things if we would fulfill the commandment, 'Love your enemies.'"[87]

That was, as the first editor had pointed out, a difficult lesson to put into practice. When the Confederate army of Robert E. Lee prepared to march into Pennsylvania in the summer of 1863, Lee issued stern orders: "The duties exacted of us by civilization and Christianity," he wrote, "are not less obligatory in the country of the enemy than in our own. . . . It must be remembered that we make war only upon armed men, and that we cannot take vengeance for the wrongs our people have suffered without lowering ourselves in the eyes of all whose abhorrence has been excited by the atrocities of our enemies, and offending against Him to whom vengeance belongeth, without whose favor and support our efforts must all prove in vain."[88]

That sounded very good, but if private plundering was restrained in some units of the Army of Northern Virginia, official requisition, without any realistic compensation, was far-reaching and voracious, sucking in virtually all the shoes, clothes, victuals, and four-legged beasts within the army's reach. Nor was private plunder and even vandalism entirely suppressed by any means, and eyewitness accounts of Confederate soldiers reported high-ranking officers, including Lee himself in at least one instance, deliberately turning a blind eye to such events as bayonet charges on poultry yards and the like. In short, the Confederate army in Pennsylvania behaved neither better nor worse than the Yankees had in Virginia. Amid the harsh demands and stark scenes of war, absence of a spirit of revenge was difficult to maintain, but Christians could try, and their trying would provide a greater degree of restraint on both sides than would have been the case had all given way to the most bitter of feelings.

The problems involved in trying to maintain a spirit of Christian charity in the midst of a bitter war were illustrated forcefully, if less violently, when contending viewpoints were representing within a single church body or worship service. Near Union-held Falmouth, Virginia, in early 1863, both Union soldiers and local Christians attended a prayer meeting in a Lutheran church building. However, when the local pastor ventured to pray for the country and President Lincoln, "two ladies left the house," an eyewitness recorded, "evidently displeased with his Union sentiments."[89] Similarly, in December 1862 when the pastor of a Methodist church in Union-held Clarksville, Tennessee, invited a Union army chaplain to preach in his pulpit, the pro-Confederate congregation simply would not attend.[90]

In Falmouth and Clarksville, Union power had left local Confederates with no stronger way of registering their religious disdain than absenting themselves. Elsewhere, they could do more. In Confederate-held Fredericksburg, Virginia, the pro-Union *Christian Banner* newspaper was shut down by Confederate authorities.[91]

St. David's Episcopal Church in Austin, Texas, presented another example. At the beginning of the war, Bishop Alexander Gregg, a recent migrant from South Carolina, demanded that all churches in his diocese include in their services a prayer that God would bring to a quick end "the unnatural war which had been forced upon us." Charles Gillete, rector of St. David's and a Union man, objected, suggesting that it would be better to let God decide for Himself who was at fault in the war, rather than dictating it to Him in prayer. For a while, Gregg relented and allowed Gillete to omit the prayer, but as the war went on and its costs—including the life of Gregg's son, a Confederate soldier—increased, the bishop became more bitter and implacable. He renewed his demand that Gillete include the offending prayer and forced Gillete to give up his position when he would not do so.[92]

The command to "Love your enemies" was not the only religious matter that proved difficult to keep straight in the midst of a fierce war. Like Northerners, some Confederates showed a tendency to think of their war almost as a jihad. As a number of Southerners came to view the war more and more as a religious crusade, the temptation, as in the North, was to begin using terminology that could produce very flawed doctrine, from a Christian point of view. Indeed, the language of "martyrs," "sacrifices," and "altars" appeared almost from the outset of the conflict. In January 1862 the *Rome Courier* referred to a deceased Confederate soldier as "another martyr to our country's cause."[93] Later that year, Edwin Fay wrote of the possibility that he might "die a martyr in my country's cause."[94] A religious newspaper wrote of the dead of First Bull Run as "the sacrifices which we have laid on the altar of our country."[95] In the spring of 1863 Reuben Pierson used much the same terminology in writing about the possibility of his own demise: "If I fall . . . and my life is sacrificed upon the altar of liberty. . . ."[96]

Miss Mollie Thompson of Clopton, Tennessee, provides an example of where this mixing of religious and civil terminology could lead. While presenting a flag to Company C, Ninth Tennessee, on behalf of the ladies who had sewn the banner, Miss Thompson could not resist one rhetorical flourish too many. "And when you come to pass from earth away," she told the assembled recruits, "whether amid the din of battle strife or in your own peaceful homes, may you, when you stand in the twilight of two worlds, be enabled to look back on this as the greatest act of your life, and may it suffice to obliterate from God's book of justice all your past offenses."[97] That may have sounded nice, but it was not Christian theology.

Miss Thompson was not alone in her patriotic heresy. In September 1861 a preacher named McClusky from McLemorsville, Tennessee, visited the camps of the Confederate forces in the western part of the state and preached to the Twelfth Tennessee. In his sermon he claimed "that the soldier fighting for a Just Cause, though wicked, if killed in battle would be saved—that he would be one of those spoken of in the scriptures whose works would be burned up but he should be saved as by fire." A devout soldier who heard the discourse was unimpressed. "I do not believe one word of it," wrote Alfred Tyler Fielder in his diary. "God is of too pure eyes to behold sin with the least degree of allowance."[98] In Fielder's reckoning, and that of orthodox Christians throughout history, heaven was for those who through faith in Christ were made righteous by God's grace. It was not for those who were devoid of God's grace—even those who might sacrifice themselves in a worthy cause.

The kind of muddled thinking manifested by Miss Thompson and preacher McClusky occurred often enough to draw notice as a theological problem. In response to it, Frances Brokenbrough, in a widely circulated tract entitled "A Mother's Parting Words to Her Soldier Boy," wrote, "Christ did not promise eternal life to those who fell in battle for their country but to those who triumphed over sin." Patriotism was a fine thing, she maintained, but it was no substitute for saving faith and submissive life. "The heroic but ungodly soldier may fill a grave honored by his nation's tears and marked by a towering monument," she warned, "but his soul, alas! must perish."[99]

Of course, the majority of Southern Christians, like the majority of Northern Christians, avoided the pitfall of thinking that participation in their war, however justified they believed it, would secure a man's acceptance with God. Their cause, they believed, was favored by God, and He would finally grant them victory over their foes. In the meantime, they must fight on bravely and maintain their grip on the larger biblical framework of their faith, trusting in God all the while. As for "the continuance of this horrid war," the Forty-fourth Virginia's Thomas Boatright wrote to his wife in February 1863, surely it was not pleasing to God, "but he in his wisdom permits it to continue and in his own good time will end it or cause it to end."[100]

Until then, Southern Christians would have to work for temporal ends without losing sight of eternal goals. One young Confederate put the contrast into words. In the summer of 1862, Rev. William M. Crumly stood beside the bed of a dying soldier in a Confederate military hospital in Richmond and heard the words the young man said, more to himself than to the minister at his side:

> I die for my country and the cause of humanity, and, with many others, have thrown my bleeding body into the horrid chasm of revolution to bridge the way for the triumphal car of Liberty which will roll over me, bearing in its long train the happy millions of future generations, rejoicing in all the grandeur of peace and prosperity. I wonder if they will ever pause as they pass to think of the poor soldiers whose bones lie at the foundation of their security and happiness? Or will the soul

be permitted from some Pizgah summit to take a look at the future glory of the country I died to reclaim from fanatical thralldom? Will the soul ever visit at evening twilight the scenes of my childhood, and listen to the sweet hymn of praise that goes up from the paternal altar at which I was consecrated to God? Though unseen, may it not be the guardian angel of my loved ones?

He stopped and, thinking a moment, seemed to dismiss what he had just said. "These are earthly desires," he continued, "which I feel gradually giving way to a purer, heavenly sympathy." At last he recited,

> Give joy or grief, give ease of pain,
> Take life or friends away,
> I come to find them all again
> In that eternal day.[101]

8

"THE BOYS LOVE HIM AS A FATHER"
Civil War Chaplains

"Our chaplain, J. D. Rodgers, is as a father to me and keeps me straight," wrote the Twenty-third Indiana's John J. Hardin in February 1862.[1] "Our chaplain appears to have forgotten us entirely," wrote Daniel Hughes of the Twenty-fifth Indiana in November of that year.[2] Chaplains were the most numerous, visible, and direct representatives of organized religion in the camps of the Civil War armies, and, as the experiences of these two Hoosiers indicates, they were men of varying attributes.

The chaplaincy was a long-established part of the American military tradition. Chaplains had accompanied the colonial militia when it marched against the Indians, the French, and, at last, the British. They accompanied the American armies through the Revolutionary War, and when the new United States established its regular army in 1783, Congress authorized one chaplain for each regiment. That pattern had continued unbroken right up to the Civil War.[3]

Not surprisingly, then, both sides in the Civil War provided for official army chaplains, whose primary task was to tend to the spiritual well-being of the soldiers. The Union did so from the outset, but the Confederate government initially made no provision for chaplains, perhaps as a result of the South's long-professed aversion to any religious

input in the things of this present world. Fairly early in the war, however, the Confederacy abandoned its original position and authorized
chaplains, though it tended to treat them shabbily. While Union chaplains received about $145 a month—the pay of a captain of cavalry—
Confederate chaplains got only $80.[4]

In both armies, the status of a chaplain was somewhat ambiguous. His
pay was comparable to that of a company-grade officer, and he could keep
and ride a horse like a field officer. However, he could not draw government forage for his horse and had to feed it out of his own resources—a
considerable drain on his purse. And despite some of the perquisites of
officer status, he drew only a private's rations and had no uniform. As
the war went on, some of these provisions changed in one way or another.
Union chaplains eventually did get government rations and forage for
their horses—but a pay cut from $1,746 to $1,200 per year. Congress also
made provision for pensions to the families of chaplains killed in action.
Whatever the perquisites of the position, however, whether a chaplain
got respect from the men of his regiment depended very much on who
they were—and who he was.[5]

Inadequacies of pay and provision and uncertainties of privilege
added to the already substantial difficulties of recruiting and keeping
an adequate number of chaplains. Chaplains were always in short supply. The lament of a Tennessee soldier in May 1862 is representative of
many others. "We had no preaching for want of a preach[er]," he wrote,
"we have made arrangements for a Chaplin the one we had having
resigned."[6]

The country had no readily available surplus of ministers on which to
call to meet the armies' needs. The great majority of such men were already serving local churches, and those churches were not simply going
to vanish for the duration of the war, even if a number of their young,
male members did enter the army. Pastors would continue to feel the need
to care for their churches back home and therefore would hesitate to
become chaplains. When young Lutheran pastor John H. W. Stuckenberg
enlisted as a chaplain in 1862, he remained deeply concerned about the
two Erie, Pennsylvania, churches of which he was pastor. While away
he corresponded voluminously with his parishioners, sending sermons
to be read in the churches and receiving numerous pleas for his return.

Concern for the home churches finally helped prompt him to resign his chaplaincy in the fall of 1863.[7]

And if some pastors were inclined to forget, for a time, their duties on the home front, denominational authorities were ready to remind them. In 1862 three Southern Methodist bishops urged their subordinate pastors to remember that "the claims of the church of God are fully as important as those of the army."[8]

Compounding the difficulties of finding enough chaplains was the fact that a sizable number of pastors who did see fit to leave their congregations and go off to war enlisted as combat soldiers. From Bishop Leonidas Polk, Maj. Gen. William N. Pendleton, and Brig. Gen. Mark Lowrey to hundreds of lower-ranking clergy, the Confederate army was replete with them. So too was the Union army. Sometimes men enlisted first as chaplains and later accepted positions as line officers. In December 1861 the Fourth Alabama found itself without a chaplain when its "Rev. Dr. Chaddick" became a major in a newly raised battalion.[9] In 1863 some 100 clergymen were enrolled in the Confederacy's Army of Tennessee, but only half of those were serving as chaplains.[10]

Once a man enlisted as a combat soldier, it was not so easy for him to shift to the role of chaplain. The armies' constant need for men on the firing line guaranteed as much. A Mississippi soldier wrote to his wife in June 1862, noting that his regiment needed a chaplain. One of his comrades was a preacher and did "pretty well" when given the chance, "but he is mustered in and consequently can not be the chaplain."[11] At the same time, a man was ineligible for the office of chaplain if he were not "ordained," that is, officially authorized by the power structure of a particular sect. From his base in the Union beachhead on the South Carolina coast, Col. Thomas Wentworth Higginson wrote, "The only preacher who is really respected here is a young lawyer from N.Y., the acting Post Chaplain who can only be 'acting' because he has never been ordained."[12]

Besides all this, the duties of chaplain were in many ways far less congenial than those of a nice, settled parish somewhere in the peaceful interior of the country. Chaplains might not be expected to live on quite the same level as the private soldiers did, but they could still expect to sleep on the ground rolled in a blanket, with canvas overhead or the stars. They might not have to march, but they would have to spend whole days in the saddle. They would be exposed to all the camp diseases the soldiers faced and, sometimes, even to hostile fire. In short, it was not a prospect that seemed likely to lure a comfortable, middle-aged parson out of his ivy-covered manse.

That being the case, one might expect that no parsons would leave settled pastorates to enter the chaplaincy. In fact, many did so, including a number of older men. One Union chaplain was nearly eighty years of age.[13] Though quite a bit younger than that, Rev. J. D. Beugless had many reasons for staying home. He had a pleasant position as a pastor in Pawtuxet, Rhode Island, with the prospect of an increasing salary, and he had recently married. Nevertheless, he determined to enlist as a chaplain "for the Cause of Truth as embodied in the great principle at issue; and for the cause of the soldiers whose welfare, present & eternal I would hope to be instrumental in promoting."[14]

Clearly, some chaplains would go out of genuine conviction. Nevertheless, there would be considerable difficulty in finding enough chaplains to tend all the armies' regiments and hospitals, and also in finding suitable ones. This was largely a factor of the peculiarly difficult demands of the chaplaincy. It was a job that required the stamina, flexibility, and robust health of a young man but also the wisdom and maturity of an older one. It should be little surprise, then, that the Civil War armies were chronically short of chaplains or that the chaplains they had were not always suitable to the position. Typical was the complaint of Clifford Anderson, a Georgia soldier serving in the Army of Northern Virginia, when he wrote one Sunday in November 1862, "We have had no religious services today, our Chaplain being sick. . . . It has been a long time since I have enjoyed the privilege of Divine Worship on the Sabbath."[15]

In June 1862 the U.S. War Department reported that only 395 of the Union army's 676 regiments had chaplains. Even those regiments with chaplains officially assigned might not necessarily enjoy their services. The same report revealed that twenty-nine chaplains were absent on detached duty, and thirteen more were absent without leave. In the Confederate army the shortage was even more acute. In 1863 the Confederate States Chaplains Association estimated that half of Southern regiments were without chaplains.[16] Stonewall Jackson complained of the same proportion of lack in his regiments during the second year of the war.[17] A

Southern minister working in army camps along the Carolina coast early in the war reported that "nearly two-thirds of the regiments that he knew were without chaplains."[18]

There were various reasons to desire a chaplain with a regiment. In June 1861, Confederate Col. Angus McDonald, recently commissioned to lead a regiment of Rebel cavalry in what would soon become West Virginia, wrote to the Confederate secretary of war requesting the appointment of Episcopal minister James B. Averitt as chaplain of his regiment. His reasons were not only that the good cleric might counteract "the demoralizing influences of campaign life" but also because "having a fully commissioned and authenticated man of God with us" would tend to prevent the unit's being labeled as "land pirates and other unenviable sobriquets" that the Federals had recently been applying to them.[19] If captured, McDonald apparently surmised, the presence of a sure-enough chaplain might be the best way to prove that one was not a common highwaymen and thus avoid hanging.

Avoiding the noose was a somewhat unusual reason for desiring the presence of a chaplain. More common was the thinking of Abraham Lincoln as reflected in the Union War Department's General Orders Numbers 15 and 16, issued in May 1861. The orders called for the selection of a chaplain for each regiment, nominated by the colonel but elected by the officers, for the purpose of maintaining "the social happiness and moral improvement of the troops" and reporting regularly on the "moral and religious condition" of the men.[20] At Lincoln's urging, Congress early in 1862 added a provision for hospital chaplains, in addition to those assigned to individual regiments.[21]

The problem was in finding men who would faithfully and effectively fulfill the duties of chaplain, and many a colonel found it a difficult problem indeed. Col. Thomas Wentworth Higginson, while organizing his new regiment of black Union troops from South Carolina, wrote a letter to Rev. James Freeman Clarke requesting that he serve as its chaplain. That position, he told Clarke, was "one of the posts easiest to fill & hardest to fill well."[22] Many an officer and soldier on both sides of the front lines would have agreed with at least the latter half of that statement.

Stories of substandard chaplains were legion in the Civil War armies. The Fifth Massachusetts's Lt. Col. Edwin Bennett estimated that "at least seventy-five per cent of the chaplains commissioned during the first year of the war were practically unfit for their work." That figure was too high by far, but there could be no denying that a number of spectacular misfits had managed to secure chaplaincies. Stealing, desertion, and gross moral turpitude brought some of them into disgrace. The chaplain of the Second Connecticut Heavy Artillery got into a game of stud poker one evening in camp and "cleaned out the whole company."[23] Milton Bailey of the Forty-third Indiana complained, "over half the preachers that our Goverment employs at such high price turns out to be the most deprave siners in the world our firs Chaplain maid no scruples to take things out of houses wher people had left them and was always in company with abandoned women, such is the case with half the Preachers that the government pays over a hunderd dolers a month." Bailey's testimony is suspect, however, because he offered it as an excuse for his own sinful manner of life. His cousin, Ann Sturtevant, had written urging him to reform. In reply, Bailey pleaded lamely, "The armey is the most outlandish place on earth no man ever live religious that comes in the army."[24]

Far more damaging is the verdict of a devout soldier like John T. McMahon. "I have come to the conclusion," McMahon wrote sadly one Sunday in 1863, "that our chaplains are a class of men that could not get employment at home and by underhanded work have got to be Chaplains. At any rate I never heard a good sermon from a Chaplain yet."[25] There was, no doubt, a grain of truth in McMahon's opinion, though he himself suggested that he had insufficient evidence to make such a broad generalization. Not all chaplains were unworthy, nor even a majority of them, but the unfit specimens stuck out like the proverbial bad lobster in a dark cellar.

There were a number of ways in which a chaplain could render himself unfit for his office. A member of the Third Alabama wrote, "We got into a little row with the Yankees a few days ago and our parson, deeming, no doubt, that 'discretion was the better part of valor,' took to his heels when the shells commenced flying and I have not seen him since." In a similar vein, a Union officer wrote that "undue susceptibility to cannon fever" was "ample grounds for the disqualification of a chaplain."[26] Abner Small was at a service shortly before the battle of Chancellorsville when the assembly came under enemy shell fire. "The danger was real enough," Small explained. "A few men of our brigade were wounded, and a few among other troops nearby were killed." All sensible soldiers would promptly take cover in such situations, but on this occasion the chaplain's headlong flight was so precipitate and prolonged as to incur the scorn of a number of soldiers.[27] It was one of the peculiar difficulties of the chaplain's office that he was free to avoid danger but had to face it if he was to have the respect of his men.

Then there were the chaplains like the one described by Daniel Hughes of the Twenty-fifth Indiana, a parson who seemed "to have forgotten us entirely," simply abandoning his duties, perhaps because of sickness and fatigue or perhaps because of mere sloth. The Twenty-eighth Alabama's Joshua Callaway wrote sadly in June 1862 that his regiment's chaplain "has never been in the Reg. more than three or four days & didn't preach then."[28] "Our Chaplain," complained one Union officer, "is good for nothing, except to relieve the government of money. He is too lazy to do anything and has preached only twice since he is with us. He never visits a sick man, but is always on hand when pay day comes."[29]

Even those chaplains who conscientiously attempted to perform their duties did not always meet with the approval of their men. Confederate soldier Philip D. Stephenson remembered with contempt the chaplain of his regiment, "a big strapping young fellow, with a dough face, big watery blue eyes that would overflow like Job Trotter's on the shortest notice in short a sniveling hypocrite and baby, who, according to the general verdict of the men ought to have been carrying a gun and was in the ministry to get out of it." Stephenson "had no use for" the man.[30]

Some chaplains had the problem of simply being dull. John Beatty noted of the Third Ohio's chaplain that "his prayers and exhortations fill me with an almost irresistible inclination to close my eyes and shut out the vanities, cares, and vexations of the world."[31] Charles B. Haydon complained of a military funeral he had attended in December 1861: "With an appropriate discourse it would have been a very solemn funeral. Chaplain May's sermon was ab[ou]t as appropriate and interesting as the dryest chapt of Coke's Commentaries would have been."[32] In fairness, however, Haydon was a fairly irreligious soldier who was not likely to be very interested in anything a chaplain had to say.

Sometimes other problems hindered the effectiveness of a chaplain. Some men simply did not have the right personality, temperament, or other qualifications necessary to gain the respect of the soldiers. The officers of one Indiana regiment elected as its chaplain the worst of the regiment's captains. A minister in civilian life, he was not much good as a line officer, so, his comrades apparently reckoned, he might as well try his hand at being chaplain.[33] Still worse was the case of a New York regiment composed mostly of German immigrants or their offspring. The regiment's officers decided that an extra surgeon would be of more use than a chaplain and so filled the latter's slot with a medical man. When a soldier died of illness, however, the medical "chaplain" found himself compelled to handle the burial service. Speaking in heavily accented English while tossing dirt into the grave, the German American surgeon intoned irreverently, "This is the first time that this man was buried in Virginia and D—n me if I ever bury him again."[34]

For many years after the war, Union general Jacob Ammen told a story about a chaplain he had seen at the battle of Shiloh, ineffectually trying to rally demoralized Union troops who were sheltering under the cover of the river bluffs near the steamboat landing. "Rally, men; rally, and we may yet be saved," the well-meaning chaplain had shouted. "Oh rally! For God and your country's sake, rally! R-a-l-l-y O-h, r-a-l-l-y around the flag of your c-o-u-n-t-r-y, my c-o-u-n-t-r-y-m-e-n!" Ammen, arriving just then with reinforcements, later claimed that he had cursed the hysterical chaplain for an old fool, threatened him, and told him to shut up. The story seems to have gained a bit in Ammen's retelling, and he retold it frequently.[35] Still, there could be no denying that some men who did well enough in a peacetime parish back home were ill equipped by personality for the rougher life of an army at war or for earning the respect of its soldiers.

Lincoln himself, who took an intense interest in the chaplaincy, expressed dismay that so many of the chaplains seemed to be more interested in their own rank, privileges, and prestige than in the souls of their men. Yet the view he got from Washington was probably jaundiced by the fact that those who made themselves heard in the capital city were generally the ones who had complaints. Lincoln would have heard little or nothing of the faithful, diligent chaplain who was successfully ministering to his regiment or hospital.[36]

Yet despite all these factors—the difficulties of recruiting chaplains and the difficulties of those who did enlist, as well as the demoralizing effects of those who were unfit for their position—a sizable number of chaplains succeeded admirably in their tasks as spiritual shepherds to their regiments. The soldiers were often quite impressed with the preaching of their chaplains. "Heard a very good sermon preached by our Chaplin," James Wren of the Forty-eighth Pennsylvania noted in his diary one Sunday in June 1862.[37] Confederate soldier James Iredell Hall wrote that his chaplain was "a wonderfully attractive preacher." Such statements were common among Civil War soldiers.[38]

Nor were all chaplains slothful—quite the contrary, the majority worked themselves at a killing pace. Between his own regiments, neighboring ones that lacked chaplains, and nearby army hospitals, the 145th Pennsylvania's John Stuckenberg sometimes conducted as many as ten services in a single Sunday.[39] David C. Dutcher of the 139th New York noted in his diary in August 1864, "Preached 5 times yesterday [and] 4 times today." It was only slightly more than his usual pace.[40]

It was not always for good preaching that soldiers appreciated their chaplains. Edward P. Stanfield of the Forty-eighth Indiana wrote a letter to his father regarding the possibility of a certain preacher from back home coming out to be the regiment's chaplain. "I think I would like him for chaplain," Stanfield wrote, "although I never liked his preaching."[41] What, then, did soldiers like Stanfield see in chaplains who could not preach to suit them? In fact, chaplains did many things besides preaching. By May 1861, the chaplain of the Eleventh Illinois had already organized a choir of some twenty-five men and had them practicing regularly in the mess hall.[42]

Of much greater importance, a good chaplain would speak personally with the soldiers. In ideal cases, such as John J. Hardin's chaplain in the Twenty-third Indiana, he became almost like a father to the young soldiers, kindly but firmly admonishing and encouraging them. There could be various styles of performing the latter duty. Thus Lucius W. Barber remembered the chaplain of the Fifteenth Illinois: "Although not a gifted man or an eloquent speaker, yet, I will venture to say that there was not a harder working chaplain in the whole army or one that did more good. With a good education, he combined goodness of heart with an indomitable energy and perseverance." Barber also recalled, "Our chaplain could not rest unless doing something for the good of the men."[43]

One of the most important duties of chaplains was praying with the men who desired it, particularly in times of distress or sorrow and, above all, when death approached. In 1865, Rev. Thomas A. Ware of the Methodist Episcopal Church, South, overheard a Confederate chaplain praying with a dying soldier and was so touched that he afterward wrote down the chaplain's words. "Oh, precious Redeemer!" prayed the minister in a low voice, kneeling and bending over the dying man as the latter lay on the ground, "We thank thee for thy abounding grace, which of late brought him from the ways of folly and sin to know and love thee, and that now makes this dark hour the brightest of his life. Be thou graciously with him to the end. Mercifully pour into the hearts of his dear ones at home that balm of thy love and sweetly resigning them to thy will bring them all at last to meet him in heaven. Amen." The soldier assured those at his side that he was "resigned and happy," ready to die.[44]

Years after the war, New York soldier Charles Bardeen remembered his chaplain, Rev. Warren H. Cudworth, as one who was "ready to pray with you at the proper time but never obtruding his piety, and always ready to help you in any way."[45] In 1863 a South Carolina soldier wrote of his chaplain, "the revrent Mr. Dool of Maryland," that "he have don much good in tending on our sic and wounded and seeing that tha was proprly tended to. He has all ways bin in the battle field ready to do his part in cearing for the wounded and have spair no pains at the hospital in seeing that tha was all promply tended to."[46]

A chaplain's duties to his regiment were in many ways similar to those a pastor performed for his parishioners back home. Besides preaching, chaplains talked privately with soldiers regarding religious matters, distributed religious literature, comforted the sick and wounded, and, if they died, conducted their funerals and often undertook the unpleasant duty of writing to inform their kinfolk back home.[47]

Chaplains also did many other things that, though no more important, had a more direct impact on the soldiers' immediate comfort or satisfaction. The chaplain of the Ninety-fourth New York, like many other army parsons, performed a service for the men of the entire brigade. When the men were paid and wanted to send some of their money to the folks back home, Chaplain Cook would carry the money to Washington for them, whence it could be sent on by express. "He carried thousands," wrote an officer in the brigade, "and I doubt a single dollar was ever lost. When I consider the responsibility he voluntarily assumed, and the great personal risk he ran when on his way to Washington through the woods and, worse, through the frauds and scoundrels who always flocked like vultures in the rear of our army, I place this chaplain among the bravest officers of his regiment."[48]

The chaplain of the Sixteenth Maine went "often from camp to Washington, usually on foot, through the mud and rain or the dust and heat, to get franked envelopes, letter paper, and other gratuities for the men," and in that he was representative of many chaplains. A non-Christian soldier in his regiment wrote of this particular chaplain that "while looking after the physical needs of his flock, [he] incurred every danger incident to a soldier's life, and bore himself like a brave man."[49] Many chaplains served as postal clerks and mail carriers for the regiments, in addition to their normal duties. The Thirty-ninth Wisconsin was typical. One of its soldiers wrote, "The chaplain is the Regimental Post Master, sending the mail for each company to its orderly sargeant for distribution to the men."[50] The chaplain of the Eleventh Illinois found time enough to spare from his additional activities as choirmaster to travel in the summer of 1862 from the regiment's camp near Jackson, Tennessee, up to the army's rear staging area at Cairo, Illinois, and bring back fifty badly needed Enfield rifles for the regiment.[51] Sometimes on hard marches, a chaplain would take turns walking and let some of the tired soldiers ride his horse, as the 145th Pennsylvania's John Stuckenberg did on the march to Gettysburg.[52] Likewise, on a difficult September 1862 march that brought the Nineteenth Iowa to Benton Barracks, Missouri, Chaplain Dennis Murphy joined the regiment's major in helping struggling soldiers "by carrying upon their horses the knapsacks and guns of many who would never [have] reached the Barracks without assistence."[53]

Sometimes a chaplain's lot might be a great deal of good old-fashioned hard work. When the Second Rhode Island built a chapel during the winter of 1863–1864, Chaplain John D. Beugless took the lead in hewing (flattening the sides of) most of the logs himself.[54] That same winter, when the Twentieth Illinois built a house of worship out in Mississippi, the regiment's chaplain "was with the boys working might and main in his shirt sleeves."[55] During the Atlanta campaign, the chaplain of the Eightieth Illinois went to the neighboring Fifty-ninth Illinois to borrow tools to bury his regiment's dead.[56]

Chaplain Thomas L. Ambrose of the Twelfth New Hampshire had been a missionary in Persia before the war. After the battle of Chancellorsville, Ambrose stayed behind with the wounded Union soldiers who fell into Rebel hands. He and a single surgeon were the only help available for a sizable encampment of badly wounded, almost helpless men, and they worked literally around the clock, bringing food and drink to the wounded, putting up tents to shelter them, and trying to keep them out of the mud and standing water during a night of torrential rain. Rice Bull of the 123rd New York also heard Ambrose comforting two soldiers of his own Twelfth New Hampshire who lay in a nearby tent dying in great pain. "The Chaplain came and remained a long time and while he was there we could hear him pray for them." With the prisoners in desperate straits for food, Ambrose walked to the headquarters of Confederate general J. E. B. Stuart, who professed to be unable to help and referred him to Lee. At Lee's headquarters he obtained the promise of a wagonload of cornmeal. Unsure of when the wagon would arrive, and knowing that some of the wounded might not last that long, Ambrose sought and received permission to carry a sack of meal back with him, some two and a half miles. "He was back in the camp at three that afternoon exhausted, for he brought with him a fifty pound sack," Bull recalled. "He was one of God's Saints," he wrote of Ambrose, "and I regard him as one of the heroes of Chancellorsville."[57]

In sharp contrast with those of civilian ministers, chaplains' duties were not necessarily performed at safe distances from the firing lines. In contrast to the weak-kneed chaplains noticed by Abner Small, Philip D. Stephenson remembered a chaplain named Markham, previously a Presbyterian pastor in New Orleans. "He was preaching one day, standing on a stump with a large crowd of soldiers around him," Stephenson recalled, "when the enemy got wind of it and began shelling. Like a bow-ing wheatfield before the wind, down would go the heads of his auditors as the shells drew nigh, but Dr. Markham kept bolt up right and would have finished his sermon if the men had stayed." But the veteran troops finally took cover.[58]

The proper role of the chaplain when his regiment went into battle was not clearly defined, and the Civil War saw great variation among chaplains in how they handled this difficult situation. Some did remain safely in the rear, but many did not. A fair number believed that their rightful place was similar to that of the rest of the regimental field and staff officers, a few paces behind the file-closers. There they would walk forward behind the regimental battle line, unarmed, ready to help the wounded when they fell. At the first battle of Bull Run, the chaplain of the Fourth Alabama went through the battle with that hard-hit regiment "and had his clothes cut by several balls."[59] In the May 1863 battle of Chancellorsville, Pvt. Henry C. Campbell of the 148th Pennsylvania was wounded and started for the rear. Just behind the battle line he met "our good old chaplain," who carried him to the field hospital. "I shall never forget him," Campbell wrote years later.[60] Chaplain John A. Brouse of the 100th Indiana was conspicuous for his courage at the battle of Missionary Ridge. "Without a thought of his personal safety he was up on the firing line assisting the wounded, praying with the dying, doing all that his great loving heart led him to do," recalled a soldier who was there. "No wonder our boys love our gallant Chaplain." Among the most seriously wounded was the chaplain's own son, Capt. Charles Brouse.[61] In the May 19, 1863, Union assault on Vicksburg, the chaplain of the Eighty-third Indiana was killed in action.[62] When the Second Rhode Island's Capt. Joseph McIntyre went down shortly after the regiment went into action at the battle of the Wilderness, Chaplain John D. Beugless was the first man to reach the fallen officer's side. Moments later the chaplain himself was wounded with a bullet to the wrist.[63] Thomas L. Ambrose, the former missionary who had tended the wounded after Chancellorsville, was mortally wounded at Petersburg on July 24, 1864.[64]

Some chaplains actually displayed a surprising propensity for battle, and a few even looked more the warrior than the cleric. "The chaplain of the Thirteenth Indiana," wrote John Beatty, "is the counterpart of Scott's Holy clerk of Copmanhurst, or the fighting friar of the times of Robin

Hood." Beatty remembered seeing this worthy churchman for the first time, standing amid a smoldering scene of martial destruction. "He had two revolvers and a hatchet in his belt and appeared more like a firebrand of war than a minister of peace."[65] Chaplain Fuller of the Sixteenth Massachusetts "was killed in the streets of Fredericksburg while carrying a gun," and one month later, at the January 1863 battle of Arkansas Post, the chaplain of the Eighty-third Indiana blazed away with a rifle of his own, repeating, each time he pulled the trigger, "God bless your soul."[66] In like manner, the chaplain of the 116th Illinois tried his hand at sharpshooting on the Vicksburg siege lines, taking five careful shots, "each time at a head which was incautiously exposed."[67]

Probably the most striking example of a chaplain who took an active hand in combat and, perhaps unlike the somewhat shocking parson of the Thirteenth Indiana, still retained the men's respect as a spiritual leader was the chaplain of the Second U.S. Sharpshooters. In this elite regiment of men specially selected for their marksmanship, Rev. Lorenzo Barber, a Methodist minister from New York State, fit right in. One soldier wrote that he was "a fine man, and one of the best shots in the regt., and doesn't hesitate to show his skill in shooting rebels."[68] Another wrote, "He is game. Always goes into the fight with the Regt. He has a Rifle of his own. . . . I think the men are scarce that have killed as many Johnnies as he has. He gets his gun up to his face then says 'God have mercy on your poor Soul' & lets her go & down comes Mr. Johnnie." Barber was wounded in December 1863 but made a full recovery. The soldiers approved of his warlike activities. Walter W. Smith of Company H wrote, "I wish the army furnished more such men. He is known all through the Corps as the fighting Chaplain."[69]

Not all soldiers necessarily felt that way. Many believed that it was somehow inconsistent for a minister of the gospel to engage in warfare. This feeling was especially strong in the South, with its lingering confusion regarding the doctrine of the "spiritual church" and the idea that spiritual and secular matters should be kept utterly separate.[70] It was one thing for a minister to enlist as a combat soldier or an officer—at least then he was not serving in his religious vocation—but some soldiers, both North and South, felt combat to be inappropriate for a chaplain who was present in the role of a minister.

Whether they went into battle with lethal intent or as fearless non-combatants, in the line of fire without firing back, chaplains also ran the risk of capture. In the Confederate prison at Danville, Virginia, Abner Small, himself not a religious man, noted "Chaplains Fowler and Emerson," who "seemed never to forget their Christian and moral obligation."[71]

Rev. William Brown Young wrote an unofficial how-to manual for Union chaplains. In it he set forth what he saw as the most important qualifications of a good chaplain. The first quality—an indispensable prerequisite—was "ardent piety." Next was the ability to teach men the Bible. Thereafter came a whole catalog of desirable personality traits: kindness, patience, generosity, cheerfulness, courtesy, resolution, and energy. Finally, Brown advised, the chaplain must have robust health and sturdy self-possession amid trying circumstances. It was a tall order, but many chaplains came impressively close to filling its many exacting demands.[72]

Just as there were good chaplains and bad chaplains, some chaplains retained more of the soldiers' respect than did others. As a group, however, chaplains performed well in the war, notwithstanding the relatively small number of obvious failures, and fared well in earning the respect of the soldiers. The chaplains who were in place when the war ended stood higher in the regard of the men of their regiments than did the average chaplain at the outset of the war. Far from becoming alienated from their chaplains, the soldiers were drawing closer to them. George A. Cooley of the Twenty-fourth Wisconsin frequently made favorable comments in his diary about his chaplain's preaching. One Sunday in January 1865 his duties kept him away from the preaching service, but "the boys say he preached a very good sermon."[73] Theodore Upson wrote in 1864, "A noble man is Chaplain Brouse and the boys love him as a Father."[74] Daniel Crotty of the Third Michigan mentioned his regiment's chaplain, "Mr. Pritchard, whom we all like, and think he can do as well in his line as any other preacher in the army." Pritchard's Sunday services were well attended by soldiers, who showed profound respect and interest.[75] Those chaplains who were not able to win that kind of respect from the men were by that time long gone.[76]

9

"TO LABOR FOR THE SOULS OF THEIR FELLOW-MEN"
Army Missionaries and the U.S. Christian Commission

Chaplains were the most obvious but certainly not the only representatives of organized religion in the camps of the Civil War armies. Many of the sermons the soldiers heard were not from chaplains but rather from missionaries to the army, ministers who had no official role in the military establishment and did not necessarily intend to remain permanently with the army. Instead, they came for a limited time to preach in various regiments and then moved on. There was a certain logic in this. The home churches might be able to spare preachers for a few weeks or months, even if they could not give them up entirely. In 1863 the three bishops of the Methodist Episcopal Church, South, announced plans to sponsor the sending of Methodist missionaries to the army. They pointed out that their denomination could not provide chaplains for every Confederate regiment "without breaking up the organization of the church at home," and that they were loath to do. They also added that their missionary program would save the Confederacy the cost of paying for additional chaplains.[1]

Another reason why the use of missionaries rather than chaplains made sense was that not all seasons of the year were equally well adapted for preaching to the soldiers. Although a quiet ministry of personal conversation, encouragement, and deeds of kindness could go on constantly, preaching was naturally suspended for the most part during active military movements. Preaching was also fairly impractical during periods of inclement weather, particularly in the winter. Except when the soldiers had access to civilian houses of worship or when they constructed special structures in which to hold their services, such affairs had to take place out under the open sky and were unlikely to be held in case of rain, sleet, snow, or bitter cold. A missionary could try to time his visits to the camps so that he would be present when the army would be stationary and the weather moderate enough to allow large outdoor meetings.

Of course, brief visits that included no heavy fighting and minimal atrocious weather were definitely a more appealing way to see the army than was constant presence in the camp and on the march in times that tried men's souls. Yet itinerant preachers and traveling evangelists had been the means of spreading the Gospel in much of the civilian world, in circumstances often as harsh as those of a soldier's life. There was more than mere love of ease involved in the churches' propensity to send such ministers to the army. In 1861, Samuel Walley, president of the Bible Society of Massachusetts, challenged the annual meeting of that organization not to neglect the souls of the many thousands of youths who were rushing to volunteer as soldiers. The churches and such Christian organizations as the various Bible societies could attend to these souls by sending the armies Bibles, tracts, and preachers, and many in both North and South purposed to do so.[2]

Stonewall Jackson expressed his views on the matter in a lengthy letter to a Southern church leader. "Each branch of the Christian Church," Jackson wrote, "should send into the army some of its most prominent ministers who are distinguished for their piety, talents, and zeal, and such ministers should labor to produce concert of action among chaplains and Christians in the army. These ministers should give special attention to preaching to regiments which are without chaplains." Jackson went on to suggest that the missionaries should help such regiments to secure chaplains, from whatever denomination their men selected, and above all should help make sure that the right sort of men were selected to fill these positions. "A bad selection of a chaplain may prove a curse instead of a blessing." Such missionaries, "prominent preachers," could accom-

plish a great deal in the army, Jackson believed, as long as "denominational distinctions" were submerged. This was not because Jackson was
indifferent to the truth claims of Christianity, but rather because he believed the army was no place for squabbles between varying beliefs within
orthodox Christianity. As he put it, the important question about any
preacher was not what denomination he belonged to but, "Does he preach
the gospel?"[3]

As in the North, so in the South, Christian denominations were quick
to dispatch missionaries to the camps of the armies. The Virginia Episcopal Mission Committee officially endorsed the effort and spent thousands of dollars each year during the war in sending missionaries to the
army. Bishop Stephen Elliott of Georgia also encouraged such efforts. By
the spring of 1863, the Baptist Board of Domestic Missions had twenty-
six missionaries serving with the Confederate armies.[4]

Missionaries found that some of the most profitable fields for their
labors were the army hospitals. It was not just that the hospital patients
represented a captive audience, but rather that sickness, wounds and near-
death experiences, the looming possibility of death in the hospital, and
the enforced inactivity both promoted serious thought and gave plenty
of time for it. Soldiers who could dismiss questions of religion amid the
rough camaraderie and animal high spirits of a camp full of healthy young
men found it much more difficult to do so through lonely hours and days
of staring death in the face. Thus, whether preaching or, more frequently,
sharing the Gospel in quiet tones by an individual soldier's bedside, missionaries to the army hospitals found a ready and receptive audience.

From the huge Chimborazo military hospital near Richmond, a missionary reported sixteen conversions within a relatively short period.
Another from the Confederate military hospitals near Atlanta reported
a number of conversions and also that his visits were a great encouragement to the Christians among the soldiers. "Some tell me that camp-life
has had a very unfavorable influence on their religious character," the
missionary wrote, "others say it has been of great service to them, that it
has bound them closer to the Savior, made them more acquainted with
their own weakness and sins, and afforded them a fine field in which to
labor for the souls of their fellow-men."[5]

In such Southern hospitals, the activities of the missionaries sometimes included not only the direct sharing of the Gospel message but also such things as teaching illiterate soldiers how to read. Rev. Joseph E. Martin wrote of teaching a wounded young man and a middle-aged Georgia soldier to read at Chimborazo and that both were using their new skill to read the Bible and various religious literature. Other duties that a missionary might find himself performing could be as simple as spoon-feeding a desperately wounded soldier who could not feed himself.[6] Nor was all missionary activity confined to hospitals. Rev. Joseph C. Stiles, a popular Presbyterian minister for many years before the war, made a number of preaching trips through the Confederate camps and met with considerable success. Many others did the same.[7]

A large part of the missionary effort in both North and South took the form of the distribution of Bibles and religious literature. A missionary whose chief role was to carry and distribute such literature was known as a colporteur, and the armies saw a number of them. Whether in camp or in hospital, soldiers often found themselves terribly bored and were eager for whatever reading material they could get. An observer in the Confederate camps in western Virginia during the first winter of the war noted, "the soldiers here are starved for reading matter. They will read anything. I frequently see a piece of newspaper, no larger than my hand, going the rounds among them."[8] An observer of the Union army gave the same testimony. "Reading was a pastime quite generally indulged in," wrote John D. Billings of the Tenth Massachusetts Battery, "and there was no novel so dull, trashy, or sensational as not to find some one so bored with nothing to do that he would wade through it. I, certainly, never read so many such before or since. The mind was hungry for something, and took husks when it could get nothing better."[9]

The purpose of the colporteurs was to offer something better, and by all accounts, there were few soldiers who did not receive their offerings eagerly. Rev. J.A. Hughes, working among the Confederate hospitals near Atlanta, wrote, "Some few hesitate to take a Testament, though they will accept a tract. One man positively refused a Testament but took the tract, 'A Mother's Parting Words to Her Soldier Boy.'" The soldier was so moved by the tract that he subsequently sought conversion. Another colporteur wrote that as he went through the hospital wards passing out tracts, "it was not uncommon for some sufferer in another part of the room to call out, 'Bring me one.'"

Rev. George Pearcy of Lynchburg, Virginia, found that he did not have to travel far to do the work of a missionary in army hospitals, as his town became the site of numerous such establishments. "I collected from Sunday Schools and individuals," he explained, "above a hundred Testaments, a few Bibles, and some books and tracts—these were placed in three large hospitals for the sick soldiers. There have been as many as 10,000 soldiers in the encampment here, hence it is a most interesting field for usefulness." All the soldiers, Pearcy asserted, "receive the tracts, and read them with delight." Rev. B. B. Ross, working among Confederate army hospitals in Mississippi, found the patients "greedy, yea ravenous, in their appetite for something to read" and quite happy to receive religious literature. They "take the tracts ... with delight," Ross reported, "and read them with avidity."[10]

The colporteur could easily find himself performing the role of a more conventional missionary. One was passing through a hospital ward handing out tracts when he came to a soldier who was in tears because he could not read and asked the colporteur, "Will you be good enough to read some of those tracts to me?" He did, beginning with that favorite of Southern soldiers, "A Mother's Parting Words," much to the delight of the illiterate soldier. Another colporteur reported a similar experience. "I was reading a few tracts to a sick soldier," he wrote from near Petersburg, "and while reading one on 'The Blood of Christ,' he became so happy that he shouted, 'Glory to God!'"[11]

Yet another colporteur, working in the camps and hospitals around Richmond, kept careful account of his activities. During a single month he handed out 41,000 pages of tracts and preached almost daily in the various hospitals. "A notice of a few minutes will give me a large congregation," he wrote. "Never in my life have I witnessed such solemn attention to the preached word." Rev. W. J. W. Crowder traveled to the army as a colporteur and in the space of several weeks distributed 200,000 pages of tracts; during the same time, he had over 2,800 "conversations on personal religion" with soldiers in the various camps and hospitals. In the Army of Tennessee's hospitals in Atlanta, colporteur S. A. Creath distributed 20,000 pages of tracts between sunup and nine o'clock one morning. In all, during his work in the Atlanta area, he estimated that he had talked to 3,000 sick men.[12]

Much of the literature that was distributed was supplied by the Evangelical Tract Society of the Confederacy, which was organized in Petersburg, Virginia, in July 1861 and supported by the various denominations throughout the South. During the course of the war, it issued more than 100 different tracts with a total print run estimated at some 50 million pages. It also printed Bibles and published a religious newspaper called the *Army and Navy Messenger*.[13] Nor was it the only source of such literature, even in the South. The Methodist Episcopal Church, South, also established its own Soldier's Tract Society, which distributed tracts, hymnbooks, and Bibles, and Methodist minister R. J. Harp published another religious newspaper called the *Army and Navy Herald*.[14] Rev. W. J. W. Crowder published over 5 million pages of thirty different tracts in Raleigh, North Carolina, during the war. In its first year of operation, the General Association of the Baptist Churches in Virginia kept precise figures: 6,187,000 pages of forty different tracts, 6,095 New Testaments, and 13,845 copies of an abbreviated hymnal called "Camp Hymns."[15] The list could go on. Suffice it to say that the effort was considerable.

And yet, amid such ink-stained diligence and the resulting avalanche of tracts and other literature, the strongest demand among the soldiers and, in the South, the greatest deficiency in supply was for copies of the Scriptures themselves. The soldiers of the Fifteenth South Carolina lost whatever Bibles or testaments they had, along with the rest of their baggage, in the Confederate debacle at Hilton Head, South Carolina, in the winter of 1862. Several weeks later, the regiment's chaplain wrote to the Bible Society of South Carolina to express thanks for replacing some of the lost Scripture portions. "The Testaments you sent to me were eagerly sought after by the men," he wrote, "many coming to me long after they were all distributed, and were much disappointed at not receiving one. Could you send us some more?" The director of the South Carolina Bible Society estimated that 20,000 copies of the Scriptures were needed at that time to meet the requests from soldiers on the South Carolina coast alone. Similarly, from a Confederate military hospital out in

Okolona, Mississippi, Rev. J. T. C. Collins wrote, "The soldiers received the [religious] books with great eagerness. I never in my life saw such a desire to get Bibles. Every ward I went into they would beg me for *Bibles and Testaments*. While they gladly received the other books, they wanted *Bibles*."

Indeed, the churches and Bible societies of the South were never able to meet the wartime demand for Bibles. As in every other area of manufacturing, the South had lagged behind the rest of the country in the business of book printing. Southern religious leaders therefore naturally looked abroad for the large numbers of copies they needed but found their efforts hindered by the Union blockade. The British and Foreign Bible Society extended to the Bible Society of the Confederate States an interest-free loan of 1,000 pounds sterling, supplying some 10,000 Bibles, 50,000 New Testaments, and 250,000 briefer portions of the Scriptures, most of which passed successfully through the blockade.

Ironically, the American Bible Society, a Northern institution, actually donated large numbers of Bibles to Southerners on several occasions, sometimes channeling its contributions through the Bible Society of Memphis and one shipment of 20,000 New Testaments through the Baptist Sunday School Board. Southern religious leaders even appealed to the general public of the South to donate any spare copies of the Scriptures they might have about their houses, and many an heirloom Bible thus found its way to the soldiers. Yet the demand in the South was never fully met. Often five or six Confederate soldiers would share a single copy of the Scriptures.[16]

The North did not experience the same problem. It had plenty of printing capacity and could easily have imported printed matter if need had arisen. Indeed, so abundant were Northern stocks that the American Bible Society could repeatedly send shipments to the enemy. Ample supply was therefore available to the Northern soldiers. Many Northern towns, like those in the South, sent their local companies off to war with ceremonies that included the distribution of a Bible or New Testament to each departing soldier. Indeed, the little town of Ashby, Massachusetts, decided to give each one of its volunteers a revolver, a bowie knife, and a Bible.[17] In contrast to the situation in the South, however, the North was able to keep up a steady flow of literature to its armies.

The Nineteenth Iowa's Benjamin F. McIntrye recorded an 1863 instance that illustrated both the great abundance of printed matter in the North and perhaps the dereliction of at least one colporteur. While his regiment was aboard the steamboat *Henry Chouteau* tied up at Genieve Mills, Missouri, a colporteur "appeared on the landing with a large box of testaments (several hundred at least) which he wished to present to the soldiers." The Iowans tried to explain to him that every soldier in the regiment already had one, but the zealous colporteur insisted on pressing the men to accept his Testaments until he had emptied the entire box. McIntrye, believing the man had done this merely so he could, with the appearance of decency, leave the war zone and get back to civilization and comfort in the North all the sooner, was not impressed. "No soldier will carry an extra copy. If he is forced to take them he will dispose of it as best he can." How the Iowans had disposed of the colporteur's unwanted largess was only too apparent. "Today testaments are sown broad cast over the boat and the entire work of mercy which has cost some society a good many dollars are kicked over board as trash or trumpery."[18] Happily, the incident was not typical.

Much of the distribution of religious literature in the Union armies—Bibles, New Testaments, hymnbooks, tracts, and the like—was carried out under the auspices of the United States Christian Commission. Organized in November 1861 at the urging of the New York Young Men's Christian Association, the U.S. Christian Commission was a national agency in which evangelical Christians from various denominations across the North could unify and coordinate their efforts to minister to the Union soldiers in an orderly, methodical way. Showing the lingering influence of the recent "Businessman's Revival," the first conference of the Christian Commission selected as the new organization's president Philadelphia merchant George H. Stuart, a Presbyterian lay leader. In the words of a later resolution by its executive committee, the Christian Commission held that there was no "more interesting and important field for missionary operations" than the army. To carry out those operations, it developed a vast organization, with field superintendents in each army corps supervising the efforts of some 5,000 volunteer delegates—the actual ministers of the Christian Commission—throughout the far-flung Union armies.[19]

The primary and overarching purpose of the work of the Christian Commission was to "persuade [the soldiers] to become reconciled to God through the blood of His Son, if they have not already done so, and if they have, then to be strong in the Lord, resolute for duty, earnest and constant in prayer, and fervent in spirit, serving the Lord." For this purpose, delegates were to cooperate with regimental and hospital chaplains in holding preaching services and prayer meetings whenever possible and encouraging the soldiers to attend. They would also distribute Bibles, tracts, and other Christian literature on a huge scale, and they would visit, comfort, and pray with the sick and wounded.[20]

Yet at the same time, the delegates were also to minister to the physical and temporal needs of the soldiers, just as their Lord had ministered to the needs of sufferers when He walked on earth and told his followers that when they did so, He counted their kindesses as if extended to Him in person. To those who objected that the Christian Commission should devote itself solely to sharing the Gospel and leave the soldiers' physical needs for other charitable organizations to address, commission president George Stuart replied that "there is a good deal of religion in a warm shirt and a good beefsteak."[21] Besides distributing literature, the delegates also gave out food items and hospital stores of various sorts.

The Christian Commission delegates also distributed stamped envelopes and stationery—both items in high demand and short supply, as the Union soldiers wrote constantly and often expended the stock of paper, stamps, and envelopes they could carry in their knapsacks. The instructions that the Christian Commission issued to its delegates enjoined them to encourage "soldiers and sailors to communicate freely and frequently with their friends, aiding them to do it, and if need be, writing for them, especially when they are sick or wounded."

The Christian Commission was profoundly methodical in its approach to taking Gospel hope and Christian comfort to the armies. Each delegate received a specially printed Christian Commission memorandum book so that he could keep note of his activities, appointments, and the like. The memorandum book also contained a large collection of useful printed information, notably a section entitled "Duties of Delegates." The directions were pointed and practical. On first arriving in his new field of labors, each delegate was to report promptly to his field agent, who was both an administrator and the conduit of the commission's bounty toward a given sector of the army. The field agent would assign the delegate the specific place or part of the army in which he was to minister and provide him with rations for himself and whatever literature, food, or other items of humanitarian aid he would be distributing to the soldiers. The instructions admonished each delegate to stick to the post his agent assigned him and use "most prayerfully all his own ingenuity, energy and enterprise in carrying on and extending the work." He was to be careful to get the permission of commanding officers and, when aiding the sick and wounded, to follow the instructions of surgeons. Except in extreme cases of dereliction on the part of a chaplain, the delegate was to cooperate with and defer to that official as well.

The instructions directed delegates that their sermons should be "brief, kind, ... earnest ... affectionate for the men, and fervent for Christ," and it warned them that the soldiers "cannot be impressed or moved by abstractions, or dry and dull discussions." When the needs of the soldiers and the assignment of his field agent sent a delegate on the march with an army on campaign or into the detritus left after battle, he "must go, on foot if necessary, notwithstanding fatigue or danger." Just as the soldiers had to carry their needs on their backs, so the delegate had to hump his relief supplies: a blanket for his own accommodation, food for himself and for the wounded—both the ordinary sort and cakes of beef bouillon to be reconstituted for those wounded men who were very weak—soap and a towel, "a bucket to carry water or coffee in, and a cup to serve it out to the wounded," a small lantern for going to the aid of wounded men lying on the battlefield at night, and a small Bible. The delegate was to give the wounded men "food and drink and everything needed to mitigate suffering and aid recovery, or if dying, point them with prayer to Jesus." He should help the surgeons and other military personnel to remove the wounded from the battlefield and try to see that the dead got a Christian burial—"in short, striving to do all that man can do to meet the wants of brethren far from home and kindred."

A final notice in the instructions reminded delegates to inform their cooperating chaplains that "by written application to the nearest office of the Commission, aid of almost any kind for their work could be obtained and sent to them free of expense"—a further reminder that just as the North was able to provide lavish equipment and supplies for its armies, so Northern Christians by their donations were able to provide an abundant supply of Bibles and religious literature of all sorts.[22]

And so they went out, and the distinctive badge of the Christian Commission, worn on broadcloth suits or various sorts of "strong, plain clothing," became a familiar sight to Union soldiers.[23] Many of the delegates had frequent opportunities to preach the Gospel. "I had the pleasure of listening to Mr. Loomis from Mass., a member of the U.S. Christian Commission," wrote a soldier of the Twenty-fourth Wisconsin in November 1863. "He is a good man and his discourse was very touching and instructive. God bless him and his labor."[24] "We will have no service in camp today," wrote James G. Theaker of the Fiftieth Ohio one Sunday in 1864, "unless some good member of the Christian commission comes over. Our Chaplain is absent, sick."[25] Many a delegate also carried Bibles, Testaments, and other literature for miles on his back to distribute to the troops. A soldier wrote of delegate George M. Smith, "I have seen him a mile from the station, among the other camps, with a haversack slung on his shoulder, filled, I suppose, with testaments and tracts that he had been giving away to the boys. He evidently understood his work, his heart was in it, and he did it well."[26]

A number of soldiers made grateful mention of the Christian Commission in their diaries, letters, and postwar reminiscences. "The Christian Commission is well got up, ably conducted and thoroughly efficient," was the verdict of Vermont soldier Wilbur Fisk. He also noted that the Christian Commission established long-term outposts with the soldiers in winter quarters, and when the army marched out to fight in the spring, "the Commission does not forsake us. It will follow us on to the field."[27] Other soldiers also gave their testimonials to the commission's work. As William McCarter of the 116th Pennsylvania lay wounded and cold in a hospital tent after the December 1862 battle of Fredericksburg, he was startled to see a man enter the tent carrying a generous supply of hot biscuits and "a tin bucket full of strong, hot coffee," items that McCarter called "God-sent luxuries." Inquiring where the good things had come from, McCarter learned that the source was the U.S. Christian Commission. It was the first he had heard of the organization, and he was deeply impressed.[28] Joseph Whitney felt most grateful for the good Christian literature the commission had given him. "It was by influence of the Commission that I came to see my wickedness and turned my steps from the path of evil," he wrote.[29]

The Christian Commission provided hospitality facilities for the comfort of soldiers in transit through Northern cities. In a letter to his wife telling of his journey to the fighting front, John Black of the Thirty-sixth Wisconsin wrote, "We changed cars ... at Pittsburg.... There we had Dinner at the Christian Commission rooms."[30] Similarly, the commission set up tent hospitality facilities closer to the fighting fronts. A desperately ill Daniel Crotty was away from his regiment, the Third Michigan, and had not the strength to get back. Staggering along, he saw "some tents pitched in front of a house close by." Making his way to the gate, he finally passed out. When he came to, he found "some kind nurses bending over me, and all looking anxiously for my recovery." These turned out to be "the ladies of the Christian Commission, who had left home and all its luxuries to administer to the poor soldier in the field. God bless all those devoted women," Crotty wrote, "and if they do not receive their reward on this earth may they receive it in heaven."[31]

Often it was the little things done by the delegates that the soldiers remembered long afterward. The stationery they provided to the soldiers appears in many collections of original soldier letters found in various repositories around the country today. "Went to the Christian Commission and got a sheet of paper and an envelope," reads an entry in the diary of the Second Iowa's John J. McKee.[32] A letter that a soldier of the Forty-third Wisconsin wrote to his parents from Decherd, Tennessee, is written on such paper and is an example of the type used. Printed at the top of the paper is a drawing of a pigeon with an envelope tied to a string around its neck. Beside this picture are the words: "The U.S. CHRISTIAN COMMISSION sends this sheet as a messenger between the soldier and his home. Let it hasten to those who wait for tidings."[33] It is not a rare specimen. Another sheet, similar to this one, was used by Theodore W. Skinner of the 112th New York to write a letter home from Chapins Farm, Virginia, in October 1864. It also featured the Bible verse: "Behold! Now is the accepted time; behold, now is the day of salvation."[34] True to their instructions, delegates were ready to write letters for those who needed such help. The Fifty-ninth Illinois's Chesley Mosman wrote in his diary that as he lay wounded in the hospital after the battle of Nashville, "Christian Commission officers come around, offer to write home for me."[35]

Another soldier recalled how "the Christian Commission used to furnish us men with Testaments and tracts and a sort of thread-and-needle case with pockets, called a 'housewife'"— much sought after by Civil War soldiers, who had to do all their own mending.[36] Allen Geer mentioned a "large stock of religious books" sent to his Twentieth Illinois Regiment by the Christian Commission, as well as several Christian Commission reading rooms in Vicksburg and Memphis in the fall of 1863. He called it "a glorious humane institution" whose workers and directors "deserve the gratitude of every American Soldier."[37] Not everyone could be satisfied all the time, of course. The job was vast, far too large for any 5,000 men, however disciplined and motivated they might be, and the more conscientious a delegate was, the more his work was never done. Not surprisingly, fatigue sometimes rendered the delegates less than sprightly in carrying out their work. An Indiana soldier who spent some time in a Memphis military hospital expressed disapproval, as he wrote his memoirs many years later, of a Christian Commission delegate who gave him a tract but did not stop to talk. "Tracts may be all right," the old soldier opined, "but a word of sympathy is sometimes better."[38] The delegate no doubt would have agreed.

The United States government encouraged the activities of the Christian Commission, and increasingly so as the war went on. The government supported the commission's efforts as much as feasible, and the leadership of the commission consistently sought official approval and cooperated with Union authorities. Lincoln himself warmly applauded the commission's efforts, and Grant seemed especially eager to further its work. On taking command of all Union forces west of the Appalachians in the fall of 1863, he issued an order that the delegates should not be hindered in their work anywhere within his command. The following spring, when all Union forces came under his command, Grant extended the same policy throughout the entire United States Army.[39]

The diaries of Christian Commission delegates speak of enthusiastic acceptance by the soldiers. One wrote of "attentive and eager listeners" and the "good respect . . . and appreciation" he received from the soldiers.

Several others gave accounts of soldiers eagerly accepting Bibles and tracts.[40]

The soldiers' writings were, if anything, even more emphatic. "I believe the soldiers like these Christian Commission delegates better than they do the regular army chaplains," wrote Wilbur Fisk, adding, "I mean as a general thing. The chaplains they say, all they care for is to come out here and see the country, hold office, get a good swad of greenbacks every pay day, perhaps preach a tolerable good sermon on Sunday, if the weather is perfectly right, distribute the mail when it comes, and then when they get tired of this contrive some way to be out of health, resign, and go home." Of course, this was terribly unfair to the majority of chaplains, who were lumped together with their worst specimens. "But these delegates," wrote Fisk, referring to the workers of the Christian Commission,

> are just the men that the army wants.... They give their time and their services, and generally work hard, and work willingly.... No missionary in any field can receive a heartier welcome than the soldier is willing to accord to the delegates of the Christian Commission.... The Christian Commission has become to be respected by all the boys. Even those who care but little about its benefits personally speak well of it, and think it a very good thing. The idea of an enterprise of such infinitude being carried on and supported by voluntary contributions from those who are interested in our welfare mainly because we belong to the common brotherhood of mankind, and have souls to save, as well as bodies to preserve, carried with it such a weight of argument for the sincerity and power of that christian principle which begets this spirit of benevolence, that no man attempts to gainsay or resist it.

As the Army of the Potomac broke up its camps in preparation for the beginning of the 1864 campaign, Fisk summed up his thoughts about the Christian Commission's ministry that winter with his own Vermont Brigade—"Vermont Station," as it was called. "We shall remember with gratitude what has been done for us here, and some will have all eternity to be grateful in."[41]

Through chaplains, independent or denominationally sponsored army missionaries, and, among the Union armies, the disciplined, methodical work of the U.S. Christian Commission, organized religion in both North and South strove to reach out to the spiritual and sometimes the material needs of the men who filled their respective armies, "to labor for the souls of their fellow-men." Yet the few hundred chaplains, 5,000 Christian Commission delegates, and smaller numbers of Southern army missionaries were dwarfed in comparison to the more than 3,300,000 men who marched off to fight as soldiers in the Civil War. The state of religion in the armies would be largely what those 3 million made of it or allowed it to be.

10

"IN THE THICKEST OF THE FIGHT"
Religion in the Camp and on the Battlefield, 1861–1862

"There is no position in which a Christian can be placed in which he may not exert much influence for good," wrote Bishop Andrew of the Methodist Episcopal Church, South, in a general letter to members who were going into the Confederate army in 1861. "You will, doubtless in camp, be surrounded by those who will have little sympathy with your religious views and feelings and who will closely and constantly scrutinize your whole conduct," the bishop warned. "Let your walk be such as to constrain them to glorify your Father in heaven. . . . Many opportunities will be afforded you of strengthening the weak, and recovering those who are just on the verge of falling. And should you so deport yourselves as to command the confidence and respect of your companions in arms, you will find many unexpected calls for advice. Strive to prepare yourself to give it. In a word, be a thorough and consistent Christian yourself, and you will be always prepared to help others."[1]

Andrew's was a more eloquent and complete version of the parting admonitions that hundreds of thousands of new recruits North and South were receiving in 1861 as they left their homes to join the army and their fathers, mothers, pastors, or concerned friends urged them to remain faithful in the midst of what were sure to be hard trials and fierce temptations. Charles O. Varnum's father "spoke about my being on my guard against temptation," when his son enlisted in the Fortieth Massachusetts.[2] The father of Confederate soldier Carlton McCarthy told his son, "I would rather hear of your death than of the shipwreck of your faith and good conscience." Similarly, in Chicago, a mother told her soldier-son that she "would rather he would be sent home dead, than that he should return alive and dissipated."[3] John C. Delano wrote to his friend Joseph Whitney, "Joseph, I want you to live a Christian life. You have a great many trials in camp, but you can have some time to be with God. Even when you go to bed, ask God to watch over you and keep you right."[4]

The concerns of parents about the moral well-being of their sons should they enter the army were sometimes reflected in patterns of enlistment. Eighteen-, nineteen-, and twenty-year-olds still needed their parents' consent to enlist, and some observers believed they saw a pattern in which parents were more likely to give that consent if they felt assured that their sons would be serving under officers who would look after their moral as well as physical well-being. Charles A. Willison, who enlisted in the Seventy-sixth Ohio with his father's consent at the age of sixteen, recalled that the captain of his company was his peacetime Sunday school superintendent, a man of about forty, well known and respected in the community. "He was a careful, moral, kindly dispositioned man," Willison wrote, "hence, if boys were determined to go to war, parents were willing it should be under such a man."[5] Similarly, when nationally known prohibitionist Neal Dow set out to raise a regiment, the Thirteenth Maine, he was virtually inundated with recruits, far more than he could accept. Dow permitted neither card playing, swearing, drinking, nor boisterous conduct. When the regiment passed through Boston, a newspaper of that city called it "the quietest regiment that has ever been seen in this city."[6]

Many of the departing soldiers purposed to remain pure, whether to please their relatives or out of sincere convictions of duty to God. Ira Pettit, a New York farm boy who joined the Eleventh U.S. Infantry, wrote to his sister, "I do not nor will not yield to the many evil influences which surround us."[7] Devout young John T. McMahon wrote in his diary upon joining the 136th New York, "I hope always to cast my influence on the side of truth and religion and to live Godly in this present evil world."[8] Naturally, there were others who openly expressed such a purpose merely to satisfy anxious relatives but felt less commitment to keep the promises they made.

Well might the families of soldiers worry about the moral effect of military service on their young men. Many of the new soldiers would be leaving their families and their home communities for the first time and going off to see sights and visit places they had only dreamed of before— Cairo, Chicago, Columbus, Harrisburg, even Washington, D.C. The traditional restraints of community expectation might not function so well in those far-off and exotic settings. Besides that, the camps and barracks of armies had long been considered notoriously degraded places. The regular United States Army, small as it was, recruited its enlisted ranks from the dregs of society, and they were a rough lot, foulmouthed, and, when they got the chance, hard drinking and loose living. The Regulars would be a tiny fraction of the citizen armies the nation was now raising, but the military culture of which they were an example was far bigger than they and could be expected to have its pervasive influence.

The new soldiers would not be coming into contact with Old Army Regulars nearly as much as they would be in unaccustomed close quarters with other volunteers like themselves—or maybe *not* so much like themselves. One of the first and most striking features of the volunteers' experience in the new citizen armies was that it brought them together, in a way they had never before experienced, with all sorts of other young men. Even though a given regiment would always come from a single state, and most companies were recruited entirely from a single community or, at most, county, their members quickly discovered that those communities had contained some remarkably dissimilar sorts of people, now represented in the company's ranks. The new recruit soon realized that he was going to spend a good deal of the next three years—if he lived that long and stayed healthy—associated with a number of young men with whom he would not have chosen to spend his leisure time back in civilian life. The young men from religious families quickly met some very different comrades in arms.

Henry Marsh of the Nineteenth Indiana wrote, "The army is a fearful place for a young christian," and later noted, "I feel that to be in the army is as if in a bar room and a gambling saloon."[9] John T. McMahon thought much the same: "The army is no place for a decent man," he wrote. "Such oaths and swearing I never heard before, and such indecent language enough to make one blush for his honor."[10] The Second Vermont's Wilbur Fisk put the same sort of thought in more eloquent terms, as he wrote from the regiment's camp early in the war: "Here are many, alas, too many, to whom you would have to listen long before you would hear a single manly thought expressed, or a single ennobling sentiment uttered. Their conversation is copiously interlarded with oaths and blasphemy, and their course jokes and vulgar obscenity is loathsome in the extreme."[11] It was. Before the Fifteenth Iowa departed the state for the seat of the war, Cyrus Boyd noted that two of its companies in particular seemed to have "some bad men," and patrols had already picked up some of those men several miles from camp "in saloons and disreputable houses."[12] The Twenty-third New York's Seymour Dexter wrote to a friend, "I have seen more drunkeness and swearing since I left Alfred [his hometown] than I have seen or heard in all my life. . . . Your cannot imagine the degradation that seems to be indelibly stamped upon at least one half the soldiers." The date was May 3, 1861, and the Twenty-third was still in New York, camped at Elmira, awaiting orders to proceed to Washington.[13] Joseph Whitney took it more philosophically. "There are all kinds of folks here," he wrote to his wife, "just the same as at home, good and bad together. If a man wants good company, he can have it, if he wants bad, he can have the same."[14] What Whitney did not mention was that though a man might choose good companions, he still had to put up with bad ones.

If anything, the situation was worse in the Confederate armies, for Christianity had traditionally been less dominant there and had prolif-erated only in more recent decades. Some enclaves of the South, and some strata of Southern society, were therefore relatively untouched by its influences. This was reflected in the experience of a missionary who in 1861 encountered three companies—then close to 300 men—among whom he could find only seven who professed to have saving faith in Christ.[15] Those numbers were unusually bad, but many Christians in both North and South were encountering in the ranks of the new volunteer regiments what to them seemed disconcerting numbers of irreligious compatriots. Confederate soldier Thomas Boatright wrote, "I am thrown among men in my tent that seem to care but little about spiritual things. . . . If I men-tion it [a religious subject] some one will bear it off as if it were unpleasant so I have to remain silent on that subject but if I bring up any other subject all is right, all take part."[16]

It all seemed to be part of the overall wickedness of the army. "There seems to be no God here," wrote Boyd, "but more than the average amount of the Devil."[17] "This is a hard kind of life," as Hoosier officer James Shanklin put it, "away from all refining influences where a church bell is scarcely if ever heard."[18] Bringing together men of every persuasion and manner of life, the army was a homogenized version of American society. For men who had been active Christians or even hangers-on of the church back home, life in the army brought close daily contact with others who openly practiced sin on a wholesale basis, and by all accounts, the encounter was a shock.

Yet if Christian recruits noticed many who were different from themselves, they also noticed some who were like them, at least in their commitment to try to live in such a way as to please God. On his first night in the barracks, Theodore Upson of the 100th Indiana noticed an older man who read quietly from his Bible, then knelt by his bunk and prayed before turning in. "I can begin to see that a man must have nerve to do that," Upson wrote in his diary. "Some of the boys are aufuly profane and some drink a good deal more than is good for them, but I believe there are a lot of good boys in the Company and they are the ones I want to tie to. I don't like smut and profanity."[19] Seymour Dexter assured his friend back in Alfred, New York, that notwithstanding the wickedness of some of his comrades, he and some others were attending prayer meetings.[20] In later years, John D. Billings of the Tenth Massachusetts Battery grew testy at many people's assumption that the army was composed exclusively of dissolute men. "That there were bad men in the army is too well known to be denied," Billings conceded, "but the morally bad soldiers were in the minority."[21] He was probably right. Thomas Boatright assured his wife that although some of his comrades had no use for religion, "it is not so with all in camp, for there are some young men here living pious lives and they have their influence."[22]

Initially, a recruit might be as likely to notice one sort of comrade as the other. Indeed, for those with religious backgrounds, the experience of living in a large group encampment might put them in mind of camp meetings they had attended in the past, complete with the blowing of a "horn" to call campers to worship or other activities. Military duties were not too pressing in those early days (compared with what they would be later on), and zealous chaplains could hold frequent meetings for worship and evangelism. In April 1861, Sgt. Dietrich Smith of the Eighth Illinois wrote to his fiancée back in Pekin, Illinois, that if she wanted to know what life in camp was like, she should "imagine yourself to be at a campmeeting where the ladies are minus where men do it all cooking washing &c."[23]

Alfred Tyler Fielder of the Twelfth Tennessee recorded in July and August 1861 that religious services took place frequently in his newly recruited regiment. On the last Sunday in July, for example, his diary records two different services, one at 10:00 A.M. and the other at 4:00 P.M. "Myself and many others felt that God was present by his spirit to the Joy and Comfort of our souls," Fielder wrote in his diary that night. Sunday services continued, though certainly not all of the regiment attended. By mid-August, Fielder was recording nightly prayer meetings at the chaplain's tent after roll call. By early September, these evening meetings were lasting until lights-out time, when military discipline required their dismissal. They featured preaching and numerous penitents seeking conversion and requesting the prayers of their believing comrades. Several of them professed conversion in what was very similar to the revival meetings or camp meetings the men had known in civilian life.[24] About that same time, Union soldier Alfred Bellard noted that one of the companies of his regiment "held a camp meeting every eve, the chaplain presiding and quite a revival was in progress."[25] Likewise, in the First Iowa during that same summer, frequent prayer meetings were one of the factors that helped men from different parts of the state gain a feeling of unity within the regiment.[26]

But things generally did not continue that way. There were dozens of corrosive influences that made it hard to continue such meetings. For one thing, the pace of military operations precluded such pursuits once active campaigning got started, and even without the movement of the armies, such activities were difficult to sustain in camp. Bellard's regiment got orders to move up to the fighting front, and that broke up the camp meeting.[27] In Fielder's Twelfth Tennessee, the chaplain went away on an extended leave. Some Christians among the soldiers tried to keep the meetings going with the help of visiting preachers, chaplains from

other regiments, and army missionaries, but the presence of such clergymen was spotty and erratic. Interest began to abate, as did the frequency
of services. "No preaching in our Camp," wrote Fielder on Sunday,
October 13, 1861, "our Chaplin has not yet returned." Three weeks later,
a guest preacher held services in the Twelfth Tennessee, with "but few
in attendance." By Sunday, December 8, Fielder was recording in his
diary, "The day past away as usual without any public worship in Camp
that I heard of. I awfully fear that religion and the worship of God is on
the retrogard [retrograde—i.e., retreat]." On Christmas Day that year he
wrote, "The Cause of sobriety, virtue, and piety have comparatively few
advocates in the army."[28]

Absence of the chaplain was also a problem in the Fifteenth Iowa. "The
Chaplain is not here now," wrote Cyrus Boyd, "and we have no preaching and Sunday goes like every other day. Men are playing cards all
through camp."[29] Christians in the Ninth Tennessee did their best to keep
up a weekly prayer meeting during the first winter of the war, despite
the absence of their chaplain, and on Sundays, whenever they could, many
went over to join the services in the Sixth Tennessee of their brigade.
The Sixth was also without a chaplain, but Lieutenant Witherspoon of
that regiment was "a devotedly pious man and a wonderfully attractive
preacher," and he led the services.[30] Texan James C. Bates was less successful. September 29, 1861, was his second Sunday in camp. That day he
wrote in his diary: "As our Chaplain is sick we have no preaching today—
after reading awhile in my Bible concluded to attend preaching about a
mile and a half from here—went & found a goodly number of soldiers
from the different companies in attendance—after waiting two hours we
were told that the preacher was sick."[31]

Another problem was the lack of good opportunities for formal worship services in an active army. Even when preachers were present, able,
and willing, they were often unable to hold religious meetings. "For three
months I have not preached a sermon," wrote a missionary to the Confederate army in Virginia in the spring of 1862. "We have no preaching
place, and I do not know when we shall have one." He had to content
himself with passing out literature.[32] Georgia soldier Clifford Anderson
noted the same problem. "Our prayer meetings in camp too have been
very irregular of late," he wrote to his wife. "We have moved about so

much that they could not be kept up with any degree of regularity & the weather too has been an obstacle."[33] Unless a civilian church building happened to be nearby, an army camp generally offered no structure large enough to accommodate corporate worship, which therefore had to be held outdoors. Cold, rain, or other inclement weather would thus compel the cancellation of meetings. "This is the Holy Sabbath Day," wrote Henry G. Ankeny from the camp of the Fourth Iowa in Rolla, Missouri, on Sunday, November 25, 1861, but he went on to note regretfully that it was "too cold for our chaplain to preach, so we have nothing to do but sit in our tents and write and freeze."[34]

Yet much religious worship did occur in the armies during the first year of the war. Vast numbers of soldiers briefly noted in their letters and diaries the occurrence of regular worship services. While it is impossible to quantify the matter with any degree of reliability, it would probably be safe to estimate that even during this first year of the war, the majority of Civil War soldiers had the opportunity to join in public worship on a fairly regular basis if they desired to do so. A significant number of the soldiers readily availed themselves of such opportunities. The soldiers' letters and diaries are replete with statements such as "The whole Regiment marched up town to Church," "Sundays we have the chance to go to church which I have improved every time," "We march to church every Sunday at two o'clock," "Got a pass and went uptown to church," "The Chaplin held service in frunt of Co. G Quarters," "The regiment assembled in front of the Chaplain's tent for Divine worship," "The same as usual Divine Service at seven oclock in the evening," "The men mostly attended church today," and the endlessly repeated notation, "Went to church."[35]

The frequent though somewhat less numerous references to the lack of religious services points up the fact that a large percentage of the soldiers, probably a majority, were accustomed to attending religious services every week in civilian life. When they found themselves without that opportunity, whether through exigencies of military operations or through lack of a chaplain, they were shocked and deeply disturbed.

When religious services did take place, they were usually outdoors. This made an impression on many of the soldiers, one they mentioned in their diaries and letters. Virginia soldier Ham Chamberlayne described in a letter to a friend a worship service held at the camp of the battered and sickly Twenty-first Virginia at Valley Mountain, Virginia, in September 1861. "It was a solemn scene, for seats the hill top, for roof, a still blue sky; to the West the view was bounded miles off, by a blue line of rugged mountains, while to the north stretched into limitless space, one rising beyond another, the dark peaks of Cheat Mountain. In some respects too the scene could remind you of the very book that was expounded [the Gospel of Luke]; for many emaciated sick, some halting along on sticks, some in the arms of their friends, came and lay along the hill to hear the Word."[36] That same month, Seymour Dexter of the Twenty-third New York wrote to a friend that in a worship service planned for that evening "the smooth ground will be our pews and the broad canopy of nature our church and the silver moon our light."[37]

Soldiers often found the outdoor services to be particularly moving. In May 1861, Capt. William Y. W. Ripley of the First Vermont wrote to his wife back in Rutland describing his regiment's outdoor worship near Fort Monroe, Virginia. "The men enjoy the Sunday service much, & it is interesting. The Regt is formed in square by division & faced inward, the singers are invited to the center & usually some 90 or 100 come out." He related that the previous Sunday quite a number had been moved to tears by the singing of one of the hymns.[38] Describing a service on the very same Sunday, an officer of the Fourth Alabama wrote of his regiment's religious observance: "It was a touching scene to see the soldiers seated on the ground, listening attentively to the beautiful religious service of the Episcopal Church."[39]

The sensation created by outdoor worship was not always a pleasant one to the soldiers. "Our first Sunday from home, and it has been a queer one to me," wrote the Second Rhode Island's Elisha Hunt Rhodes in his diary in June 1861, but he added, "The scene to me was a solemn and impressive one."[40] That same month, Allen Geer of the Twentieth Illinois "attended preaching" on his first Sunday in camp, and its difference from the conventional indoor services he had known every Sunday for as long as he could remember struck him forcefully with the realization of how different his life was going to be. "Everything seemed so very different from home that a sense of desperate homesickness came over me," he wrote, "but I determined to stand up to duty and preserve my manhood and honor let come what may."[41]

Even when a chaplain was present and held meetings, observers often noted the disturbingly close juxtaposition of the godly and the ungodly within the enforced proximity of an army's camps. "While Parson Strong and a devoted few are singing the songs of Zion," wrote Union colonel John Beatty in October 1861, "the boys are having cotillion parties in other parts of the camp."[42] In the civilian world back home, the irreligious often showed more respect than that for the close proximity of those worshipping God. They had seemed ashamed of their sins and practiced them in more out-of-the-way places, far from the disapproving gaze of devout persons. Sometimes in the army, shame seemed gone, and it was likely to be the devout who came in for disapproving looks. It was the same in the Confederate army. A young soldier of the Army of Northern Virginia told a missionary, "You know not how difficult it is to stem the tide of corruption in the army. Many of our officers drink and swear, and discourage all manifestations of religious feeling."[43]

All things considered, many observers agreed that army life during the first year or so of the war was not having a good moral and religious effect on the soldiers. One soldier wrote, "War is pretty sure to relax the morals of everybody it comes in contact with."[44] The sentiment was widespread. "Stripped of all the restrictions and influences of home, of society and immediate friends, the natural inclinations and characteristics of a man are sure to speedily develop themselves," wrote a minister who served with the Fifth Maine. "I know of no surer test upon which to apply a man's character then to place him in a volunteer army."[45] Even the irreligious Charles Haydon wrote, "It is doubtful whether the effect which war has upon the morals of a people is not more to be regretted than its more ostensible evils."[46]

Union officer John William De Forest noticed that his troops were getting tougher as soldiers, "but" he added, "the men are not so *good* as they were once; they drink harder and swear more and gamble deeper." De Forest thought the reason for this was inherent in the duty of soldiers to kill their fellow men in time of battle: "De Quincey is right," De Forest wrote, "in his statement that if homicide is habitually indulged in, its leads to immorality." De Forest believed officers were not exempt from this phenomenon. "It is wonderful how profane an army is," he wrote. "Officers who are members of the church, officers who once would not even play a game of cards, have learned to rip out oaths when the drill goes badly, or when the discipline 'gets out of kilter.'"[47] The Fifteenth Iowa's Cyrus Boyd summed it up: "War is *hell* broke *loose* and benumbs all the tender feelings in men and makes of them *brutes*."[48]

Most of the evidence the soldiers left behind indicates that De Forest and Boyd were right in some ways and wrong in others. A great many soldiers were indeed becoming more wicked, but not necessarily for the reason De Forest believed. It was not exposure to combat, per se, that debauched men, but rather the temptations that came when a young man left, often for the first time, the restraining influences of home and community. For many a young soldier, the opportunity to seek imagined pleasures and practice forbidden vices in the relative anonymity of distant places, large groups, and uniform clothing was more than he cared to resist. "Vice grows" in an army camp "like plants in a hot bed," wrote Southern preacher William W. Bennett, "and yields abundant and bitter fruits.... The temptation to recklessness is strong among all soldiers. Religion is supposed to be well suited to the pursuits of peaceful life, but not to rough uncertain army life."[49] On top of that, many an adolescent wrongly supposed that such vices as cursing, drinking, gambling, and wenching might make him appear more manly and tough; and manliness—whether to face the fire of the enemy or merely to hold his own among the male society of army life—was something about which a young soldier might well be insecure. "The roving, uncertain life of a soldier has a tendency to harden and demoralize most men," wrote John Beatty. "The restraints of home, family, and society are not felt."[50]

For many, this led to a loosening of sexual morals. Capt. Charles B. Haydon of Michigan claimed that there were three types of people in Washington, D.C.—soldiers, politicians, and prostitutes—the latter two being "about equal in numbers, honesty & morality." The prevalence of prostitution brought its usual results, and venereal disease flourished. "A comrade said to me there yesterday," wrote Haydon, "that he used to dote a great deal on some day marrying a virtuous wife but had concluded that if he could find one who hadn't got the _____ [*sic*] he would not look any farther."[51] Haydon inserted the blank at that point to indicate what he called "the clap"—venereal disease. Union medical records for the war indicated that slightly more than 8 percent of Federal soldiers suffered from sexually transmitted diseases.[52]

The national capital had not cornered the market on debauched classes (except perhaps the politicians). Lucius W. Barber wrote in 1862 that although his regiment, the Fifteenth Illinois, enjoyed its encampment near Memphis, Tennessee, moving away from the city was a good thing for the troops. "Too many of the boys were becoming too dissipated to attend to their ordinary duties," Barber explained. "So foul had the pestilential breath of the city become that decent ladies were not seen on the streets. The city itself was beautiful but it harbored more vice and was more steeped in degradation and filth than any city I had yet seen, but we will draw a veil over this scene."[53] Other cities, North and South, suffered similar evil ferment if the armies remained long near them.[54] Cyrus Boyd wrote in his diary that same year, "Corinth [Mississippi] is full of 'fast womin' who have come in within a few days and are demoralizing many of the men and with the help of bad whiskey will lay many of them out."[55]

Another way in which war and life in the army were corrosive to good morals was that they seemed to blur previously clear-cut moral boundaries. Back in their hometowns, as historian Mark Grimsley points out, few of the men who had become Civil War soldiers "would have dismantled houses, stolen fence rails, or coerced meals from unwilling hosts."[56] But what if the people around them were enemies, possibly deserving of punishment? Or suppose the soldier's needs, in the service of his country, were extreme. In fact, for one justification or another, Civil War soldiers, Union and Confederate, generally resorted to dismantling houses if they needed building materials to make a bridge or huts to shelter themselves from winter weather. They burned fence rails when they wanted dry, seasoned firewood, and they took or demanded food whenever they thought they could get away with it. There might truly be a moral difference between foraging off the enemy and mere plundering and freebooting, but they looked disturbingly similar, and the practice could dull a man's conscience with regard to other matters as well.

Sometimes consciences seemed to require but little loosening before becoming almost completely flaccid. When soldiers of the Fifteenth Illinois arrived in St. Louis on August 14, 1861, they had missed the previous two meals. "As they were passing along market St.," recalled Lucius Barber, "and noticed its richly laden viands, etc., they pitched in and helped themselves, much to the indignation of the proprietors."[57] Elliott McKeever of the Ninth Ohio Cavalry later admitted that when he enlisted he had thought "that a part of soldier life was to take about everything one could."[58] Ohioan Lyman D. Ames observed Union soldiers "drinking and swearing and tearing about to the great annoyance of most of the people" in an occupied Southern town and lamented, "O! what a school is war. It is the field of Satan."[59] Similarly, Union surgeon H. H. Penniman wrote to his wife from camp, "The army is a school of bad morals; about nine-tenths of the troops, entering the army irreligious, become worse and worse."[60]

Alcohol was another item that dismayed Christians saw as debauching their fellow soldiers. Even non-Christian Charles Haydon was disturbed at what he saw. "In many of our men who are fine fellows now," he wrote, "I can see the exact pictures of worthless drunkards five years hence. They are so surely on the road that nothing will stop them."[61] Confederate Philip D. Stephenson remembered that the first Christmas of the war "was unhappily the most noted illustration of camp dissipation. On that occasion, everyone got beastly drunk—officers and men, the whole army indeed, as far as I can remember!" With some exaggeration, Stephenson claimed that he and his brother "were about the only sober men in the regiment and spent our time carrying men to their tents." Looking back on those times years later, Stephenson believed that the encampment that first winter of the war was "the most wicked, drunken and disorderly of my whole army experience."[62]

Similarly, Alfred Fielder wrote in his diary on that same twenty-fifth of December, "The cause of sobriety, virtue, and piety have comparatively few advocates in the army but as for myself though it may be unpopular I am determined by Gods grace to advocate them all and remonstrate with those who say and act differantly. There was quite a number drunk in the encampment and this evening I have heard of several fights and one man in a drunken quarrel cut the throat of an other." Fielder himself "staid close about" his own quarters, went to bed at his usual early hour, and "felt to thank God for his sustaining grace and goodness towards my self."[63]

A man's observations of dissipation in the army depended much on his particular unit, for practices varied widely throughout both armies. Most members of James Iredell Hall's company of North Carolinians took an abstinence pledge early in the war and kept it so faithfully that later in the war official issues of whiskey (for medicinal purposes) were poured out on the ground.[64] Clearly, the armies were not mere conglomerations of sots, although the presence of a large sprinkling of those who gave way to the temptations of dissipation proved alarming to many of their comrades.

Moral problems were widespread enough to provoke extensive comment. Allen Geer noted gambling binges and drunken riots in the Twentieth Illinois during the summer of 1861, and Charles B. Haydon recorded similar activities in his Michigan regiment, along with the unsuccessful efforts of some of the officers to rid the camp of "lewd women." He added, "We are beginning to lose all recollection of Sunday."[65]

Cyrus Boyd summed up many different aspects of army life's corrosive moral effect in a lament written in his diary one Sunday in March 1862. "There is Sunday in the almanac," Boyd wrote, "but in military affairs there seems to be no sacred day. All is work. The men are playing cards swearing and dancing just as on other days." Boyd could put up with such behavior by his comrades on weekdays, but on Sunday, the day above all others set aside as holy, the presence of such shameless wickedness all around him seemed unbearable. He was also appalled at the change for the worse in the moral practices of some whom he had previously known in civilian life. "Men that four months ago would not use a profane word can now outswear many others," Boyd wrote, "and those who would even shun a checker board now play cards for profit." Perceptively, he added, "The descent looks gradual from the top but how fast they seem to go as everything seems to hurry on the downward grade. If the war should last a year or two how degraded some of these men will become. How eager they seem to abandon all their early teachings and to catch up with everything which tends to debase."[66]

As men gave in to various temptations and engaged in practices they had been taught were displeasing to God, the next step was for those same men to deny the existence of God altogether or at least to deny that He took any interest in the affairs of man. In March 1862, Fielder wrote, "I find there is more infidelity in the army than I had immagened. Many of the officers and men deny the special providince of God or that prayers will avail in temporal affairs." These same irreligious men scoffed at "the idea that we ought to humble ourselves before God." Fielder was dismayed but unshaken in his faith. "Notwithstanding men in high position hold such opinions," he concluded, "I for one am still determined to put my trust in God and make my prayers daily unto him through the merits of Christs death."[67]

Obviously, there were many in the armies who succumbed more or less entirely to the novel temptations of soldier life. There were others, like Fielder, who at least tried to fight them. "I feel for one I ought to live a far different life from what I do," wrote John Henry Jenks of the Fourteenth New Hampshire. "I make resolutions that I will, but how frail I am, how soon do I forget them. It is hard to live a christian life when at home, under the influence of a christian wife and family, under the preached gospel, and surrounded by many christian friends, but oh how much harder in the army away from all these influences, but," he concluded, "I pray God I may be kept from sin."[68] His fellow New Englander Elisha Hunt Rhodes of the Second Rhode Island, reflecting in March 1862 on his first ten months of military service, wrote, "I feel to thank God that he has kept me within his fold while so many have gone astray, and trust that he will give me Grace to continue to serve Him and my country faithfully."[69] Most impressive, perhaps, was the Ninth Tennessee's Bob Gibbs. During the first winter of the war, his commander came upon Gibbs in the quarters holding evening prayers with members of his mess, all of whom were older than he and none of whom professed to be Christians. Gibbs's officers were so impressed they made him color-bearer.[70]

Army hospitals were places particularly likely to yield large numbers of soldiers who were taking religion seriously. "Hundreds are here on beds of suffering," wrote missionary J. C. Clopton from a Confederate army hospital in Charlottesville, Virginia, "and consequently disposed to consider things that make for their peace." The sick soldiers listened attentively to the Christian message and eagerly read the Bibles and tracts Clopton gave them. In another hospital, this one in Lynchburg, Rev. George Pearcy spoke with a suffering young soldier who "told me that at home he was a steady, sober man, never swore; but that becoming a soldier, he did as many others did—threw off restraint, and did wickedly." The young man now realized how wrong all that had been. "I have done swearing, and will seek the salvation of my soul," he told Pearcy. Colporteur M. D. Anderson worked in Confederate army camps and hospitals near Fredericksburg. "Much of my time," he related, "has been spent with the sick in the hospitals." There he had an experience like Pearcy's in Lynchburg. A soldier told him "that at home he had been a prominent member of the Church; but that since he had been to camp he had wandered off and brought reproach upon his profession [i.e., Christianity], but that this sickness, from which he was then suffering, had been blessed to his soul, and that he should, with divine help, live a new life and consecrate himself to the cause of God."[71]

Outside the hospitals, missionaries and Christian Commission delegates found somewhat less enthusiastic receptions—at first. The experience of combat, however, actually tended to incline most soldiers toward religion rather than away from it, as John William De Forrest had mistakenly supposed. Whitfield Stevens of the Eighth Georgia was deeply moved after the first battle of Bull Run, or Manassas, as his side would come to call it. His regiment had been all but cut to pieces there, losing almost half its strength in half an hour. Stevens, who had been raised by pious Methodist parents, had been living of late as if there were no God. Impressed that God had spared his life amid the horrible scenes of the battle, Stevens was filled with gratitude. That evening, he found a bit of relative solitude in the woods, knelt there, and prayed, seeking and finding reconciliation with God.[72]

In like manner, the following spring Alfred Fielder experienced his first major battle at Shiloh. At the close of the first day's bloody fighting, only a handful of men remained in his company, and one of them suggested that Fielder, a known Christian, read from the Bible and lead them in a hymn. Fielder read the Seventy-first Psalm, which begins with the verses:

In thee, O Lord, do I put my trust;
  Let me never be put to confusion.
Deliver me in thy righteousness, and cause me to escape:
  Incline thine ear unto me, and save me.
Be thou my strong habitation, whereunto I may continually resort:
  Thou hast given commandment to save me;
  For thou art my rock and my fortress.

The reading of the psalm concluded, Fielder led the company in singing a Charles Wesley hymn commonly called "Safety," the first verse of which seemed especially appropriate:

> God of my life, whose gracious power
> Through varied deaths my soul hath led,
> Or turned aside the fatal hour,
> Or lifted up my sinking head.

The battle was renewed next day, and again Fielder survived without a scratch. Reflecting on the dangers through which he had passed unharmed, he wrote, "My soul appeared to be almost melted within me in thankfulness to God for his preserving Care." And though already devout, he added, "I intend to be a better man."[73]

The battle of Shiloh had a powerful effect on other soldiers as well. A Christian in the Thirty-eighth Tennessee wrote after the battle that he had "continually raised my heart to him, in prayer, and in the thickest of the fight, I envoked His protection." The soldier's deliverance from harm in the battle moved him to seek God even more earnestly than he had before. To his wife he wrote, "I have struggled and prayed to God until I am altogether another person. . . . Oh, I feel as I have not felt in years."[74]

Heavy fighting began in the eastern theater of the war later that spring and continued into the summer. There, too, it had an effect on the soldiers' religious state of mind. In midsummer a Baptist missionary to the Army of Northern Virginia reported, "Since the battle of Seven Pines, I have conversed with probably five hundred who, having passed through the recent bloody scenes, have told me with different degrees of emphasis that they had resolved to lead a better life." Another minister wrote of the heavy fighting, "I do believe that these solemn visitations of Providence have been His chosen way of touching many a heart. There are earnest desires awakened in many a bosom, which I trust will lead them to the Cross." "Strange as it may appear to some," wrote a Confederate chaplain, "scores of men are converted immediately after great battles. This has become so common that I as confidently look for the arrival of such patients as I do for the wounded."[75]

The same chaplain explained why this was: "Before they went into battle they had been serious and thoughtful. Here God covered their heads, and their preservation was a manifestation of his power and goodness that humbled their souls." Another minister put it this way:

> There is something irresistible in the appeal which the Almighty makes when he strikes from your side, in the twinkling of an eye, your friend and comrade. . . . [A]nd when, at the termination of the conflict, he finds himself exempted from the awful fiat that has brought death to his very side, and all around him, his gratitude to his Creator is alloyed, though it may be but dimly, with a holier emotion, which for the time renders him a wiser and a better man. In this respect, the recent battles have done more to make religious converts than all the homilies and exhortations ever uttered from the pulpit. A man who has stood upon the threshold of eternity, while in the din and carnage of a fight, has listened to eloquences more fiery than ever came from mortal lips."[76]

The soldiers themselves also gave explanations for turning to God after great battles: "What cause for gratitude to God that I was not cut down when my comrades fell at my side"; "But for God I would have been slain"; "I do not see how I escaped; I know that I am under renewed obligations to love him, and am resolved to serve him"; "God preached to us as all the preachers on earth could not do"; "After the battle at Malvern Hill, I was enabled to give my soul to Christ—this war has made me a believer in religion, sir."[77]

Reuben Allen Pierson expounded the thought more fully. "Our company has been much more fortunate than any other in the regiment," he explained in a letter to a kinsman, and we should all be thankful to him who rules all things according to his own good will and pleasure, for our preservation through so many dangers. I have often thought of the prayers and petitions rendered up in our behalf by fond and loving Christian friends at home. This may seem strange notions for a soldier to be indulging in surrounded by wickedness on every side, but yet the heart that can remain unmoved and stubborn after passing through as many dangers & making so many miraculous escapes must truly be made of adamantine. When others fall around on the right and left and are momentarily hurried into eternity the question naturally arises what protects me from a similar fate, the only answer being one Who gives life and Who alone can take it away.[78]

The same trend was occurring among Union as well as Confederate soldiers. The heavy fighting of 1862 coincided with a growing religious awakening in both armies. Jasper Laughlin of the Seventy-eighth Ohio had long been a devout Presbyterian. Nevertheless, he was moved to tell his chaplain, Thomas M. Stevenson, "I never before felt the importance of religion as I do here. Cut off from home and the public means of grace, I feel the necessity of leaning exclusively on the Savior, and committing myself entirely to a kind and good Providence."[79]

Other Union soldiers, like their Confederate counterparts, were quick to see God's hand in their protection from harm in battle and were sobered by the presence of death. When a soldier of the 145th Pennsylvania died in an army hospital, one who stood by was moved to record, "The fact that I must die became to me living and real."[80] Pvt. Moses A. Parker of the Third Vermont felt gratitude to God for preserving his life in battle. "It was pretty close dogging for me to have a shell pass between my arm and side," he wrote, "and I think none but a Divine hand directed it."[81] William H. Walling expressed a similar sentiment in a letter to his sister. "Many of our braves fell by the 'destruction that wasteth at noonday,'" Walling wrote, quoting the Ninety-first Psalm, a passage on God's protection. "I can but rejoice that I came out of the fights (three in all) without a scratch," he continued. "He who numbers the very hairs of our head and notes even the fall of the sparrow shielded me in the hour when bullets rained like hail around me."[82] "God is good," wrote Peter Welsh of the Twenty-eighth Massachusetts, "He brought me safe out of this last battle."[83]

This gratitude produced similar results among Union soldiers as it did among Confederates. At the time of his enlistment, Union soldier Frederick Pettit had been impressed with the ungodliness of the army, writing of war that "It makes men wicked" and noting, "I dread to see the day when this army goes home. Religion will be driven from the country." Now, however, he found it "as easy to serve God here as at home. . . . Disappointment, danger, and temptation," he explained, "seem to drive me nearer the cross."[84] Likewise, a private in the Twenty-fifth Massachusetts wrote of his feelings in battle: "I felt the need of religion then if I ever did."[85] Col. John Beatty noted on the eve of an anticipated battle, "Theological questions, which before had attracted little or no attention, now came uppermost in our minds."[86]

The horrors of war turned men's hearts toward God not only in gratitude for His protection in battle or in pursuit of His help in facing hardships, but also because soldiers were impressed with the peace and happiness of dying Christians among their fellow soldiers. In Columbus, Mississippi, the chaplain of the Thirty-seventh Alabama wrote that summer that "many of those who have died were happy and triumphant."[87] Henry Fogg was mortally wounded at the battle of Mill Springs and suffered greatly before he died several days later. "Until four hours before his death," wrote an eyewitness, "between the paroxysms of pain he would sing hymns and seemed patient and resigned to the last."[88] A soldier dying in Virginia in the summer of 1862 told an attending chaplain, "Thank God that by his grace I am a Christian. Oh, what would I do now if I was not a Christian! I know that my Redeemer liveth. I feel that his finished work has saved me. And, chaplain, thank God for giving me dying grace. He has made my bed feel 'soft as downy pillows are.' Thank him for the promised home in glory. I'll soon be there—there, where there is no more war, nor sorrow, nor desolation, nor death—where I'll see Jesus and be forever with the Lord." The mention of "downy pillows" was in reference to a gospel song, popular at that time, that began, "Jesus can make a dying bed soft as downy pillows are."[89]

One dying soldier in the summer of 1862 sang hymns while his strength lasted. Asked if he had any final messages for his family, he requested, between gasps, that those standing by tell his father "that Christ is now all my hope, all my trust, and that he is precious to my soul. Tell him that I am not afraid to die—all is calm." He asked the chaplain to read a hymn, and the minister read "Nearer, My God, to Thee." Repeatedly during the reading, the soldier gasped, "Oh, Lord Jesus, thou art coming near to me." On another occasion when a Christian soldier died in an army hospital in the summer of 1862, obviously happy and without fear, a number of those present were deeply impressed. One remarked, "I never prayed until last night; but when I saw that man die so happy, I determined to seek religion too!"[90]

How could these believing soldiers express such peace and even triumph in their dying moments? Naturally, all of them were subsequently unavailable for comment. The only ones who could leave written records were those who recovered. A Christian soldier badly wounded at the battle of Gains's Mill believed he was dying and later described his feelings at the time. "Immediately there came over my soul such a burst of the glories of heaven, such a foretaste of its joys as I have never before experienced. It was rapturous and ecstatic beyond expression. The new Jerusalem seemed to rise up before me in all its beauty and attractiveness. I could almost hear the songs of the angels. My all-absorbing thought, however, was about the Divine Redeemer, whose arms were stretched out to receive me. So completely overwhelming and exclusive was the thought of heaven, that I was wholly unconscious of any tie that bound me to the earth."[91]

As an increased interest in and awareness of religious matters grew among the soldiers, so too did interest in public worship. Although during the first year of the war religious services had taken place with a fair degree of regularity, if not quite that which prevailed in civilian life, their frequency increased during 1862. Several regiments built special places for religious worship, though usually not enclosed, all-weather facilities. The Twenty-third New York, along with the other regiments of its brigade, set up "stands and seats . . . for church exercises" in a pleasant grove near their camp.[92] Some of the soldiers of the Union's celebrated Iron Brigade built "a shelter of poles covered with pine boughs," where their chaplains held meetings every Tuesday, Friday, and Sunday evening that summer when other duties permitted.[93] The chaplain of the Thirty-seventh Alabama held a "protracted meeting" and, at the end of the first week of nightly services, could report nineteen conversions within the regiment.[94] In the Twelfth Tennessee, nightly meetings continued through August and September 1862, even as the regiment took part in Braxton Bragg's march into Kentucky. A typical entry for this period in Alfred Fielder's diary notes the occupation of Barboursville, Kentucky, in the morning and adds, "Our Chaplin preached at night." Fielder considered the attendance and response to the meetings very good.[95] Similarly, during the same period and in the same theater of the war, Union soldier Julius Birney Work, of the Fifty-second Ohio, attended frequent services and heard preaching by his own regiment's chaplain, as well as those of the 105th Illinois and Seventy-ninth Ohio.[96]

In August 1862, Melvin Dwinell of the Eighth Georgia in Robert E. Lee's Army of Northern Virginia wrote, "There has been a very decided change in the religious tone of the army, going on during the past six months. There has been no great public demonstration in the way of revival meetings, or any thing or that sort. Yet a quiet but deep work has evidently been going on in the hearts of large numbers" of the Confederate soldiers. "Prayer meetings are now held, in many of the Regiments, every night, and they are much better attended than formerly." Dwinell believed that the countenance and general demeanor of the soldiers indicated a pious state of mind. The soldiers, he believed, felt gratitude to God "for his gracious mercy shown in preserving their lives from the ravages of disease, and the awful conflicts of the bloody field." The men were reading their Bibles more now—those who had them—and they were using a great deal less profanity. "May the good work go on," Dwinell concluded, "until not only profanity, but all other immoralities shall cease in the Confederate army, and having enlisted under the banner of Christ, every man feel a calm and holy reliance in the protection of Providence, and be willing to live or die as an all wise and just God shall determine."[97]

The good work was going on simultaneously throughout the army, and, to a greater or lesser degree, in most of the other armies. Hymn singing could be heard in many of the camps even on weekdays, and nightly prayer meetings became common. That same summer, Rev. J. M. Stokes, a chaplain in Wright's Georgia brigade, wrote, "I believe sincerely that there is less profanity in a week, now, than there was in a day, six months ago. And I am quite sure there are ten who attend religious exercises now to one who attended six months ago." He knew this was true in his own regiment, and he had heard reports that the same conditions prevailed elsewhere.[98] Another Georgian, Pvt. Sam Brewer of the Eighth Georgia, wrote to his wife about the difference he had noticed in a comrade. "You never saw such a change in a boy as there is in Bob [Harben]," Brewer wrote. "He is very sober and has become a professor of religion [i.e., one who professes to have saving faith in Jesus Christ]. I heard him pray in public last night at prayer meeting."[99]

The upsurge in religious interest in the armies by no means eradicated the presence of vice and dissipation in the camps. "I know there are dreadful exhibitions of deliberate wickedness," wrote a missionary to the Confederate armies, "but Satan ever delights in placing his abominations in the porch of God's temple."[100] The new religious interest did, however, create a more than counterbalancing influence to the sin that abounded in the armies.

In October 1862, James M. Simpson of the Thirteenth Alabama wrote to his mother from Winchester, Virginia, and spoke of the horrors of war, with its terrible loss of life. "How many brave and noble men are hurried into eternity. How much more need has a soldier have for Christianity for he knows not what hour or minute he may meet his God and there is no place where you can find more depravity & wickedness than here, all around me are men gambling, swearing & fighting and it does seem to me that our Regt. is more so than ever." Largely deprived of the opportunity to take part in public worship, as he had in time past, Simpson found particular comfort in the Eighty-fourth Psalm. "I find many beautiful passages addressed to those depressed in spirits and they never fail to make me feel happy and my heart invariably exclaims, 'How amiable are thy tabernacles O Lord God of hosts' and every day that I live I see that passage verified that says 'Blessed is the man who trusteth in Thee, O God.'" He related the difficulties he faced in publicly professing his faith in the midst of unbelievers. "When put in rooms with strangers I would often find myself revolving in my mind whether to attend to my daily devotions, reading [the Bible] and saying my prayers. Often they would be cursing and drinking around me but thank God I . . . resisted the inclination not to acknowledge my Saviour before men, and each time I felt a renewal of strength, and then I remembered the passage where our Saviour says, 'If any man be ashamed of me before men of him will I be ashamed before my father in heaven.'"[101]

11

"A GREAT REVOLUTION HAS BEEN WROUGHT"
Religion in the Camp and on the Battlefield, 1862–1863

"Last night," wrote Lt. Chesley Mosman of the Fifty-ninth Illinois, "we heard one preacher preaching in the Rebels lines and another preaching in our lines."[1] The date was September 29, 1863, and the Union Army of the Cumberland had only nine days before it fought one of the war's bloodiest battles with the Confederate Army of Tennessee. Now the two armies faced each other in their entrenched lines just outside the town of Chattanooga. The Union army was experiencing a continued, intense interest in religion. The shocking thing for Mosman and his fellow blue-coat soldiers was to realize that their gray-coat foes in the opposite lines were enjoying a similar revival of religion.

One striking feature of the soldiers' religious experience was the stark reality of encountering the enemy's religion. The religion of one's enemy was shocking when it differed from one's own. Americans of the Civil War generation sometimes found an even greater shock in discovering ways in which their enemies' religion was just like their own. Either way, the encounter was usually disturbing and thought-provoking. Such encounters began almost as soon as Union soldiers began coming into contact with Confederate civilians at the outset of the war. They were especially numerous in the middle portion of the war, which brought large Union armies deep into the heartland of the South.

Ira Blanchard and his fellow soldiers of the Twentieth Illinois had no difficulty with such matters during the time their regiment spent in Vicksburg in the late summer of 1863. Blanchard and other soldiers attended the Methodist church, "which was some times presided over by our Army Chaplain, and some times by their regular pastor, a southern man." Blanchard and other Union soldiers even joined the choir and had quite a good time.[2] Perhaps by this time, after the fall of Vicksburg to a six-week Union siege, the city's inhabitants were suitably chastened, though one might as readily expect them to have been embittered. Then again, during that same month, August 1863, the officers of the Second Rhode Island attended the civilian church in the town of Warrenton, Virginia, apparently without incident.[3] In December of that year, soldiers of the Union Thirteenth Corps worshipped with the Methodist church in Brashear City, Louisiana, and when they prepared to depart for other fields of service, they took up a collection for the local minister, both "for his services and for the use of the house. The amount taken was over thirteen dollars"—an amount equal to a Union soldier's monthly pay.[4] Clearly, sometimes Northern and Southern Christians could worship together in harmony.

Such experiences were a sharp contrast to what Blanchard and his fellow members of the Twentieth Illinois had experienced the previous year when stationed in Jackson, Tennessee. "We attended the Methodist Church," Blanchard wrote, "the soldiers occupying two thirds of the seats." The local churchgoers seemed quite surprised by this, apparently assuming that the heathen Yankees would not attend worship. "The ladies would no more come near us than they would a snake," Blanchard continued, "although we were now brushed up and looked quite respectable." The pastor seemed to be quite a talented preacher, but the Union soldiers "soon learned from his tone and manner that he was a rank secesh." Their solution was simply to keep on attending, and finally their very presence, sitting respectfully in the pews, became an unbearable affront to the Southerners. The pastor "skipped the town," and few of his flock continued attending. "We put our own Chaplain in charge," wrote Blanchard, and so carried on worship in what was, for the moment, an otherwise abandoned church building.[5]

In Natchez, Mississippi, local reaction was similar. A townswoman expressed in her diary her disdain for the Union soldiers who attended services at her church. She had to admit that the Union garrison behaved well and had not committed depredations in the area, but she abhorred the thought of worshipping with them. "The Yankees come to our church in crowds and are by degrees filling the pews up with their hateful blue coats," she wrote. "I cannot bear to be nearer than three or four pews. They are such dirty creatures."[6] It was, of course, not the Union soldiers' hygiene that bothered her, but rather their allegiance.

Sometimes the religious features of the conflict seemed difficult to sort out. In September 1863 the Fifty-ninth Illinois was stationed in Chattanooga, Tennessee, and Chesley Mosman and some of the others got permission to attend church in town. In the Methodist church they heard a local preacher pray, "Oh Lord, if thou hast any mercy for the rebels let them have it, I pray thee, but if thou has not I pray thee send them to hell in a minute." Mosman took this to mean that the preacher actually wanted the Confederacy to succeed but most of all wanted the war to end at once. If the Rebels were not going to win, then he hoped they would lose quickly and thus minimize the damage.[7] It is possible, however, that Mosman had the man figured all wrong and that he was in fact a Unionist.

Sometimes differences arising out of the sectional conflict could lead to serious religious problems. In Memphis, Tennessee, a Methodist church was operated with such strong "southern principles," that the Federal authorities in control of the town confiscated the building and turned it into a "Union Church." Northern nurse Emilie Quiner thought, "It looked rather queer to see a church decorated with pictures of Washington and Clay and festooned with flags."[8] It did indeed. Such government intervention in church matters was out of line with both American tradition and the Constitution. Nonetheless, Union authorities in the occupied South were reluctant to allow a hostile church to go on fomenting rebellion in their very midst. In nearby La Grange, Tennessee, Federal authorities in a similar case forbade Rev. John Waddel to conduct services, and the Union provost marshal denounced him in a letter: "You have hitherto used all the means in your power to aid this wicked Rebellion. . . . Instead of being an Humble follower of our Saviour . . . You have stirred up Dissension . . . and urged Vile Treason toward the best Government that God ever created on Earth."[9] Like others in the occupied South, it was a difficult case.

Often, members of the opposing sides were contemptuous of each other's religion. When the Second Rhode Island returned to its old camps after the Bristow Station campaign, it found that the Confederates had taken possession of that spot in the interim. "Since we were here the 2nd and 11th Mississippi Regiments have occupied our quarters, and they made things look bad," wrote Elisha Hunt Rhodes. "They burned up the seats we used for church gatherings and destroyed all of our boards."[10] A worship area, even a rough, outdoor one, could hardly be mistaken for anything else. Despite the fact that the Southerners were experiencing a lively spiritual awakening in their own camps, they were contemptuous enough of the Yankees' religion to vandalize their place of worship.

At Camp Chase, a prisoner of war camp in Ohio, the Union commandant was a Colonel Moody. Moody was a Methodist preacher from that state and made an earnest effort to minister to the prisoners in his charge. He "brought us bundles of little tracts," recalled one of the Rebel prisoners, "which were sometimes rejected and sometimes received with ill-concealed disdain." Moody "prayed over the sick in the prison hospital till great tears rolled down his cheeks." The prisoners treated him with "very scant civility," but "he seemed to be unaware of the daily insults which were offered him." The Rebel prisoner put that down to what he deemed Moody's "ignorance of good breeding."[11] For some Confederates, at least, some things were more important than a supposedly mutually shared religion.

Another new experience for the soldiers—at least the Northern ones—was their encounter with the religious practices of the black slaves. "I attended today a church of coloured people," wrote Melvin Clark of the 101st Pennsylvania in March 1863. "Their meetings are very interesting so I think at least."[12] The most immediately noticeable characteristic of black worship, in contrast to that of white Southerners and even more so to that of white Northerners, was the high level of emotion in their services. Many Union soldiers found this to be inappropriate and very disturbing. Jabez Alvord of Connecticut called the blacks' prayer meetings "howlings," and another Union soldier wrote of the blacks at worship with the remark, "Sum of them fell Down an hollard as loud as they cold ball."[13]

Others, like Capt. Ralph Ely of the Eighth Michigan, found the displays of emotion entertaining. "Attended a Negro Shout in the evening," he wrote, "which was new and novel to me." Of another slave religious meeting he attended, Ely wrote that he was "very much amused with their singing and manner of Worship, etc."[14]

Ira Blanchard and his friends of the Twentieth Illinois attended a black service that met on Sunday afternoons in the basement of the Vicksburg church building the Union soldiers had unintentionally taken over from its white Southern occupants. Blanchard confessed that his main reason for going was curiosity, and he was amused to see slaves "who had toiled all the week with bare head and back in the cotton fields" coming to church in fine clothes. The novelty of the service, however, turned out to be more than he and his friends had bargained for. "At the opening hymn we almost thought we were caught up into the third heavens," he wrote, "such a swell of melody came from a hundred voices as they chanted,"

> Bredren dear dont get a weary
> Bredren dear dont get a weary
> Bredren dear dont get a weary
> Your work be almost done.

After that, the slaves sang, "I'm gone away to glory hallaluyah," which Blanchard thought "still more inspiring." Before it was over, a number of the slave women were on their feet, clapping their hands and shouting "glora," as Blanchard spelled it, and, he added, "one more earnest than the rest would jump up full two feet from the floor every time they came to the 'hallaluyah.'" The Northerners did not know quite what to think of all this. "Thus the racket was kept up for half an hour," Blanchard concluded, "singing, shouting, jumping and clapping of hands." A white Southerner was present to try to lead the meeting, but he could not get in more than a few words at a time before pandemonium would break loose again.[15]

Some were inclined to be favorably impressed with the blacks' manner of worship. Edwin W. Keen of the Third Rhode Island Heavy Artillery wrote to his uncle from Union-held Hilton Head, South Carolina,

"The darkies out here know how to have good meetings. I went the other night to one." There Keen heard the quaint but touching prayer of a black preacher for the Union troops that had recently arrived in their district. The old man "pray[ed] for their new masters that came from a foreign clime and wanted them to get religion for said he how do you know but this night will be the last day you will ever see."[16] Some Northern soldiers especially noticed the warmth and sincerity of the slaves' worship. A Massachusetts chaplain who was inclined to be disdainful of the unlearned sermons of black preachers nonetheless had to admit that they were "honest and in earnest in their devotions." Union soldier Alva Griest wrote that he had heard "an able sermon by a negro, which although in crude language was deeply felt by all and I firmly believe he was more sincere in his preaching than our Chaplain often is, for his words seemed to go right to the heart." In general, the more a Northern soldier was inclined toward abolitionism, the more likely he was to take at least a partially favorable view of the slaves' worship.[17] This was true for more than just the obvious reason. Abolitionism tended to be particularly strong among evangelical Christians in the North, whereas the more staid, upper-class churches, with their self-consciously intellectual clergy and formalized worship style, would be naturally hostile both to abolitionism and to the spontaneous sort of worship found among the slaves.

The religious message that Northern whites delivered to the slaves and erstwhile slaves was one of patience and hopeful anticipation. During the summer of 1862, the chaplain of the Twentieth Illinois began preaching to large crowds of blacks who flocked to the regiment's camp on Sundays. "He always exhorted them to remain quietly at home and obey their masters and see what the hand of the Lord would do for them by way of their deliverance from slavery," recalled Ira Blanchard, but the slaves continued to take matters into their own hands, regardless of risk. "They constantly crowded our camps," wrote Blanchard, "always desiring to go along with the Yankees."[18]

Meanwhile, as the bloody campaigns of 1862 drew toward a close, religious interest among the soldiers continued to grow. Soldiers' diaries and letters from the period report an increasing number of preaching services and prayer meetings taking place within the camps. Sunday services were held with great regularity in many regiments, the troops meeting in whatever locations were available. The men of the Forty-eighth Pennsylvania gathered around their chaplain in the shade of a large straw stack on the Sunday after the hard-fought battle of Antietam.[19] Chaplain Button of the Twentieth Illinois climbed on a stump or a barrel to preach at frequent evening meetings while the regiment was camped at La Grange, Tennessee, in November 1862. Stumps were platforms of necessity for many other preachers in both armies.[20]

Some soldiers wrote home complaining that they had not been "to church" for a long time, but by this they usually meant that they had not entered a church building. Charles A. McCutchan of the Eleventh Indiana was one such. Writing to a friend back in Vanderburgh County, Indiana, McCutchan complained, "You could not believe how lost I am [with] no chance of going to church at all." His meaning became clear, however, when he immediately added, "I have not been inside of a church for one year."[21] John J. Warbinton of the Fifty-ninth Ohio felt much the same. "It has been so long since I was in a church," he wrote to his aunt in October 1863, then added, "We have no churches in camp; have to set out doors when we go to Preaching."[22]

Religiously inclined soldiers took advantage of every opportunity to worship in established houses of worship, joining in the services of local congregations as James Iredell Hall and some of his friends from the Ninth Tennessee did when passing through Glasgow, Kentucky, during Braxton Bragg's fall 1862 Kentucky campaign.[23] About the same time, Chesley Mosman of the Fifty-ninth Illinois was attending a civilian church in Nashville. "Good sermon," he noted in his diary.[24] Aurelius Voorhis regularly attended a local church in Helena, Arkansas, where his Forty-sixth Indiana was stationed.[25]

Sometimes soldiers more or less commandeered nearby church buildings or at least put empty structures to their intended use. Theodore Skinner of the 112th New York wrote to his parents that the regimental chaplain preached every Sunday afternoon in the church in occupied Suffolk, Virginia. Skinner did not specify whether the congregation in those cases was composed of soldiers, local citizens, or both.[26]

Soldiers were not always permitted to go out of camp to attend worship in nearby churches. With the Eighty-third Ohio bivouacked at Camp Price, Kentucky, in November 1862, Isaac Jackson fretted that he could hear bells ringing at the church in an adjacent village but was not free to attend. "What a pity we have to stay right here in Camp and not allowed to go to church when it is right at hand. It would not take me five minutes to walk there," Jackson wrote, "if I were only allowed to. I tell you, when a man goes in the army he sacrifices a great many privileges that he enjoyed at home."[27] By December 1863, soldiers of the Forty-sixth Indiana, veterans of Grant's victorious Vicksburg army, were not inclined to let such things stand in their way. "There was a meeting in the church tonight," wrote Aurelius Voorhis one Wednesday that month. "The guards that are stationed between here and the church have orders not to pass anyone so we had to go around through the graveyard."[28]

Worshipping on Sunday was traditional. Most of the soldiers had been attending such meetings all their lives. More significant was the fact that increasing numbers of soldiers began gathering to meet at additional times during the week. Berea Willsey wrote in late September 1862 that the new chaplain in his Massachusetts regiment was going to hold prayer meetings at his tent three nights a week. "I went this evening," Willsey wrote one Saturday. "We had a good meeting."[29] Alburtus Dunham of the 129th Illinois wrote to his wife in November 1862 from Bowling Green, Kentucky, "I have attended two prayer meetings last week, and heard a sermon today, and expect to attend another this evening."[30] Alfred Fielder of the Twelfth Tennessee attended Tuesday and Friday evening prayer meetings on a regular basis beginning in January 1863 and continuing right into summer. He also usually attended three services on Sundays during this period. By April, he was up to four prayer meetings a week, besides Sunday services, and he reported them as well attended. For a good part of August, there were nightly preaching services.[31]

By the spring of 1863, a soldier in Kershaw's South Carolina Brigade could write that they were having preaching three times on Sunday and twice during the week.[32] In like manner, Aurelius Voorhis reported nightly meetings. Of one Saturday evening event he wrote, "The young men's prayer meeting was largely attended tonight in the fields in front of our brigade. The interest seems to increase." The next day, Sunday, he wrote of attending three services at the Methodist church. "The house was filled each time an hour before the time of preaching. . . . I think the religious feeling is increasing. Hope it may continue."[33]

Chaplain W. C. Dunlap of the Eighth Georgia noted his regiment's rising interest in spiritual matters, an interest that had been steadily increasing ever since the close of the peninsula campaign in July 1862. "I have held prayer-meetings in my own regiment until ten o'clock many a night," Dunlap wrote, "and, after closing, the brethren would all retire to the woods, frequently accompanied by a half-dozen mourners [those seeking to become Christians], and there, with no other covering save the open canopy of heaven, pour out their souls in humble supplication at the throne of grace, often remaining until after midnight."[34]

Members of the Twenty-seventh North Carolina continued holding prayer meetings in camp even when they had no chaplain to lead them.[35] The case was the same in the Third Alabama, where Capt. Richard H. Powell wrote, "For two months we have held prayer-meetings regularly, when military duties have not prevented, three times a week." Interest was steadily growing, Powell reported, and all of this was "in the absence of a chaplain." The Second Rhode Island had been without a chaplain for several months when Rev. John D. Beugless, formerly pastor of the Pawtuxet Baptist Church, arrived one night in October 1863. He "found many of the men in a grove holding a prayer meeting."[36] The men of the Forty-eighth Georgia had their chaplain with them, but Rev. William Hauser could hardly have been in attendance at all the meetings being held in several different companies on a nightly basis.[37]

The religious awakening had begun to grow among the soldiers in 1862, and clearly it continued unabated into and through the following year. The Sixteenth Mississippi's David Holt remembered, "We had more church services that winter [1863–1864] than we had had during the whole war [up to that time] put together."[38] Large numbers of religious meetings throughout the week indicated something beyond the normal. In the religious terminology of that time, it was a revival.

Increased interest in religion and, on the part of some, devotion to Christ continued to coexist with much open practice of sin on the part of others within the camps of all the armies. This situation of contrasting behaviors was visible in stark relief in late 1862 and early 1863. Chaplain Edward P. Stone of the Sixth Vermont complained to his family of being compelled "to listen to such profanity and obscenity" in the camps, and Lt. Thomas Boatright of the Forty-fourth Virginia wrote, "Wickedness pervades our camp still." Boatright pointed out hopefully that "some of the men in the regiment are deeply concerned on the subject of religion." He also noted that his tent mate, Lieutenant Miller, was for the first time in the war willing to join him in evening devotions in their tent.[39]

Chaplains continued to warn against prevalent vices and no doubt had good reason to do so. Chaplain N. G. Collins of the Fifty-seventh Illinois warned the troops in the summer of 1863, "I believe we have a more fearful enemy to encounter than the rebels of the South, enemies from abroad, or Copperheads at home. . . . Nothing will so soon or certainly corrupt an army or people as the free use of intoxicating drinks." Collins was particularly eager to combat the widely held belief that the consumption of alcohol helped maintain good health. "The idea of drinking for health in the army or at home," he continued, "is moonshine—a mere pretense. The more men drink the sicker they get."[40] But of course, many continued to get drunk just the same. In February 1863, Cyrus Boyd could still write, "Whiskey and sexual vices carry more soldiers off than the bullet."[41] That, at least, was nothing new in the history of warfare.

The chaplains' preaching against sin was not always well received, especially by regimental commanders who were much given to cursing, drunkenness, and other vices. In one Confederate regiment the colonel took the chaplain severely to task for preaching against profanity, accusing him of "having taken advantage of his position to lecture him [the colonel] on swearing." The colonel promised that he would attend no further preaching by that chaplain.[42] Other forms of opposition were also evident. The Fifteenth Iowa's Cyrus Boyd recorded in his diary his indignation at some of his fellow soldiers' scoffing. "This evening there was a *mock prayer meeting* in Co. "K." They sang and prayed in blasphemous mockery. This work ought to be stopped by an officer—but they only *laughed*."[43]

Still, an overall increase in interest in Christianity continued to take place in the armies' camps, right alongside the persistent presence of sin. Chaplains and missionaries eagerly strove to add to the impetus of the revival movement, but they were not its source or even its indispensable channels. Its origins could be traced much more in the soldiers themselves, and even the prolonged absence of a chaplain could not stanch their intense interest in spiritual things. The chaplain of the Third South Carolina was away from the regiment for several weeks in 1863 due to the needs of his family back home, some of whom were sick. The chaplain was popular, "much liked," as soldier J. Miles Pickens recorded, and had the confidence of the Christians in the regiment. Nevertheless, even in his absence there was "quite a revival in the regt." Naturally, that revival was helped along by preaching from visiting missionaries and chaplains from other regiments, but early in the war, such efforts had not been adequate to keep up religious observance in regiments without regular chaplains present. Pickens added, "Still the good work is going on, and I pray it may extend through the whole army."[44]

It did just that. Fellow Third South Carolina soldier Tally N. Simpson wrote that the movement encompassed their entire brigade. "Every morning at 9 o'clock," he wrote in August 1863, "one of the regimental chaplains holds forth in a place convenient for the whole brigade." Visiting missionaries also preached for the men and were well received.[45] By April 1863, the Forty-fourth Virginia had so many new converts that the chaplain set up a special class for them led by Thomas Boatright, who helped those who had recently professed repentance and trust in Christ to become grounded in the faith. In July the regiment held its first baptismal service of the war, at which a number of new converts were immersed in water, publicly symbolizing their identification with Christ in His death, burial, and resurrection. All of that represented a considerable accretion to the numbers of Christians within a single regiment. As Boatright put it, "A great change has been wrought among our regt."[46]

Much the same situation prevailed elsewhere in Lee's army. In October 1862, Presbyterian army missionary Joseph Stiles reported intense seeking after God in Pryor's and Lawton's brigades, and in Early's division as well as Pickett's. Others reported like conditions in most of the army's other units. The chaplain of the army hospital at Farmville, Virginia, reported "a most interesting revival" with many converts, and similar reports came in from Confederate army hospitals in Lynchburg, Charlottesville, and Petersburg and from Richmond's vast Chimborazo hospital. Scores of conversions were reported in almost every brigade and army hospital.[47]

At first, those seeking God's favor had to contend with moderate amounts of scoffing and with "the loud whistling, talking, hallooing, cooking, eating, and constant moving about the camp" of other soldiers not attending the religious meetings. This problem, however, proved short-lived. Soon numerous chaplains and missionaries were writing such reports as, "The most perfect decorum is observed during divine service, and the most perfect respect is manifested for those who serve God." Sometimes from a single place in the camps one could hear several different services in progress in the distance, and many Christian soldiers were reminded of prewar camp meetings. One described affairs in his division as "one great Methodist Camp Meeting—they build log fires, sing, pray and preach, and when they ask for the morners they come in hundreds some falling on the ground crying for mercy."[48]

A typical meeting might begin with a chaplain or missionary and a number of soldiers gathering in some promising place near camp— a grove of trees, perhaps, or a specially prepared arbor. They would begin to sing hymns, and rapidly a large crowd of soldiers would gather. Sometimes a "horn" or a drum would call interested soldiers to worship. Singing followed in any case. Favorite hymns included "How Firm a Foundation" and "Am I a Soldier of the Cross." Once the singing was concluded, the preacher addressed the assembly, taking a text from the Bible and endeavoring to convey its meaning to the listeners fully, clearly, and powerfully. Texts varied widely, as the Bible presents a great deal of material from which to choose. Favorites included "Except ye repent ye shall all likewise perish," "What must I do to be saved?" and "The wages of sin is death, but the gift of God is eternal life through Jesus Christ our Lord." A preacher once described his message to the soldiers, stating, "I pointed them to the blood of Jesus as the only atonement for sin, and to his righteousness as our only ground of acceptance with God the Father." Alfred Fielder wrote after hearing such a sermon out in Tennessee, "The sermon was plain and pointed and I trust will tell for good in eternity."[49]

During the sermon, the soldiers listened with rapt attention in complete silence. The quietness of the congregations was often mentioned by observers. Chaplain William Hauser of the Forty-eighth Georgia called it "a silent yet precious revival of religion." Chaplain F. S. Petway of the Forty-fourth Tennessee wrote of the "marked attention and deep solemnity of the vast crowds to whom we preach." Another minister noted, "They listen with a quiet, deferential respect to the Word." Joseph Stiles described the soldiers as "exhibiting the most solemn and respectful earnestness." And yet another wrote, "Not one word is spoken, not even in the outskirts of the congregation; but every man is looking intently at the minister, catching every word that falls from his lips."[50]

At the close of the sermon, the minister might well give some sort of invitation to those who wished to seek salvation to declare themselves, usually by coming forward to pray, often in a designated area known as "the altar." Alfred Fielder described a service in which the preacher "gave an oppertunity for those who felt convicted for having sined and were inquiring what they must do to be saved to designate it by coming forward."[51] By the fall of 1862, the responses were often amazing even to the preachers, and for the next year they generally increased. "The altar was crowded from day to day with seekers of religion," the Sixtieth Georgia's chaplain Samuel S. Smith wrote of meetings he held during October 1862. Rev. Joseph Stiles wrote of a meeting in which "we had some sixty or seventy men and officers come forward and publicly solicit an interest in our prayers, and there may have been many more who, from the press, could not reach the stand." A Reverend W. H. Browning in the Confederate camps near Chattanooga, Tennessee, in 1863 wrote that he had seen "from sixty to seventy-five penitents at the altar each night" for some five weeks.[52] South Carolinian Samuel C. Clyde, visiting a neighboring Mississippi brigade, once counted about 150 men at the altar.[53]

The number who came forward to pray did not equal the number of conversions. The prevailing religious belief of the time held that a man had to feel complete inward assurance that he truly repented of his sins and genuinely trusted in Christ alone to save him. He had to perceive within himself the Holy Spirit, Third Person of the Trinity, witnessing that God had indeed accepted him for Jesus' sake. Such assurance, and the awareness of such an inward witness, probably would not come at the first bidding. It had to be sought diligently, persistently. Those who were in that process were referred to as "seekers" or "mourners." Those who received the sought-after assurance and inward witness could then publicly profess themselves to have been converted. Thus, observers of the services commonly recorded such notations as, "There was a number of mourners. Several made an open profession of faith in Christ," or, "Quite a number came forward—one made an open profession of his having found peace by believing in Christ."[54]

After a time of prayer with the mourners, and perhaps exuberant testimonies and even shouts of joy from those who were sure that Christ had accepted them, the minister would usually close with a benediction. That did not, however, necessarily mean the end of religious activities for the night. The men might continue praying and singing for some time. Samuel Clyde wrote of the meeting he visited in the Mississippi brigade, "I came away after the benediction, leaving them still singing, shouting & praising God."[55]

A meeting might also include a number of individual soldiers sharing in a few homely words their personal experiences of what God had done for them through Jesus Christ. These might be in addition to a regular preaching service, or the entire time might be given over to what was called "an experience meeting." Recent converts might also be called upon to share their Christian experiences before being baptized. "At about 8 oclk," wrote Alfred Fielder, "the experiances of three young men were heard who were going to be baptised. . . . Immediately after hearing their Christian experiance a number of us repaired a short distance to a stream where our Chaplin baptised them by Immersion." Such occasions were very happy ones for believers. "I can say of a truth," added Fielder, "that I have this day been enabled to rejoyce with that Joy inexpressable and full of glory—This world is not my home but I look by faith to heaven as my home."[56]

Another type of meeting was the prayer meeting. True to its name, it included a great deal of praying on the part of various Christians among the soldiers. It would probably also include the singing of several hymns and possibly a brief devotional message by one of the soldiers or the chaplain, if the latter was present. At the height of the revival, prayer meetings might even include invitations to seek God, just like the more evangelistically oriented preaching service. Fielder, ever the diligent diarist, wrote of one prayer meeting in April 1863, "Had prayer meeting. Several presented themselves (when an opperturnity was given) as desireing an interest in the prayers of the people of God."[57]

During the winter and early spring of 1863, Confederate soldiers stationed in the immediate vicinity of Fredericksburg had the privilege of attending meetings in the church buildings of that town. Rev. J. D. Stiles described the situation there:

We held three meetings a day—a morning and afternoon prayer meeting, and a preaching service at night. . . . Our sanctuary has been crowded—lower floor and gallery. Loud, animated singing always hailed our approach to the house of God; and a closely packed audience of men, amongst whom you might have searched in vain for one white hair, were leaning upon the voice of the preacher, as if God himself had called them together to hear of life and death eternal. At every call for the anxious, the entire altar, the front six sets of the five blocks of pews surrounding the pulpit, and all the spaces thereabouts ever so closely packed, could scarcely accommodate the supplicants.

Forty or fifty conversions took place every week, and Stiles concluded that the building was simply becoming too small for their purposes.[58]

Meetings of one sort or another took place on a weekly basis (often several times a week) in a great many regiments and brigades, whenever the exigencies of weather and the movements of the army did not intervene, from about the middle of 1862 onward for almost the next two years. "Congregations large—interest almost universal," wrote Virginia chaplain G. R. Talley. By the fall of 1863, a chaplains' meeting of the Army of Northern Virginia estimated that approximately 500 conversions were taking place every week.[59]

The revival was not confined to the Army of Northern Virginia. West of the Blue Ridge, in middle Tennessee, Philip Stephenson remembered a large revival in the Army of Tennessee in the spring of 1863. The soldiers erected "a great arbor" under which many of the larger meetings were held, "attended by hundreds of the soldiers, with great earnestness and feeling. Many professed the Savior."[60] Army missionary Rev. S. M. Cherry wrote from the camps of the Army of Tennessee that spring that "revivals are reported in several brigades," though chaplains were "still scarce." One chaplain who was present, Rev. W. T. Bennett of the

Twelfth Tennessee, wrote, "Our regiment is being greatly blessed. We meet from night to night for exhortation, instruction, and prayer. Already there have been upwards of thirty conversions. Most of them have joined the Church. There are yet a large number of inquirers." Chaplain Strick of the Fifty-ninth Tennessee wrote ecstatically, "God is at work among our men. Many are earnestly seeking the pardon of their sins. . . . Our nightly prayer-meetings are well-attended by anxious listeners, and my tent is crowded daily by deeply penitent souls." In Cleburne's division alone, chaplains tallied up some 478 conversions. Two regiments of McCown's division yielded another 140 between them. Reports of revival also came from the small Confederate army in east Tennessee and the forces posted on the coast near Charleston, South Carolina, and Mobile, Alabama. Stationed at the latter city, the Thirty-eighth Alabama had "held nightly meetings almost uninterruptedly, whenever the weather permitted, ever since last October, with large attendance, much interest, and good results." They had "a large arbor with seats." In the spring of 1863 they were transferred to the Army of Tennessee but started up their nightly meetings there. In one meeting, despite the interruption of rain, some thirty soldiers requested prayer that they might soon find salvation in Christ.[61]

The Great Revival, as it came to be called, grew and flourished in nearly all the armies, North and South, East and West. It had no particular birthplace, and though religious awakening might spread from one regiment to another, it is impossible to trace any particular geographic flow or progression in a movement that seemed as spontaneous as the blooming of prairie wildflowers in the spring.

The Thirtieth Wisconsin was still organizing at Camp Randall in Madison, Wisconsin, in the spring of 1863. Nevertheless, there too, revival prevailed. "We have been having some of the most interesting meetings, here in Madison, for three weeks past, that I ever attended in my life," wrote soldier Albert M. Childs. "A great many have been brought from darkness into light, and have been . . . converted to Christ. And many more are still inquiring what they must do to be saved."[62] Meanwhile, in the Forty-sixth Indiana down in Louisiana, a soldier wrote, "There are quite a number in our Regt. that have lately come out on the Lord's side."[63]

Military activity generally interrupted the outward manifestations of revival in the armies. Chaplain Stone of the Sixth Vermont lamented the fact that for several Sundays in a row during times of active campaigning he had been unable to preach at regular Sunday services. "We can do nothing but pray," he told his family.[64] On the march or in battle, the soldiers had little time and less energy for large regular services, though in some cases they did endeavor to hold small, relatively informal prayer meetings at the close of the day's march.

Occasionally they found opportunity for more. After the repulse of Pickett's Charge at Gettysburg on July 3, 1863, the major of the Sixty-fourth New York requested Chaplain John Stuckenberg of the 145th Pennsylvania to hold services in his regiment. "The men were behind their breastworks," Stuckenberg recorded in his diary that night. "I stood in front of them. Brisk skirmishing was going on all the time, rebels and our men . . . could be seen running and firing. A rebel flag was also seen at the edge of the woods. Worship at such a place, at such a time, with fearful scenes just enacted and being enacted, was very solemn. I thanked God that we had been spared, prayed for the many wounded and remembered the relatives and friends of the killed. The soldiers felt deeply and many were moved to tears."[65]

A similar situation occurred in the autumn of 1863 as the Confederate Army of Tennessee maneuvered against its foes in the hills of southeastern Tennessee and northwestern Georgia. "We are preaching and laboring for the spiritual good of the soldiers as much as the situation will allow," wrote Rev. C. W. Miller. "The troops are in line of battle, and we assemble a regiment or two around their camp-fires at night and speak to them the Word of Life. The soldiers receive gladly the truth, and are always anxious to hear preaching." A few weeks later, Rev. J. B. McFerrin wrote from the same army, "The revival in the army progressed up to the time of the Chickamauga fight; and even since, notwithstanding the condition of troops moving to and fro, or engaged in erecting fortifications, the good work in some regiments still goes on."[66]

Military operations brought battles, and battles brought death. In these conflicts, Christian soldiers continued to die with peace and confidence, as others had during the first year of the war. For some who died in the battles of 1863, the confidence with which they faced death was a result of the revivals that year. In a makeshift army hospital in Chattanooga, Tennessee, Jim McCollum of the Thirteenth Illinois lay dying of a wound received in the assault on Missionary Ridge. The regimental chaplain was a good friend of McCollum's and was deeply moved by the young soldier's suffering. At McCollum's request he sang one of the latter's favorite hymns:

> Come sing to me of Heaven,
> When I'm about to die;
> Sing songs of holy ecstasy,
> To wait my soul on high.

The chaplain asked McCollum "if it was well with his soul." "Oh! God is so good," the soldier replied. "He has received me in Christ." He died the next day, "resigned to God's will."[67]

For some, battle meant dying. For others, it meant killing. The fact that the soldiers had grown up on the old King James translation of the Bible became a problem for some. The 1611 translators had rendered the Sixth Commandment, "Thou shalt not kill," instead of the more correct, "You shall not murder." An understanding of the context would have shown soldiers that the Bible frequently affirmed the taking of human life in a just war, but many soldiers lacked such an understanding, and a few of them could not get past what appeared to be a blanket prohibition. At the battle of Chickamauga, Val C. Giles of the Fourth Texas "saw a fellow shooting straight up in the air and praying as lustily as ever one of Cromwell's Roundheads prayed. . . . When Lieutenant Killingsworth remonstrated with him about it," Giles continued, "he paid no attention to him whatever. Captain Joe Billingsley threatened to cut him down with his sword if he didn't shoot at the enemy, for the woods in front were full of them. He retorted to the Captain: 'You can kill me if you want to, but I am not going to appear before my God with the blood of my fellow man on my soul.'" The soldier kept steadfastly to his resolve, "exposed to every volley of the enemy's fire," but never firing back.[68] Most devout soldiers on both sides took quite a different view of matters, as the bloody combats of 1863 demonstrate. More typical was a case described by a soldier of the Twelfth Virginia in the heat of a furious battle in that state: "I heard one fellow praying and firing at the same time. He was a tall tallow-faced boy named John Adkins, of Sussex County, who expected to be killed in every fight, yet never missed one."[69] The general consensus in the Civil War armies was that a good Christian was a good soldier.

Interruptions in religious activities due to active military operations were temporary for those who survived them. Given the opportunity to hold prayer meetings and preaching services, the soldiers who marched back into camp after the campaigns were over quickly resumed their frequent religious activities with the same fervor they had shown before the armies marched off to battle. "Wherever the troops remain long enough in one place," wrote Confederate army missionary J. B. McFerrin, "religious services are observed with great effect."[70] In the Union Army of the Potomac, Elisha Hunt Rhodes noted in his diary that same month, October 1863, that his regiment would be starting up its Sunday school (in this case, Bible study for the soldiers) for the first time "in some weeks as our movements have prevented."[71]

The revivals in the various armies were the sum total of a great many personal revivals in individual soldiers. Aurelius Voorhis of the Forty-sixth Indiana experienced such an awakening in his own life. Like many soldiers, he had enjoyed a Christian upbringing at home. Once in the army, he had experienced many temptations, and, he admitted regretfully in his diary, he had succumbed to some of them. Specifically, he had been guilty of "the use of foolish and obscene language, the playing of foolish games, such as dominoes, checkers, chess and I regret to say sometimes handling the vile cards." However, on the night of Wednesday, October 22, 1862, he heard someone singing an old hymn he had known well in time past. This set him to thinking, and he ended up re-committing himself to God's service. He would quit the questionable practices he had picked up in the army, and he would strive to display a patient, contented, pleasant demeanor to those around him. He wrote it all down in his diary in order "to impress it more forcibly on my mind." "I think by watching close and trusting in the Lord (not in myself)," he added, "I can do better." A week after his resolution, he could write, "[I] think God is helping me."[72]

During the revivals, many soldiers became followers of Christ who had never been such back in civilian life. A badly wounded Confederate soldier testified from his hospital bed that winter, "When I was at home, I was wild and wicked, but since I have been in the army, I have tried to change my life, and since I have been wounded I have been able to trust my soul in the hands of God, and I feel that if he should call me to die, all will be well." A Georgia soldier, dying of his wounds in a Confederate army hospital, similarly told those at his bedside that since entering the army he had trusted in Christ for the salvation of his soul and, as a witness recorded, "with tears of joy, praised God in full hope of heaven."[73]

Confederate soldier Reuben Pierson wrote to inform his father of his newfound faith in Christ. He was not, he assured his father, "a profane or wicked man," but he knew that he still needed divine atonement for his sins. "I have determined to seek Christ who died for sinners."[74] A captain wrote that "between forty and fifty" men had been converted in his company, which must have been very nearly a clean sweep. They were now, he said, "very happy in hope of a blissful and peaceful immortality. Some of the hardest hearts, long-lived and desperate sinners, have been melted under the power of the truth, and, like little children, have come to Jesus."[75]

For many soldiers who participated in the revivals in the army, the effect was not to bring them for the first time to faith in Christ nor to renew those who had fallen away but rather to confirm and strengthen their previous resolve to live a life that was pleasing to God. Chaplain Samuel S. Smith of the Sixtieth Georgia wrote of the meetings in his regiment, "Many souls were renewed and encouraged, [and] several were made happy in the love of God."[76] "I am resolved to live nearer to Christ this year than I did last year," wrote Joseph Whitney to his wife in June 1863.[77] After "a good meeting" in June 1863, Alfred Fielder wrote, "I was enabled to feel that God was still my father and friend and in my soul there was a peace the world can neither give nor take away."[78]

As the revivals progressed in the various armies, the behavior of the soldiers began to change. Reports begin to appear in the spring of 1863 that many of the soldiers were living out some of the practical results of their faith in Christ. In April of that year, Chaplain Stuckenberg noted the change in the 145th New York. "There is little gambling or drunkenness in the regt.," he recorded in his diary, "and profanity has greatly decreased since we entered the field."[79]

A chaplain in Benning's Georgia brigade of the Army of Northern Virginia wrote that same spring, "The moral tone of our brigade is rapidly changing. Card-playing is fast playing out, swearing is not heard so much as formerly, and attendance on preaching increases." Similarly, Rev. William Hauser, chaplain of the Forty-eighth Georgia, recorded, "Swearing, and all other crimes incident to an army, are evidently diminishing, and deep piety is on the increase," and the Twelfth Tennessee's chaplain W. T. Bennett wrote, "The moral tone of the regiment seems rapidly changing for the better." Another Confederate soldier reported, "When we first came into camp, swearing was a common practice; but now, thank God, an oath is seldom heard. Our men seem to feel as if they ought to be more observant of God's law." An Alabama soldier who had gone home on furlough because of severe illness in March 1863 returned that fall to a much changed regiment. Whereas before "you could scarcely meet with any one who did not use God's name in vain," and gambling was rampant, now "I found at least three-fourths of my company not only members of the Church of the living God, but professors of religion [i.e., openly avowed Christians]." It was the same throughout his whole brigade. A soldier from another brigade in the same division made a similar observation about his own unit: "A great revolution has been wrought in the moral tone of the brigade."[80]

Later that summer, Rev. W. H. Browning summed up the situation among the Confederate troops encamped near Chattanooga, who were probably as representative as any. "The most careless observer can but notice the marked change that has taken place in the regiments," Browning wrote. "Instead of oaths, jests and blackguard songs, we now have the songs of Zion, prayers and praises to God. True, there are yet many profane, wicked, and rude, yet the preponderance is decidedly in favor of Christianity. I verily believe that the morals of the army are now far in advance of those of the country. And instead of the army being the school of vice, as was once supposed, and really was, it is now the place where God is adored, and where many learn to revere the name of Jesus."[81]

As Browning pointed out, the moral changes in the overall tone of the armies would never be absolute. Some soldiers would be halfhearted about their professed conversions, and others, at least a large minority, would not convert at all. What one thought of the morals of the Civil War armies during and after the Great Revival depended on the particular part of those armies one observed. Numerous soldiers testified of continuing evil in their regiments, including gambling, sexual immorality, and rampant theft.[82] Still, the chaplains and missionaries, those who considered it their business to observe the morals of the soldiers as a whole, were often convinced that the situation was improving as the war went on.[83]

Even as religious awakening suffused the various armies of both sides, soldiers read frequently in letters from their families and friends that revivals were breaking out in their home counties. Aurelius Voorhis learned in a letter from his sixteen-year-old brother Albinus that a revival was in progress back home in Cass County, Indiana, and that Albinus and their sister Percina were among the fifty new converts. "They have had a glorious meeting," Aurelius wrote in his diary. "That is good news; all the young folks and some of the aged has started in the good cause. I hope they will prove faithful Christians."[84]

The phenomenon was remarkably widespread and virtually simultaneous throughout the country, particularly in the North. From the Twenty-fifth Iowa's camp near Vicksburg in late winter 1863, William H. Nugen wrote that he was "glad to heare they are having such a revival" in his hometown of New London.[85] Isaac Jackson wished he could be in attendance at the revival he heard about back home in Harrison, Ohio. "I only [wish] I was home to attend those meetings you speak about," he wrote to his wife in February 1863.[86] Samuel Ensminger of the 158th Pennsylvania wrote to his family, "I here that thare was a big revivle in town. I hope thare has bin some good don."[87] From Harrison, Ohio; Cumberland County, Pennsylvania; Maquon, Illinois; and other places throughout the Northern states, soldiers heard of religious movements in their home districts.[88]

Those who became Christians back home usually became members of local churches almost immediately after their conversion. That was natural, since Christians had the command of Scripture to assemble together for worship and mutual support and encouragement, and the inclination to do so was one that Christians had always found natural. In this respect, however, the soldiers in the army were in an awkward situation. Those who were Christians before joining the army were already members of particular churches back home—mostly Methodist, Baptist, or Presbyterian. The new converts would, upon returning home at the end of the war, be making their choices among the several denominations. Many of them expressed such an allegiance while still in the army. It would be absurd to set up separate Methodist, Baptist, and Presbyterian churches within a single regiment or even a brigade, and churches that encompassed larger formations—divisions or corps—might well be broken up by the exigencies of military operations. Expedience called for one church within a regiment or, at most, a brigade. Yet what sort of church could accommodate all the various doctrinal preferences?

The most popular answer in the Confederate armies was the Christian Association, an arrangement that allowed soldiers to come together organizationally for worship and mutual encouragement but did not compromise any of the various denominations' doctrinal distinctions. On Sunday, June 21, 1863, Joshua K. Callaway wrote to his wife that his regiment, the Twenty-eighth Alabama, was "following the example of the others and getting up the 'Christian Association,' a kind of church. It is a good thing and I hope will prosper."[89] Another soldier described his regiment's Christian Association as "a kind of substitute for a church."[90]

The Christian Association of the Fourteenth South Carolina, established in the spring of 1863, was typical. Its constitution declared it to be for the purpose of being "helpers of each other's joy in Christ, and laborers together with God" in the promotion of His cause. "We covenant together," it continued, "with each other and with Christ to strive to grow in grace ourselves, to use all means in our power to promote the growth of grace in each other, and to be instrumental in bringing others to a saving knowledge of the truth as it is in Jesus."

Anderson's Georgia brigade, part of John B. Hood's famous division of the Army of Northern Virginia, set up a unified Christian Association for the whole brigade, the Seventh, Eighth, Ninth, Eleventh, and Fifty-ninth Georgia regiments. "It has drawn out and developed all the religious element among us," wrote one of the Georgians. "It has created a very pleasant, social feeling among the regiments, and has blended them into one congregation." The five regiments of the brigade had only three chaplains among them, and by means of the association, these three were able not only to help one another in their work but also to provide chaplain services for the two regiments that lacked ministers. By the fall of

1863, the association's membership within the brigade numbered over 400, or probably about a third of its total strength.

In setting up the Christian Association in Anderson's brigade, the soldiers formally elected a president, vice president, and secretary. They also issued a statement about what they were doing and why. They had felt the need of something similar to the churches back home and therefore "determined to form an Association which would supply this want and be acceptable to all orthodox denominations." To make this explicit, they added their affirmation of the truths contained in the so-called Apostle's Creed, the fundamental statement of orthodox Christianity. "All members of the Association," they continued, "are required to conform themselves to the rules of faith and Christian conduct as laid down in the revealed word of God; and when any brother is charged with being in disorder, his case shall be referred to the brethren of the same faith and order with himself" for adjudication. "All members are required to attend meetings of the Association ... and when they fail to do so are expected to state the reasons at the next meeting."

Large numbers of Confederate soldiers took very seriously the mission of the Christian Associations. In a declaration accompanying the founding of a Christian Association in the Third Alabama, the soldiers formally explained its purpose: "Being engaged in a constant warfare with 'spiritual wickedness in high places,' beset on every side, and most sorely tempted, man needs the advice and encouragement of a brother who similarly tempted and tried, by a word fitly spoken, or a consistent upright walk and godly conversation, may strengthen him in his determination to serve God." What they needed was "the genial, soul-cheering, heart-comforting influence of the communion of saints." The Christian Association of Buford's brigade, in the Confederate Army of Mississippi, proceeded without the help of any chaplain or missionary at all. The association met every Wednesday evening, and the soldiers held additional prayer meetings every night of the week. "Having no chaplain or preacher," wrote one of the soldiers, "we feel that the work of the Lord devolves upon the lay members," and thus they bestirred themselves more vigorously to do it.[91]

Not all Confederate soldiers, even Christian ones, saw at once the need or the benefit of the Christian Associations. When the Twelfth Tennessee organized its Christian Association in April 1863, Alfred Fielder wrote in his diary, "I did not go into it." He went on to explain that he was a member of the Methodist Episcopal Church, South, and that he feared that the Christian Association and its rules might somehow come into conflict with those of the church. Of course, such concerns were exactly what had prompted the creation of Christian Associations as organizations in which Christians of different denominations could come together for mutual edification without compromising their allegiance to their individual denominations. Fielder eventually saw this and came on board.[92]

Within the Confederacy, the trans-Mississippi was always a bit different, and by mid-1863, it was already well on its way to being practically cut off from the rest of the South in many ways and for various reasons. Not surprisingly, then, customs there differed somewhat with regard to the organization of Christians in the army. Instead of instituting Christian Associations in the various regiments or brigades of the Confederate army there, Christians in the ranks set up a unified Church of the Army, Trans-Mississippi, a sort of nondenominational denomination, with articles of faith that spelled out the fundamental doctrines of Christianity on which all orthodox believers could agree.

The "Articles of Faith" of the Church of the Army were such that virtually all Christians, East and West, North and South, could have signed on to them:

I. We believe the Scriptures of the Old and New Testament to be the Word of God, the only rule of faith and obedience.

II. We believe in one God, the Father, the Son, and the Holy Ghost; the same in substance; equal in power and glory.

III. We believe in the fall in Adam, the redemption by Christ, and the renewing of the Holy Spirit.

IV. We believe in justification by faith alone, and therefore receive and rest upon Christ as our only hope.

V. We believe in the communion of all saints, and in the doctrine of eternal rewards and punishments.[93]

Soldiers in the Union armies did not form Christian Associations as such, but they did worship for the most part in nondenominational meetings. In some ways, the U.S. Christian Commission may have met the same needs in Northern armies that the Christian Associations did for those of the South. Other near equivalents were set up here and there throughout the Union armies on an ad hoc basis. Christians in the Second Rhode Island organized "a Union Church" in January 1864.[94]

Aside from the harmonizing effect of the various Christian Associations, one of the most striking aspects of the prolonged and intense religious awakening in the various Civil War armies was that they were virtually everywhere and at all times, both North and South, characterized by a great deal of gracious forbearance and brotherly kindness among members of the various denominations. For example, in January 1863, the Twelfth Tennessee's Alfred Fielder heard an Episcopal minister, Charles T. Quintard, preaching in a Methodist church. The next week he heard another Episcopal minister, "Rev. Mr. Peas," preaching in the Presbyterian church. On a national fast day several weeks later, it was a Cumberland Presbyterian minister speaking in the Methodist church, and various regimental chaplains spoke from the different pulpits in the area interchangeably. Of course, Fielder also frequently heard Methodist preachers speaking in the Methodist church, but there was nothing unusual about that.[95]

Many soldiers, like Fielder, were staunch adherents of particular denominations, and forbearance did not always come easily. Still, they made the effort. Fielder, for one, preferred Methodist to Episcopal styles of worship. "Everything about their worship is too formal for me," he wrote, speaking of the Episcopalians, "but I suppose it is just as one has been raised." And he was willing to make allowances for those who had been raised differently than he had in such relatively inconsequential matters.[96]

Perhaps more remarkably, ministers also strove for interdenominational harmony. During the revival in the Confederate camps around Shelbyville, Tennessee, in the spring of 1863, chaplains and other ministers arranged for the various converts to be baptized according to the tenets and procedures of whichever denomination they chose and then worked together to accommodate them. When an appeal was given at a Friday, May 1, meeting, twenty-two candidates presented themselves for baptism, ten as Methodists, ten as Baptists, and two as Cumberland Presbyterians. The chaplain, a Baptist who believed strongly that any mode of baptism other than immersion was unbiblical and therefore wrong, nevertheless made arrangements for those who preferred to be baptized according to the practices of the other denominations, by pouring, the next Sunday, while he baptized the ten Baptists by immersion in the river. A week later, at the same place, the Baptist chaplain baptized two by immersion, and a Methodist baptized one by pouring and two by immersion in the same meeting.[97] Such goings-on may sound trivial to many in the twenty-first century, but they represented an unusual degree of tolerance for nineteenth-century Baptists and Methodists on the issue of the proper mode of baptism.

In prewar years, the two denominations had squabbled over this issue to an unseemly degree. Now, at least, they seemed to have more important things in mind. When early in 1863 a rumor surfaced that the Baptist Tract Society in the South had been churning out tracts arguing for the Baptist position on baptism, the denomination's leading periodical, the *Religious Herald,* denied that such was the case and assured readers that Baptists were not seeking sectarian advantage. Likewise, the Methodist Episcopal Church, South, was accused of attempting to advance its own position, but this too was proved to be false. Throughout the war, both denominations concentrated on teaching "the great cardinal doctrines and duties of religion."[98]

This spirit of cooperation extended throughout both armies and to a wide range of issues. A Confederate army missionary in Chattanooga wrote in the fall of 1863, "During a ministry of a fourth of a century I have never witnessed a work so deep, so general, and so successful. It pervades all classes of the army ... and elicits the cooperation of all denominations. We know no distinction here. Baptists, Cumberlands, Old Presbyterians, Episcopalians, and Methodists, work together, and rejoice together at the success of our cause." Chaplain P. A. Johnson of the Thirty-eighth Mississippi wrote in the spring of 1863, "The partitions are well-nigh broken down that have heretofore kept Christians so far apart. We know each other here only as Christian brethren traveling to a better world."[99]

The same freedom from denominational rancor characterized the revivals in the Union armies as well. Christian Commission delegate George M. Smith explained, "There appeared to be ... entire unanimity among" the soldiers. "No sectarianism or bigotry marred the harmony of the meetings. Nobody inquired of another if he was a Methodist, a Baptist, or an Episcopalian, and no one seemed to care for religious preferences. If a man was a Christian, it was enough."[100]

The revival continued to grow in breadth and intensity. It became especially intense in the Northern armies around the time of the Chattanooga campaign, in the late fall of 1863.[101] The Forty-sixth Indiana's Aurelius Voorhis wrote that fall, "The interest taken in religious meetings in this division is increasing."[102] In contrast, prior to August 1863, the revival, as such, had hardly touched the Second Rhode Island, where religious observances remained about as normal. Then things began to change. "About three weeks ago," explained Elisha Hunt Rhodes in early September, "three of our men who are Christians attended a religious meeting at one of the camps in Gen. Wheaton's Brigade. On the way home they kneeled down in the woods and prayed that God bless our Regiment. The next week six of them met for prayer, and last week about thirty were present." That night, the meeting started with about fifty men, but by the time it was over, "nearly every officer and man of our Regiment" had come into the grove where the Christians were meeting. "I never saw such a prayer meeting before," wrote Rhodes, "and I know the Spirit of the Lord was with us." The chaplain of the First Rhode Island Cavalry came over to preach to them. In the coming days, the men of the Second Rhode Island set about fixing up their grove for services. "We have made seats by splitting long logs in halves and hewing them smooth." The awakening continued to grow in the regiment, and by November, the nightly prayer meetings were still drawing 150 men.[103]

Another late-starting regiment was the Twenty-seventh Alabama, which also saw the first stirrings of revival in August 1863 in the piney woods of east-central Mississippi. As elsewhere, in both armies, nightly preaching services were well attended. "Fat pine knots were scattered in profusion all over the woods," wrote a soldier. "We gathered these into piles and, when ignited, they illuminated the meeting grounds which was attended by large numbers every night. Hundreds of penitents gathered around the altar and many were converted. A Christian Association was organized embracing all denominations. . . . This association was continued through the war."[104]

The revival movement varied in intensity from place to place and regiment to regiment. The large and more culturally diverse Union armies may well have experienced a more gradual, steady, and less explosive religious awakening, though the difference, if any actually existed, was at most one of degree. Christians among the Northern ranks also had to cope with peculiar disadvantages beginning in the second half of 1863. These were posed by the influx of large numbers of conscripts and substitutes into the armies. As a group, these men were drawn from the absolute dregs of Northern urban society, the most debauched and spiritually hardened class of people on the continent. Chaplain John Stuckenberg of the 145th Pennsylvania complained in September 1863, "There has been gambling and stealing and drunkenness in the regt for the last eight days, [more] I believe, than for the whole year we were out before. It does not seem like the same regt; it being completely changed by the subs or conscripts (or convicts as some call them) for the worse." The guardhouse was full now, and officers had to institute harsh punishments to control the riffraff. The old members of the regiment felt ashamed of the way the "godless subs" had "lowered the moral of the regt.," but there was little they could do.[105]

Austin C. Stearns of the Thirteenth Massachusetts noted the same problem. The situation as he described it was much like that at the beginning of the war—good men thrown together with bad—only worse. "We received our first installment of substitutes," he wrote not long after the battle of Gettysburg." Their "conversation was foul, with almost every other word an oath. Gambling was a favorate ammusement with them; some would gamble all day, and then all night." Then he went on even more emphatically:

To think that men and towns of the loyal north should send down such to be companions and associates of in many instances theirs sons and brothers and then say the army was corrupting the morals of the young men. Life in the army was very different from life at home. In the one place we could chose our companions and those we wished to associate with, but in the army how different. Here we were of necessity thrown together; there was no choosing. When we took our place in the ranks perhaps it was between two of those desperate characters.

We also had to draw rations with each other, and although we need not lay under the same blanket, yet we could not lay very far apart, and is it a thing to be wondered at that the boys should to a certain extent inhale into their system some of this poisonous element when the atmosphere all around was filled with it.[106]

Many Union regiments had to deal with similar problems, and it remained a hindrance to religious efforts among them. Christians among the Union ranks could only soldier on.

As cold, wet weather closed in near year's end 1863 and brought a halt to most military operations, religious activities proliferated in the camps as if the summer and fall campaigns had not brought their many interruptions nor the battles promoted many of the previous participants in the revivals to the more immediate presence of God. In the camp of the Twentieth Illinois on the banks of the Big Black River in Mississippi, the soldiers decided to build themselves a house of worship so that their meetings would not be interrupted by the winter's rain and storms. "Getting a permit from Colonel Bradley, and a score of axes from our Quartermaster, we soon made the Southern Forest ring with the felling of trees and the shouts of laughter," recalled Ira Blanchard. "Our Chaplain was with the boys working might and main in his shirt sleeves, and he stated emphatically that he never built a church under so favorable circumstances or with so little difficulty to obtain subscriptions." "Worked hard to finish our church," wrote Allen Geer in his diary on November 28. "Finished chimney, chinked and mudded cracks, made seats etc." Blanchard happily noted that it was the best soldier-constructed church building he had ever seen. "We covered our edifice with a huge tent, built a log fireplace with a stick chimney at one end, then splitting some logs in half we made pews, and with a barrel for a pulpit, we were ready for business." On the next Sunday they held the service of dedication for the new building, and "every log was occupied."[107]

Blanchard might not have been so confident of the architectural superiority of his regiment's chapel if he had seen the one constructed by the Second Rhode Island in Virginia that winter. "The building is made of logs hewn smooth on one side and built up cob fashion," wrote Elisha Hunt Rhodes. "The roof is covered by a large canvas, presented by the

Christian Commission. Inside we have a fireplace and tin reflectors for candles on the walls. A chandelier made from old tin cans, or the tin taken from cans is in the center. The pulpit or desk is covered with red flannel, and the ground or floor is carpeted with pine boughs." A detail of men from the regiment had gone to an abandoned church building in the vicinity and taken out the pews for use in their chapel, fighting a skirmish with Rebel guerrillas on the way. "In recognition of God's goodness to us we have named it 'Hope' Chapel." At the formal dedication of the building in January 1864, four visiting chaplains joined the Second's own John D. Beugless in conducting the service.[108] The Sixteenth Maine's chapel was not completed until February 1864, but it too was "built of hewn logs and roofed with canvas. The interior was decorated with evergreens, which were hung in festoons and fashioned into crosses, anchors, and circles upon the walls. Familiar Bible texts met the eye from over the pulpit."[109]

Many other regiments took steps toward securing reliable places to worship. When the Sixty-seventh Indiana camped at New Iberia, Louisiana, after the Bayou Teche campaign of late 1863, its men "found an old abandoned sugar house nearby and converted [it] into a church house in which rousing religious meetings were held almost nightly" that winter.[110] The Seventy-fifth and Eightieth Illinois had no sooner dedicated their new chapel in January 1864 when they found it too small—packed full— and many disappointed soldiers were turned away.[111] In the Confederate camps around Dalton, Georgia, that winter, many brigades built crude log chapels in which to worship. In Brown's brigade, the place of worship had to be enlarged twice to accommodate the ever-larger crowds in attendance.[112] In the Army of Northern Virginia alone, some forty chapels were built that fall, and a missionary reported that "men may be seen an hour before services running to the [meeting] house, in order that they may procure seats."[113] One of the chapels was large and commodious enough to boast six chimneys. Thus, as the Twenty-seventh North Carolina's Samuel P. Lockhart explained, "we can have service when it is cold and be very comfortable."[114]

The Great Revival of 1862 and 1863 changed the nature of the Civil War armies. In part, it undid some of the coarsening and going astray that had led many devoutly raised youths into sin during their first months in the army. In part, the revivals went beyond even that, converting many who had not previously taken Christianity seriously. The religious awakening was more dramatic in the Confederate than in the Union armies but was no less pervasive in the latter, where Christian influence seems to have been more widespread at the outset.

The revivals were not universal in their effect. Many soldiers remained practical pagans with, in most cases, only a bare nod of respect for Christianity. These men would continue all the unsavory practices that Christians since the outset of the war had deplored in the army. Nonetheless, the overall moral and spiritual condition of the armies would never again be as bad as it had been in 1861.

12

"IF WE FALL ON THE FIELD OF STRIFE"
Religion in the Camp and on the Battlefield, 1864–1865

"I never knew the comfort there is in religion so well as during the past month," wrote a soldier of the 100th Pennsylvania after the bloody battles of the Wilderness and Spottsylvania in May 1864. "Nothing sustains me so much in danger as to know that there is one who ever watches over us." The final year of the war brought fighting even more ferocious and bloodshed even more appalling than all that had gone before. Many soldiers were enabled to face such horrors and continue doing their duty in large part through "the comfort there is in religion."[1]

The religious revival in the armies continued right up to and even through the commencement of active campaigning. The movement was stronger than ever in the Union camps, East and West. Charles C. Parker, a Christian Commission delegate at Vermont Station, a tent chapel that was the commission's outpost with the Vermont brigade of the Army of the Potomac that winter, wrote of an enthusiastic "experience" or "testimony" meeting in February 1864. "We have had a very interesting meeting—some four or five new persons rising to speak." On another winter Sunday he wrote of a meeting "not as interesting as the others" because many of the troops who would have attended were out of camp on a military operation, "yet two young men who had not spoke before—spoke

very finely & touchingly of themselves & of their interest in these meetings & of their purpose to renew their Christian life."[2]

The tent would hold about 200 men and was usually filled to overflowing. Indeed, it was not unusual for large numbers of men to be turned
away because there was simply no room for them. Religious meetings
relieved the boredom of camp life, but attendance also reflected a sincere interest on the part of many, and some who came out of curiosity
found themselves growing interested as well.[3] Of yet another meeting at
the tent Parker wrote, "In the evening we had a very precious meeting—
With the utmost readiness & heartiness ten soldiers spoke. . . . Some spoke
of their wanderings & asked the forgiveness of their comrades—Others
spoke of the preciousness of Jesus & the power of his religion to cheer &
sustain the heart in all the perils & exposures of a soldiers life—the
march—the watch—the battlefield—There were many moistened eyes
& trembling lips—That meeting rewarded me a thousand fold for all that
I have done or endured in coming to the army."[4]

"The meetings commence at half past six and are held till the drum
calls us to roll call at eight," wrote the Second Vermont's Wilbur Fisk.
"One of the delegates preaches a short sermon, or rather makes a few
practical remarks founded upon some text of Scripture, and then the time
is occupied by any one who wishes to speak, sing or pray. Generally the
time is fully occupied, and often two or more rise to speak at once. . . .
Some have spoken there that never spoke in meeting before." Fisk added
that the delegates held "a sort of Bible class" every day at the tent chapel
and also distributed much literature.[5]

Dozens of similar meetings were taking place throughout the army,
and soldier diaries of the period speak of "Very exciting meeting," "best
meeting I ever attended in the Army," and "Spoke in meeting at night."[6]
"The religious interest continues," wrote Elisha Hunt Rhodes in his diary
that February.[7] At a gathering of Christian Commission delegates for the
Army of the Potomac that month, "reports were most cheering." Many
delegates reported that at their stations "there has been & is still a deep
& extensive work of grace—Many have been hopefully converted—
many wandering professors reclaimed—Both classes are numbered by
hundreds."[8] The work continued unabated, and in April, Rhodes was
still making notations in his diary such as, "Tonight we had a very in-

teresting religious meeting, and about twenty took part in remarks or prayer."[9]

In the Union armies of the West, Chesley Mosman of the Fifty-ninth Illinois wrote that winter of a meeting near Chattanooga at which "between 50 and 60 men spoke of their religious experience and five or six men stood up and asked to be prayed for."[10] Iowa soldier Jacob Gantz recorded twenty-seven soldiers becoming church members on a single day in February.[11] The 129th Illinois's LaForest Dunham wrote to tell his mother that he was among those who had converted that spring. "Ma I feal as iff God was on my side. . . . I have resolved to be a christon the rest of my life."[12]

In Algeirs, Louisiana, George S. Marks of the Ninety-ninth Illinois wrote of frequent services, including a celebration of the Lord's Supper, adding "We had a grand time; God was Present with us."[13] In the same vicinity, Aurelius Voorhis of the Forty-sixth Indiana was particularly moved by a service at which the Lord's Supper was administered. He estimated the attendance between seventy-five and one hundred and wrote, "It was truly a solemn sight." He also mentioned numerous converts, including one who "was so happy he could hardly talk but managed to say that he felt that blessed assurance that God had pardoned all the sins and owned him for his child." Of a February 4 meeting he wrote, "It was impossible for all to speak who wished to. . . . The interest appears to grow very fast." And grow it did, with nightly meetings, numerous conversions, and masses of soldiers eagerly seeking spiritual help. Sometimes the chaplain could hardly dismiss the meeting, so many soldiers wanted to remain afterward for prayer and counseling.[14]

Still farther west, camped at Point Cavallo on the Texas coast, Union troops of the Thirteenth Corps continued to experience revival. "The religious spirit that came over the camp while on the Teche [the previous autumn] had not abated," wrote R. B. Scott of the Sixty-seventh Indiana, "but on the contrary had spread over the whole army and daily meetings and baptisms seemed to be the order of the day. At one of these meetings, while the beach was covered with the assembled throng, Chaplain Chittenden led down into the water and baptized sixty converts."[15]

Even in the camps of instruction, where new regiments were organizing in preparation for going to the front, the same spirit prevailed. "We are still blest with good meetings of some kind every night in the week," wrote the Thirty-sixth Wisconsin's John Black from Camp Randall, near Madison.[16] In the same regiment, David Coon wrote, "It is really refreshing for we have most pleasant and intersting meetings. It is really affecting to hear men get up and tell of their companions at home praying for them." Interestingly, the revival was not confined to those of Anglo-Saxon ancestry or American birth. Immigrants and American Indians (those who were at least partially assimilated into white society) were touched by it. Of the revival at Camp Randall, Coon wrote of seeing "foreigners and even Indians get up and in broken English tell of their love for the Savior."[17]

In the late winter and spring of 1864, Col. Cullen Battle of the Third Alabama remembered frequent baptisms, "an immense brush arbor near brigade headquarters" with large and frequent services, and a vast combined celebration of "the Christian Association of the Army," at which a large number of conversions took place.[18] In March 1864, Samuel P. Lockhart of the Twenty-seventh North Carolina wrote to his sister, "We are having a very nice little meeting going on at this time; there were four made a profession last night." It struck Lockhart that the worshippers and converts were very quiet and subdued, yet still quite earnest. "Surely the Lord is with us," he wrote. Chaplain J. M. Stokes of the Third Georgia described the situation in his regiment, which was typical of the army: "We have had several conversions, and there were, I reckon, fifty mourners at the altar for prayer last evening. Our chapel seats between 300 and 400, and is full every night unless the weather is very inclement."[19]

In April 1864 the highlight of religious observances in the Army of Northern Virginia was a large outdoor meeting at which the Lord's Supper, or Holy Communion, as some called it, was celebrated. It took place in a large clearing near the Rapidan River. Some fifteen chaplains were on the platform, and thousands of soldiers sat around on stumps and logs. Naturally, few of the soldiers had hymnbooks, so the hymns were "given out." That is, a preacher would read out the words to two verses of the hymn at a time. Since most of the men were already familiar with those hymns, they were able to remember the words to the two verses and sing them. Then the next two verses would be read out. At this particular service, the crowd was so vast that two chaplains stood, one on each side of the platform, and each gave out the hymns to the soldiers on his side. Then the whole assembly would sing the hymn together.

When the time came for praying and preaching, the same pattern was used, with one chaplain on each side of the platform, which was large enough, according to the Sixteenth Mississippi's David Holt, so that "there was no confusion"—the soldiers on each side of the crowd could hear, for the most part, only their own preacher. Then the chaplains blessed the bread—crumbled pieces of hardtack—and the wine, the former on tin plates and the latter in tin cups, and distributed them to a large number of helpers, who passed through the mass of soldiers, handing out the elements to all those who wished to partake. For a time, the only sounds were the low murmurs of the servers, "The body of the Lord," and "The blood of the Lord," as they offered the bread and wine.

The service was completed, and the benediction pronounced. The men stood up to leave. Then an old chaplain waved his hands and shouted from the platform, "Attention, wait a minute!" The crowd stood still in silence. "Men, before we part," the old man went on,

> let us sing, "How Firm a Foundation Ye Saints of the Lord." I know full well that this is the last communion for many of you. The next campaign will be the hardest fought and bloodiest of all. It will be the extreme test. Many of you in the pride and vigor of early manhood will be laid low in death, and all your fond ambitions for the future, expectancy of home, wife and children, will be blotted out in your blood. But, Oh! This simple feast that we have just eaten is a token and a pledge of the undying love and power of our God. It is also an earnest of the feast and joy of the World to come. May the remembrance of it console you in your deepest distress, and comfort your hearts with a sense of the personal love and presence of your Lord.

The old chaplain then gave out the hymn:

> How firm a foundation ye saints of the Lord,
> Is laid for your faith in his excellent word.

And so on. "Everyone sang with a will," recalled Holt. He looked at the "glowing faces" of the men all around him, and he too felt that Christ was spiritually present among them as they sang verse after verse, each recounting some promise of Scripture. "I never heard such singing in my life."

> The soul that on Jesus hath leaned for repose
> I will not, I will not, desert to his foes.
> That soul, though all hell should endeavor to shake,
> I'll never, no, never, no, never forsake.

"The hymn ended the service," Holt recorded, and the soldiers, "in small groups, went their different ways without words."[20]

Farther to the west, across the Appalachians in the Army of Tennessee, the revival continued with equal force. In Gist's brigade, in addition to nightly preaching services, the newly organized Christian Association met each morning at 8:30. The new converts were organized into small-group prayer meetings that met at 7:00 A.M. The beat of a drum called those who wanted to attend the evening preaching service at about sunset. The crowds for this event had grown so large by spring that the men took advantage of the pleasant weather and brought the pulpit and benches out of their chapel to the bare hillside, so as to accommodate more worshippers. The service would usually continue until the beating of tattoo, which sent the men to their quarters. There, however, many of them continued praying, singing, and helping anxious seekers. Some 140 were converted in the space of two weeks.[21]

It was much the same in Brown's brigade. Flavel C. Barber of the Third Tennessee wrote in March 1864, "The religious revival still goes on in the brigade, and several of our best young soldiers have manifested a deep interest. Indeed I think there is quite an improvement in point of morals throughout our whole army." Brown's brigade, like Gist's, had just that spring got around to organizing a Christian Association—something many brigades and regiments had done the preceding summer and fall. In early April, Barber again noted the continuing revival and added that it was "producing some good fruits." Among the "good fruits" of the revival, Barber believed, was an end to desertions. Also, "the soldiers seem better satisfied than they have been before, although their discipline is stricter than usual. They seem happy and contented with their rough fare," and optimistic about the coming campaign.[22]

Indeed, it was the same all through the Army of Tennessee, with chaplains and army missionaries reporting chapels overflowing, scores of seekers, and dozens of converts—"weakness and vice seem restrained," as a missionary described it, and "members of the churches are becoming revived."[23] Notwithstanding the continued lack of sufficient numbers of chaplains, many regiments held nightly prayer meetings without them. On an average day at the height of the revival, some fifty soldiers might be baptized.[24]

A strange incident marred the revival in the Army of Tennessee at Dalton that spring. While a number of seekers were praying in the altar area after a preaching service on the night of April 29, 1864, a large tree fell among them, fatally crushing ten members of Strahl's brigade. Sumner A. Cunningham of the Forty-first Tennessee believed that the event was a "lesson" to him, that by it, God was awakening him to the "uncertainty of life" and the need to seek salvation. Cunningham had lost his lifelong close friend Henry Newsom in the incident and wrote afterward, "During the four years of war there was hardly an incident that created more general sorrow throughout the army."[25]

Hanging over all the troops was the impending campaign, which all knew would be the most desperate and bloody the war had yet produced. In many parts of the country, as had been the case in the Army of Northern Virginia, one of the reactions of devout soldiers was a desire to partake of the Lord's Supper. On the first Sunday of April at Vermont Station, the delegates of the Christian Commission administered the ordinance to members of what would become one of the Army of the Potomac's premier combat brigades during the coming year of fighting. At that service, eleven men made profession of faith and three were baptized.[26] Army missionary A. G. Haygood administered the Lord's Supper to soldiers of the Army of Tennessee that same month. Tears streamed down the faces of the hardened veterans as they sang

> That doleful night before his death,
> The Lamb for sinners slain,
> Did, almost with his dying breath,
> This solemn feast ordain.

Then they knelt along a large log—a rough altar improvised for the occasion—to receive the bread and wine.[27]

The Christians among the Second Rhode Island received the Lord's Supper on Sunday, April 24, and then gathered along the banks of nearby Hazel Run, along with members of the Thirty-seventh Massachusetts and Battery G, First Rhode Island Artillery, for the baptism of four soldiers. The regiment was already under orders to break up its winter camp when, on the night of April 26, Chaplain Beugless preached the final sermon in the Hope Chapel, whose logs he had helped the men hew out. His sermon, "Our duty in the coming campaign," had a very attentive audience. The next morning, the canvas roof came off the chapel and was sent to storage. Then, in the best hurry-up-and-wait tradition of the army, the Second sat awaiting marching orders. No one had any doubt that the orders would come within a few days, and no one could be uncertain as to their meaning. "Our move means fight," wrote Elisha Hunt Rhodes. "May God grant us the victory." Then on May 3, Rhodes wrote, "Our turn has come. . . . I feel very calm, trusting in God that his protecting care will be over me. While I do not feel that I am more safe than others, yet I have a firm reliance upon my Heavenly Father and am willing to leave all to him."[28]

Daily services were still being held in the Union armies in the West. On April 28, the chaplain of the Ninth Indiana preached a "splendid sermon," and "twenty-three stood up asking for prayers." At an "experience meeting" later that day, "some 40 professing Christians spoke." Men of the Fifty-ninth Illinois and nearby regiments celebrated the Lord's Supper on Sunday, May 1, and saw eight men baptized at the same service. That afternoon, the regiment drew new Springfield rifles, an obvious indication of what was to come. In the evening, Chesley Mosman went to hear the chaplain of the Ninth Indiana preach but wrote, "We could not get inside for the crowd so sat down on the outskirts."[29]

At Lookout Station, Tennessee, the 129th Illinois was "having quite a revival" in late April. Many attended a prayer meeting at the regiment's log chapel on Saturday, April 30, and then preaching the next morning. "Thare was to be preaching at three o'clock this afternoon," wrote LaForest Dunham in a letter home, "but we have got marching orders." After a few hours to prepare, the regiment was drawn up in line, and the chaplain led the men in prayer. Then they marched off, never to return.[30] Similarly, in the Army of Northern Virginia's Third Corps, a preaching service that Sunday was interrupted by orders "to strike tents, cut them up and distribute them among men, cook up rations and hold ourselves in readiness to march."[31]

For troops in most parts of the country, the final campaigns began in early May. On May 4 the Army of the Potomac crossed the Rapidan, only a few miles in space and a couple of weeks in time from the great Confederate communion service along its banks. That evening, the Eleventh New Jersey had a prayer meeting on the field of the previous year's battle of Chancellorsville.[32] The next morning, the Army of the Potomac and the Army of Northern Virginia clashed and were henceforth locked in a death grapple that would last until the war ended eleven months hence. On the night of May 6, a soldier of Wilcox's Alabama Brigade found himself lying in the tangled underbrush of the Wilderness, badly wounded and, it seemed, near death. Desperately thirsty and with a mouth so dry that he could not even cry out, he gazed up through the foliage and saw a star shining in the night sky. That made him think. "Who made the stars?" he thought to himself, and answered, "My Father which art in Heaven made the stars, and I know Him as my Father." He went on in his reverie:

> Then I thought of the suffering of Christ, and how He said, "In me ye shall have peace, but in the world ye shall have tribulation. But fear not for I have overcome the world." The Christ Himself was not exempt from tribulation. He bore His suffering with the fortitude of faith because it was the divine plan of God. As God's child also I must bear what comes by the divine plan with the fortitude of faith, knowing that the very hairs of our heads are all numbered and we are of the greatest value in the sight of our Heavenly Father. As the pure and quiet light of the star fell upon my sight, so the peace of God fell upon my heart, and, in spiritual joy, I forgot my bodily pain.

He fell asleep and awakened when his comrades found him.[33]

In the midst of the fierce campaigns of the summer of 1864, many soldiers tried to keep up religious activities. "We have prayer meetings whenever circumstances will permit," wrote James Iredell Hall of the Ninth Tennessee in June.[34] In mid-July, when the Twenty-seventh Alabama was rotated out of the lines to a reserve position in the rear, J. P. Cannon recorded in his diary, "We had preaching and prayer meetings day and night," with strong interest among the soldiers and additional conversions. The meetings were held in the woods by moonlight. "Part of the command is allowed to attend each service," the rest being held in readiness for immediate action.[35] At the outset of the campaign, a number of Christians in the Richmond Howitzers covenanted together that "during the coming campaign, every evening, about sunset, whenever it was at all possible, we would keep up our custom, and such of us as could get together, *wherever we might be,* should gather for prayer." William Dame, one of those believers, wrote after the war was over:

I may remark, as a notable fact, that this resolution was carried out *almost literally.* Sometimes, a few of the fellows would gather in prayer, while the rest of us fought the guns. Several times . . . we met *under fire.* Once . . . a shell burst right by us, and covered us with dust; and, once . . . a Minie bullet slapped into a hickory sapling . . . not an inch above my head. . . . But, however circumstanced, in battle, on the battle line, in interims of quiet . . . we held that prayer hour every day, at sunset, during the entire campaign. And some of us thought, and *think* that the strange exemption our Battery experienced, our little loss, in the midst of unnumbered perils, and incessant service, during that awful campaign, was that, in answer to our prayers, "the God of battles covered our heads in the day of battle" and was merciful to us, because we "called upon Him."[36]

That widespread religious meetings could go on in the midst of almost continuous combat was a surprise to many, including some of the chaplains and the top generals. When army missionary J. W. Beckwith wrote to Lt. Gen. William J. Hardee, commander of one of the corps in the Army of Tennessee, asking if he should leave the army hospitals at Atlanta to join the army itself north of the city, Hardee responded that he had better stay where he was. "He says," Beckwith explained, "that if the men were brought together for service it wd. at once attract the attention of the enemy [who] would open fire upon us, break up the congregation & cause a useless sacrifice of life." The perceived impossibility of preaching in the army even led some of the Army of Tennessee's regular chaplains to leave their regiments and go back to the hospitals at Atlanta, where they believed they would find more opportunities to minister.[37]

According to at least some testimony, they—and Hardee—may have been mistaken. On a single Sunday that summer, in one division of the army, "eight sermons were preached in full sight of the Federal lines, and even within range of small arms." Indeed, an active revival continued in the Missouri brigade, with some sixty men becoming church members in the space of a week. Army missionary S. M. Cherry conducted a meeting along the front lines that August. He selected a location that would be handy to the lines of three different Confederate brigades, but regretted that "not a single tree or shrub was to be found to screen us from the intense heat of an August sun." He went on to describe the meeting: "Soon the singing collected a large congregation of attentive soldiers. A caisson served for a pulpit, while the cannon, open-mouthed, stood in front of the foe. We were in full range and in open view of the enemy, but not a single shell or minnie-ball was heard hissing or hurtling near during the hour's service. The soldiers sat on the ground, beneath the burning sun, listening seriously to the words of life." On July 18 army missionary L. R. Redding reported from the lines near Atlanta, "A most gracious revival is in progress in Gist's brigade. We have built a bush-arbor in rear of our line of battle, where we have services twice a day." Up to that point, another twenty-five members of the brigade had become church members, "and penitents by the score are found nightly at the altar." Similar reports came from other parts of the army. Rev. L. B. Payne reported holding "prayer meetings in the breastworks several times" and preaching under such circumstances several more times.[38]

Some of Sherman's Federals were prepared to respect their foes' religious observances, at least so far as not to fire on them. They too were attending religious services when possible behind their lines outside Atlanta.[39] In a letter headed "Camp in the woods north of Atlanta, July 16, 1864," the 129th Illinois's LaForest Dunham wrote, "We have prair meating evry eavening now while we ar in camp and it is a dooing a great deal of good."[40] "We had a good meeting at night," wrote Chesley Mosman in

August 1864, "but it seems strange to have the prayers punctuated by the vicious hiss or the dull thud of the Minnie ball flying overhead or striking some object." The Union soldiers were not necessarily prepared to accept the validity of their enemy's worship of God, however. "We can hear the Johnnies singing, 'Come thou fount of every blessing,'" wrote Mosman that same month. That was the first line of a hymn, and the second was, "Tune my heart to sing Thy grace." Mosman did not believe the Rebels were fit to be praising God. "How," he wondered, "could he [God] tune their savage 'hearts to sing thy praise.'"[41]

Restraint toward the religion of one's foes was not absolute, especially if the enemy openly attempted to enlist religion in his cause. Elsewhere in the camps of the Union armies around Atlanta that same month, Charles B. Loop of the Ninety-fifth Illinois recorded a similar incident with a different conclusion. "Last night our skirmishers advanced a little and broke up a Rebel prayer meeting," he explained in a letter to his wife. "They were asking the Lord to paralize the Yankees and wipe them from face of the earth & all within hearing distance of our main line but behind a small ridge from the skirmish line and only a few rods from them." The Union soldiers listened to the prayers for their destruction until they grew tired of it. Then "the boys crept up to the top of the ridge and poured several vollies into them and they 'dried up' very quick and went to shooting."[42]

To a soldier who faced death almost every day, as many did in the 1864 campaigns, the state of a man's soul and his eternal destiny when this life was over were matters of urgent importance. In August of that year, a chaplain was called to the hospitals of the Union Twenty-third Corps "in great haste to see a dying man. I asked what do you want?" the chaplain recounted. "He said, 'I want Christ.'" Earnestly the chaplain did his best to explain to the soldier the way of salvation. Fifteen minutes later, the soldier was dead. In the same hospital a few days later, a soldier died with the words, "God be merciful to me a sinner," while yet another's final words were "Lord Jesus receive my spirit."[43]

On Monday, July 18, 1864, Alfred Fielder noted in his diary that the Twelfth Tennessee "had preaching at sun rise" and at "night had prayer meeting." At the latter event, "quite a number of mourners presented themselves," and sixteen men became members of the Methodist Epis-

copal Church, South. Among those who officially signified their possession of saving faith was Fielder's nephew, A. M. J. Fielder, known as
Marion in the family. Four days later, the Twelfth Tennessee took part
in the desperate battle of Atlanta. Young Marion carried the regiment's
colors and was the first man upon the Union works, waving the flag and
shouting, "Boys follow the flag of your country," before leaping over,
followed by the regiment en masse. They were eventually repulsed, and
Alfred Fielder was wounded. Lying in the Confederate field hospital, he
received word that Marion had also been wounded—through the abdo-
men—and wanted to see him. The chaplain of the Thirteenth Tennessee came to his aid. He rounded up several other able-bodied men, and
together they carried Fielder to his nephew's side. "Uncle Alfred," said
Marion, taking his hand, "I am dying . . . I feel that I am prepared to die
and I want you to tell all my relations and friends not to grieve after me
but to meet me in heaven." Alfred Fielder noted in his diary, "about 9 oclk
he breathed his last."[44]

The testimonies of dying soldiers like Marion Fielder emphasized the
degree to which Christianity had increased during the course of the war.
Another Confederate dying of wounds during the final year of the war
assured those who attended him that he was prepared to meet his maker.
"I entered the army a wicked man," he explained, but he had been moved
to place his trust in Christ through the influence of his sister, exerted
through her frequent letters. When an army missionary asked another
dying soldier, one who had become a Christian in the army revivals of
the preceding year, if there was anything he could do for him, the man
asked him to write to his wife. "What shall I write?" asked the missionary. "Say to my dear wife," the man replied in a weak voice, "it's all right."
The missionary wrote that down, then asked, "What more shall I write?"
The soldier answered, "Nothing else—all's right." And then he died.[45]

Maj. Pickens B. Bird of Florida was mortally wounded near Richmond
that summer. When the surgeons informed him that he was not expected
to live, he replied, "But for leaving my wife and children, I should not
feel sad at the prospect of dying. There is not cloud between me and God
now." Some time later he tried to sing, "Jesus can make a dying bed" but
had not the strength. He lay resting for a few moments and then said
quietly, "Jesus can make a dying bed feel soft as downy pillows are."[46]

The inner peace exhibited by dying Christians never failed to impress those who saw their final moments. A Confederate surgeon responded to an invitation for seekers at a service that summer. To the chaplain who came to pray with him, he explained that he had had a religious upbringing but after extensive education had become "a skeptic and scoffer of religion." Now, however, he had discovered something at which he could not scoff. "I see such a difference between the death of the believer and the unbeliever." Day and night his mind could not get away from the nagging question, "What makes the difference?" Finally, he had dug in his trunk and brought out a little-used Bible his mother had given him years before, determined to find the answer to his question. Searching through the book, he came to the verse, "Precious in the sight of the Lord is the death of his saints." That was enough. "I came here tonight," he explained to the chaplain, "resolved to accept, publicly, the invitation of the gospel which, for two days and nights, you have so earnestly urged upon this congregation. Oh that I had submitted my stubborn heart to God years ago! I thank God that I am spared to bear testimony here tonight that Christ is able and willing to save the chief of sinners."[47]

After the fall of Atlanta on September 1, 1864, there came a lull in military operations in Georgia. Soldiers lost no time in returning to religious pursuits. "Preaching services were held between the hours of duty today," wrote J. P. Cannon of the Twenty-seventh Alabama on September 11. "An attempt is being made to renew the revival that has been interrupted for so long a time." The attempt was successful. Cannon was soon referring to the "big meeting" and noting as many as twenty-five baptisms in a single day, with twenty more the next. "Interest in the revival grows," he noted on the thirteenth. "Many penitents at the altar. Preaching and drilling takes up about all our time."[48] On the Union side of the lines, diaries from this period frequently mention, "We had a good meeting at night," "We had a right good meeting at night," "We had a splendid meeting. Very well attended."[49] From Atlanta itself, the 129th Illinois's LaForest Dunham wrote, "We have preaching in camp now most evry eavening."[50]

In Virginia, operations had settled down to a siege of Petersburg and Richmond. Again the soldiers tried to attend religious services whenever possible. "We had preaching this morning in the trenches," wrote Virginia soldier William Russell one Sunday in September. "I attended meeting & herd a fine sermon." On another Sunday that month, he listened to the sermon but could not actually be part of the meeting because he was on watch. "While I am standing here on my post, looking out for the enemy," he wrote, "there is preaching going on within my hearing about twentifive yards to my right, in the trenches. Brother Wm. Wiatt is preaching the word of God to my comrades in arms."[51] Other Confederate soldiers were occasionally permitted to avail themselves of the nearby town of Petersburg to attend services in the churches there.[52] Union soldiers also showed a willingness to attend religious services, even under less than ideal conditions. Daniel Sober of the Sixth Pennsylvania Heavy Artillery noted in his diary on September 4, 1864, "Was at Prayer meeting and preaching in camp. Attended service in the roaring rain."[53]

As it had been the previous year, the religious interest in the armies was remarkably widespread. From Fort Rice, Dakota Territory, where his Thirtieth Wisconsin had been sent to watch the restless Sioux, Albert M. Childs wrote, "We now have prayer meetings every evening and preaching once or twice on the sabbath and another prayer meeting or a kind of a speaking meeting for the other service. . . . I have been abundantly blessed in attending these meetings. I find God the same here in Dakota that I found him at home."[54]

Soldiers in all the armies on both sides generally tried to keep the days of religious observance declared by their respective presidents. Both presidents, Lincoln and Davis, declared a number of days of fasting and prayer or of thanksgiving, as seemed appropriate. On August 5, 1864, for example, several Union soldiers noted, "The President's fast day was generally observed in the Army. We held services at Brigade Headquarters," and "Fast day. . . . Our whole Division went to church." Because such observances drew in soldiers by the command of their officers rather than by their own choice, the assemblies included those who had never accepted Christianity and were not well disposed toward it, and there was correspondingly less unanimity of feeling. Samuel Clear of the 116th Pennsylvania wrote of some of the men sitting on the ground and "playing mumble meg" during the sermon.[55]

Strong religious interest continued in both the Union and Confederate armies throughout the final year of the war. The Confederate lines

around Petersburg that last winter of the war were dotted with chapels—
one observer said that there was one every 600 to 800 yards—just as the
winter camps had been the previous year.[56] It was much the same on the
Union side, when circumstances permitted. After the war was over, Rev.
William W. Bennett, who had served as an army missionary in the Army
of Northern Virginia, made a study of the revivals in the Confederate
armies. He estimated that 150,000 conversions took place during the war
and that "fully one-third of all the soldiers in the field were praying men
and members of some branch of the Christian Church."[57] Modern scholars have but little modified Bennett's estimate, allowing that "at least
100,000 were converted." Conversions in the Union armies were even
more numerous, with estimates ranging from 100,000, corresponding to
the low estimate for Confederate conversions, all the way up to twice that
many. The total Union conversions would thus equal roughly 5 to 10
percent of all those who wore blue.[58] The Confederate armies being
smaller, their percentage of conversions was higher, perhaps 10 percent
or better. By any standard, the religious happenings of those four years
were remarkable.

As always, evil remained present in the armies to a greater or lesser
degree, even alongside intense religious interest. The revivals never became so all-pervasive as to produce a decisive effect on all the soldiers.
As Wilbur Fisk explained, "Camp life must always present peculiar and
powerful temptations. An army collects a great many very bad men, and
their example here is all the more pernicious, because it has a wider range
of liberty to develop itself, and there is no public sentiment to crush it.
Away from the restraints of society, and of home, it is the easiest thing in
the world to drop in with the current, call it the 'soldier style,' 'live while
you do live,' and let the end take care of itself."[59] In short, evil would never
be eradicated from the army, and what evil there was would tend to appear in its boldest colors in that setting.

Whether an observer thought the extent of evil remaining in the army
was greater or lesser depended much on who his comrades were—and
who he was. David C. Dutcher, a chaplain, found that he had to work with
a number of profane and wicked surgeons in a nearby army hospital. He
was also subject to bouts of discouragement, especially when the weather
was bad. "In the field," reads his diary for November 21, 1864, "and yet it

rains." If Dutcher's view of the world was bleak, it is one with which most people who have had to live under canvas and rainy skies can sympathize. It was in this state of mind that Dutcher wrote, "Religion is not very popular in the army." But others would have taken a different view, and indeed Dutcher himself may have done so—when the sun came out. In fact, two days after writing his gloomy comment, Dutcher attended a prayer meeting and afterward wrote, "It was a good meeting. God is very good to me."[60]

Encounters between Northern and Southern Christians continued to occur during the final phase of the war, and in ever-increasing numbers as more of the South was overrun by Union armies. In October 1864, Elisha Hunt Rhodes and his Second Rhode Island found themselves in Winchester, Virginia. Rhodes and some of his fellow officers decided to take advantage of the opportunity to worship with the Episcopal church in town, the only church whose building was not being used as an army hospital. The first Sunday, Rhodes noted that "the music was good, and we enjoyed it, but the sermon was a little rebellious." The sermon was on the importance of receiving "all afflictions as from the hand of God." "No matter how diabolical the agents sent might be," Rhodes summarized, "the people should remember that the Lord sent them." Here Rhodes interjected in his diary, "How are you, diabolical Yank?" The Lord's Supper was served, and one of the Union soldiers present, a private, partook. Rhodes noted, "Most of the ladies were dressed in black, and it seemed almost like a funeral." He felt sorry for these people, "but when I remembered that they brought their troubles upon themselves . . . I could not help feeling that their punishment was just."

Not deterred, the Union officers returned the following week and heard another "rebellious" sermon. At the close of the service, the minister made an announcement: "A Chaplain of a New York Regiment will hold service in this church this evening at early candle light, but as we have no way of lighting up perhaps he will not want this notice given." The locals smiled at the joke, but Rhodes and his friends determined to attend the evening service "if each of us had to hold a candle in our hand."

Rhodes and his friends kept coming back, despite the rebellious preaching. "Attended church this morning," he wrote in his diary, "but I can hardly say 'worship' for . . . the minister is a regular old Rebel." Rhodes's prayers were answered when the next week another church, the Lutheran one, was opened in town. He attended but was disappointed. "The minister prayed for peace and unity and then preached a rebellious sermon. There is not much difference in the ministers of this town." He never found a satisfactory church there.[61]

Union soldiers elsewhere in Virginia were also made to feel unwelcome in local churches. The chaplain of the Second Vermont had an appointment to preach in a local church building on a Sunday afternoon but was preempted by the funeral of a Confederate officer. The chaplain postponed his service to a later hour and, taking part of the regiment's choir with him in case they might be needed, attended the funeral. The choir was emphatically not needed, and the Yankees sat quietly through the service. As for the Virginians, "It was easy to see from their manner," wrote one of the Vermonters, "that they cared but little for the presence of Union soldiers."[62]

In December 1864, Sherman's armies captured Savannah and moved into the city to remain for several weeks. During that time, some of the soldiers took the opportunity of attending local civilian churches. In one church, identified by a soldier only as "a fashionable church with ushers," a large crowd—"a good many citizens and a great many soldiers"—filled the seats one Sunday morning. The fashionable ushers "paid no attention" to the Union soldiers and "did not show us to seats." As the service began, the minister rose and prayed for "the success of our arms" and that "the health and life of our President be preserved." It was fairly obvious that he was referring to the Confederate arms and to the health and life of Jefferson Davis. Perceiving this, a Union soldier wrote out a note and handed it to an usher to give to the minister. The note demanded that the minister henceforth, and as long as Sherman's men were in town, include in his prayers "the President of the United State and for all in power." The pastor, however, got the better of them, for at the end of the service he said, "We are taught in Holy Writ to pray for our enemies," and then prayed that "the life of the President of the United States may be spared to the close of this cruel war, in order that his eyes may be opened to the right" and that Sherman "may be as merciful and wise in the government of the city as he has been successful in waging a devastating war." The Union soldiers took it indulgently.[63]

General Sherman himself, along with his staff, attended St. John's Episcopal Church, which was also packed with both townspeople and Union soldiers. The minister there avoided difficulty by simply omitting the portion of the Episcopal liturgy that included a prayer for the president—either of the Confederate States or of the United States.[64]

In the final weeks of the war, large numbers of Sherman's soldiers attended civilian churches in Fayetteville, North Carolina, after capturing that town. "We heard a pretty good sermon," wrote the 100th Indiana's Theodore Upson, "all about loving ones enemies which I think the Southerners will have hard work to do. But they would have not had any enemies if they had not tried to break up the Union. If they will give up that crazy notion and stop fighting us, we will be their best friends."[65]

All wars are destructive, but the generation of Americans who lived through the Civil War considered it to be especially so. Compared with anything in their previous experience—or indeed, anything in the experience of previous Americans, with the exception of those New Englanders who had fought for their lives in King Philip's War in the late seventeenth century—the Civil War was surpassingly horrible. Two particular aspects of the war's horrors particularly impressed participants.

First of these was the terrible loss of life, unparalleled in percentage in any of America's other wars up to that time or, for that matter, any time since. The Christian faith of many soldiers helped them endure the repeated loss of comrades and the constant threat of death. The man who, through repentance and faith, places all his trust in the Lord Jesus Christ is assured of eternal life in heaven after this life on earth is ended. Thus, death in battle is not the end of one's existence, nor is it the worst thing that could befall. This assurance was probably of most help to the men during the long periods between battles rather than in the heat of action itself, when urgent activity left little time for thought. The frequent references in soldiers' letters and diaries to the comfort of their hope of salvation leave no room for doubt that this affected their morale—both their willingness to remain in the ranks, forgoing desertion, and their readiness to go into battle again when ordered.[66]

A second aspect of the war's virulence was the destruction of civilian property it entailed. Chastising the enemy's populace and countryside is as old as the history of warfare, but that was little comfort to the Civil

War generation, who had never before experienced it in their own lives. Both North and South carried out such destruction as they had opportunity. Initially, the practice was almost as shocking to the soldiers as it was to the civilians—all the more so, since in most ways the civilian targets of plundering looked and acted very much like the civilians the men had known back home. Back there, taking another man's pigs, cows, horses, honey, or apples was unequivocally stealing, and most of the boys, especially the Christians, had been brought up not to do this. Many of them expressed reservations about doing it in wartime too.

John D. Billings of the Tenth Massachusetts Battery wrote of "the presence in the army of a large number of men who had learned the ten commandments, and could not, with their early training and education, look upon this taking to themselves the possessions of others without license as any different from stealing." Billings added that in the early days of the war "these soldiers would neither forage nor share in the fruits of foraging," but by the later stages, they had mostly gotten over their scruples.[67] In some cases, this meant that they did not give up their conviction against stealing, but they did learn to differentiate between stealing and foraging. "We had . . . been brought up not to steal or lie, and I despise a thief or liar now," wrote Elisha Stockwell of the Fourteenth Wisconsin. "When we foraged, though, we thought of it as a part of war and punishment of the enemy."[68]

In other cases, they never learned to make that distinction but did join their comrades in the appropriation and destruction of civilian property, plagued all the while by a guilty conscience. Alva C. Griest of the Seventy-second Indiana wrote dolefully of the destruction wrought by his regiment, adding his belief that he "was doing wrong all the time we were at it."[69]

Still others came down somewhere in between the first two positions, remaining ambivalent about the rough use the army gave to civilian property. William Henry Walling of the 142nd New York wrote to his sister from North Carolina in March 1865, near the end of Sherman's march through the Carolinas. Foraging, he explained, was a "favorite pasttime to many of the men," but Walling himself found "no attractions" in it. He had been on only one foraging expedition thus far. "Cattle and sheep were all we took by authority that day," he explained. He believed the men took too much from the civilians. "All is taken and the people are left in many instances with broken furniture or none at all and in perfect destitution." Walling was not quite sure what to think of this. "If the saying be true that all things are right in times of war which distress ones enemies then the warfare of Gen. Sherman is the one after all for me (though I cannot admit in clear conscience). Where he has been there will be no seed time, consequently there can be no harvest. He seems to be the avenger of the slave as well as his liberator. You see I believe and I do not believe. May God bless him, him and us."[70]

Contrary to legend, Confederates behaved much the same way when they got the chance. When Lee's army marched north into Pennsylvania in 1863, his soldiers foraged liberally off the rich countryside. Confederate general William Dorsey Pender wrote to his wife, "Our people have suffered from the depradations of the Yankees, but if we ever get into their country they will find out what it is to have an invading army amongst them. Our officers—not Genl. Lee—have made up their minds not to protect them and some of our chaplains are telling the men they must spoil and kill." Similarly, a Confederate soldier, H. C. Kendrick, wrote, "I don't think we would do wrong to take horses, burn houses, and commit every depredation possible upon the men of the North."[71] In fact, the Confederates did not kill many civilians (two murders and one rape were later reported as the total for the entire campaign), nor did they burn many houses. They did, however, take clothes, shoes, horses, and about all they could find in the way of food. Lee himself occasionally looked the other way when his orders against plunder were being deliberately flouted.

Yet while foraging and destruction of civilian property might go too far for even the wartime scruples of some of the Christians among the soldiers, the overriding moral sense of the soldiers, strongly shaped by Christianity, put limits to what they did. Severity was directed toward those whom the soldiers believed to be guilty and therefore deserving of punishment.[72] That punishment was limited to the loss of property. As with the Confederates in the Gettysburg campaign, so with Union troops in their marches through the South; murders and rapes were extremely rare in this war. Finally, when the war ended, the soldiers did not, as some had feared they would, turn their newly developed foraging propensities to outright crime. Instead, most of them showed a sharp awareness of the difference between stealing and taking things as part of warfare. Even Sherman's renowned foragers knew when to quit. Illinois soldier Charles W. Wills wrote that the march of Sherman's men through North Carolina and Virginia after the Rebels' surrender "was splendidly conducted, no straggling, and the peace orders were faithfully lived up to. It seems like the early days of my soldiering to see the citizens all at home, their horses and mules in the stables, and gardens full of vegetables passed untouched. When a man can pass an onion bed without going for them, and they did a number of them today, no one need talk to me of total depravity. The soldier goes more on onions than any other luxury."[73]

The strong religious interest in the camps remained constant right down to the end of the war. In March, Aurelius Voorhis of the Forty-sixth Indiana noted of a weeknight prayer meeting, "There was an unusual number present," and at Sunday services, "attendance was good."[74] That same month, the Fifty-ninth Illinois's Chesley Mosman went to church one Sunday "but could not get in" because of the crowd.[75] That same month, Daniel G. Crotty of the Third Michigan wrote that the Sunday worship services in his regiment were "well attended, and all listen with the greatest attention to the sermons and join in the hymns that are sung."[76]

The efforts of army missionaries and the Christian Commission continued unabated. At the Sixth Corps hospital at City Point, Virginia, in March 1865, Wilbur Fisk of the Second Vermont wrote, "We are having some very excellent religious meetings here at our new chapel. Last evening there was a crowded house. I should think there was nearly if not quite 500 men present." Several delegates of the Christian Commission spoke, with obvious effect on the listeners. "The interest and feeling appeared to be deep and earnest," wrote Fisk. These particular delegates happened to be from Chicago, and the last of them to speak, a young preacher by the name of Dwight L. Moody, made a particularly strong impression. At the end of the service, at Moody's invitation, some fifty men rose, indicating their request that Christians pray for their salvation.[77]

While chaplains, missionaries, and Christian Commission delegates continued to be effective in their ministries, there were never enough of them. This shortfall was increasingly made up in the last year of the war by soldiers themselves, a number of whom began displaying a gift for preaching. In August 1864, Chesley Mosman heard a corporal of the Eightieth Illinois preach. The following January, a private from Company C of his own Fifty-ninth Illinois preached "a very good discourse."[78] Soldiers of the Thirty-second Wisconsin, lacking a chaplain, nevertheless held regular meetings in a grove near their camp.[79]

The revivals in the armies, beginning in the summer of 1862 and continuing more or less through the end of the war, had been an amazing phenomenon. Such a thing never occurred in any other American war. Although it was customary to refer to what happened in the armies as a series of revivals, it is really more accurate to think of it as a single large revival, approximately two and a half years long, occasionally interrupted by military operations. Although one segment of the military population lived in a state of continuous blatant sin, another large and steadily growing segment was constant and energetic in its spiritual pursuits throughout the war. One soldier did not think that the movement should be referred to as a revival at all. The Second Vermont's Wilbur Fisk wrote in 1864, "Some who have been with us and seen how easily great results are obtained, have called it a revival, when really it is not a revival, it is only what can be done anywhere in the army, at anytime by the same means."[80] In short, the Civil War armies contained a great many young men who were hungry for spiritual fulfillment and hope in the life to come.

While the revival continued in the armies, other revivals continued back home. In February 1864, Eunice Snow of Greenwich, Connecticut, wrote to her son Henry, in the Twenty-first Connecticut, "Their has been some verry interesting Meetings in this Town their has been a great a number of convertions. . . . Their were a number spoke and told what the Lord had done for them."[81] In January 1865, Isaac Jackson of the Eighty-third Ohio wrote to his brother back in Harrison, Ohio, "I was glad to learn of the grand result of your protracted meeting."[82] In March, William Henry Walling of the 142nd New York wrote to his sister expressing his happiness at the good news he had received from their hometown of Gouverner, New York, where a religious revival was flourishing. He rejoiced at "what God hath done for members there," and particularly over those who had converted. "Oh that the good work may not cease," he wrote in closing.[83] James G. Theaker of the Fiftieth Ohio wrote to his sister back home in Belmont County, Ohio, "I hear there has been a great revival at Mt. Pleasant," and asked for more information.[84] From the camp of the Forty-third Wisconsin in Decherd, Tennessee, Lewis Chase wrote to a friend back in Platteville, Wisconsin, rejoicing to hear that the Sunday school there was thriving and growing.[85]

Even as the war came down to its close, the soldiers' spiritual interests remained as strong as ever. As the Army of the Potomac prepared for its final, April 2, 1865, assault on the Confederate lines at Petersburg, a soldier of the Eighty-sixth New York—one who had come to Christ while in the army—wrote in his diary, "Jesus owns me, O, how sweet to feel that if we fall on the field of strife, we only fall to rise to higher and more perfect bliss than this world can give. My object is to live for heaven."[86] Elisha Hunt Rhodes, who in his four years in the army had risen from private to colonel, had anticipated this grand assault two days before. In his diary he wrote, "I am not fearful of death, and I may be one of the number. My trust is in God, for he doeth all things well."[87]

Wilbur Fisk was still in the Sixth Corps hospital at City Point on that day, a Sunday. "At the close of the afternoon service," he wrote, "at the Chapel of the Christian Commission," the Army of the Potomac's provost marshal general Marsena Patrick came in and announced that the army had early that morning broken Lee's lines around Petersburg in several places. According to the most recent dispatch he had received, the battle was still raging, with the issue in doubt. "He told us to pray every man of us to the God of battles, for the men who were fighting at that moment, as it was not only fitting, but our solemn duty to do so." At the urging of the presiding minister, Patrick himself led in prayer and did so very impressively.[88] That evening, after darkness had fallen on the field of the successful and truly decisive Union assault, the thoughts of those who had fought the battle also turned toward God. The officers of the Second Rhode Island gathered and joined in singing "Praise God from Whom All Blessings Flow."[89]

In Joseph E. Johnston's small Confederate army in North Carolina, nightly preaching services continued even while Lee's army, scarcely a hundred miles to the north, was in its death throes. On Friday, April 7, Alfred Fielder noted the text of the sermon and that "the audience was large and attentive and there were several mourners." The next evening saw additional seekers and conversions, and on Sunday, April 9, while Lee and Grant met in the McLean home at Appomattox, three soldiers in Johnston's army were baptized, and a Reverend Mr. Burr preached on the first eight verses of the twelfth chapter of 1 Corinthians.[90] On the other side of the lines, in the Fifty-ninth Illinois, Lt. Chesley Mosman went to church on Thursday, April 13, and found "the house was crowded so I must stand." On Sunday, April 16, the day that news of Lincoln's death was confirmed for the Union troops in North Carolina, Mosman attended church in a nearby town, where a Union sergeant preached on the text, "I am not ashamed of the gospel of Christ."[91]

The impending collapse of the Confederacy was no reason not to continue seeking more important things. Indeed, if the present life seemed bleak, that was more reason to look to the life to come. On Sunday, April 30, with the surrender of Johnston's forces agreed on and the men only waiting for completion of the last formalities to allow them to go home, Rev. J. B. McFerrin preached to one of the brigades of Johnston's army on Hebrews 13:14—"For here have we no continuing city, but we seek one to come." Alfred Fielder, who heard the sermon, wrote in his diary, "I felt that my abiding home would be in heaven."[92]

13

"GOD HAS CHASTENED US"
Northern Christians View the Concluding Stages of the War

"Notwithstanding all these difficulties and discouragements," proclaimed Chaplain N. G. Collins of the Fifty-seventh Illinois, "as we review the history of the past two years, we have abundant cause to exclaim, 'Behold, what hath God wrought!' We have conquered more than half the rebel territory, which we still hold, have been successful on almost every battle-field. . . . We have taken all the strong-holds of the enemy, from one end of the Mississippi River to the other, upon which Jeff Davis has staked the issue of the struggle; and, thank God, we will soon have all along the Atlantic coast. In view of these facts what cause for thanksgiving to Almighty God, and courage to arm us for new victories."

It was August 3, 1863, and Collins was addressing the men of Bane's brigade at Corinth, Mississippi, in honor of a national day of thanksgiving proclaimed by President Lincoln in observance of the recent Union victories at Vicksburg, Port Hudson, Helena, Tullahoma, and, out on the eastern fringe of the war's operations, Gettysburg. These victories seemed harbingers of the beginning of the end of the rebellion. Collins's sermon, one of many delivered that day from the various camps of the armies of the great Republic from the Atlantic to the Great Plains, expressed the predominant outlook of Union soldiers toward the religious aspects of the war as the nation braced itself for what all believed would be the final struggle to crush the evil Confederacy.

"The cause of God, and right, will succeed," Collins flatly declared, citing examples from both the Bible and secular history. "Our Government, I believe, was given us of God, and he has a destiny for us that will illumine with its brightness the whole world, and pour its blessings of peace and freedom upon nations yet unborn. Sooner than see this Government overthrown would I expect to see the mighty river rolling its vast volume of water up the mountain side, the laws of nature everywhere reversed, and all giving evidence that God had forsaken the helm of this part of the universe." About such matters there could be no doubt; final Union victory was assured.

Equally clear and certain were the rights and wrongs of the contest. "This dreadful war was not the choice of the North," Collins continued, "nor was it commenced by the North." Rather, it was the South that had foolishly and wickedly rebelled. "This war presents the pleasing fact to us that the North are fighting for the right, the perpetuation of intelligence and human freedom, while the South are fighting for human bondage as the chief corner-stone of their government, and the perpetuation of ignorance as an inevitable result." Now "the Southern Confederacy has been weighed in the balance and found wanting." The North was fighting to free the slaves, and "when the cause (slavery) which has produced this war shall have been removed and not till then, shall we have a permanent peace." He concluded, "I was never prouder of being an American citizen than today. In the midst of the confusion of war we have abundant cause for thanksgiving to God, that he has caused light to shine out of darkness, and brought order out of confusion, upon the subject of American slavery which has hitherto darkened almost every ray of light in our political heavens."[1] Collins's sermon summed up succinctly much of what Union soldiers in late 1863 thought about God and the war.

Like Chaplain Collins, Union soldiers believed emphatically in the rightness of their cause. Speaking of Union successes in Middle Tennessee in the summer of 1863, James A. Connolly of the 123rd Illinois exulted, "God speeds the right."[2] Early the following spring, Alfred L. Hough wrote from the Union camps around Chattanooga, "This is a terrible ordeal we are going through, but out of this darkness we will appear brighter and better, so I believe, and every day I have a more religious feelings, that this war is a crusade for the good of mankind." Hough was especially impressed by the progress made in helping the newly freed slaves learn to read.[3] The Second Vermont's Wilbur Fisk also saw the slaves as central to the issue of right and wrong in the war. "Compromise with Slavery, and restore the Union with Slavery in it still!" he wrote indignantly in April 1864, "as well might Jehovah compromise with Satan and give him back part of Heaven. . . . With Slavery for a corner stone they [the Rebels] hope to rob our government of her honor, and erect within our borders a rival government, which every attribute of the Almighty must detest." In his letter, which was intended for publication in a newspaper back home, Fisk then turned to the charge leveled by some that the Union was fighting solely to free the slaves. Fisk said that there was much more involved, but that fighting to free the slaves was certainly a good and proper motive. "I verily believe that He who when He was on the earth healed foul leprosy, gave sight to the blind beggars, and preached the gospel to the poor, would not be ashamed to act from such a motive. And if he would not, why should I?"[4]

Religion lay very close to patriotism in the minds of a great many Union soldiers. During the winter and spring revivals in the camps, soldiers of the Sixty-seventh Indiana sometimes drifted across the line from the expression of one to the expression of the other. "It was not unfrequent," wrote R. B. Scott, "when a rousing sacred meeting was at its highest pitch that a tune would be switched off into an outburst of patriotism, when the very walls would tremble and roof shake with the soul-stirring strains" of patriotic music.[5]

As the armies made obvious preparations for the opening of the 1864 campaigns, Union soldiers expressed continued and even enhanced confidence in the rightness of their cause and its ultimate success. "We will conquer in our holy cause," wrote George W. Shingle of the Fifty-third Pennsylvania in April of that year, "for I am sadisfyed that God is on our side."[6]

Throughout the months of almost constant fighting, they continued to say the same. An officer of the 142nd New York believed his men fought better because of their assurance that the Union cause was just. "I know my men fought bravely," he wrote near the end of May, "and why should they not since our cause is so good and just."[7] From the battle lines around Atlanta in August, a soldier of the 105th Ohio wrote that the "*big idea* which is at stake" was not only "the principles of Liberty, [and] Justice" but also "of the Righteousness which exalteth a Nation."[8]

It almost went without saying that if the cause was right and pleasing to God, then the side that espoused that cause must certainly be victorious—but the soldiers said it all the same, perhaps to buck up their own confidence. In July 1864, with Sherman's armies stalled in front of Atlanta after three hard battles, James Connolly wrote that he was certain the city would fall. "Our reliance is in God and a just cause," he wrote, "and 'by that sign we conquer.'"[9]

But some doubted, at least a little. They seemed not to question the rightness of their cause or that it was pleasing to God. They did, however, express some uncertainty as to whether God would see fit to intervene to assure its victory. Pvt. Henry Kauffman of the 110th Ohio was typical of many soldiers when he wrote, "I hope that God will be with the right."[10] It was a common phrase. Some, both then and now, might well ask who else God would conceivably be with, but that did not answer the doubts. Sometimes in past centuries, God had allowed just causes to go down to defeat for the accomplishment of greater good and the fulfillment of His will over vast stretches of time. For some Union soldiers, the question remained as to whether He might not do this in their case, withholding His intervention while their cause failed.

As had begun to be the case during the first half of the war, the cause could sometimes take on a life of its own in the minds of its adherents. Some Union soldiers, especially those who were not actually Christians, tended to raise their cause to the status of the ultimate good. As some had begun to do in the first half of the war, these men asserted their own concept of eternal rewards and punishments. John Roberts of the Eighty-third Indiana had, in his words, "never . . . professed Christianity," yet as he lay sick and near death, he thought of God and reflected, "Won't he give me some credit for my life blood and service for the best Government on earth." Later, in his memoirs, he somewhat retreated from the implied heresy of his delirious thoughts. "I don't say that every soldier will be saved."[11] Others, however, were more blatant in stating heretical beliefs. "I couldn't imagine the soul of a soldier who had died in the defense of this country being consigned to an orthodox hell," wrote David Cornwell of the Eighth Illinois, "whatever his opinion might be of the plan of salvation."[12]

Such heretical ideas could creep into discourse in various forms and to differing degrees. Some enterprising printer issued patriotic stationery for soldiers' use picturing at the top an image of the flag and the Constitution, with two clasped hands and arching above this composite picture the words: "The Rock of Our Salvation."[13] That term had a very definite meaning within Christianity and referred to Jesus Christ. As had been the case earlier in the war, however, such departures from orthodoxy remained distinctly a minority view.

If the Union cause was that of God in the eyes of both orthodox Christian Northerners and their heterodox compatriots, it followed naturally what the Confederate cause was. Union soldiers continued to be emphatic in stating their thoughts on the matter. "This wicked rebellion" and "This unholy rebellion" were common expressions among soldiers.[14] It was sometimes difficult, even for a devout Christian like Elisha Hunt Rhodes, to prevent his loathing of the "wicked rebellion" from spilling over into personal feelings toward the Rebels. "May God forgive the men who brought about this war," Rhodes wrote in the summer of 1864, "I fear that I shall yet hate them."[15] But hate was considered the proper motivation not for God's people, fighting for truth, but for His enemies, the Rebels. "We fight because we love our government," wrote Wilbur Fisk, "and they fight because they hate it."[16]

The wickedness of the South was a recurring theme in the writings of Union soldiers and the preaching of their chaplains in the latter stages of the war. On May 6, 1865, James K. Newton of the Fourteenth Wisconsin attended a preaching service in the Alabama capitol at Montgomery, the very building where, more than four years before, Jefferson Davis had been chosen as president of the Confederate States. The sermon was preached by a Union chaplain, who took as his text, "And they laughed him to scorn." Newton described the sermon in a letter he wrote to his parents the next day: "He enumerated the many ways in which God was laughed to scorn, & instanced the rebellion as one. He also spoke of the time when in that very room the solemn compact made by our fathers was laughed to scorn by the south."[17]

Letters from home emphatically seconded the idea that the Rebel cause was hellish. "I was afraid," wrote the mother of Sylvanus T. Harrison to her son, "you had been captured or killed by those heathenish wretches who are skulking about that and every other Secesh region, like the enemy of souls, seeking whom he may devour."[18] The "enemy of souls," of course, is Satan.

Not surprisingly, in view of all this, another theme often repeated in the writings of religiously inclined Northern soldiers during the final months of the war was that of punishment. That concept, however, was capable of a number of different applications. The most straightforward was the punishment of the South for its sins of slavery and secession. In February 1864, Maj. P. J. Arndt of the Thirty-first Wisconsin wrote to his parents, "Truly may it be said that the South are reaping a most fearful retribution for the sin of cecession and rebellion."[19] That same month, J. N. DeForest wrote that the reason Jefferson Davis and other Confederate leaders did not sue for peace was that "God Almighty won't let them until slavery has been fully abolished and these men have wrought out their own destruction."[20] In October 1864, Cpl. George J. Howard of the Fifth Vermont expressed his ideas on this matter in a letter to his wife. Referring to the Union war dead up to that time, he wrote, "Ah! Those three hundred thousand fresh soldiers graves in these slave states call for redress at our hands; and as true as God has a principal they shall have it, and woe to those unhappy people of this wicked rebellious conspiricy if they do not soon return to their allegiance."[21] Five months later, William Henry Walling of the 142nd New York wrote to his sister from the vicinity of Raleigh, North Carolina, at the conclusion of Sherman's two great campaigns through the interior of the conquered South, describing "the absolute emptiness of this Southern country. . . . If ever a people have been brought low," wrote Walling, "it is here." This he saw as the result of their "crimes against God, humanity and good government."[22]

As the war came down to its final weeks, Lincoln in his Second Inaugural Address enunciated the thought he had long been turning over in his mind, a thought that had been on the minds of many Union soldiers since the second year of the war. He suggested that God had His own purposes in allowing the war to come and in allowing it to continue as long as it did. Perhaps the war was not only a punishment on the South for embracing the institution of slavery and trying to break up the Union but also a punishment on the North for a wrongful national pride and its reluctance to come to the point of striking for the obliteration of slavery. God could have given the North a quick and relatively bloodless victory. He did not. As the bloodshed went on, month after month, to ever more appalling proportions, Lincoln was haunted by the question of why God allowed this. His conclusion was that God was using the war for His own purposes, and those purposes might be different from the initial war aims of either the North or the South. "If the Almighty shall have ordained," Lincoln stated in his Second Inaugural Address, "that the war continue until all the wealth amassed by the bondsman's 250 years of unrequited toil be sunk and every drop of blood drawn with the lash be atoned with another drawn with the sword, then as was said by the prophet 2,000 years ago so it must be said again, 'The judgments of the Lord are true and righteous altogether.'"

Lincoln restated his basic premise a week and a half later in a letter to Republican political manager Thurlow Weed: "Men are not flattered by being shown that there has been a difference of purpose between the Almighty and them. To deny it, however, in this case, is to deny that there is a God governing the world. It is a truth which I thought needed to be told; and as whatever of humiliation there is in it, falls most directly on myself, I thought others might afford for me to tell it."[23]

The concept that God was using the war to punish the North as well—perhaps for tolerating slavery, perhaps for a wrongful national pride, materialism, and the like—had been raised by the North's Episcopal bishops in a joint letter in October 1862. "God has loaded us with benefits," the bishops wrote, "and with our benefits have grown our ingratitude, our self-dependence, and self-sufficiency, our pride, our vain-glorying." The war, therefore, was God's "chastening Providence."[24]

The same idea was also present with the Union soldiers from time to time in the latter half of the war. In July 1863, Maj. Samuel Duncan of the Fourteenth New Hampshire read such ideas in a letter from his father back in Meriden, New Hampshire. "Now as to this wicked and unholy war," his father had written, "I will say I believe it is a judgment upon us for our great national and individual sins and although grievous we must be submissive to the divine will, there is mourning all over the land for

there is scarcely a place but what some one has lost a friend or an acquaintance either in battle or the Hospital. . . . May God in mercy grant
us victory and put an end to the Rebellion."[25]

The soldiers themselves spoke of it sometimes. One soldier wrote,
"This war is sent by our Lord and if the People are punished enough for
their national sin then it will soon be settled." Benjamin Ashefelter of the
Thirty-fifth Pennsylvania had similar ideas. "Soon as the Nation becomes
Humbled in the sight of God the war will end and no sooner."[26] In a similar vein, David Humphrey Blair wrote to his sister in June 1864 saying
that he hoped the war would end soon. "Still," he added, "we must not be
too sure. I fear the nation has not yet recd just punishment yet. . . . We
must acknowledge the hand of the Almighty God in warfare and should
be patient at his hand."[27]

That fall, Orson Young of the Ninety-sixth Illinois put the case as plainly
as anyone could. The war was a punishment for sin, and the North felt that
punishment as well as the South because the North had been part of a nation
that had for four score and seven years tolerated slavery. "Four millions of
human beings are suffering under the chain and the lash," Young wrote,
speaking of the slaves. "They have been appealing for years to the Almighty
God for justice. In the anguish of their hearts, the slaves almost thought
that there was no God. But God heard their prayers. We are now paying
the price of our national sin. Shall we be so rash as to allow slavery to continue and call the wrath of a just God upon us again?"[28]

Sometimes the faith of the soldiers was simply that God was using the
war to accomplish his purposes but that those purposes—not necessarily emancipation or the punishment of anybody—were probably un-
knowable at the present time. Richard R. Crowe of the Thirty-second
Wisconsin took this simpler view. On the same day Lincoln gave his
Second Inaugural Address, but hundreds of miles away, he wrote, "An
all wise Providence will end the strife and misery, as soon as the purposes for which it was ordained is accomplished."[29] In like manner,
James G. Theaker of the Fiftieth Ohio wrote to his sister in April 1864,
"I believe that He [God] will yet over rule this war for good, and that
He has a great purpose to accomplish."[30]

Those who thought along the same lines Lincoln did—that God might
have other purposes in the war besides those of the Northern people, and

that one of those purposes might be the just chastisement of the North for certain sins—were not questioning the rightness of the Union cause or the propriety of their own fighting for it. Rather, they were seeking to explain why God allowed such a long and painful struggle before the triumph of His righteous cause was achieved. The general consensus of the Union soldiers was still that their cause was just and favored by God. Wilbur Fisk, for example, in reflecting on the fact that his own Sixth Corps was not transferred out of the Shenandoah Valley before the October 1864 battle of Cedar Creek but remained there to help win the Union victory, stated, "Can there be any doubt on whose side God's Providence was there?" Two and a half months later, at the turn of the year, Fisk wrote, "A revolution against such a Government as ours is too foul a thing for God to permit. The Confederacy is doomed." He conceded that the South might win another victory or two, but such victories would be "feeble" and could at most "lengthen out the contest a short time." What was more important than the precise timing was the final outcome. "Trusting in God," Fisk wrote, "we know the issue cannot be doubtful."[31]

Other soldiers also expressed this confidence that no matter how long and rough the path by which God might lead the nation, He would eventually bring it out not only victorious but also strengthened and purified. The difficulties and setbacks along the way would be His means of doing this. Vermont soldier Joseph C. Rutherford did not approve of the lenient terms on which William T. Sherman accepted the surrender of Joseph E. Johnston's army in North Carolina in late April 1865. Nevertheless, he assured his wife, "So much have I become to believe in the ultimate designs of the great Ruler of all things that I feel it was intended that greater good might accrue to the nation from it."[32]

It had not always been easy to have such faith. During the dark days of late summer 1864, when Grant's army appeared to be stalled outside of Richmond and Sherman's outside of Atlanta, and as Union casualty lists grew to hideous length, doubt had stalked the North, tempting some to despair and believe that God would not grant them victory over the Rebels. On the whole, the soldiers resisted that temptation better than the civilians back home, but the feeling of discouragement in late summer was just as real for both.

Many soldiers expressed their feelings in writing as they clung doggedly to their faith. That August, Pennsylvania soldier John Harmer wrote that even if the Rebels "whip Grant and drive Sherman to the Ohio and burn the citties of Pa. I will still believe that they must be finally destroyed. I cannot believe that Providence intends to destroy this Nation."[33] A soldier of the Fifty-fourth Pennsylvania used some of the same words: "I cannot believe Providence intends to destroy this Nation," he wrote, "this great asylum for the oppressed of all other nations and build a slave oligarchy on the ruins thereof."[34] Writing in early September, before the fall of Atlanta was known in Virginia, William Henry Church of the Second Wisconsin surveyed the dismal situation for the North. Worst of all was the prospect that the Democratic Party, which Church considered disloyal, might win the upcoming election. "But," he concluded, "I trust in God to protect the Right & bring us through this trial in honor & safety."[35] Just three weeks later, William Henry Walling of the 142nd New York mentioned "the depression that was felt both by the army and the country" after the July 30 Union debacle at the battle of the Crater, near Petersburg. By the time of his writing, however, much had changed, and among the most important changes was Sherman's capture of Atlanta. "Now," Walling wrote, "that cloud has past away. Providence veiled his face and tried our faith. The country and the army trusted Him in the night time and since then He has blessed us with glorious victories. The sky is cloudless today and every heart is full of hope that we are his people whom he will never forsake."[36]

As always, it was sometimes difficult for soldiers who had such faith to sort out what was God's responsibility and what was their own. If God could be counted on to ensure Union victory, did it matter whether the soldiers did their part or not? The 110th Ohio's Henry Kauffman took a stab at explaining this in a letter to his brother and sister. It was crucial, he wrote in August 1864, that Lincoln be reelected. Then he added, "It is no use for us to talk about it, for if we trust in God he will make it all right, yet although we must do our part and do it right."[37] More experienced theologians than the twenty-one-year-old Kauffman have wrestled long and hard with such questions.

Belief that service to the Union cause was service to something greater than one's own self-interest—indeed, service to God Himself—was one of the more powerful motivations in keeping the Union soldiers to their task to the very end. The Ninety-sixth Illinois's Orson Young admitted in the fall of 1864 that he sometimes asked himself, "What was the use of it to me, if the union was saved and my life was lost?" A man might risk his life in the hope of living a better life in a victorious nation, but what if the risk of one's life turned into the loss of that life? Young's answer to himself was unequivocal: "Then my conscience would ask me what I was born for—just to live for myself alone? No, I cannot believe that."[38] At the end of the day, it was pleasant and proper that a man lay down his life not only for his country but also for the accomplishment of God's will and the purposes for which God had brought that man into the world in the first place.

Northern soldiers were not slow to see God's hand in the final Union victories. When Sherman took Atlanta in September 1864, James Connolly wrote, "The 'God of Israel' is wielding his sword in our behalf and we know no such word as fail." The next month, when he learned that the Republicans had carried key Northern states in the fall 1864 elections, Connolly exulted, "Thank God for it! He is giving our old flag victories with the ballot as well as with the bullet."[39] When Petersburg fell, the Fifty-seventh Massachusetts's George Barton wrote to his mother, "Glory to God and his brave boys!"[40] "Glory to God in the highest," exalted Elisha Hunt Rhodes on April 9, 1865. "Peace on earth, good will to men! Thank God Lee has surrendered, and the war will soon end."[41] Gen. David S. Stanley, commanding the Fourth Corps at Greeneville, Tennessee, announced the news of Appomattox to his troops in a general order that then "recommended that chaplains of the Regiments hold service in their respective places of worship; to render thanks to Almighty God for his goodness and mercy in preserving us as a nation and giving us this great victory over our enemies." Stanley concluded his order, however, by striking the same thoughtful note that Lincoln had in his Second Inaugural Address. "Let us reflect," read Stanley's order, "and we may profit by so doing, that great national, as great personal sins, must be atoned for by great punishments."[42]

Lincoln's assassination was profoundly disturbing to Northerners. Wilbur Fisk wrote that the president had been "murdered by the same fiendish spirit, begotten in hell, and fed by slavery on earth, that has brought forth this rebellion." It was all very well, of course, to say that Lincoln's assassin had been satanically inspired, but why had a sovereign God allowed it? "Why did a just and merciful Providence permit this thing to happen? . . . It seemed almost impossible," Fisk wrote, "to submit to it as a dispensation of Divine Providence." The only answer he could give was Lincoln's own answer to all the previous bloodshed of the war: "We must quote, in view of this event, the same words that Mr. Lincoln quoted in his second inaugural, 'The judgements of the Lord are true and righteous altogether.'"[43] In short, the assassination of Lincoln was yet another punishment on the nation as a whole.

Pvt. Henry E. Dunbar of the Third Massachusetts Heavy Artillery believed that he knew why God had allowed Lincoln's assassination. Rather than as a punishment of the North, God had permitted the tragedy to motivate the North to a more thorough and relentless punishment of Southerners, "the *incarnate Devils,*" as Dunbar called them. Speaking of his fellow soldiers, he wrote, "We are all ready here for a *complete annihilation* of the whole *cursed race,* & I am about willing to believe that God would justify such a Policy. If not," he asked, "why should He permit the *fiends* to murder our good president[?]"[44]

Justus M. Silliman of the Seventeenth Connecticut had a different interpretation of the assassination. In his view, God had allowed the assassination in order to keep the people of the North from idolatry, to keep them from setting up Lincoln as their great deliverer when in fact their deliverance had come from God. Silliman and his comrades "then reflected that our cause was still in the hands of the Supreme Ruler who has thus far guided us through our troubles, and that he might have removed from us the Father of our Country that we might be induced to place our whole reliance on the God of our fathers, and not in man as perhaps has been done by a large portion of the people."[45]

Some Northern soldiers came to see Lincoln as a special servant of God for the accomplishment of the great work of emancipation and the preservation of the Union. Speaking of Lincoln's assassination, George Allen of the Fourth Rhode Island wrote, "His great work upon earth was ended, his mission fulfilled, and the angels of heaven, bending over his dying bed, softly whispered, 'Well done, good and faithful servant; enter thou into the joy of thy Lord.'"[46] Similarly, the Third Michigan's Daniel

Crotty wrote that Lincoln "was called to receive the reward that is meted out by the just Judge of all those that doeth his will." Lincoln would be remembered, Crotty opined, "as the great martyr of our country's freedom."[47] Yet Lincoln's personal religious beliefs remained somewhat obscure to the end.[48] He may have come to Christ late in his presidency, in late 1863 or 1864, but the evidence is unclear.

Just as Chaplain Collins's sermon summed up the soldiers' religious thoughts about the conflict just beyond the midpoint of the war, so Chaplain George Wells of the Eleventh Wisconsin preached a sermon in April 1865 that captured the essence of what Union soldiers believed were the spiritual issues of the war they had just fought. Wells began by alluding to the causes of the war. "A faction of fanatics made fanatical by their blind devotion to and superstitious reverence for the institution of slavery" had endeavored to break up the United States. "As men, patriots, and Christians it was our duty to sustain the honor of the flag." Yet something far more was at stake. "Principals were involved," Wells asserted. "There was then to begin a grand struggle between truth and error. Right and wrong were to meet face to face, and the great battle between glorious heavenly liberty and hell born, hell bound slavery was to be fought." The final result of such a contest could never be in any real doubt, but, Wells admitted, "it has not always appeared so." He rehearsed the history of Union setbacks and the determined perseverance that had led to victories on the battlefield and finally the complete victory they now enjoyed. God had given them these victories—by raising up great leaders such as Lincoln and the victorious Union generals, by stirring the hearts of millions of Northern men to enlist as soldiers, and by providing the North with abundant material resources. The triumphant Northerners were now obligated to show their gratitude to God not only in words but in actions too—first of all, by prayer. "Pray therefore that God would still continue and preserve us a nation. . . . Pray for those whose hearts are made sad by war's desolation. . . . Pray that God would bestow consolation, and give the oil of joy for mourning with the garment of praise for the spirit of heaviness." They should also do what they could to help relieve those who were suffering and sad. "But in praying," Wells added, "do not forget your own need of pardoning mercy, and a regenerated nature. Pray that God would forgive the past and give you 'A heart in every thought renewed / And full of love divine.'"

Finally, they could show their gratitude to God through holy living. "If we are grateful to a friend we show it by corresponding acts, and if we are in earnest in thanking God for our successes we shall show it not by rebelling against His will but by keeping His commandments, walking in His statutes, and living to love Him." As he approached the conclusion of his sermon, Wells spoke in terms that resonated with the ideas of the early Puritans who came to America with a vision of a "city upon a hill" and an awareness of a divine covenant by which blessing lay before them as a reward for faithfulness and a curse awaited them if they forsook their covenant with God. "As a nation," Wells stated, "we have passed through a very fiery ordeal, and it ought to purify us as gold is purified by fire. God has chastened us, not for our distruction, but to correct and make us a holy people that we may serve Him forever. If we will learn that lesson and obey the teachings of our Almighty Friend our future will be great and glorious beyond our most sanguine expectations, but if we will not serve Him we may expect distruction, for the nation that will not serve God shall perish."

How should the soldiers then live in the now peaceful and victorious United States that their arms had helped to save? Wells offered his answer: "The laws of our country are so constituted that every man wields an influence. You and I, my friends, have a power, and we can use it to good advantage if we so choose. Then let us show our gratitude and at the same time benefit our country by living a holy life and exerting a Christian influence around. Let it be said of the 11th Wisconsin that besides expressions of thanks, they yielded themselves servants to God, and thereby manifested sincere and hearty thanks to God for giving us the victory. Amen."[49]

14

"THE LORD HAS FORSAKEN HIS PEOPLE"
Southern Christians View the Concluding Stages of the War

"Our cause is Just and will bring us off Conquerors," wrote the Twelfth Tennessee's Alfred T. Fielder in his diary. "Lord, help us as a nation to humble ourselves under thy mighty hand."[1] The date was July 4, 1863. Though Fielder could not yet know it, Lee's army was beginning its forlorn retreat from Gettysburg, and Confederate forces under Lt. Gen. Theophilus H. Holmes that day suffered repulse in an attempt to take Helena, Arkansas. Fielder's own Army of Tennessee had just been maneuvered almost entirely out of the state whose name it bore, and worst of all, Vicksburg and an entire Confederate army of 30,000 men had just surrendered to Ulysses S. Grant. The Southern people were clearly going to have plenty of occasion to humble themselves under God's hand, but it took considerable faith for a soldier like Fielder to believe that they would still come off as conquerors. Yet this faith, based on the belief that the Confederate cause was right, was one shared by vast numbers of Southerners both in and out of the army.

Confederates were sure they were right. Most Southerners had come to accept as unquestionable truth their section's oft-repeated assertions that the Bible sanctioned slavery. If that was the case, then the slave system they had started this war to perpetuate was in fact ordained by

God. To many Southerners, the Confederate war effort took on a strong religious significance, and fighting for the Confederacy was an act of devotion to God.[2] This view was strengthened by the overt and enthusiastic support of Southern clergy, who repeatedly and vehemently equated the Confederate cause with that of God. Southern Methodist leaders claimed that the "maintenance of pure Christianity on this continent" and "the very existence of our churches" depended on Confederate victory.[3]

A firm faith in the divine assurance of Confederate victory required some explaining in the late summer of 1863, for things had not gone well for the South for several months past. The explanation that was on the lips—and pens—of many Confederates that summer was that God was chastening his people, punishing them for their sins and purifying them for their glorious future existence as an independent country. It was remarkably like the thinking of many Northerners, as they also wondered why God allowed the war to go on. Similarly, only in this manner could Southerners explain why God delayed giving them the triumph they deserved and allowed bloody and heart-rending setbacks along the way. "How long, oh God, how long?" asked Flavel C. Barber of the Third Tennessee in the biblical words of martyred souls in heaven who called upon God to avenge their blood. What Barber asked of God, however, in this late July 1863 diary entry was how long "wilt Thou suffer such tyranny upon the earth?" He believed that the Southern people, for unnamed sins, "deserved all we have suffered, but," he pleaded, "spare the rod of Thy anger before we are utterly destroyed. Chasten us, but do not entirely destroy us."[4]

Some other soldiers shared Barber's discouragement. In July 1863, Joshua Callaway of the Twenty-eighth Alabama wrote to his wife, "Of course you have heard all about the fall of Vicksburg and I need not say a word about it.... I confess that I tremble with apprehension. But our trust is in God and our cause is just."[5] Maryland Confederate soldier Randolph McKim wrote concerning the recently lost battle of Gettysburg, "I went into the last battle feeling that victory must be ours—that such an army could not be foiled, and that God would certainly declare himself on our side. Now I feel that unless He sees fit to bless our arms, our valor will not avail."[6]

Despite the widespread belief that God was chastening the South, most Confederates continued to feel assured that however severe their punishment might be, God would not, after all, "entirely destroy" the South, His chosen people. Johnny Green of the Ninth Kentucky, part of the "Orphan Brigade," wrote, "Our reverses at Vicksburg & at Gettysburg were severe blows, but not to our faith. Our cause is just & will surely prevail. We must have been a little too puffed up with pride & confidence in our own powers; justice may be delayed but it will come."[7] That same July 1863, the Ninth Louisiana's Reuben A. Pierson wrote to his father that since the "news of the sad misfortune" at Vicksburg "a dark pall is thrown over" the Confederacy's prospects. Nonetheless, Pierson believed, "Our hopes must rest on the God of battles who hath assured us that the race is not to the swift nor the battle to the strong. I have but little fear of the final result. Adverse fortune may for awhile darken our prospects but in the end we will come out conquerors."[8]

Likewise, in that dark July, the Third South Carolina's Tally Simpson wrote to his sister that even if Charleston, Savannah, and Richmond should fall, that would be "no reason why we should despair. . . . We profess to be a Christian people, and we should put our trust in God. He holds the destiny of our nation, as it were, in the palm of his hand. He it is that directs the counsel of our leaders, both civil and military, and if we place implicit confidence in Him and go to work in good earnest, never for a moment losing sight of Heaven's goodness and protection, it is my firm belief that we shall be victorious in the end." Like some Northerners who wondered why God allowed the war to continue so long and with so much bloodshed before bringing about their victory, Simpson speculated that the Almighty might have some purpose to be attained by the prolonging of the war. That, however, did not shake his ultimate confidence. "Let the South lose what it may at present, God's hand is certainly in this contest, and he is working for the accomplishment of some grand result, and so soon as it is accomplished, He will roll the sun of peace up the skies and cause its rays to shine over our whole land." Simpson agreed that the South's current problems were the result of God's chastening, which was well deserved. "We were a wicked, proud, ambitious nation, and God has brought upon us this war to crush and humble our pride and make us a better people generally." He only wished that the task of his country's betterment might quickly be completed. "The sooner this happens the better for us," he added.[9]

Southern leaders expressed the same message in their official proclamations. Jefferson Davis, in his proclamation making August 21, 1863, a fast day, pointed to the South's sin and resulting chastisement almost with relief. The concept made it possible to think of the recent disasters in terms other than divine rejection of the Confederate cause. "Who then will presume to complain that we have been chastened," Davis wrote, "or to despair of our just cause and the protection of our Heavenly Father?"[10] Robert E. Lee, in a proclamation to his troops that same month, wrote, "We have sinned against Almighty God. We have forgotten his signal mercies, and have cultivated a revengeful, haughty and boastful spirit. We have not remembered that the defenders of a just cause should be pure in His eyes; that 'our times are in his hands'—and we have relied too much on our own arms for the achievement of our independence. . . . Let us confess our many sins, and beseech Him to . . . hasten the time when war, with its sorrows and sufferings, shall cease."[11] This was to be the predominant, almost sole theme of Confederate religious utterance, public and private, civilian and military, right down to the end of the war.

In speaking and writing of God's chastening, His punishment of his people in order to correct their wrongdoing, Southerners believed they had a very good idea of at least one of the sins that had merited God's displeasure. By the middle of the war, Southern preachers and editors had begun a hue and cry of excoriation that was to be constant for the remainder of the conflict. The targets of these denunciations were "a heartless, rapacious horde of speculators and extortioners, who, like ravenous wolves, are preying upon the life-blood of the people and the Government."[12] In every Southern state and community of any size, their name was legion. "All classes, all trades, all professions, and both sexes alas! seemed infected by the foul contagion," lamented Rev. W. W. Bennett.[13] The people of the South had, through the actions of their government, become the corrupters of themselves. The Confederate government financed the war with credit and the printing press. Predictably, the value of Confederate scrip dropped like the proverbial rock, which meant that everyone had to charge higher prices for his goods and services or else accept a much lower value—often a value so low as to make continued economic activity impossible.

As the inexorable laws of economics drove prices higher, patriotic Southerners, few of whom understood those laws or what drove them, loathed themselves for the higher prices they could not avoid charging. Especially, however, they loathed their fellow citizens, those never quite identifiable others who were unnecessarily jacking up prices to make a wartime killing and thus forcing their godly and patriotic neighbors to raise prices a little bit too. It provided endless material for the jeremiads of the preachers, a nagging cause of guilt to many good Confederates, and an even greater source of mutual recrimination. Southerners never thought of blaming the unjust system created by their government's method of financing the war. If wrong had been done, it must have been by individual, not corporate, actions. Those individuals were the elusive speculators, and within that framework, suspicion could fall on virtually everyone engaged in economic activity. In the economic sense, the Southern people had met the enemy, and it was themselves. The soldiers blamed the civilians, and the civilians blamed each other.

Energetic civilians tried organizing "Confederate Societies," voluntary organizations of citizens who would compact to accept Confederate money at par with gold and sell all their produce at the cost of production. It was no use. Confederate money simply was not worth that much gold, and selling at production cost was not a long-term plan for economic viability. Inevitably, such schemes collapsed, and the people, who could not function otherwise, were plagued with the denunciations of moralists who demanded, "Are there no self-denial and self-sacrifice to be made, or has God in his wrath delivered us over to a doom worse than death?"[14] Similarly, a writer in a religious newspaper decried the situation in western Georgia: "Speculators and extortioners are, true to their instincts, ravaging this country, monopolizing every article of prime necessity as soon as it begins to get a little scarce. They seem to have forgotten the awful denunciations of God's word against all such characters and proceedings." Well might a people despair who found themselves trapped between economic reality and "the awful denunciations" thus wrongly held over them. If the South was plagued by guilt during the war, and if we take Southerners' own written testimony about its source and nature, it was not guilt over the sin of slavery but rather guilt for imagined economic sins. Bennett believed that these sins "finally broke the spirit of the people and the army."[15]

As for guilt about the institution of slavery itself, Southerners expressed none. A few, however, did express reservations about some of the ways that slaves were treated. Rev. Nelson Head of Virginia feared that Southerners were not providing adequate religious instruction to their slaves. "The moral and religious condition of our servants are by far too much neglected," he wrote in the *Richmond Christian Advocate* in the fall of 1863. "Perhaps God has a controversy with us on this subject. And the sooner we submit and learn the lesson He would teach us, the better for us as a people, and it may be the sooner the present troubles of our land will pass away in the so earnestly courted blessing of peace and independence for our beloved Confederate States."[16] The soldiers themselves scarcely mentioned slavery at all. Slavery lay behind the South's difficulties with those whom the soldiers frequently denounced as "abolitionists," but when speaking of their own cause, they preferred to use terms such as "liberty" and "independence."

Notwithstanding any nagging problems of guilt, Southerners in the second half of the war actually found what they believed to be a cause for even greater assurance of the rightness of their cause: the alleged barbarity of the evil Yankee invaders.[17] As the *Richmond Christian Advocate* put it in the fall of 1863, "The demon spirit of selfishness and greed of gain is undermining us within," but "the diabolical vandals of the North are burning and devastating our homesteads and fair land from without."[18] Naturally, there had always been the usual litany of how wrong the enemy was. J. Trooper Armstrong of the Ninth Arkansas wrote to his wife of "this unjust & unholy war that has been waged against us," and there were many more like him.[19] That was to be expected and had been so since the outset.

By the midpoint of the war, however, Union forces were treating Southerners less like friendly civilians and more like an enemy populace. The Federals did not, to be sure, treat Southerners like the rebels and traitors that Northerners believed them to be, but even treatment as hostile civilians was a shock to Americans, who had known little of the passage of enemy armies. Southerners soon took up the cry of atrocity and quickly made it part of their propaganda for the rightness of their cause. In July 1863, the *Rome Courier* reprinted a report from the *Richmond Sentinel* regarding a number of churches in northern Virginia that the Yankees had allegedly vandalized or destroyed. "Can the history of the world present a similar record of outrage?" foamed the editor.[20] Of course, the history of the world could present a long and dismal list of wartime destructions far exceeding the wear and tear in northern Virginia, but they had happened in far-off lands and so did not count. For good Confederates, such alleged actions by some of the Union soldiers proved the exceeding wickedness of their cause. "No war was ever prosecuted against any people with the same fiendish and malignant hate, or was ever attended by the same savage and revolting cruelties, as that waged by the United States against the people of this Confederacy," whined the *Richmond Whig*. The *Richmond Christian Advocate* smugly saw in this the harbinger of Northern doom: "The malice of our enemies encourage us in our confidence of their utter failure in their purposes. It is a bad sign for them; but a good sign for us. We have only to keep cool, do our duty, trust in God."[21]

Confederates continued to pray for victory and peace and that their enemies the Federals would see the light and realize the justice of the Southern cause. Alfred Fielder spent Sunday, August 23, 1863, in meditation and prayer for his family, his "country," as he called the Confederacy, and even "for my enemies that God would show them their error and that they might be better men." He prayed that God would cause the war to cease without further fighting, but if fight they must, he prayed God to nerve the arms of Confederate soldiers and enable them to drive the enemy from "the soil of the Confederate States." While in the hospital after being wounded at the battle of Missionary Ridge, Fielder recorded a similar prayer. "Oh! That this cruel war would come to an end and that our enemies would be content to let us alone in the enjoyment of those rights and privilages we so much desire and which we believe is garanteed to us by God himself."[22] Rev. J. B. McFerrin, an army missionary, wrote in the *Southern Christian Advocate* that winter, "Let my enemies North revile, yet, from 'my heart of hearts' I can pray God to have mercy on them and lead them to repentance and salvation."[23]

Not quite all Confederates took this view regarding God and the war. One fascinating exception is Joshua Callaway. Throughout the first two years of the war, Callaway mentioned several times in his letters to his wife his strong desire for peace "on our own terms." Late in 1863, Callaway became one of many Confederates who had come to Christ and felt assured of his future salvation. A few weeks after his conversion, he stated in a letter to his wife, "May the Lord give us peace, upon His own terms." He elaborated the thought further in a letter he wrote to a friend that same day in late October 1863. "I agree to your proposition to pray for peace," Callaway wrote, "but I am disposed [to] let the Good Lord decide upon what terms we have it. We have been pray[ing] for peace upon our own terms for three years and the prospect becomes more gloomy. Now let us accept it on his terms and trust his goodness to do us well. We know he will give us justice, or our rights. Let us not ask more." It was a striking change and may have indicated that Callaway was becoming reconciled to the idea that God's will might not include the fulfillment of all the demands Southerners had been making. How his views would have developed over the remainder of the war is a mystery. One day shy of a month after penning those letters, Callaway was killed in action at the battle of Missionary Ridge.[24]

Most Confederates, however, believed that the great revivals, culminating in the winter of 1863–1864, were a pledge of God's intent to save the Confederacy. Surely the righteousness of all the newly converted soldiers would so cleanse the Southern cause that God would now see fit to grant them victory. "While we have such men as these and fight in a holy and just cause we need have no fears of being enslaved by so brutal and cruel enemies as those against whom we are fighting," Reuben A. Pierson wrote to his father. "God who rules the destiny of all things and is a God of wisdom and justice will never suffer a determined and Christian people to be overcome by a cruel Tyrant but will be their deliverer as in the days of old He led the children of Israel dry-shod through the Red Sea."[25] North Carolina chaplain Richard Webb wrote, "I am of the candid opinion that this will be the last year of this cruel war, and my opinion is based on the fact that God has given us so many tokens of good in converting so many hundred soldiers, and still the work goes on all through this army. I don't believe that God will deliver us over into the hands of our enemies while we take Him to be our refuge and strength."[26]

One definite effect of the revival atmosphere that winter was to promote the reenlistment of soldiers whose three-year terms were about to
expire. Philip D. Stephenson described the strong religious overtones of
a mass reenlistment rally at Dalton, Georgia, that winter. "All of the ardor
that so splendidly opened their career as soldiers, tempered and deepened by the stern and terrible experience they had afterwards undergone,
was shown that wonderful night. They moved under the power of a force
within themselves, the capacities of which they little knew, the force of
the Soul aroused by a Divine influence."[27]

As the cold, snowy winter of 1864 melted away and spring came round
again, all knew that the most titanic conflicts of the war lay just ahead,
and Confederate soldiers, like their Union counterparts, strove to prepare themselves spiritually. April 8 was one of the many national days
of fasting, humiliation, and prayer set aside by the Confederate president and congress. Chaplain Chapman of the Thirty-second Tennessee preached to his own and neighboring regiments on the subject of "the
influence of individual sin upon our national success."[28] That was typical of Southern piety. In the Southern Christian way of thinking, well
trained by long-practiced connivance at slavery, social systems were
givens; they were not proper topics for critique, being simply beyond the
possibility of judgment as things good or evil. Only individual sins mattered, and therefore only they could be the source of divine displeasure.[29] The fast day, at any rate, seemed to be a success. Flavel Barber
thought the day was "very generally observed throughout the regiment
and brigade."[30]

It was so observed in other brigades as well. Army missionary S. H.
Smith was with Gordon's brigade that day and wrote of the observances
in rapturous terms, tightly weaving spiritual devotion with the prospects
of Confederate victory. "I have no idea that ever before was there such a
day realized by the present generation," Smith enthused. "Old professors of religion expressed a degree of confidence in God, of an early
deliverance from the bloody revolution, that astonished themselves. Who
can tell but that yesterday was the birthday of Southern independence?
Oh! If we could have ascended above the earth and looked down upon a
nation upon their knees before God, confessing their sins and suing for
mercy. I imagine we could have heard the shouts of the redeemed and

the songs of the angels as they exclaimed 'Peace on earth and good will to men.'"[31]

The soldiers generally looked with confidence toward the coming campaign. This confidence had been greatly enhanced by the continuing army revivals of the preceding winter. Now they translated their increased faith in God into an increased faith that He would favor their cause. Ted Barclay of the Fourth Virginia wrote, "Our cause we believe to be a just one, and our God is certainly a just God, then why should we doubt." The Thirteenth Virginia's F. Stanley Russell wrote, "I cannot but think that if we are true to ourselves and do our whole duty that a just and almighty God will crown our efforts with success and peace." Many others said the same.[32]

George Phifer Erwin of the Sixtieth North Carolina was perhaps less sanguine than most of his comrades. "If it is necessary that our beloved South should be still more severely chastised," he wrote in a letter to his father near the end of April, "we can only bow the head and receive unflinchingly and with awe, the merited punishment of our shortcomings." Still, even Erwin believed that this would be only chastisement, not final judgment and destruction, and he went on to express the hope that the war might be concluded victoriously before the year was out.[33]

Implicit in most of the statements about God's present chastisement and certain final elevation of the Confederate people in victory was an important proviso. God would thus bless the Confederacy if, and only if, its people would repent of the sins that had brought on the chastisement in the first place. If, however, they continued in their sins and showed themselves unworthy of the holy cause (liberty, true religion, or whatever) for which they conceived themselves to be engaged in war, then God might turn from them and leave them to their destruction. In April 1864, the Christian Association of the First Virginia Artillery published an appeal to the Confederate people. "We believe this war which is now desolating our land is a righteous judgment and chastisement from the hand of a just God for the various sins of which we have been and are still guilty." Under these circumstances, the soldiers urged that "frivolities or pleasures" and "sounds of joy and rejoicing" were not appropriate for the Southern people. Rather, this should be a time for "that proper feeling of sorrow and gravity which belongs to a people so deeply afflicted."[34] If they would humble themselves before God, perhaps He would consider the punishment thus far meted out to be sufficient. A Georgia soldier expressed the same thought: "If the hearts of our People will get right God will give us Peace and not before."[35]

Throughout the summer's fighting, Confederates continued to think of the war in terms of the righteousness of their own cause. "We are now fighting in the most just & honorable cause a nation ever engaged in and, our cause being just, I have no doubt of our ultimate success," wrote the Ninth Arkansas's J. Trooper Armstrong, adding, "I only pray that we may speedily see an end."[36] Since the Confederate cause was one of sublime righteousness, fighting for the Confederacy became a virtual religious rite. Reuben Pierson of the Ninth Louisiana wrote, "Many of our best men have already sacrificed their lives on the altar of Freedom."[37] Cullen Battle of the Third Alabama referred to the Confederate dead of Petersburg as having "offered up their lives on the hallowed altar of their Country. They went to the battlefield not as adventurers and mercenaries, but as God Commissioned Apostles of Liberty, and their translation was glorious."[38] Some pious Southern soldiers believed that the sublime moral excellence of those who had given their lives for the cause was itself an assurance of the purity and righteousness of the Confederacy, the fountain of redeeming virtue to offset the venality of those nameless speculators back home, and the key to God's eventual intervention on the South's behalf. Similarly, as many Confederates had begun to do during the first half of the war, during its latter phases, some Southerners continued to look to the piety and Christian character of Robert E. Lee as proof of the rightness of their cause.[39]

In the heat of the summer battles, some Confederates actually began to assert that God willed that Southerners should perpetrate atrocities on their foes. When Brig. Gen. William Mahone persuaded his men to stop murdering black Union prisoners of war at the July 30 battle of the Crater, the *Richmond Enquirer* reacted with dismay and urged Mahone, at the next such opportunity, to "let the work, which God has entrusted to you and your brave men, go forward to its full completion that is, until every negro has been slaughtered."[40] Confederate soldier Philip D. Stephenson wrote years later that the "poor Negro" was "an inevitable victim for the reluctant yet righteous resentment and retaliation of the

South."[41] A Virginia woman writing to her soldier-husband did not limit her wrath to black Federals. "Shoot them, dear husband, every chance you get. . . . They are devil furies who thirst for your blood and who will revenge themselves upon your helpless wife and children. It is God's will and wish for you to destroy them. Your are his instrument and it is your Christian duty."[42]

The fighting of 1864 involved a number of serious blows to the South. Yet once again, the same interpretive scheme determined how Confederates thought about these defeats. In July 1864 a Confederate soldier defending Atlanta wrote to his wife, "It seems like the Lord has turned his face from us and left us to work out our own destruction." It might seem so, but the soldier clung tenaciously to his faith that the Confederate cause was ultimately God's cause and that God would finally save it as soon as the Southern people were sufficiently punished for the various individual sins they had committed. "Oh that he would give the people to see the error of there ways as he did the children of Israel," concluded the same soldier, "and save us from everlasting destruction."[43] Southern Presbyterian minister William T. Hall wrote that Confederate defeat would be "the only inexplicable anomaly of history."[44] Soldiers need not concern themselves with anomalies of history. For them, at least, the matter seemed simple. Ignatius W. Brock wrote his sister, "All that we can do is fight and pray the blessing of God upon our efforts."[45]

Throughout the winter of 1865, with the Confederate cause all but beyond human hope of recovery, Southerners took comfort and encouragement from their Christian faith and their added belief that God would deliver them from their enemies. Sometimes this assurance could take bizarre forms. On his way back from a furlough, Alfred Fielder stopped overnight at the home of one Jack Taylor, who was, he vouchsafed, writing a book on the subject of Bible prophecies and their application to the Confederacy. "He affirms," wrote the nonplussed Fielder, "that the Confederate States is ancient Israel restored and declares that according to the scriptures the independence of the Confederacy is a fixed fact." Better yet, there was not to be much more fighting in the South, but lots of fighting in the North, either among the Northerners or between them and some unspecified foreign invaders. "He may be said to be a maniac upon the subject," Fielder dryly observed.[46]

Other Confederates also made the connection—a popular one—between the Southern people and the Old Testament nation of Israel. On Sunday, January 1, 1865, Rev. H. H. Kavanaugh preached to the Ninth Kentucky and took as his text Christ's assurance to his disciples, "Let not your hearts be troubled, ye believe in God believe also in me." A soldier who was present described the sermon, which included several themes popular with the Christians of the Civil War generation. The preacher "made it very plain that all we had to do was to have faith, keep our powder dry & take good aim & that finally the victory would be ours. He said the ways of God are past finding out, but 'He doeth all things well.' The Israelites were doomed to wander in the wilderness forty years but finally they gained the promised land."[47]

Still other Southerners continued to express the old standard doctrine that the South was being chastened and purified but was on the side of right and would finally win. Some Confederate soldiers wondered, however, just how far God would go with this chastisement before He poured out on the Yankees the fiery judgment they so richly deserved. Tennessee soldier George Phifer Erwin was optimistic on that score. In late January 1865 he wrote, "Our prospects look gloomy, don't they? . . . We may deserve severe chastisement from Providence for our national sins, but it appears to me that the Yankees deserve it the most and I believe they will meet it in good time. We are suffering now; our time to see the Yankees in the same situation will come soon. The strong alone cannot gain the victory. A higher power rules the course of events. The enemy are the mere instruments. I believe our nation will rise purified & innobled by this struggle & march on to its destiny, the highest place on the role of nations."[48]

Kentuckian Johnny Green clung desperately to his Confederate faith. "Our cause is just & surely God will not let us fail. The Lord loveth whom he chasteneth & we must renew our faith in him, meekly, faithfully serve him, never faltering, never wavering in courage and devotion . . . he will yet lead us to victory." It was not easy to overlook the signs of collapse all around him, but Green did his best. "It is darkest just before day," he added hopefully. "Day must be near at hand for us, for it certainly is dark."[49]

A few Southern religious leaders appeared to be hedging their bets, however, and were beginning to assert that perhaps the Confederacy and the kingdom of God were not quite the same thing. After the fall of Atlanta, Methodist minister James D. Anthony met William T. Sherman. Sherman told him, "You preachers ought to be out preaching peace and submission to the best government in the world." In reply, Anthony flatly lied. "My dear sir, we preachers down South let politics alone. We preach Christ Jesus and the Gospel of peace, and leave to Caesar the things of state."[50] In a February 1865 article, the *Southern Advocate* rather belatedly complained that Southerners had come to equate service to their country with service to God. If they had, the *Advocate* had certainly done its part to create that impression. Its editors had previously been vigorous in urging Southern Christians, for the good of the church and true religion, to fight to preserve "our national life."[51]

As the end approached, Southerners continued to hope that they might by some means win God's favor and His intervention on their behalf. Jefferson Davis, in accordance with a resolution of the Confederate congress, declared Friday, March 10, 1865, as a day of fasting, humiliation, and prayer. "Let the hearts of our people turn contritely and trustfully unto God," Davis exhorted in his proclamation. "Let us recognize in his chastening hand the correction of a Father, and submissively pray that the trials and sufferings which have so long borne heavily upon us may be turned away by his merciful love . . . that the Lord of Hosts will be with our armies, and fight for us against our enemies; and that he will graciously take our cause into his own hand and mercifully establish for us a lasting, just, and honorable peace and independence."[52]

Alfred Fielder wrote in his diary that day, "Oh that it may be indeed and in truth a national fast and may the heart of the nation be so humbled before God that in mercy he may turn aside the dark cloud of war that now hovers over our nation and that peace and prosperity may smile upon us." Fielder himself carefully kept the fast, eating nothing until after sundown that night. At 10:30 A.M. he went to St. John's Methodist Church and heard the pastor, a Reverend Mr. Evens, preach from 1 Samuel 7:3–4 and 13–14, a passage of Scripture that told how the prophet Samuel had challenged the people of Israel, if they would "return to the Lord with all [their] hearts," to put aside their worship of idols and then God would "deliver [them] out of the hand of the Philistines." They did, and God did. The Philistines were driven out, and the cities they had taken were restored to Israel. "The sermon," Fielder noted, "was well adapted to the occasion." When the day was over, he opined that it had "been more generally observed than any fast yet proclaimed by our presadent."[53]

Many pious Confederates continued to expect divine deliverance up to the very end. The battlefield defeats that piled one atop another in the Confederacy's last months were in their eyes but temporary setbacks, more of God's chastening and purifying, but never a sign that His cause was not their own. They kept fighting, always telling themselves that if they were faithful enough, God would at last come to their aid.[54] In March 1865, Col. Samuel Hoey Walkup of the Forty-eighth North Carolina wrote lamenting the long odds faced by his men in the Army of Northern Virginia. "The sea before us, the mountains on each side, behind us a mighty and desperate enemy. Where can we look for help but upwards[?]"[55] The reference to being hemmed in by mountains, sea, and an enemy army behind was a direct allusion to the situation in which the people of Israel had found themselves when departing Egypt. God had opened a miraculous way of escape for them, and Walkup's implication was that God would do so for the Confederacy as well.

The persistence of the Southern belief that after chastening them God would turn on their enemies is nothing short of amazing. That belief simply would not be surrendered, regardless of circumstances. To do so, as they saw it, would have been to display a lack of faith in God. Once they had established the paradigm early in the war for understanding and explaining the events happening around them, Southerners found that paradigm to be a sufficiently useful tool to account for even the most appalling sequences of disasters, with complete disregard for reality. That paradigm went like this: (1) The Confederate cause is right, (2) God will give victory to the cause of right, and therefore (3) anything bad that happened was merely an incident along the way to Confederate victory, painful perhaps, but ultimately inconsequential. At least this is what a forceful and vocal segment of Southern society expressed. Others may have seen it differently and simply left the army to return quietly to their homes. At any rate, Northern Christians would have disagreed hotly with the first premise of this unspoken Confederate syllogism, and many Christians throughout history might have suggested numerous caveats to the second premise as well.

That spring, the men of five brigades of Georgia troops in the Army of Northern Virginia joined in adopting resolutions on the subject. "We hereby acknowledge the sinfulness of our past conduct as a just and sufficient ground for the displeasure of Almighty God," the resolutions stated. They went on to set forth that the soldiers had now repented of their sins and asked their friends and relations back in Georgia to pray for "the salvation of our souls; that God may preserve our lives through the coming campaign, nerve our arms in freedom's contest, and crown our labors, privations, and toils, with Southern independence, peace, and prosperity."[56] The implication, of course, was that now that they had repented, God would certainly do just that. The same month, March 1865, Confederate artillery officer William Pegram expressed much more confidence. "He has his good purpose in chastising us now," Pegram wrote, "which I doubt not, when it is revealed to us, we will find to have been to *our good*."[57] Somehow, at last, God would deliver them from their enemies.

But divine deliverance did not come. For Confederate soldiers and civilians, the final realization that they had lost the war came at different times, depending on their particular circumstances. For the citizens of Richmond, it came on Sunday, April 2, 1865. Those attending St. Paul's Episcopal Church that morning noticed that Jefferson Davis was summoned out of the service. Then other high-ranking government figures left. Finally, many others, sensing the approach of doom, began to slip out of the service. Later that day, the situation was plain to all the citizens of Richmond, as columns of Confederate troops marched through the city in retreat. "Oh it is hard, hard, hard," wrote a foreign observer, "for your men whose brave comrades have died for honor to see their noble city given up." The citizens seemed to take it even worse. "They cannot believe it," the same observer wrote. "Heaven will interfere. It never can be! But lo the hour approaches & as the last soldiers come up to take a long adieu perhaps for ever, the long pent up tide of emotions bursts forth & the poor girls fling themselves on down on their sofas & chairs & weep & sob till their hearts seem breaking."[58]

For most Confederate soldiers, whenever and however the realization came, it was devastating to grasp that God had allowed them and their supposedly sacred cause to be utterly crushed. For Edwin H. Fay, it was a slow dawning. On May 5, 1865, he wrote his wife from Opelousas, Louisiana, "Oh my God why dost thou so afflict my beloved country. Is thy arm shortened so that it cannot save." Ten days later, he had faced the truth and wrote, "Truly the Lord has forsaken his people—I fear the subjugation of the South will make an infidel of me. I cannot see how a just God can allow people who have battled so heroically for their rights to be overthrown."[59]

In a similar state, Philip D. Stephenson reeled as his entire world seemed to collapse. "I had lost all interest in life and faith in humanity and well nigh lost all faith in God," Stephenson wrote years later. "I was really in great danger of confirmed cynicism and skepticism. Life's prospects stretched before me, a dreary sterile flat, and I looked on it with loathing. I felt that force, fraud, fawning, falseness had triumphed and were 'on top,' and that all good and genuineness were crushed out of sight." The fact was that Stephenson, like many Rebel soldiers, blamed God for forsaking the Confederate cause, and for some time, he was unable to get over his bitterness. A large measure of relief came eighteen months after the war. "God's grace visited my heart," Stephenson explained, "put a new light on the past, the present, and the future. It 'restored my soul' to a healthy normal state, put before me once more an object in life, and within me a motive impelling to it. And so I was saved."[60]

15

"WE SHALL NOT EASILY FORGET"
The Soldiers' Religion and the Impact of the Civil War

"All the church bells were melted down for cannons," wrote former Confederate soldier James Whitehorne in 1865, "but the preachers are back from the army and services [will be held] as usual tomorrow."[1] The war had left its mark on more than just the physical edifices of the church in America, but with its ending, religious life could begin to return to life "as usual."

For Southerners like Whitehorne, however, it would be far less "usual" than for those in the North. The destruction wrought by the war, the elimination of slave property, the revolution of the social system, and perhaps worst of all the lingering awareness of defeat left their marks not only on the Southern landscape but also on the hearts and minds of its people. Many church buildings were destroyed. Many members were dead, and others were financially ruined. Across the South, the Methodist denomination, for example, suffered a 30 percent loss in membership and a 50 percent loss in some types of charitable giving. The war may also have had a negative impact on Christianity among the Southern civilian population.[2] Disillusionment over defeat, guilt over "speculation," or possibly even the elusive, never-mentioned guilt over slavery may have been the reasons. Then too, throughout much of the war it had been inconvenient and sometimes downright dangerous to go out to church services in many regions of the South, veritable no-man's-lands where neither side could exercise solid authority and keep down the banditti. Had it not been for the great revivals in the Confederate armies and the large influx of newly converted soldiers into the home churches after the war, the cause of religion would have suffered severely in the South of the 1860s. In the years that followed, however, evangelical Christianity prospered in the region, as many found solace in the midst of discouraging secular situations.[3]

Another Southern response to the war and to the Confederate defeat was that in matters of religion, the South would continue to assert that it had been right about all the moral questions of the era. In 1865 several Southern Methodist bishops in a pastoral address declared, "The abolition, for military and political considerations, of the institution of domestic slavery in the United States does not affect the moral question" that had previously separated Southern Methodists from their Northern brethren. That same year, a group of Methodist laymen in Macon, Georgia, argued that the Southern Methodists must not reunite with the Northern church, because doing so would "yield the position we have so often taken, admit the charges we have so often refuted, and . . . compromise the essential principles of the gospel."[4] Likewise, Southern Presbyterian minister Robert L. Dabney never tired, decade after decade, of denouncing the North and attempting to vindicate the South. Slavery, he argued, had been good and benevolent. The war had been "caused deliberately" by Northerners who "with calculated malice invaded our rights, goaded us to resistance, and refused all compromise, . . . to revolutionize the government, establish their own faction, and gratify their spite."[5] In short, the South had been right, even if it lost.

The former Confederate soldiers tended to agree. Pvt. James A. Scott of the Third Virginia Cavalry was typical when he insisted after the war, "We were engaged in a just and holy war." It was unthinkable that so many Southern men had died for a cause that was wrong. "It's hard to think that our glorious old Confederate banner—which we have borne high aloft unconquered so long—must now be furled—but I doubt not—in his own good time God will give us a new & more beautiful one which shall float proudly and wide over all of our foes. Let us put our trust in Him."[6]

Just as the need to protect slavery had kept Southern religion, like every other aspect of Southern life, fixed and immovable throughout the half century before the war, so the determination to vindicate one's own actions, and then the actions of one's fathers and forefathers, kept the religion of the South locked to every previously asserted position. As had been the case before the war, this phenomenon would cause the preservation of both good and bad aspects of religion and society. Indeed, as it pertained to the foundational teachings of Christianity, such rigid stasis was entirely good, for at the heart of the Christian religion are certain basic truths and doctrines that do not change. Thus, by the late twentieth century, the South had become the nation's bastion of Christian orthodoxy, a role that had never been particularly its own in the nineteenth. Still, for the first few generations after the war, the reason Southern beliefs did not change was not so much an adherence to "the faith once delivered to the saints" for its own sake but rather a determination to vindicate "the Cause" for which the war generation had died—and killed— to the combined total of 620,000 lives.

In many ways, the war reinforced the old prewar doctrine of "the spirituality of the church," with its teaching that Christianity had nothing to say to the broader society and was blissfully unconcerned about what happened to it.[7] In the humiliation of defeat, Southerners like Alfred Tyler Fielder could take comfort in the reflection "that my abiding home would be in heaven."[8] Yet, as had been the case before the war, the application of such teachings would be uneven. Southern Christians certainly remained more "otherworldly" and less socially engaged than their Northern counterparts, but they never fully withdrew from society. Indeed, a few years after the war, a Georgia Methodist laymen would urge Methodists to "Christianize society," and another urged Christians to "vote as we pray."[9]

The South's drive to justify its actions in launching the great rebellion eventually took the form of what came to be called the myth of the "Lost Cause." As the tongues, pens, and, soon enough, typewriters of myriad Lost Cause advocates told the story in the decades after the Civil War, the South had been right all along. God for His own mysterious reasons had chosen to allow it to go down fighting nobly for eternal truths, but then had not God's own sinless and pure Son suffered and died at the hands of evil men in order to fulfill God's plan? Now the South by its suffering had been transformed into an even more pure and noble society, impoverished by the malice of its enemies, to be sure, but more than ever fit to be the great advocate of all that was pure and eternal. This, of course, was nonsense, but it still resonates in much writing on the Civil War and the Old South.

As part of the Lost Cause myth, Southerners began to assert that the war had been about something—anything—other than slavery. They elevated Robert E. Lee—a towering figure in his own right—to the status of demigod. Even Jefferson Davis, though much maligned by his own people during the war, became in the long twilight of his life a hero in the South. Lost Cause writers depicted both men as Christ figures who suffered for their people, a shocking departure for a people who had once recoiled in horror at the implied blasphemy of a "battle hymn" that likened the Union army to "the coming of the Lord." Lost Cause mythmakers asserted that the Southern soldier was braver, purer, nobler, tougher, and a better shot than his Yankee counterpart. In short, he was the bluecoat's superior in everything except perhaps cleanliness, and that he could not help, because the army was short of soap and new uniforms—another aspect of the overwhelming Union material and numerical superiority that supposedly decided the outcome.

Especially, the Southern soldier was represented as being his Yankee cousin's superior in piety, and this led to the development of an entire subgenre of Lost Cause literature—the religion of the Lost Cause. In the years after the war, Southern clergymen such as William W. Bennett, with his *Narrative of the Great Revival in the Southern Armies,* and John William Jones, with *Christ in the Camp,* gathered from fellow preachers and religious newspapers vast numbers of genuine anecdotes of the real religious awakening that took place in the Confederate armies during the war.[10] The factual information gathered was sound, but the goal in compiling it was to support a false claim that the South had been more devoted to God and therefore must have been right in the cause for which it fought. Bennett expanded on the superior nobility, purity, and spirituality of the Confederate soldiers and noted with satisfaction that the South had not been bothered with the presence of several heresies that plagued Christianity in the North.[11]

Northern religious leaders, not feeling the need to prove their own region's religious superiority, made no similar efforts.[12] One result of this has been that in the popular conception of the Civil War, and even in such a scholarly effort as Bell Irvin Wiley's *The Life of Billy Yank*, the great revivals in the camps are generally held to have been primarily or even totally Southern affairs.[13] In fact, the religious awakenings occurred about equally on both sides of the lines, and the average Union soldier was at least as devout as his Confederate counterpart, if not more so. Perhaps the greatest myth in the constellation of myths that formed the Lost Cause was that which claimed superior piety for the Confederate soldier.[14]

The North did not have to deal with the stigma of defeat, yet the war left great bitterness in many hearts. Northerners mourned some 360,000 dead, and as a crowning tragedy, they suffered the assassination of a president that many of them were just coming to recognize as the wise leader he was. The soldiers had lived for years with death all around them, and now they could not imagine that the killing would stop until full vengeance was taken. After learning of Lincoln's assassination, the Second Iowa's John J. McKee wrote in his diary, "This Day I sware eternal vengence against all copperheads and will shoot a man for saying anything against A. Lincoln."[15] William Henry Walling of the 142nd New York feared "the assassin's knife will be unsheathed for a long time to come." He had talked to recently released Union prisoners of war and wrote, "Many of our fellows who have suffered every indignity while in Southern prisons from officials openly declare they will [get] vengeance the first time they meet their man no matter what the circumstances may be."[16] Many Union soldiers had, during the war, promised that when they got home they would kill all the local copperheads. Yet none of this happened. There were, no doubt, many reasons why old scores were not paid off, but one reason was the pervasive influence of Christianity, which did not approve of taking vengeance.

The North never developed its own equivalent of the Lost Cause myth. It had no need. Instead, the North could look somewhat complacently on the war as a triumph of right and a purification of the Republic. Lincoln was elevated into another of the Christlike figures of the war, but more because, as one historian put it, he "represented a perfect fulfillment of everything the North had hoped to gain; he had destroyed slavery, preserved the Union, and provided an image of sacrifice and rebirth."[17]

For many Christians among the soldiers, the end of the war brought an awareness of a job well done and a duty faithfully performed for both God and country. "I trust I entered the Army with pure motives and from love of country," wrote Elisha Hunt Rhodes as he looked back over a four-year army career that had taken him from a nineteen-year-old private to colonel of the Second Rhode Island. "I have tried to keep myself from evil ways and believe that I have never forgotten that I am a Christian. Thank God no spiritous liquors have ever passed my lips as a beverage, and I feel that I can go home to my family as pure as when I left them as a boy of 19 years. I have been successful in my Army life simply because I have always been ready and willing to do my duty. I thank God that I have had an opportunity of serving my country freeing the slaves and restoring the Union."[18]

Many soldiers came out of the war with their faith strengthened. Others found faith in Christ for the first time during the war. Very few gave signs of becoming embittered or losing their faith.[19] Historian Reid Mitchell notes that whereas widespread disillusionment followed the bloodbath of the First World War, no such general loss of faith and meaning followed the Civil War, with its own appalling death toll. Mitchell suggests that this was the result of "northern imagery of the home and family."[20] Perhaps, but it undoubtedly owed at least as much to the Christian faith of many thousands of Americans, a faith that gave meaning to life and death, good and evil, and held out hope beyond the grave.

Indeed, one of the most remarkable aspects of the Civil War may be how little it changed, rather than how much. The idea that the Civil War wrought significant changes in the foundation of the American Republic may be the greatest illusion of U.S. history. Contrary to the musings of exuberant Northern liberals and the bitter fulminations of Southern agrarians, the conflict was not the beginning and triumph of a new age in which the American political landscape was swept clear of fixed values and eternal verities. Rather, it was the culmination of an old but vital and vigorous worldview, the completion of the original American vision of a society ordered according to divine principles. It was more the working out of the thought of John Winthrop, Thomas Hooker, and Jonathan

Edwards than it was a harbinger of the ideas of William James, Lester Frank Ward, or Oliver Wendell Holmes, Jr.

On the national political scene, the Civil War freed the slaves—that was the big change, of course—and the system of federalism was somewhat weakened. Yet states' rights did not die and showed no signs of serious illness until about the beginning of the twentieth century. Culture and society in North and South changed relatively little—far less than ambitious Northern politicians thought the power of government could achieve during the Reconstruction period. Real change in culture and society comes only with the change of people's most fundamental beliefs. The beliefs that transcend all others and lie at the very foundation of one's worldview are religious. This is equally true whether one's religion is Christianity or atheism and whether the object of one's worship is the infinite, personal God or one's own self-gratification. The core presuppositions that provide what philosopher Francis Schaeffer called "the wellspring" for the "flow [of] history and culture" are religious.[21] In the religious world of the Civil War soldiers, and that of the families to which they returned when the war was done, nothing fundamental had changed. With remarkable continuity, that world was still, at the most basic level, the world of Charles G. Finney, William McCreedy, George Whitefield, Jonathan Edwards, John Winthrop, and William Bradford. With the foundation remaining unchanged, so too did the most fundamental aspects of culture and society.

The ideas of Darwin and Marx, the so-called German higher criticism, and other strange winds of thought might already be blowing on foreign shores, but their tainted breath was scarcely to touch America for another generation. For Americans of the 1860s whose faith rested on a firm foundation, the passing incidents of life, even including wars and rumors of wars, could be understood, endured, and overcome, for, as they would have quoted, "This is the victory that overcometh the world, even our faith." Thus, when the guns fell silent and the smoke cleared, the bands played, and the young men in blue or gray or butternut marched home to the same America they had known—changed, to be sure, in circumstance and condition, but the same at the heart of its being. Little of real importance had changed in the religious world of the Civil War soldiers.

Likewise, little had changed in the Christian ideal for America, a vision that stretched all the way back to the first Puritan settlers. As the Civil War came to a close, Northern soldiers of Christian faith liked to believe that the fiery trial through which they had passed, a trial that Abraham Lincoln said would "light [them] down to the last generation" as a spectacle for all ages to observe and consider, had also purified them and prepared the nation to continue being what it was meant to be, fulfilling its God-given purpose as the "city upon a hill" of Puritan vision, a light and example to the world.

In just those terms wrote the Second Connecticut Artillery's Henry Hoyt in May 1865 from his regiment's camp near Burkeville Junction, Virginia, where he and his comrades were waiting to be mustered out and sent home. "This is indeed a great age to live in," wrote Burke. "We have lived years in the past few months. I cannot find language to express my feelings in regard to events that are transpiring. My heart swells within me at the thought of them. We have been taught lessons which we shall not easily forget. Although they seem severe yet they are for our own good." Then in words that John Winthrop would have affirmed, Hoyt concluded, "This nation will be an example for the whole world."[22]

NOTES

Abbreviations

AHC   Atlanta History Center

IHS   Indiana Historical Society, Indianapolis

ISHL   Illinois State Historical Library, Springfield

OR   U.S. War Department, *The War of the Rebellion: Official Records of the Union and Confederate Armies,* 128 vols. (Washington, D.C.: Government Printing Office, 1881–1901)

PLDU   Perkins Library, Duke University, Durham, North Carolina

SHC   Southern Historical Collection, University of North Carolina, Chapel Hill

SHSW   State Historical Society of Wisconsin, Madison

USAMHI   United States Army Military History Institute, Carlisle Barracks, Pennsylvania

VHS   Virginia Historical Society, Richmond

Preface

1. Warren B. Armstrong, *For Courageous Fighting and Confident Dying: Union Chaplains in the Civil War* (Lawrence: University Press of Kansas, 1998).

Chapter 1. "In Such a Country as This"

1. Luther H. Cowan Diary, November 30, 1862, Luther H. Cowan Papers, SHSW.

2. Susan Leigh Blackford and Charles Minor Blackford, *Letters from Lee's Army: Memoirs of Life in and out of the Army in Virginia During the War Between the States* (New York: A. S. Barnes, 1947), 176.

3. Ira Blanchard, *I Marched with Sherman: Civil War Memoirs of the 20th Illinois Volunteer Infantry* (San Francisco: J. D. Huff, 1992), 93.

4. Quoted in Mark Noll, "The Puzzling Faith of Abraham Lincoln," *Christian History* 11 (1992): 10–15.

5. William W. Bennett, *A Narrative of the Great Revival in the Southern Armies During the Late Civil War Between the States of the Federal Union* (Philadelphia: Claxton, Remsen and Haffelfinger, 1877), 227.

6. Chesley A. Mosman, *The Rough Side of War: The Civil War Journal of Chesley A. Mosman, 1st Lieutenant, Company D, 59th Illinois Volunteer Infantry Regiment,* ed. Arnold Gates (Garden City, N.Y.: Basin Publishing, 1987), 93.

7. John Eidsmoe, *Christianity and the Constitution: The Faith of Our Founding Fathers* (Grand Rapids, Mich.: Baker, 1987), 208–9.

8. Keith McNeil and Rusty McNeil, *Colonial and Revolution Songs with Historical Narration* (Riverside, Calif.: WEM Records, 1989), audio recording.

9. John B. Boles, *The Great Revival, 1787–1805* (Lexington: University Press of Kentucky, 1972), 71.

10. David Holt, *A Mississippi Rebel in the Army of Northern Virginia,* ed. Thomas D. Cockrell and Michael B. Ballard (Baton Rouge: Louisiana State University Press, 1995), 43–44.

11. Julius Birney Work Diary, January 31–February 18, 1863, Civil War Miscellaneous Collection, USAMHI.

12. Timothy L. Smith, *Revivalism and Social Reform: American Protestantism on the Eve of the Civil War* (Baltimore: Johns Hopkins University Press, 1980), 42.

13. John T. McMahon, *John T. McMahon's Diary of the 136th New York, 1861–1864,* ed. John Michael Priest (Shippensburg, Pa.: White Mane, 1993), 2, 21.

14. Wilbur Fisk, *Hard Marching Every Day: The Civil War Letters of Private Wilbur Fisk, 1861–1865,* ed. Emil Rosenblatt and Ruth Rosenblatt (Lawrence: University Press of Kansas, 1992), 190; James A. Connolly, *Three Years in the Army of the Cumberland: The Letters and Diary of Major James A. Connolly,* ed. Paul M. Angle (Bloomington: Indiana University Press, 1959), 214.

15. Marvin Olasky, *The Tragedy of American Compassion* (Washington, D.C.: Regnery, 1992); Marvin Olasky, *Abortion Rites: A Social History of Abortion in America* (Washington, D.C.: Regnery, 1995).

16. Olasky, *Abortion Rites.*

17. Tim Stafford, "The Abolitionists," *Christian History* 11, no. 1 (1992): 21.

18. Ibid., 22–23.

19. Ibid.

20. Ibid., 25.

21. Charles G. Finney, *Revival Lectures* (reprint, Old Tappan, N.J.: Fleming Revell, 1970), 336–37; David Barton, *The Myth of Separation* (Aledo, Tex.: WallBuilder Press, 1991), 265.

22. Henry C. Sheldon, *History of the Christian Church,* 5 vols. (1895; reprint, Peabody, Mass.: Hendrickson Publishers, 1988), 5:243.

23. Stafford, "The Abolitionists," 25.

24. A recent example is David Williams, *Rich Man's War: Class, Caste, and Confederate Defeat in the Lower Chattahoochee Valley* (Athens: University of Georgia Press, 1998), 27–28.

25. Mark A. Noll points out that the overwhelming majority of American Christians interpreted the Bible in its literal sense, but he claims that on that basis Southerners had an edge in their defense of slavery. Nonetheless, Noll does not deny that antislavery Christians attacked the institution on the basis of a literal interpretation of Scripture. Mark A. Noll, "The Bible and Slavery," in *Religion and the American Civil War,* ed. Randal M. Miller, Harry S. Stout, and Charles Reagan Wilson (New York: Oxford University Press, 1998), 43–73.

26. Williams, *Rich Man's War,* 27; Eugene D. Genovese, *A Consuming Fire: The Fall of the Confederacy in the Mind of the White Christian South* (Athens: University of Georgia Press, 1998), 4.

27. Noll, "The Bible and Slavery," 62–66.

28. Gardiner H. Shattuck, Jr., *A Shield and Hiding Place: The Religious Life of the Civil War Armies* (Macon, Ga.: Mercer University Press, 1987), 3; Christopher H. Owen, *The Sacred Flame of Love: Methodism and Society in Nineteenth-Century Georgia* (Athens: University of Georgia Press, 1998), 63–64.

29. Owen, *Sacred Flame of Love,* 89.

30. Genovese, *Consuming Fire,* 5, 28–29; Owen, *Sacred Flame of Love,* 87.

31. Genovese, *Consuming Fire,* 113.

32. Ibid., 113–14.

33. Owen, *Sacred Flame of Love,* 61–62.

34. Genovese, *Consuming Fire,* 76, 81–85; Owen, *Sacred Flame of Love,* 78, 82.

35. Sheldon, *History of the Christian Church,* 5:241.

36. Owen, *Sacred Flame of Love,* 55.

37. Boles, *Great Revival,* 195–97.

38. Olasky, *Abortion Rites,* 61–82.

39. Gideon W. Burtch Diary, March 4, 1865, Civil War Miscellaneous Collection, USAMHI.

40. McMahon, *Diary,* 22.

41. David H. Blair to "Dear Sister," September 29, 1864, and David H. Blair to "My Dear Lizzie cousin," September 30, 1864, David Humphrey Blair Papers, Civil War Miscellaneous Collection, USAMHI.

42. Allen C. Guelzo, *Abraham Lincoln: Redeemer President* (Grand Rapids, Mich.: Eerdmans, 1999), 149–50.

43. Ibid., 156.

44. Smith, *Revivalism and Social Reform*, 60–69.

45. Ibid., 63–74; Owen, *Sacred Flame of Love*, 77.

46. Smith, *Revivalism and Social Reform*, 67–72.

47. Ibid., 17.

Chapter 2. "A Merciful Providence"

1. John T. McMahon, *John T. McMahon's Diary of the 136th New York, 1861–1864,* ed. John Michael Priest (Shippensburg, Pa.: White Mane, 1993), 3–4.

2. Alfred Tyler Fielder, *The Civil War Diaries of Capt. Alfred Tyler Fielder, 12th Tennessee Regiment Infantry, Company B, 1861–1865,* ed. Ann York Franklin (Louisville, Ky.: privately published, 1996), 130.

3. Thomas F. Boatright to "My Dear Wife," February 4, 1863, Thomas F. Boatright Papers, SHC.

4. Levi Y. Lockhart to "Dear Sister," June 12, 1863, Hugh Conway Browning Papers, PLDU.

5. James A. Connolly, *Three Years in the Army of the Cumberland: The Letters and Diary of Major James A. Connolly,* ed. Paul M. Angle (Bloomington: Indiana University Press, 1959), 118–19.

6. Henry Matrau, *Letters Home: Henry Matrau of the Iron Brigade,* ed. Marcia Reid-Green (Lincoln: University of Nebraska Press, 1993), 43, 59.

7. Jeffrey D. Marshall, ed., *A War of the People: Vermont Civil War Letters* (Hanover, N.H.: University Press of New England, 1999), 100. Another good example of this thought is found in Alfred Lacey Hough, *Soldier in the West: The Civil War Letters of Alfred Lacey Hough,* ed. Robert G. Athearn (Philadelphia: University of Pennsylvania Press, 1957), 132.

8. William H. S. Burgwyn, *A Captain's War: The Letters and Diaries of William H. S. Burgwyn, 1861–1865,* ed. Herbert M. Schiller (Shippensburg, Pa.: White Mane, 1994), 43.

9. James G. Theaker, *Through One Man's Eyes: The Civil War Experiences of a Belmont County Volunteer,* ed. Paul E. Rieger (Mt. Vernon, Ohio: Printing Arts Press, 1974), 118–19.

10. James Maynard Shanklin, *Dearest Lizzie: The Civil War Letters of Lt. Col. James Maynard Shanklin,* ed. Kenneth P. McCutchan (Evansville, Ind.: Friends of Willard Library Press, 1988), 196–97.

11. Henry Hoyt to "Dear Ones Home," June 30, 1864, Henry Hoyt Letters, Civil War Miscellaneous Collection, USAMHI.

12. William Winters, *The Musick of the Mocking Birds, the Roar of the Cannon: The Civil War Diary and Letters of William Winters,* ed. Steven E. Woodworth (Lincoln: University of Nebraska Press, 1998), 31.

13. Theaker, *Through One Man's Eyes,* 99.

14. George Rogers to "My Dear Friend," April 12, 1862, from the collection of Wiley Sword, printed in *In Camp on the Rappahannock: The Newsletter of the Blue & Gray Education Society* 4, no. 2 (fall 1998): 14.

15. Fielder, *Civil War Diaries*, 43; the words of the hymn are from *The Free Methodist Hymnal*, ed. William B. Olmstead et al. (Chicago: Free Methodist Publishing House, 1910), 318.

16. Edwin H. Fay, *"This Infernal War": The Confederate Letters of Sgt. Edwin H. Fay*, ed. Bell Irvin Wiley (Austin: University of Texas Press, 1958), 226.

17. Dick Simpson and Tally Simpson, *"Far, Far from Home": The Wartime Letters of Dick and Tally Simpson, Third South Carolina Volunteers,* ed. Guy R. Everson and Edward H. Simpson, Jr. (New York: Oxford University Press, 1994), 202.

18. Thomas W. Cutrer and T. Michael Parrish, eds., *Brothers in Gray: The Civil War Letters of the Pierson Family* (Baton Rouge: Louisiana State University Press, 1997), 186.

19. Letter of February 4, 1865, William Henry Walling Letters, Civil War Miscellaneous Collection, USAMHI.

20. Ibid., October 21, 1862.

21. Aurelius Lyman Voorhis Diary, September 4, 1863, IHS.

22. Fay, *This Infernal War,* 123, 380.

23. Hough, *Soldier in the West,* 179; Henry Kauffman, *The Civil War Letters of Private Henry Kauffman: The Harmony Boys Are All Well,* ed. David McCordick (Lewiston, N.Y.: Edwin Mellen Press, 1991), 6.

24. W. H. L. Wallace to Ann Wallace, March 8, 1862, Wallace-Dickey Family Papers, ISHL.

25. This point has been misunderstood in previous studies of the Civil War soldiers' beliefs. Gerald F. Linderman wrote, "The common understanding was that the more complete the soldier's faith, the greater would be God's care. Perfect faith seemed to offer the possibility of perfect safety." Although a few misguided souls may have thought so, this strange conceit was far from being the "common understanding" of the Civil War soldiers. Gerald F. Linderman, *Embattled Courage: The Experience of Combat in the American Civil War* (New York: Free Press, 1987), 9.

26. McMahon, *Diary,* 20.

27. Jim Leeke, ed., *A Hundred Days to Richmond: Ohio's "Hundred Days" Men in the Civil War* (Bloomington: Indiana University Press, 1999), 170.

28. Hough, *Soldier in the West,* 36.

29. Letter of October 29, 1861, William Henry Walling Letters, Civil War Miscellaneous Collection, USAMHI.

30. William W. Bennett, *A Narrative of the Great Revival in the Southern Armies During the Late Civil War Between the States of the Federal Union* (Philadelphia: Claxton, Remsen and Haffelfinger, 1877), 383–84. Similar expressions of trust are almost numberless. Several especially good ones are found in Marshall, *War of the People,* 51, 194; and John W. McGill to D. Lewis, August 17, 1864, Camden Lewis Papers, Civil War Miscellaneous Collection, USAMHI.

31. Aurelius Lyman Voorhis Diary, IHS.

32. David Humphrey Blair Diary and Letters, Civil War Miscellaneous Collection, USAMHI.

33. Simpson and Simpson, *Far, Far from Home*, 207.

34. Levi Y. Lockhart, to "Dear Sister," December 12, 1862, Hugh Conway Browning Papers, PLDU; N. H. R. Dawson to Elodie Todd, June 8, 1861, N. H. R. Dawson Papers, SHC.

35. Theaker, *Through One Man's Eyes*, 38.

36. Marquis Townsend to "Dear Sister Eliza," April 15 and July 12, 1863, Townsend Family Papers, PLDU.

37. David Humphrey Blair to "My Dear Sister Lizzie," February 23, 1864, David Humphrey Blair Papers, Civil War Miscellaneous Collection, USAMHI.

38. Robert T. Coles, *From Huntsville to Appomattox: R. T. Coles's History of the 4th Regiment, Alabama Volunteer Infantry, C.S.A., Army of Northern Virginia*, ed. Jeffrey D. Stocker (Knoxville: University of Tennessee Press, 1996), 115.

39. Richard R. Crowe to "Dear Mammy," May 19, 1864, Richard Robert Crowe Papers, SHSW.

40. Sidney A. Bean to "Dear Mother," August 4, 1862, Sidney A. Bean Papers, SHSW. Another forceful expression of this trust is in William Ross Stillwell to "My Dear Molly," September 10, 1862, in *In Camp on the Rappahannock: The Newsletter of the Blue & Gray Education Society* 4, no. 3 (spring 1999): 12.

41. Abner R. Small, *The Road to Richmond: The Civil War memoirs of Maj. Abner R. Small of the 16th Maine Vols.: With His Diary as a Prisoner of War*, ed. Harold Adams Small (Berkeley: University of California Press, 1959), 145.

42. Marshall, *War of the People*, 56.

43. Bennett, *Narrative of the Great Revival*, 164–69.

44. James W. Bacon to "Dear Friend," October 20, 1862, Hugh Conway Browning Papers, PLDU.

45. Thomas F. Boatright to "My Dear Wife," February 4, 1863, Thomas F. Boatright Papers, SHC.

46. Burgwyn, *A Captain's War*, 95.

47. Simpson and Simpson, *Far, Far from Home*, 98–99.

48. J. T. Armstrong to "My dearest Cousin," January 26, 1862, J. T. Armstrong Papers, SHC.

49. Henry Hoyt to "Dear Ones at Home," June 2, 1864, Henry Hoyt Letters, Civil War Miscellaneous Collection, USAMHI; Seymour Dexter, *Seymour Dexter, Union Army: Journal and Letters of Civil War Service in Company K, 23rd New York Volunteer Regiment of Elmira*, ed. Carl A. Morrell (Jefferson, N.C.: McFarland, 1996), 19–20; Shanklin, *Dearest Lizzie*, 42; Cutrer and Parrish, *Brothers in Gray*, 27–28; James C. Bates, *A Texas Cavalry Officer's Civil War: The Diary and Letters of James C. Bates*, ed. Richard Lowe (Baton Rouge: Louisiana State University Press, 1999), 112; Marcus A. Stults Papers, Civil War Miscellaneous Collection, USAMHI; Wilbur Fisk, *Hard Marching Every Day: The Civil War*

Letters of Private Wilbur Fisk, 1861–1865, ed. Emil Rosenblatt and Ruth Rosenblatt (Lawrence: University Press of Kansas, 1992), 58; Kelly Family Papers, Civil War Miscellaneous Collection, USAMHI.

50. Simpson and Simpson, *Far, Far from Home,* 207.

51. Peter Welsh, *Irish Green and Union Blue: The Civil War Letters of Peter Welsh, Color Sergeant, 28th Regiment Massachusetts Volunteers,* ed. Lawrence Frederick Kohl and Margaret Cosse Richard (New York: Fordham University Press, 1986), 71–72.

52. Winters, *Musick of the Mocking Birds,* 50–51.

53. "Jim A." Letters, VHS.

54. Fay, *This Infernal War,* 295.

55. Joshua K. Callaway, *The Civil War Letters of Joshua K. Callaway,* ed. Judith Lee Hallock (Athens: University of Georgia Press, 1997), 19.

56. Allen C. Guelzo, *Abraham Lincoln: Redeemer President* (Grand Rapids, Mich.: Eerdmans, 1999), 102–42; Mark Noll, "The Puzzling Faith of Abraham Lincoln," *Christian History* 11 (1992): 15.

57. Samuel McIlvaine, *By the Dim and Flaring Lamps: The Civil War Diaries of Samuel McIlvaine,* ed. Clayton E. Cramer (Monroe, N.Y.: Library Research Associates, 1990), 136.

58. Franklin Aretas Haskell, *Haskell of Gettysburg: His Life and Civil War Papers,* ed. Frank L. Byrne and Andrew T. Weaver (Madison: State Historical Society of Wisconsin, 1970), 154–55.

59. Charles W. Bardeen, *A Little Fifer's War Diary* (Syracuse, N.Y.: author, 1910), 137.

60. James M. McPherson, *For Cause and Comrades: Why Men Fought in the Civil War* (New York: Oxford University Press, 1997), 64–67. Other good examples of balanced orthodox Christian views of providence on the part of Civil War soldiers are found in Leeke, *A Hundred Days to Richmond,* 69; and Shanklin, *Dearest Lizzie,* 57–58.

Chapter 3. "In the Light of God's Throne and the Presence of Jesus"

1. Thomas Wentworth Higginson, *The Complete Civil War Journal and Selected Letters of Thomas Wentworth Higginson,* ed. Christopher Looby (Chicago: University of Chicago Press, 2000), 86.

2. James C. Bates, *A Texas Cavalry Officer's Civil War: The Diary and Letters of James C. Bates,* ed. Richard Lowe (Baton Rouge: Louisiana State University Press, 1999), 88.

3. Hamlin Alexander Coe, *Mine Eyes Have Seen the Glory: Combat Diaries of Union Sergeant Hamlin Alexander Coe* (Rutherford, N.J.: Fairleigh Dickinson University Press, 1975), 68.

4. Seymour Dexter, *Seymour Dexter, Union Army: Journal and Letters of Civil War Service in Company K, 23rd New York Volunteer Regiment of Elmira,* ed. Carl A. Morrell (Jefferson, N.C.: McFarland, 1996), 45.

5. Andrew B. Wardlaw to "My Dear Wife," February 5, 1865, Andrew B. Wardlaw Letters, Civil War Miscellaneous Collection, USAMHI.

6. John Beatty, *Memoirs of a Volunteer, 1861–1863* (New York: W. W. Norton, 1946), 93.

7. George S. Marks Papers, Civil War Miscellaneous Collection, USAMHI.

8. Thomas W. Cutrer and T. Michael Parrish, eds., *Brothers in Gray: The Civil War Letters of the Pierson Family* (Baton Rouge: Louisiana State University Press, 1997), 201.

9. Thomas F. Boatright to "My Darling Wife," March 18, 1863, Boatright Papers, SHC.

10. Jeffrey D. Marshall, ed., *A War of the People: Vermont Civil War Letters* (Hanover, N.H.: University Press of New England, 1999), 311–12.

11. Aurelius Lyman Voorhis Diary, April 2, 1865, IHS.

12. Nancy Richardson to M. V. Barkley, June 13, 1864, Barkley Family Papers, SHC; Joseph Whitney, *Kiss Clara for Me: The Story of Joseph Whitney and His Family, Early Days in the Midwest, and Soldiering in the American Civil War,* ed. Robert J. Snetsinger (State College, Pa.: The Carnation Press, 1969), 58, 67.

13. Coe, *Mine Eyes Have Seen the Glory,* 40.

14. David H. Blair to "Dear Mother & Father," August 8, 1864, David Humphrey Blair Papers, Civil War Miscellaneous Collection, USAMHI.

15. Dick Simpson and Tally Simpson, *"Far, Far from Home": The Wartime Letters of Dick and Tally Simpson, Third South Carolina Volunteers,* ed. Guy R. Everson and Edward H. Simpson, Jr. (New York: Oxford University Press, 1994), 293.

16. Henry Morgan to Ellen Morgan, January 14, 1865, Henry T. Morgan Letters, Civil War Miscellaneous Collection, USAMHI.

17. Cutrer and Parrish, *Brothers in Gray,* 160; James G. Theaker, *Through One Man's Eyes: The Civil War Experiences of a Belmont County Volunteer,* ed. Paul E. Rieger (Mt. Vernon, Ohio: Printing Arts Press, 1974), 159; Wilson S. Covill to "Dear sister" [May 1862], Wilson S. Covill Letters, SHSW; Marshall, *War of the People,* 68; Henry Kauffman, *Civil War Letters of Private Henry Kauffman: The Harmony Boys Are All Well,* ed. David McCordick (Lewiston, N.Y.: Edwin Mellen Press, 1991), 62; John Blair to David Blair, January 31, 1864, David Humphrey Blair Papers, Civil War Miscellaneous Collection, USAMHI; Alburtus A. Dunham and Charles LaForest Dunham, *Through the South with a Union Soldier,* ed. Arthur H. DeRosier, Jr. (Johnson City: East Tennessee State University Research Advisory Council, 1969), 138; James W. Bacon to "Dear Friend" [December 1861], Hugh Conway Browning Papers, PLDU; Thomas F. Boatright to "My Dear Wife," March 10, 1863, Boatright Papers, SHC; Horace Currier Diary, August 15, 1863, Horace Currier Papers, SHSW.

18. For other examples, see Joshua K. Callaway, *The Civil War Letters of Joshua K. Callaway,* ed. Judith Lee Hallock (Athens: University of Georgia Press, 1997), 167; Whitney, *Kiss Clara for Me,* 118; Ignatius W. Brock to "My Dear Sister," June 22, 1863, Ignatius W. Brock Papers, PLDU.

19. Alfred Tyler Fielder, *The Civil War Diaries of Capt. Alfred Tyler Fielder, 12th Tennessee Regiment Infantry, Company B, 1861–1865,* ed. Ann York Franklin (Louisville, Ky.: privately published, 1996), 55–56.

20. Emily Elliott Diary, October 18, 1864, Jonas Denton Elliott Papers, Civil War Miscellaneous Collection, USAMHI.

21. Simpson and Simpson, *Far, Far from Home,* 293.

22. Callaway, *Civil War Letters,* 156.

23. William W. Bennett, *A Narrative of the Great Revival in the Southern Armies During the Late Civil War Between the States of the Federal Union* (Philadelphia: Claxton, Remsen and Haffelfinger, 1877), 161.

24. Emily Elliott Diary, October 16, 1864, Jonas Denton Elliott Papers, Civil War Miscellaneous Collection, USAMHI.

25. J. T. Armstrong to "My Darling Wife," October 26, 1861, J. T. Armstrong Papers, SHC.

26. George A. Cooley Diary, June 18, 1864, SHSW.

27. Isaac Jackson, *Some of the Boys: The Civil War Letters of Isaac Jackson, 1862–1865* (Carbondale: Southern Illinois University Press, 1960), 145.

28. Samuel P. Lockhart to "Dear Sister," January 18, 1863, Hugh Conway Browning Papers, PLDU. For additional expressions of this idea, see Thomas M. Davis to "Dear and respected wife," December 4, 1861, Thomas M. Davis Letters, Civil War Miscellaneous Collection, USAMHI; and Dunham and Dunham, *Through the South,* 96.

29. James Maynard Shanklin, *Dearest Lizzie: The Civil War Letters of Lt. Col. James Maynard Shanklin,* ed. Kenneth P. McCutchan (Evansville, Ind.: Friends of Willard Library Press, 1988), 79–80.

30. Whitney, *Kiss Clara for Me,* 124; James M. McPherson, *For Cause and Comrades: Why Men Fought in the Civil War* (New York: Oxford University Press, 1997), 70–71.

31. D. J. Benner to "Dear Uncle," April 9, 1862, Luther H. Cowan Papers, SHSW.

32. Emily Elliott Diary, October 31, 1864, Jonas Denton Elliott Papers, Civil War Miscellaneous Collection USAMHI.

33. Robert Y. Walker to "Cousin Ellen," August 27, 1864, Hugh Conway Browning Papers, PLDU.

34. Marshall, *War of the People,* 311–12.

35. Callaway, *Civil War Letters,* 153–54.

36. Samuel J. Marks to "Dear Carrie," September 12, 1864, Samuel J. Marks Papers, Civil War Miscellaneous Collection, USAMHI.

37. Emily Elliott Diary, October 16 and November 25, 1864, Jonas Denton Elliott Papers, Civil War Miscellaneous Collection, USAMHI.

38. Samuel P. Lockhart to "Dear Sister," June 24, 1862, Hugh Conway Browning Papers, PLDU.

39. Daniel Crotty, *Four Years Campaigning in the Army of the Potomac* (Kearny, N.J.: Belle Grove, 1995), 128.

40. Coe, *Mine Eyes Have Seen the Glory,* 164.

41. William Henry Walling to "Sisters," January 17, 1862, William Henry Walling Letters, Civil War Miscellaneous Collection, USAMHI.

42. James Henry Gooding, *On the Altar of Freedom: A Black Soldier's Civil War Letters from the Front,* ed. Virginia Matzke Adams (Amherst: University of Massachusetts Press, 1991), 26.

43. The quotation is from *The Soldier's Prayer Book* (Philadelphia: Protestant Episcopal Book Society, n.d.), 62, in the Matthew Bracken Black Papers, Civil War Miscellaneous Collection, USAMHI; McPherson, *For Cause and Comrades,* 70–71.

44. Aurelius Lyman Voorhis Diary, December 20, 1862, and March 10, 1863, IHS.

45. Berea M. Willsey, *The Civil War Diary of Berea M. Willsey: The Intimate Daily Observations of a Massachusetts Volunteer in the Union Army, 1862–1864,* ed. Jessica H. DeMay (Bowie, Md.: Heritage Books, 1995), 130–31.

46. Louisa D. Miller to "Dear husband," March 19, 1865, Reynolds Laughlin Papers, Civil War Miscellaneous Collection, USAMHI.

47. Levi N. Walling to "Ever Kind & remembered Sister," May 17, 1864, Levi N. Walling Letters, Civil War Miscellaneous Collection, USAMHI.

48. Wilbur Fisk, *Hard Marching Every Day: The Civil War Letters of Private Wilbur Fisk, 1861–1865,* ed. Emil Rosenblatt and Ruth Rosenblatt (Lawrence: University Press of Kansas, 1992), 183.

49. John W. Compton to "Dear Wife & daughter," March 26, 1865, John W. Compton Letters, Civil War Miscellaneous Collection, USAMHI.

50. Whitney, *Kiss Clara for Me,* 93.

51. Samuel E. Piper to "My Dear Wife," November 25, 1862, Samuel E. Piper Letters, Civil War Miscellaneous Collection, USAMHI.

52. Emily Elliott Diary, February 7, 1864, Jonas Denton Elliott Papers, Civil War Miscellaneous Collection, USAMHI.

53. Dunham and Dunham, *Through the South,* 134.

54. William H. Walling to "My Dear Sister," June 12, 1864, William Henry Walling Letters, Civil War Miscellaneous Collection, USAMHI.

55. Thomas F. Boatright to "My Dear Wife," February 17, 1863, Boatright Papers, SHC.

56. Alan D. Gaff, *On Many a Bloody Field: Four Years in the Iron Brigade* (Bloomington: Indiana University Press, 1996), 145.

57. Ira S. Pettit, *The Diary of a Dead Man: Letters and Diary of Private Ira S. Pettit,* ed. Jean P. Ray (New York: Acorn Press, 1979), 101–2.

58. Sumner A. Cunningham, *Reminiscences of the Forty-first Tennessee Regiment,* ed. John A. Simpson (Nashville: Vanderbilt University Press, 1997), 42.

59. John J. McKee Diary, August 14, 1864, Civil War Miscellaneous Collection, USAMHI.

60. Bennett, *Narrative of the Great Revival,* 142.

61. Ignatius W. Brock to "Dear Sister," July 22, 1862, Ignatius W. Brock Papers, PLDU.

62. Bennett, *Narrative of the Great Revival,* 318.

Chapter 4. "Peace with God"

1. David Humphrey Blair to "Dear Mother & Father," August 8, 1864, David Humphrey Blair Papers, Civil War Miscellaneous Collection, USAMHI.

2. John T. McMahon, *John T. McMahon's Diary of the 136th New York, 1861–1864*, ed. John Michael Priest (Shippensburg, Pa.: White Mane, 1993), 16.

3. Thomas W. Cutrer and T. Michael Parrish, eds., *Brothers in Gray: The Civil War Letters of the Pierson Family* (Baton Rouge: Louisiana State University Press, 1997), 186.

4. Joshua K. Callaway, *The Civil War Letters of Joshua K. Callaway*, ed. Judith Lee Hallock (Athens: University of Georgia Press, 1997), 158.

5. Elisha Hunt Rhodes, *All for the Union: The Civil War Diary and Letters of Elisha Hunt Rhodes*, ed. Robert Hunt Rhodes (New York: Orion Books, 1985), 65–66.

6. Specimen in Edward W. Allen Papers, SHC.

7. Gideon W. Burtch Papers, Civil War Miscellaneous Collection, USAMHI.

8. Cutrer and Parrish, *Brothers in Gray*, 230.

9. Thomas F. Boatright to "My Dear Wife," February 17 and April 8, 1863, Boatright Papers, SHC.

10. Cutrer and Parrish, *Brothers in Gray*, 230.

11. David H. Blair to "My Sister Lizzie," July 2, 1864, David Humphrey Blair Papers, Civil War Miscellaneous Collection, USAMHI.

12. Callaway, *Civil War Letters*, 133.

13. David Holt, *A Mississippi Rebel in the Army of Northern Virginia*, ed. Thomas D. Cockrell and Michael B. Ballard (Baton Rouge: Louisiana State University, 1995), 235.

14. Emily Elliott Diary, February 14, 1864, Jonas Denton Elliott Papers, Civil War Miscellaneous Collection, USAMHI.

15. Samuel P. Lockhart to "Sister Ellen," November 13, 1863, Hugh Conway Browning Papers, PLDU.

16. Chesley A. Mosman, *The Rough Side of War: The Civil War Journal of Chesley A. Mosman, 1st Lieutenant, Company D, 59th Illinois Volunteer Infantry Regiment*, ed. Arnold Gates (Garden City, N.Y.: Basin Publishing, 1987), 262.

17. William T. Stewart to "My own dear wife," January 23, 1865, Anderson-Capehart-McCowan Family Papers, Civil War Miscellaneous Collection, USAMHI.

18. N. H. R. Dawson to Elodie B. Todd, June 17, 1861, N. H. R. Dawson Papers, SHC.

19. Jeffrey D. Marshall, ed., *A War of the People: Vermont Civil War Letters* (Hanover, N.H.: University Press of New England, 1999), 80–81.

20. Edwin H. Fay, *"This Infernal War": The Confederate Letters of Sgt. Edwin H. Fay*, ed. Bell Irvin Wiley (Austin: University of Texas Press, 1958), 419.

21. Warren Wilkinson, *Mother, May You Never See the Sights That I Have Seen: The Fifty-seventh Massachusetts Veteran Volunteers in the Army of the Potomac, 1864–1865* (New York: Harper and Row, 1990), 335.

22. Joseph Whitney, *Kiss Clara for Me: The Story of Joseph Whitney and His Family, Early Days in the Midwest, and Soldiering in the American Civil War*, ed. Robert J. Snetsinger (State College, Pa.: Carnation Press, 1969), 98.

23. Joseph Hart, "Come Ye Sinners, Poor and Needy," in *The Free Methodist Hymnal*, ed. William B. Olmstead et al. (Chicago: Free Methodist Publishing House, 1910), 115.

24. Abner R. Small, *The Road to Richmond: The Civil War Memoirs of Maj. Abner R. Small of the 16th Maine Vols.: With His Diary as a Prisoner of War*, ed. Harold Adams Small (Berkeley: University of California Press, 1959), 218.

25. Levi Y. Lockhart to "Dear Sister," September 18, 1862, Hugh Conway Browning Papers, PLDU.

26. Gideon W. Burtch Papers, Civil War Miscellaneous Collection, USAMHI.

27. Fay, *This Infernal War*, 222–23.

28. Thomas F. Boatright to "My loving wife," April 8, 1863, Boatright Papers, SHC.

29. Alfred Tyler Fielder, *The Civil War Diaries of Capt. Alfred Tyler Fielder, 12th Tennessee Regiment Infantry, Company B, 1861–1865*, ed. Ann York Franklin (Louisville, Ky.: privately published, 1996), 191.

30. Rhodes, *All for the Union*, 71.

31. Ignatius W. Brock to "My Dear Sister," November 11, 1863, Ignatius W. Brock Papers, PLDU.

32. John A. Simpson, *S. A. Cunningham and the Confederate Heritage* (Athens: University of Georgia Press, 1994), 39.

33. Oliver Wendell Holmes, Jr., *Touched with Fire: Civil War Letters and Diary of Oliver Wendell Holmes, Jr., 1861–1864*, ed. Mark de Wolfe Howe (Cambridge, Mass.: Harvard University Press, 1947), 27–29.

34. Ignatius W. Brock to "Dear Sister," March 25, 1863, Ignatius W. Brock Papers, PLDU.

35. James C. Bates, *A Texas Cavalry Officer's Civil War: The Diary and Letters of James C. Bates*, ed. Richard Lowe (Baton Rouge: Louisiana State University Press, 1999), 305.

36. Luther H. Cowan Papers, SHSW.

37. Warren Wilkinson and Steven E. Woodworth, *A Scythe of Fire: The Civil War Story of the Eighth Georgia Regiment* (New York: HarperCollins, in press).

38. Mary Livermore, *My Story of the War* (Hartford, Conn.: A. D. Worthington, 1890), 196–97.

39. William W. Bennett, *A Narrative of the Great Revival in the Southern Armies During the Late Civil War Between the States of the Federal Union* (Philadelphia: Claxton, Remsen and Haffelfinger, 1877), 108, 161–62.

40. Gideon W. Burtch Diary, March 11, 1864, Civil War Miscellaneous Collection, USAMHI.

Chapter 5. "His Grace Is Ever Sufficient for Me"

1. William W. Bennett, *A Narrative of the Great Revival in the Southern Armies During the Late Civil War Between the States of the Federal Union* (Philadelphia: Claxton, Remsen

and Haffelfinger, 1877), 205–6; Alfred Tyler Fielder, *The Civil War Diaries of Capt. Alfred Tyler Fielder, 12th Tennessee Regiment Infantry, Company B, 1861–1865,* ed. Ann York Franklin (Louisville, Ky.: privately published, 1996), 59.

2. Thomas Wentworth Higginson, *The Complete Civil War Journal and Selected Letters of Thomas Wentworth Higginson,* ed. Christopher Looby (Chicago: University of Chicago Press, 2000), 65.

3. Henry Matrau, *Letters Home: Henry Matrau of the Iron Brigade,* ed. Marcia Reid-Green (Lincoln: University of Nebraska Press, 1993), 75.

4. Samuel E. Piper to "My Dear Wife," April 7, 1863, Samuel E. Piper Letters, Civil War Miscellaneous Collection, USAMHI.

5. Aurelius Lyman Voorhis Diary, May 21, 1862, IHS.

6. James Maynard Shanklin, *Dearest Lizzie: The Civil War Letters of Lt. Col. James Maynard Shanklin,* ed. Kenneth P. McCutchan (Evansville, Ind.: Friends of Willard Library Press, 1988), 111.

7. William H. S. Burgwyn, *A Captain's War: The Letters and Diaries of William H. S. Burgwyn, 1861–1865,* ed. Herbert M. Schiller (Shippensburg, Pa.: White Mane, 1994), 3; Ira S. Pettit, *The Diary of a Dead Man: Letters and Diary of Private Ira S. Pettit,* ed. Jean P. Ray (New York: Acorn Press, 1979), 27, 55–56; Joseph Whitney, *Kiss Clara for Me: The Story of Joseph Whitney and His Family, Early Days in the Midwest, and Soldiering in the American Civil War,* ed. Robert J. Snetsinger (State College, Pa.: Carnation Press, 1969), 49; Aurelius Lyman Voorhis Diary, April 6, 1862, IHS.

8. Warren Wilkinson and Steven E. Woodworth, *A Scythe of Fire: The Civil War Story of the Eighth Georgia Regiment* (New York: HarperCollins, in press).

9. Recollections of Mrs. Sarah L. Clark, Melvin L. Clark Papers, Civil War Miscellaneous Collection, USAMHI.

10. John Morton to "Dear Mother," September 16, 1861, John Morton Letters, Civil War Miscellaneous Collection, USAMHI.

11. James Wren, *From New Bern to Fredericksburg: Captain James Wren's Diary,* ed. John Michael Priest (Shippensburg, Pa.: White Mane, 1990), 66.

12. Evan Morrison Woodward, *Our Campaigns: The Second Regiment Pennsylvania Reserve Volunteers, 1861–1864,* ed. Stanley W. Zamonski (Shippensburg, Pa.: Burd Street Press, 1995), 63.

13. John Henry Wilburn Stuckenberg, *I'm Surrounded by Methodists: Diary of John H. W. Stuckenberg, Chaplain of the 145th Pennsylvania Volunteer Infantry,* ed. David T. Hedrick and Gordon Barry Davis, Jr. (Gettysburg, Pa.: Thomas Publications, 1995), 21.

14. Bennett, *Narrative of the Great Revival,* 150.

15. David Humphrey Blair Papers, Civil War Miscellaneous Collection, USAMHI.

16. Philip Daingerfield Stephenson, *The Civil War Memoir of Philip Daingerfield Stephenson, D.D.,* ed. Nathaniel Cheairs Hughes, Jr. (Baton Rouge: Louisiana State University Press, 1995), 147. Another story of a Bible saving a soldier's life is found in Rufus B. Buxton, "The Buxton Journal," *Licking Countian* 7, no. 35 (March 13, 1986).

17. William A. Moore Memoirs, Civil War Miscellaneous Collection, USAMHI.

18. John Hampden Chamberlayne, *Ham Chamberlayne, Virginian: Letters and Papers of an Artillery Officer in the War for Southern Independence, 1861–1865* (Richmond, Va.: Dietz, 1932; reprint, Wilmington, N.C.: Broadfoot, 1992), 123.

19. David Holt, *A Mississippi Rebel in the Army of Northern Virginia*, ed. Thomas D. Cockrell and Michael B. Ballard (Baton Rouge: Louisiana State University Press, 1995), 263.

20. John T. McMahon, *John T. McMahon's Diary of the 136th New York, 1861–1864*, ed. John Michael Priest (Shippensburg, Pa.: White Mane, 1993), 7.

21. John Howes Burton Letter, Civil War Miscellaneous Collection, USAMHI.

22. Thomas F. Boatright to "My Dear Wife," March 9, 1863, Boatright Papers, SHC.

23. Marcus A. Stults to "Mr. Lymmes," July 19, 1861, Marcus A. Stults Papers, Civil War Miscellaneous Collection, USAMHI.

24. Joshua K. Callaway, *The Civil War Letters of Joshua K. Callaway*, ed. Judith Lee Hallock (Athens: University of Georgia Press, 1997), 29.

25. Levi Y. Lockhart to "Dear Sister," July 16, 1863, Hugh Conway Browning Papers, PLDU.

26. Emily Elliott Diary, Jonas Denton Elliott Papers, Civil War Miscellaneous Collection, USAMHI.

27. Henry Hoyt to "Dear Ones at Home," May 17, 1864, Henry Hoyt Papers, Civil War Miscellaneous Collection, USAMHI.

28. N. H. R. Dawson to Elodie Todd, July 25, 1861, N. H. R. Dawson Papers, SHC.

29. Bennett, *Narrative of the Great Revival*, 110.

30. Seymour Dexter, *Seymour Dexter, Union Army: Journal and Letters of Civil War Service in Company K, 23rd New York Volunteer Regiment of Elmira*, ed. Carl A. Morrell (Jefferson, N.C.: McFarland, 1996), 129.

31. Thomas W. Cutrer and T. Michael Parrish, eds., *Brothers in Gray: The Civil War Letters of the Pierson Family* (Baton Rouge: Louisiana State University Press, 1997), 200.

32. James G. Theaker, *Through One Man's Eyes: The Civil War Experiences of a Belmont County Volunteer*, ed. Paul E. Rieger (Mt. Vernon, Ohio: Printing Arts Press, 1974), 118–19.

33. Edwin H. Fay, *"This Infernal War": The Confederate Letters of Sgt. Edwin H. Fay*, ed. Bell Irvin Wiley (Austin: University of Texas Press, 1958), 254.

34. Henry T. Morgan to "Dear Ellen," April 4, 1863, Henry T. Morgan Letters, Civil War Miscellaneous Collection, USAMHI.

35. William N. Tyler, *Memoirs of Andersonville* (Bernalillo, N.M.: Joel Beer and Gwendy MacMaster, 1992), 19–20. This story is corroborated by the William A. Miller Reminiscences, Civil War Miscellaneous Collection, USAMHI. Incredible as it may seem, Gerald F. Linderman asserts that at Andersonville, "Religious sensibility seemed almost to disappear . . . and prayer diminished" (*Embattled Courage: The Experience of Combat in the American Civil War* [New York: Free Press, 1987], 259). Obviously, my findings do not support his assertion.

36. Henry Hitchcock, *Marching with Sherman: Passages from the Letters and Campaign Diaries of Henry Hitchcock*, ed. M. A. de Wolfe Howe (New Haven, Conn.: Yale University Press, 1927; reprint, Lincoln: University of Nebraska Press, 1995), 19–20.

37. Callaway, *Civil War Letters*, 147.

38. Albert M. Childs to "Dear Brother," January 22, 1863, Albert M. Childs Papers, SHSW.

39. Henry T. Morgan to "Dear Ellen," March 9, 1865, Henry T. Morgan Papers, Civil War Miscellaneous Collection, USAMHI.

40. Callaway, *Civil War Letters*, 17.

41. McMahon, *Diary*, 5.

42. Holt, *Mississippi Rebel*, 145.

43. Shanklin, *Dearest Lizzie*, 114–15.

44. Wilkinson and Woodworth, *Scythe of Fire*.

45. William B. Olmstead, John M. Critchlow, A. T. Jennings, and Thoro Harris, eds., *The Free Methodist Hymnal* (Chicago: Free Methodist Publishing House, 1910), 111.

46. Stuckenberg, *I'm Surrounded by Methodists*, 13–14.

47. McMahon, *Diary*, 29.

48. Charles B. Haydon, *For Country, Cause and Leader: The Civil War Journal of Charles B. Haydon*, ed. Stephen W. Sears (New York: Ticknor and Fields, 1993), 154.

49. Gideon W. Burtch Diary, May 1, 1864, Gideon W. Burtch Papers, Civil War Miscellaneous Collection, USAMHI.

50. R. M. Campbell Diary, July 6, 1862, AHC.

51. James C. Bates, *A Texas Cavalry Officer's Civil War: The Diary and Letters of James C. Bates*, ed. Richard Lowe (Baton Rouge: Louisiana State University Press, 1999), 90.

52. William Homan Diary, August 31, 1862, Civil War Miscellaneous Collection, USAMHI.

53. Aurelius Lyman Voorhis Diary, February 8, 1863, IHS.

54. Dexter, *Seymour Dexter*, 11; Chesley A. Mosman, *The Rough Side of War: The Civil War Journal of Chesley A. Mosman, 1st Lieutenant, Company D, 59th Illinois Volunteer Infantry Regiment*, ed. Arnold Gates (Garden City, N.Y.: Basin Publishing, 1987), 261–62.

55. Daniel Hughes Diary, November 30, 1862, IHS.

56. Cyrus F. Boyd, *The Civil War Diary of Cyrus F. Boyd, Fifteenth Iowa Infantry, 1861–1863*, ed. Mildred Thorne (Millwood, N.Y.: Kraus, 1977), 47.

57. Fielder, *Civil War Diaries*, 70.

58. Jeffrey D. Marshall, ed., *A War of the People: Vermont Civil War Letters* (Hanover, N.H.: University Press of New England, 1999), 67.

59. Bates, *Texas Cavalry Officer's Civil War*, 125.

60. Charles W. Wills, *Army Life of an Illinois Soldier* (Carbondale: Southern Illinois University Press, 1996), 213. For a similar expression from a soldier, see Wilbur Fisk, *Hard Marching Every Day: The Civil War Letters of Private Wilbur Fisk, 1861–1865*, ed. Emil Rosenblatt and Ruth Rosenblatt (Lawrence: University Press of Kansas, 1992), 239.

61. William Henry Walling to "Maryetta & Cassen," October 13, 1861, William Henry Walling Papers, Civil War Miscellaneous Collection, USAMHI.

62. Allen Morgan Geer, *The Civil War Diary of Allen Morgan Geer: Twentieth Regiment, Illinois Volunteers*, ed. Mary Ann Andersen (Denver: Robert C. Appleman, 1977), 49.

63. Bates, *Texas Cavalry Officer's Civil War,* 125.

64. William Henry Walling to "Maryetta & Cassen," October 13, 1861, William Henry Walling Papers, Civil War Miscellaneous Collection, USAMHI.

65. Gideon W. Burtch Diary, February 14, 1864, Civil War Miscellaneous Collection, USAMHI.

66. Aurelius Lyman Voorhis Diary, November 22, 1863, IHS.

67. Isaac Jackson, *Some of the Boys: The Civil War Letters of Isaac Jackson, 1862–1865* (Carbondale: Southern Illinois University Press, 1960), 59.

68. Haydon, *For Country, Cause and Leader,* 154.

69. Henry A. Kircher, *A German in the Yankee Fatherland: The Civil War Letters of Henry A. Kircher,* ed. Earl J. Hess (Kent, Ohio: Kent State University Press, 1983), 119.

70. Berea M. Willsey, *The Civil War Diary of Berea M. Willsey: The Intimate Daily Observations of a Massachusetts Volunteer in the Union Army, 1862–1864,* ed. Jessica H. DeMay (Bowie, Md.: Heritage Books, 1995), 19.

71. N. H. R. Dawson to Elodie Todd, August 4, 1861, N. H. R. Dawson Papers, SHC.

72. Mosman, *Rough Side of War,* 100.

73. Tracy J. Power, *Lee's Miserables: Life in the Army of Northern Virginia from the Wilderness to Appomattox* (Chapel Hill: University of North Carolina Press, 1998), 4–5.

74. William McCarter, *My Life in the Irish Brigade: The Civil War Memoirs of Private William McCarter, 116th Pennsylvania Infantry,* ed. Kevin E. O'Brien (Campbell, Calif.: Savas, 1996), 71–72.

75. Thomas F. Boatright to "My Dear Wife," February 16, 1863, Boatright Papers, SHC.

76. Fisk, *Hard Marching Every Day,* 127–28.

77. Aurelius Lyman Voorhis Diary, October 4, 1863, IHS.

78. Fielder, *Civil War Diaries,* 68–69.

79. Jackson, *Some of the Boys,* 70.

80. Marshall, *War of the People,* 62.

81. David Coon to "Dear Son," April 16, 1864, David Coon Papers, SHSW.

82. McCarter, *My Life in the Irish Brigade,* 87.

83. Bennett, *Narrative of the Great Revival,* 79.

84. Aurelius Lyman Voorhis Diary, April 13, 1862, IHS.

85. Johnny Green, *Johnny Green of the Orphan Brigade: The Journal of a Confederate Soldier,* ed. A. D. Kirwan (Lexington: University of Kentucky Press, 1956), 122.

86. Theodore F. Upson, *With Sherman to the Sea: The Civil War Letters, Diaries and Reminiscences of Theodore F. Upson,* ed. Oscar Osburn Winther (Bloomington: Indiana University Press, 1977), 123.

87. James I. Robertson, Jr., *Soldiers Blue and Gray* (Columbia: University of South Carolina Press, 1988), 95.

88. Green, *Johnny Green of the Orphan Brigade,* 122.

89. Nina Silber and Mary Beth Sievens, eds., *Yankee Correspondence: Civil War Letters Between New England Soldiers and the Home Front* (Charlottesville: University Press of Virginia, 1996), 132–33.

90. Ibid., 115.

91. Albert M. Childs to Elsworth Childs, March 27, 1864, Albert M. Childs Papers, SHSW.

92. Silber and Sievens, *Yankee Correspondence*, 99.

93. Holt, *Mississippi Rebel*, 4.

94. Allen C. Guelzo, *Abraham Lincoln: Redeemer President* (Grand Rapids, Mich.: Eerdmans, 1999), 152.

95. Geer, *Civil War Diary*, 151.

96. Burgwyn, *Captain's War*, 75, 114.

97. Higginson, *Complete Civil War Journal*, 156.

98. William Henry Walling to "My Dear Sister," April 8, 1865, William Henry Walling Letters, Civil War Miscellaneous Collection, USAMHI.

99. McMahon, *Diary*, 3–4.

Chapter 6. "We Are the Sword in the Hand of God"

1. Emilie Quiner Diary, April 20 [21], 1861, SHSW.

2. Lincoln Papers, Library of Congress, microfilm roll 21, mounting numbers 9137–42, 9151–52, 9201–2, 9208.

3. James I. Robertson, Jr., *Soldiers Blue and Gray* (Columbia: University of South Carolina Press, 1988), 22.

4. Emilie Quiner Diary, September 12, 1861, SHSW.

5. Quoted in Reid Mitchell, *The Vacant Chair: The Northern Soldier Leaves Home* (New York: Oxford University Press, 1993), 118–19.

6. Reid Mitchell argues that McAllister's statement amended "thoroughly the traditional meaning of the United States' role in history. Where Americans had hoped that their country's example was one of liberty, McAllister held the nation up as an emblem of power" (*Vacant Chair*, 119). Obviously, I would contend that no such either-or distinction should be made.

7. Reid Mitchell, *Civil War Soldiers* (New York: Viking, 1988), 20.

8. William A. Clebsch, *Christian Interpretations of the Civil War* (Philadelphia: Fortress Press, 1969), 6–8.

9. Gardiner H. Shattuck, Jr., *A Shield and Hiding Place: The Religious Life of the Civil War Armies* (Macon, Ga.: Mercer University Press, 1987), 17–18.

10. "Dear Brother," August 10, 1861, Edward and Mary Ann Craig Papers, ISHL.

11. James Maynard Shanklin, *Dearest Lizzie: The Civil War Letters of Lt. Col. James Maynard Shanklin*, ed. Kenneth P. McCutchan (Evansville, Ind.: Friends of Willard Library Press, 1988), 178.

12. Ibid., 195.

13. An example of the stationery can be found in the Daniel Buck Letter, SHSW.

14. This can be found in the Richard Robert Crowe Papers, SHSW.

15. Gerald F. Linderman, *Embattled Courage: The Experience of Combat in the American Civil War* (New York: Free Press, 1987), 109.

16. Lester A. Miller to Abraham Lincoln, April 16, 1861, Lincoln Papers, Library of Congress, microfilm roll 21, mounting number 9133.

17. Nathaniel Cheairs Hughes, Jr., *The Battle of Belmont: Grant Strikes South* (Chapel Hill: University of North Carolina Press, 1991), 78.

18. John Beatty, *Memoirs of a Volunteer, 1861–1863* (New York: W. W. Norton, 1946), 60.

19. William Henry Walling Papers, Civil War Miscellaneous Collection, USAMHI.

20. William McCarter, *My Life in the Irish Brigade: The Civil War Memoirs of Private William McCarter, 116th Pennsylvania Infantry*, ed. Kevin E. O'Brien (Campbell, Calif.: Savas, 1996), 89–90.

21. Elisha Hunt Rhodes, *All for the Union: The Civil War Diary and Letters of Elisha Hunt Rhodes*, ed. Robert Hunt Rhodes (New York: Orion Books, 1985), 21.

22. Ira Blanchard, *I Marched with Sherman: Civil War Memoirs of the 20th Illinois Volunteer Infantry* (San Francisco: J. D. Huff, 1992), 24.

23. Seymour Dexter, *Seymour Dexter, Union Army: Journal and Letters of Civil War Service in Company K, 23rd New York Volunteer Regiment of Elmira*, ed. Carl A. Morrell (Jefferson, N.C.: McFarland, 1996), 72; Nathan W. Daniels, *Thank God My Regiment an African One: The Civil War Diary of Colonel Nathan W. Daniels*, ed. C. P. Weaver (Baton Rouge: Louisiana State University Press, 1998), 102; James Henry Gooding, *On the Altar of Freedom: A Black Soldier's Civil War Letters from the Front*, ed. Virginia Matzke Adams (Amherst: University of Massachusetts Press, 1991), 16; John Henry Wilburn Stuckenberg, *I'm Surrounded by Methodists: Diary of John H. W. Stuckenberg, Chaplain of the 145th Pennsylvania Volunteer Infantry*, ed. David T. Hedrick and Gordon Barry Davis, Jr. (Gettysburg, Pa.: Thomas Publications, 1995), 60–61.

24. Berea M. Willsey, *The Civil War Diary of Berea M. Willsey: The Intimate Daily Observations of a Massachusetts Volunteer in the Union Army, 1862–1864*, ed. Jessica H. DeMay (Bowie, Md.: Heritage Books, 1995), 11–12.

25. Douglas Hapeman Diary, April 13, 1862, ISHL.

26. Allen Morgan Geer, *The Civil War Diary of Allen Morgan Geer: Twentieth Regiment, Illinois Volunteers*, ed. Mary Ann Andersen (Denver: Robert C. Appleman, 1977), 28.

27. Chesley A. Mosman, *The Rough Side of War: The Civil War Journal of Chesley A. Mosman, 1st Lieutenant, Company D, 59th Illinois Volunteer Infantry Regiment*, ed. Arnold Gates (Garden City, N.Y.: Basin Publishing, 1987), 10.

28. Henry G. Ankeny, *Kiss Josey for Me*, ed. Florence Marie Ankeny Cox (Santa Ana, Calif.: Friss-Pioneer Press, 1974), 59.

29. William Henry Walling to "My Dear Sisters," November 20, 1862, William Henry Walling Papers, Civil War Miscellaneous Collection, USAMHI.

30. The words of Christ quoted by Walling are from Mark 16:15. The additional portion of Christ's words are from Matthew 28:20, a passage that reports the same scene, some of Christ's final instructions to his disciples.

31. Nina Silber and May Beth Sievens, eds., *Yankee Correspondence: Civil War Letters Between New England Soldiers and the Home Front* (Charlottesville: University Press of Virginia, 1996), 85.

32. Edward Watson to "Dear Lil," April 12, 1862, Edward Watson Papers, Civil War Miscellaneous Collection, USAMHI.

33. Wesley W. Bierly Diary, August 22, 1861, Civil War Miscellaneous Collection, USAMHI.

34. Lincoln Papers, Library of Congress, microfilm roll 23, mounting numbers 10186–87.

35. Ibid., microfilm roll 22, mounting numbers 9730–34.

36. Ankeny, *Kiss Josey for Me*, 11.

37. Shanklin, *Dearest Lizzie*, 50, 64.

38. Mitchell, *Vacant Chair*, 119–20.

39. Silber and Seivens, *Yankee Correspondence*, 78.

40. Gerry Harder Porris and Ralph G. Poriss, *While My Country Is in Danger: The Life and Letters of Lieutenant Colonel Richard S. Thompson, Twelfth New Jersey Volunteers* (Hamilton, N.Y.: Edmonston Publishing, 1994), 63.

41. Willsey, *Civil War Diary*, 19.

42. James Magill to "Dear Mother," February 1, 1863, James Magill Papers, Civil War Miscellaneous Collection, USAMHI.

43. Luther H. Cowan to "My Dear Ones," March 30, 1862, Luther H. Cowan Papers, SHSW.

44. Andrew Roy, *Fallen Soldier: Memoir of a Civil War Casualty*, ed. William J. Miller (Birmingham, Ala.: Elliott and Clark, 1996), 59.

45. Joseph Whitney, *Kiss Clara for Me: The Story of Joseph Whitney and His Family, Early Days in the Midwest, and Soldiering in the American Civil War*, ed. Robert J. Snetsinger (State College, Pa.: Carnation Press, 1969), 47.

46. Wilbur Fisk, *Hard Marching Every Day: The Civil War Letters of Private Wilbur Fisk, 1861–1865*, ed. Emil Rosenblatt and Ruth Rosenblatt (Lawrence: University Press of Kansas, 1992), 65–66.

47. Mitchell, *Civil War Soldiers*, 77.

48. Thomas Wentworth Higginson, *The Complete Civil War Journal and Selected Letters of Thomas Wentworth Higginson*, ed. Christopher Looby (Chicago: University of Chicago Press, 2000), 86.

49. R. W. Lloyd to Robert C. Blair, January 4, 1863, Richard Emerson Blair Papers, IHS.

50. McCarter, *My Life in the Irish Brigade*, 27.

51. Dexter, *Seymour Dexter*, 108.

52. George H. Allen, *Forty-six Months with the Fourth R.I. Volunteers, in the War of 1861–1865* (Providence, R.I.: J. A. and R. A. Reid, 1887), 109.

53. Ibid., 148.

54. Charles B. Haydon, *For Country, Cause and Leader: The Civil War Journal of Charles B. Haydon*, ed. Stephen W. Sears (New York: Ticknor and Fields, 1993), 180, 183.

55. William Garrett Piston and Richard W. Hatcher III, *Wilson's Creek: The Second Battle of the Civil War and the Men Who Fought It* (Chapel Hill: University of North Carolina Press, 2000), 237.

56. Gooding, *On the Altar of Freedom,* 21–22.

57. Mitchell, *Vacant Chair,* 146–47.

58. Richard E. Blair to R. C. Blair, January 26, 1863, Richard Emerson Blair Papers, IHS.

59. Stephen V. Ash, *When the Yankees Came: Conflict and Chaos in the Occupied South, 1861–1865* (Chapel Hill: University of North Carolina Press, 1995), 114.

60. Beatty, *Memoirs of a Volunteer,* 119–20.

61. William A. Bennett, *A Narrative of the Great Revival in the Southern Armies During the Late Civil War Between the States of the Federal Union* (Philadelphia: Claxton, Remsen and Haffelfinger, 1877), 234.

62. N. P. Tallmadge to Lincoln, April 22, 1861, Lincoln Papers, Library of Congress, microfilm roll 21, mounting numbers 9352–62.

63. James M. McPherson, *For Cause and Comrades: Why Men Fought in the Civil War* (New York: Oxford University Press, 1997), 12.

64. John T. McMahon, *John T. McMahon's Diary of the 136th New York, 1861–1864,* ed. John Michael Priest (Shippensburg, Pa.: White Mane, 1993), 23–24.

65. Samuel McIlvaine, *By the Dim and Flaring Lamps: The Civil War Diaries of Samuel McIlvaine,* ed. Clayton E. Cramer (Monroe, N.Y.: Library Research Associates, 1990), 146–47.

66. Peter Welsh, *Irish Green and Union Blue: The Civil War Letters of Peter Welsh, Color Sergeant, 28th Regiment Massachusetts Volunteers,* ed. Lawrence Frederick Kohl and Margaret Cosse Richard (New York: Fordham University Press, 1986), 65–67.

67. William H. Walling to "My Dear Sisters," October 25, 1862, William Henry Walling Papers, Civil War Miscellaneous Collection, USAMHI.

68. Ibid.

69. Cyrus F. Boyd, *The Civil War Diary of Cyrus F. Boyd, Fifteenth Iowa Infantry, 1861–1863,* ed. Mildred Thorne (Millwood, N.Y.: Kraus, 1977), 18.

70. Quoted in McPherson, *For Cause and Comrades,* 129.

71. Mitchell, *Civil War Soldiers,* 187.

72. Shattuck, *Shield and Hiding Place,* 16–17.

73. Fisk, *Hard Marching Every Day,* 66–67.

74. Quoted in Mitchell, *Civil War Soldiers,* 186–87.

75. Jefferson Newman to Caroline Newman Kirkpatrick, May 20, 1863, Samuel Cotter Kirkpatrick Letters, SHSW.

76. Silber and Sievens, *Yankee Correspondence,* 69–70.

77. Quoted in McPherson, *For Cause and Comrades,* 130.

78. Quoted in Mitchell, *Civil War Soldiers,* 187.

79. George W. Johnson Letter, Civil War Miscellaneous Collection, USAMHI.

80. Fisk, *Hard Marching Every Day,* 70.

81. Jack K. Overmyer, *A Stupendous Effort: The 87th Indiana in the War of the Rebellion* (Bloomington: Indiana University Press, 1997), 56.

82. Alan D. Gaff, *On Many a Bloody Field: Four Years in the Iron Brigade* (Bloomington: Indiana University Press, 1996), 232.

83. Whitney, *Kiss Clara for Me*, 34.

84. Jefferson Newman to Caroline Newman Kirkpatrick, May 20, 1863, Samuel Cotter Kirkpatrick Letters, SHSW.

85. Rice C. Bull, *Soldiering: The Civil War Diary of Rice C. Bull, 123rd New York Volunteer Infantry*, ed. K. Jack Bauer (San Rafael, Calif.: Presidio Press, 1977), 86.

86. Thomas Francis Gallwey, *The Valiant Hours*, ed. W. S. Nye (Harrisburg, Pa.: Stackpole, 1961), 35.

87. John M. Roberts, "A Pioneer's Story," John M. Roberts Reminiscences, IHS.

88. Ash, *When the Yankees Came*, 171–72.

89. Silber and Sievens, *Yankee Correspondence*, 144.

Chapter 7. "God Has Favored Our Cause"

1. Robert Manson Myers, ed., *The Children of Pride: A True Story of Georgia and the Civil War* (New Haven, Conn.: Yale University Press, 1972), 690; Warren Wilkinson and Steven E. Woodworth, *A Scythe of Fire: The Civil War Story of the Eighth Georgia Regiment* (New York: HarperCollins, in press).

2. Avery O. Craven, *The Growth of Southern Nationalism, 1848–1861* (Baton Rouge: Louisiana State University Press, 1953), 374.

3. Christopher H. Owen, *The Sacred Flame of Love: Methodism and Society in Nineteenth-Century Georgia* (Athens: University of Georgia Press, 1998), 91–92, 97.

4. Val C. Giles, *Rags and Hope: The Recollections of Val C. Giles, Four Years with Hood's Brigade, Fourth Texas Infantry, 1861–1865*, ed. Mary Lasswell (New York: Coward-McCann, 1961), 22–23.

5. Owen, *Sacred Flame of Love*, 95.

6. Ibid., 92.

7. James Oscar Farmer, Jr., *The Metaphysical Confederacy: James Henley Thornwell and the Synthesis of Southern Values* (Macon, Ga.: Mercer University Press, 1986), 11.

8. Owen, *Sacred Flame of Love*, 107; George Rable, *The Confederate Republic: A Revolution Against Politics* (Chapel Hill: University of North Carolina Press, 1994), 135.

9. Rable, *Confederate Republic*, 123–24.

10. Eugene D. Genovese, *A Consuming Fire: The Fall of the Confederacy in the Mind of the White Christian South* (Athens: University of Georgia Press, 1998), 3–4.

11. David Williams, *Rich Man's War: Class, Caste, and Confederate Defeat in the Lower Chattahoochee Valley* (Athens: University of Georgia Press, 1998), 57–58.

12. United States War Department, *The War of the Rebellion: Official Records of the Union and Confederate Armies*, 128 vols. (Washington, D.C.: Government Printing Office, 1881–

1901), series 1, vol. 4, pp. 522, 539 (hereafter cited as *OR;* except as otherwise noted, all references are to series 1).

13. Ibid., 368–69.

14. N. H. R. Dawson to Elodie Todd, December 4, 1861, N. H. R. Dawson Papers, SHC.

15. J. Roderick Heller III and Carolynn Ayres Heller, eds., *The Confederacy Is on Her Way up the Spout: Letters to South Carolina, 1861–1864* (Athens: University of Georgia Press, 1992), 39.

16. Owen, *Sacred Flame of Love,* 107.

17. Kurt O. Berends, "Wholesome Reading Purifies and Elevates the Man: The Religious Military Press in the Confederacy," in *Religion and the American Civil War,* ed. Randall M. Miller, Harry S. Stout, and Charles Reagan Wilson (New York: Oxford University Press, 1998), 131–66.

18. Owen, *Sacred Flame of Love,* 105.

19. Gardiner H. Shattuck, Jr., *A Shield and Hiding Place: The Religious Life of the Civil War Armies* (Macon, Ga.: Mercer University Press, 1987), 36.

20. William C. Davis, *A Government of Our Own: The Making of the Confederacy* (New York: Free Press, 1994), 75.

21. Genovese, *Consuming Fire,* 3–4.

22. Owen, *Sacred Flame of Love,* 103–4.

23. William W. Bennett, *A Narrative of the Great Revival in the Southern Armies During the Late Civil War Between the States of the Federal Union* (Philadelphia: Claxton, Remsen and Haffelfinger, 1887), 88–90.

24. Williams, *Rich Man's War,* 57–58.

25. Owen, *Sacred Flame of Love,* 95.

26. William Garrett Piston and Richard W. Hatcher III, *Wilson's Creek: The Second Battle of the Civil War and the Men Who Fought It* (Chapel Hill: University of North Carolina Press, 2000), 21.

27. James I. Robertson, Jr., *Soldiers Blue and Gray* (Columbia: University of South Carolina Press, 1988), 185.

28. Stewart Sifakis, *Who Was Who in the Civil War* (New York: Facts on File, 1988), 498; David Holt, *A Mississippi Rebel in the Army of Northern Virginia,* ed. Thomas D. Cockrell and Michael B. Ballard (Baton Rouge: Louisiana State University Press, 1995), 231.

29. James Iredell Hall Papers, SHC.

30. Mark P. Lowrey Autobiography, Civil War Miscellaneous Collection, USAMHI.

31. Owen, *Sacred Flame of Love,* 104–5.

32. Williams, *Rich Man's War,* 58; *Rome Courier,* March 25 and April 8, 1862.

33. Owen, *Sacred Flame of Love,* 99–100.

34. Robertson, *Soldiers Blue and Gray,* 173.

35. Genovese, *Consuming Fire,* 48.

36. *Rome Courier,* May 19, 1862.

37. James Iredell Hall Papers, SHC.

38. *Rome Courier,* April 22, 1862.

39. R. M. Campbell Diary, June 18, 1862, AHC.

40. Alfred Tyler Fielder, *The Civil War Diaries of Capt. Alfred Tyler Fielder, 12th Tennessee Regiment Infantry, Company B, 1861–1865,* ed. Ann York Franklin (Louisville, Ky.: privately published, 1996), 52–53; Silas T. Grisamore, *The Civil War Reminiscences of Major Silas T. Grisamore,* ed. Arthur W. Bergeron, Jr. (Baton Rouge: Louisiana State University Press, 1993), 54.

41. William Ross Stillwell to "My Dear Molly," September 10, 1862, in *In Camp on the Rappahannock: The Newsletter of the Blue & Gray Education Society* 4, no. 3 (spring 1999): 12.

42. Flavel C. Barber, *Holding the Line: The Third Tennessee Infantry, 1861–1864,* ed. Robert H. Ferrell (Kent, Ohio: Kent State University Press, 1994), 101.

43. Thomas W. Cutrer and T. Michael Parrish, eds., *Brothers in Gray: The Civil War Letters of the Pierson Family* (Baton Rouge: Louisiana State University Press, 1997), 190–91.

44. Dick Simpson and Tally Simpson, *"Far, Far from Home": The Wartime Letters of Dick and Tally Simpson, Third South Carolina Volunteers,* ed. Guy R. Everson and Edward H. Simpson, Jr. (New York: Oxford University Press, 1994), 237.

45. Bennett, *Narrative of the Great Revival,* 116.

46. Ibid., 174–76.

47. Ibid., 91–92.

48. Ibid., 224–25.

49. Ibid., 92.

50. Ignatius W. Brock to "My Dear Sister," June 22, 1863, Ignatius W. Brock Papers, PLDU.

51. Gary W. Gallagher, *Lee and His Generals in War and Memory* (Baton Rouge: Louisiana State University Press, 1998), 7, 117.

52. Bennett, *Narrative of the Great Revival,* 90–91.

53. Letter reprinted in *Rome Courier,* February 13, 1862.

54. N. H. R. Dawson to Elodie Todd, May 10, 1861, N. H. R. Dawson Papers, SHC.

55. *OR,* 2:97.

56. Ibid., 482, 542, 574.

57. Bennett, *Narrative of the Great Revival,* 111.

58. Ibid., 112.

59. N. H. R. Dawson to Elodie Todd, July 23, 1861, N. H. R. Dawson Papers, SHC.

60. *OR,* 3:329.

61. Quoted in Bennett, *Narrative of the Great Revival,* 128–29.

62. Stephen V. Ash, *When the Yankees Came: Conflict and Chaos in the Occupied South, 1861–1865* (Chapel Hill: University of North Carolina Press, 1995), 38.

63. Owen, *Sacred Flame of Love,* 98.

64. Simpson and Simpson, *Far, Far from Home,* 201.

65. Robert G. Tanner, *Stonewall in the Valley: Thomas J. "Stonewall" Jackson's Shenandoah Valley Campaign, Spring 1862* (Mechanicsburg, Pa.: Stackpole, 1996), 414.

66. George Phifer Erwin to "My dear Sister," July 10, 1862, George Phifer Erwin Papers, SHC.

67. William Ross Stillwell to "My Dear Molly," September 10, 1862, in *In Camp on the Rappahannock: The Newsletter of the Blue & Gray Education Society* 4, no. 3 (spring 1999): 12.

68. *Rome Courier,* September 12, 1862.

69. Melvin Dwinell letter of November 24, 1862, printed in *Rome Courier,* December 5, 1862.

70. Cutrer and Parrish, *Brothers in Gray,* 66.

71. N. H. R. Dawson to Elodie Todd, December 22, 1861, N. H. R. Dawson Papers, SHC.

72. Letter of June 5, 1863, Barkley Family Papers, SHC.

73. Simpson and Simpson, *Far, Far from Home,* 136.

74. Barber, *Holding the Line,* 107.

75. Reid Mitchell, *Civil War Soldiers* (New York: Viking, 1988), 10–11.

76. Bennett, *Narrative of the Great Revival,* 89–90.

77. Andrew Roy, *Fallen Soldier: Memoir of a Civil War Casualty,* ed. William J. Miller (Birmingham, Ala.: Elliott and Clark, 1996), 48.

78. *OR,* 3:576–77.

79. Ash, *When the Yankees Came,* 68–69.

80. N. H. R. Dawson to Elodie Todd, May 25 and 26, 1861, N. H. R. Dawson Papers, SHC.

81. Cutrer and Parrish, *Brothers in Gray,* 77.

82. James R. Arnold, *Grant Wins the War: Decision at Vicksburg* (New York: John Wiley and Sons, 1997), 146.

83. Joshua K. Callaway, *The Civil War Letters of Joshua K. Callaway,* ed. Judith Lee Hallock (Athens: University of Georgia Press, 1997), 34.

84. Mitchell, *Civil War Soldiers,* 80.

85. Evan Morrison Woodward, *Our Campaigns: The Second Regiment Pennsylvanian Reserve Volunteers, 1861–1864,* ed. Stanley W. Zamonski (Shippensburg, Pa.: Burd Street Press, 1995), 118–19.

86. Bennett, *Narrative of the Great Revival,* 94.

87. Ibid.

88. Quoted in Gerald F. Linderman, *Embattled Courage: The Experience of Combat in the American Civil War* (New York: Free Press, 1987), 181.

89. John Henry Wilburn Stuckenberg, *I'm Surrounded by Methodists: Diary of John H. W. Stuckenberg, Chaplain of the 145th Pennsylvania Volunteer Infantry,* ed. David T. Hedrick and Gordon Barry Davis, Jr. (Gettysburg, Pa.: Thomas Publications, 1995), 59.

90. Benjamin Franklin Cooling, *Fort Donelson's Legacy: War and Society in Kentucky and Tennessee, 1861–1863* (Knoxville: University of Tennessee Press, 1997), 160.

91. Seymour Dexter, *Seymour Dexter, Union Army: Journal and Letters of Civil War Service in Company K, 23rd New York Volunteer Regiment of Elmira,* ed. Carl A. Morrell (Jefferson, N.C.: McFarland, 1996), 70.

92. James Marten, *Texas Divided: Loyalty and Dissent in the Lone Star State, 1856–1874* (Lexington: University of Kentucky Press, 1990), 53–55.

93. *Rome Courier,* January 21, 1862.

94. Edwin H. Fay, *"This Infernal War": The Confederate Letters of Sgt. Edwin H. Fay,* ed. Bell Irvin Wiley (Austin: University of Texas Press, 1958), 92–93.

95. Bennett, *Narrative of the Great Revival,* 109–11, 162–63.

96. Cutrer and Parrish, *Brothers in Gray,* 201.

97. James Iredell Hall Papers, SHC.

98. Fielder, *Civil War Diaries,* 8.

99. Genovese, *Consuming Fire,* 66.

100. Thomas F. Boatright to "My Dear Wife," February 21, 1863, Boatright Papers, SHC.

101. Bennett, *Narrative of the Great Revival,* 213–21.

Chapter 8. "The Boys Love Him as a Father"

1. John J. Hardin to John Hardin, February 17, 1862, John J. Hardin Papers, IHS.

2. Daniel Hughes Diary, November 16, 1862, IHS.

3. Warren B. Armstrong, *For Courageous Fighting and Confident Dying: Union Chaplains in the Civil War* (Lawrence: University Press of Kansas, 1998), 2.

4. Ibid., 8; Gardiner H. Shattuck, Jr., *A Shield and Hiding Place: The Religious Life of the Civil War Armies* (Macon, Ga.: Mercer University Press, 1987), 52.

5. James I. Robertson, Jr., *Soldiers Blue and Gray* (Columbia: University of South Carolina Press, 1988), 174–75; Shattuck, *Shield and Hiding Place,* 52.

6. Alfred Tyler Fielder, *The Civil War Diaries of Capt. Alfred Tyler Fielder, 12th Tennessee Regiment Infantry, Company B, 1861–1865,* ed. Ann York Franklin (Louisville, Ky.: privately published, 1996), 53.

7. John Henry Wilburn Stuckenberg, *I'm Surrounded by Methodists: Diary of John H. W. Stuckenberg, Chaplain of the 145th Pennsylvania Volunteer Infantry,* ed. David T. Hedrick and Gordon Barry Davis, Jr. (Gettysburg, Pa.: Thomas Publications, 1995), 8.

8. Christopher H. Owen, *The Sacred Flame of Love: Methodism and Society in Nineteenth-Century Georgia* (Athens: University of Georgia Press, 1998), 106.

9. N. H. R. Dawson to Elodie Todd, December 8, 1861, N. H. R. Dawson Papers, SHC.

10. Robertson, *Soldiers Blue and Gray,* 175.

11. Edwin H. Fay, *"This Infernal War": The Confederate Letters of Sgt. Edwin H. Fay,* ed. Bell Irvin Wiley (Austin: University of Texas Press, 1958), 94–95.

12. Thomas Wentworth Higginson, *The Complete Civil War Journal and Selected Letters of Thomas Wentworth Higginson,* ed. Christopher Looby (Chicago: University of Chicago Press, 2000), 211.

13. Armstrong, *For Courageous Fighting and Confident Dying,* 5.

14. Elisha Hunt Rhodes, *All for the Union: The Civil War Diary and Letters of Elisha Hunt Rhodes,* ed. Robert Hunt Rhodes (New York: Orion Books, 1985).

15. Clifford Anderson to "My Dear Wife," November 16, 1862, Clifford Anderson Papers, SHC.

16. Robertson, *Soldiers Blue and Gray,* 176.

17. William W. Bennett, *A Narrative of the Great Revival in the Southern Armies During the Late Civil War Between the States of the Federal Union* (Philadelphia: Claxton, Remsen and Haffelfinger, 1877), 51–52.

18. Dick Simpson and Tally Simpson, *"Far, Far from Home": The Wartime Letters of Dick and Tally Simpson, Third South Carolina Volunteers,* ed. Guy R. Everson and Edward H. Simpson, Jr. (New York: Oxford University Press, 1994), 237 n. 1.

19. *OR,* 2:952–54.

20. Shattuck, *Shield and Hiding Place,* 52.

21. Armstrong, *For Courageous Fighting and Confident Dying,* 4.

22. Higginson, *Complete Civil War Journal,* 227.

23. Robertson, *Soldiers Blue and Gray,* 176–77.

24. Milton A. Bailey to Ann Sturtevant, August 4, 1863, Ann Sturtevant Letters, Civil War Miscellaneous Collection, USAMHI.

25. John T. McMahon, *John T. McMahon's Diary of the 136th New York, 1861–1864,* ed. John Michael Priest (Shippensburg, PA: White Mane, 1993), 60.

26. Robertson, *Soldiers Blue and Gray,* 176–77.

27. Abner R. Small, *The Road to Richmond: The Civil War Memoirs of Maj. Abner R. Small of the 16th Maine Vols.: With His Diary as a Prisoner of War,* ed. Harold Adams Small (Berkeley: University of California Press, 1959), 85.

28. Joshua K. Callaway, *The Civil War Letters of Joshua K. Callaway,* ed. Judith Lee Hallock (Athens: University of Georgia Press, 1997), 33.

29. Stuckenberg, *I'm Surrounded by Methodists,* 103.

30. Philip Daingerfield Stephenson, *The Civil War Memoir of Philip Daingerfield Stephenson, D.D.,* ed. Nathaniel Cheairs Hughes, Jr. (Baton Rouge: Louisiana State University Press, 1995), 42.

31. John Beatty, *Memoirs of a Volunteer, 1861–1863* (New York: W. W. Norton, 1946), 66–67.

32. Charles B. Haydon, *For Country, Cause and Leader: The Civil War Journal of Charles B. Haydon,* ed. Stephen W. Sears (New York: Ticknor and Fields, 1993), 144.

33. James Maynard Shanklin, *Dearest Lizzie: The Civil War Letters of Lt. Col. James Maynard Shanklin,* ed. Kenneth P. McCutchan (Evansville, Ind.: Friends of Willard Library Press, 1988), 47.

34. Reid Mitchell, *Civil War Soldiers* (New York: Viking, 1988), 56.

35. Beatty, *Memoirs of a Volunteer,* 124–25.

36. Armstrong, *For Courageous Fighting and Confident Dying,* 4.

37. James Wren, *From New Bern to Fredericksburg: Captain James Wren's Diary,* ed. John Michael Priest (Shippensburg, Pa.: White Mane, 1990), 39.

38. Some examples are Adam S. Bright and Michael S. Bright, *"Respects to All": Letters of Two Pennsylvania Boys in the War of the Rebellion,* ed. Aida Craig Truxall (Pittsburgh: University of Pittsburgh Press, 1962), 4; Rhodes, *All for the Union,* 141; James Iredell Hall Papers, SHC.

39. Stuckenberg, *I'm Surrounded by Methodists,* 20.

40. David C. Dutcher Diary, August 10, 1864, David C. Dutcher Papers, PLDU.

41. Edward P. Stanfield to "Dear Father," March 20, 1862, Edward P. Stanfield Papers, IHS.

42. W. H. L. Wallace to Ann Wallace, May 12, 1861, Wallace-Dickey Family Papers, ISHL.

43. Lucius W. Barber, *Army Memoirs of Lucius W. Barber, Company "D," 15th Illinois Volunteer Infantry* (Chicago: J. M. W. Jones Stationery and Printing Co., 1894), 103.

44. Bennett, *Narrative of the Great Revival,* 416.

45. Charles W. Bardeen, *A Little Fifer's War Diary* (Syracuse, N.Y.: author, 1910), 45.

46. J. Roderick Heller III and Carolynn Ayres Heller, eds., *The Confederacy Is on Her Way up the Spout: Letters to South Carolina, 1861–1864* (Athens: University of Georgia Press, 1992), 96. For another example, see Val C. Giles, *Rags and Hope: The Recollections of Val C. Giles, Four Years with Hood's Brigade, Fourth Texas Infantry, 1861–1865,* ed. Mary Lasswell (New York: Coward-McCann, 1961), 27.

47. Armstrong, *For Courageous Fighting and Confident Dying,* 19–27.

48. Small, *Road to Richmond,* 189.

49. Ibid., 32, 189.

50. Hamlin L. Chapman Reminiscences, SHSW.

51. Douglas Hapeman Diary, July 7, 1862, ISHL.

52. Stuckenberg, *I'm Surrounded by Methodists,* 75.

53. Benjamin Franklin McIntrye Diaries, September 5, 1862, PLDU.

54. Rhodes, *All for the Union,* 139.

55. Ira Blanchard, *I Marched with Sherman: Civil War Memoirs of the 20th Illinois Volunteer Infantry* (San Francisco: J. D. Huff, 1992), 110–11.

56. Chesley A. Mosman, *The Rough Side of War: The Civil War Journal of Chesley A. Mosman, 1st Lieutenant, Company D, 59th Illinois Volunteer Infantry Regiment* (Garden City, N.Y.: Basin Publishing, 1987), 207.

57. Rice C. Bull, *Soldiering: The Civil War Diary of Rice C. Bull, 123rd New York Volunteer Infantry,* ed. K. Jack Bauer (San Rafael, Calif.: Presidio Press, 1977), 70–81.

58. Stephenson, *Civil War Memoir,* 230.

59. N. H. R. Dawson to Elodie Todd, August 4, 1861, N. H. R. Dawson Papers, SHC.

60. Henry C. Campbell Recollections, Civil War Miscellaneous Collection, USAMHI.

61. Theodore F. Upson, *With Sherman to the Sea: The Civil War Letters, Diaries and Reminiscences of Theodore F. Upson,* ed. Oscar Osburn Winther (Bloomington: Indiana University Press, 1977), 87, 102–5.

62. John M. Roberts, "A Pioneer's Story," John M. Roberts Reminiscences, IHS.

63. Rhodes, *All for the Union,* 144.

64. Bull, *Soldiering*, 70.

65. Beatty, *Memoirs of a Volunteer*, 42–43.

66. Bardeen, *Little Fifer's War Diary*, 45; John M. Roberts, "A Pioneer's Story," John M. Roberts Reminiscences, IHS.

67. James R. Arnold, *Grant Wins the War: Decision at Vicksburg* (New York: John Wiley and Sons, 1997), 268.

68. James M. McPherson, *For Cause and Comrades: Why Men Fought in the Civil War* (New York: Oxford University Press, 1997), 74.

69. Jeffrey D. Marshall, ed., *A War of the People: Vermont Civil War Letters* (Hanover, N.H.: University Press of New England, 1999), 196.

70. Shattuck, *Shield and Hiding Place*, 71.

71. Small, *Road to Richmond*, 174–75.

72. Armstrong, *For Courageous Fighting and Confident Dying*, 16–17.

73. George A. Cooley Diary, January 15, 1865, SHSW.

74. Upson, *With Sherman to the Sea*, 102–5.

75. Daniel G. Crotty, *Four Years Campaigning in the Army of the Potomac* (Kearny, N.J.: Belle Grove, 1995), 171.

76. See Armstrong, *For Courageous Fighting and Confident Dying*, throughout. The assertion of Gerald F. Linderman (*Embattled Courage: The Experience of Combat in the American Civil War* [New York: Free Press, 1987], 254) that chaplains in general lost respect and came to be held in contempt by the end of the war simply does not square with the preponderance of the evidence, notwithstanding the few exceptional cases that he adduces as evidence. For additional examples of soldiers' favorable opinions of their chaplains, see William Russell Diary, September 25, 1864, PLDU; George S. Johnson to "Dear Mother," February 8, 1864, George S. Johnson Papers, IHS; George A. Cooley Diary, January 22, 1865, SHSW; Daniel Chisholm, *The Civil War Notebook of Daniel Chisholm: A Chronicle of Daily Life in the Union Army, 1864–1865*, ed. W. Springer Menge and J. August Shimrak (New York: Orion, 1989), 59; Marshall, *War of the People*, 249; Aurelius Lyman Voorhis Diary, September 4, 1864, IHS; Tracy J. Power, *Lee's Miserables: Life in the Army of Northern Virginia from the Wilderness to Appomattox* (Chapel Hill: University of North Carolina Press, 1998), 125–26.

Chapter 9. "To Labor for the Souls of Their Fellow-Men"

1. Christopher H. Owen, *The Sacred Flame of Love: Methodism and Society in Nineteenth-Century Georgia* (Athens: University of Georgia Press, 1998), 106.

2. Gardiner H. Shattuck, Jr., *A Shield and Hiding Place: The Religious Life of the Civil War Armies* (Macon, Ga.: Mercer University Press, 1987), 22–23.

3. William W. Bennett, *A Narrative of the Great Revival in the Southern Armies During the Late Civil War Between the States of the Federal Union* (Philadelphia: Claxton, Remsen and Haffelfinger, 1877), 51–52.

4. Ibid., 75, 279.

5. Ibid., 79–80.

6. Ibid., 57, 80.

7. Dick Simpson and Tally Simpson, *"Far, Far from Home": The Wartime Letters of Dick and Tally Simpson, Third South Carolina Volunteers,* ed. Guy R. Everson and Edward H. Simpson, Jr. (New York: Oxford University Press, 1994), 273–74 n. 1.

8. Bennett, *Narrative of the Great Revival,* 120–21.

9. John D. Billings, *Hardtack and Coffee: Or, The Unwritten Story of Army Life* (1887; reprint, Lincoln: University of Nebraska Press, 1993), 65.

10. Bennett, *Narrative of the Great Revival,* 78–82, 140, 150.

11. Ibid., 78–81.

12. Ibid., 101.

13. Ibid., 74–75.

14. Owen, *Sacred Flame of Love,* 99.

15. Bennett, *Narrative of the Great Revival,* 75–76.

16. Ibid., 46–49, 131.

17. Billings, *Hardtack and Coffee,* 274.

18. Benjamin Franklin McIntrye Diaries, June 5, 1863, PLDU.

19. Shattuck, *Shield and Hiding Place,* 26–29.

20. Christian Commission memorandum book, David C. Dutcher Papers, PLDU.

21. Shattuck, *Shield and Hiding Place,* 26–29.

22. Christian Commission memorandum book, David C. Dutcher Papers, PLDU.

23. Ibid.

24. George A. Cooley Diary, November 22, 1863, SHSW.

25. James G. Theaker, *Through One Man's Eyes: The Civil War Experiences of a Belmont County Volunteer,* ed. Paul E. Rieger (Mt. Vernon, Ohio: Printing Arts Press, 1974), 91.

26. Wilbur Fisk, *Hard Marching Every Day: The Civil War Letters of Private Wilbur Fisk, 1861–1865,* ed. Emil Rosenblatt and Ruth Rosenblatt (Lawrence: University Press of Kansas, 1992), 211–12.

27. Ibid., 213–14.

28. William McCarter, *My Life in the Irish Brigade: The Civil War Memoirs of Private William McCarter, 116th Pennsylvania Infantry,* ed. Kevin E. O'Brien (Campbell, Calif.: Savas, 1996), 205.

29. Joseph Whitney, *Kiss Clara for Me: The Story of Joseph Whitney and His Family, Early Days in the Midwest, and Soldiering in the American Civil War,* ed. Robert J. Snetsinger (State College, Pa.: Carnation Press, 1969), 157.

30. John Black to "My Dear Jane," May 14, 1864, John Black Letters, SHSW.

31. Daniel G. Crotty, *Four Years Campaigning in the Army of the Potomac* (Kearny, N.J.: Belle Grove, 1995).

32. John J. McKee Diary, August 26, 1864, Civil War Miscellaneous Collection, USAMHI.

33. Letter of March 19, 1865, Lewis Chase Papers, SHSW; letter of August 4, 1864, Edward D. Allen Papers, SHC.

34. Letter of October 3, 1864, Theodore W. Skinner Letters, Civil War Miscellaneous Collection, USAMHI.

35. Chesley A. Mosman, *The Rough Side of War: The Civil War Journal of Chesley A. Mosman, 1st Lieutenant, Company D, 59th Illinois Volunteer Infantry Regiment* (Garden City, N.Y.: Basin Publishing, 1987), 321.

36. Robert Hale Strong, *A Yankee Private's Civil War*, ed. Ashley Halsey (Chicago: H. Regnery, 1961), 77.

37. Allen Morgan Geer, *The Civil War Diary of Allen Morgan Geer: Twentieth Regiment Illinois Volunteers*, ed. Mary Ann Andersen (Denver: Robert C. Appleman, 1977), 129, 132, 143.

38. John M. Roberts, "A Pioneer's Story," John M. Roberts Reminiscences, IHS.

39. Shattuck, *Shield and Hiding Place*, 29–31.

40. Ibid., 32–33.

41. Fisk, *Hard Marching Every Day*, 212–14.

Chapter 10. "In the Thickest of the Fight"

1. William W. Bennett, *A Narrative of the Great Revival in the Southern Armies During the Late Civil War Between the States of the Federal Union* (Philadelphia: Claxton, Remsen and Haffelfinger, 1877), 97–98.

2. Charles O. Varnum to "Dear Father," November 16, 1862, Charles O. Varnum Letters, Civil War Miscellaneous Collection, USAMHI.

3. Gerald F. Linderman, *Embattled Courage: The Experience of Combat in the American Civil War* (New York: Free Press, 1987), 86–87.

4. Joseph Whitney, *Kiss Clara for Me: The Story of Joseph Whitney and His Family, Early Days in the Midwest, and Soldiering in the American Civil War*, ed. Robert J. Snetsinger (State College, Pa.: Carnation Press, 1969), 56.

5. Charles A. Willison, *Reminiscences of a Boy's Service with the 76th Ohio* (1908; reprint, Huntington, W.V.: Blue Acorn Press, 1995), 10.

6. James I. Robertson, Jr., *Soldiers Blue and Gray* (Columbia: University of South Carolina Press, 1988), 23.

7. Ira S. Pettit, *The Diary of a Dear Man: Letters and Diary of Private Ira S. Pettit*, ed. Jean P. Ray (New York: Acorn Press, 1979), 97.

8. John T. McMahon, *John T. McMahon's Diary of the 136th New York, 1861–1864*, ed. John Michael Priest (Shippensburg, Pa.: White Mane, 1993), 24.

9. Alan D. Gaff, *On Many a Bloody Field: Four Years in the Iron Brigade* (Bloomington: Indiana University Press, 1996), 104.

10. McMahon, *Diary*, 25–26.

11. Wilbur Fisk, *Hard Marching Every Day: The Civil War Letters of Private Wilbur Fisk, 1861–1865*, ed. Emil Rosenblatt and Ruth Rosenblatt (Lawrence: University Press of Kansas, 1992), 5.

12. Cyrus F. Boyd, *The Civil War Diary of Cyrus F. Boyd, Fifteenth Iowa Infantry, 1861–1863*, ed. Mildred Thorne (Millwood, N.Y.: Kraus, 1977), 16.

13. Seymour Dexter, *Seymour Dexter, Union Army: Journal and Letters of Civil War Service in Company K, 23rd New York Volunteer Regiment of Elmira*, ed. Carl A. Morrell (Jefferson, N.C.: McFarland, 1996), 11–12.

14. Whitney, *Kiss Clara for Me*, 33.

15. Bennett, *Narrative of the Great Revival*, 101.

16. Thomas Boatright Papers, SHC. See also Larry J. Daniel, *Soldiering in the Army of Tennessee: A Portrait of Life in a Confederate Army* (Chapel Hill: University of North Carolina Press, 1991), 115–16.

17. Boyd, *Civil War Diary*, 23.

18. James Maynard Shanklin, *Dearest Lizzie: The Civil War Letters of Lt. Col. James Maynard Shanklin*, ed. Kenneth P. McCutchan (Evansville, Ind.: Friends of Willard Library Press, 1988), 72.

19. Theodore F. Upson, *With Sherman to the Sea: The Civil War Letters, Diaries and Reminiscences of Theodore F. Upson*, ed. Oscar Osburn Winther (Bloomington: Indiana University Press, 1977), 23.

20. Dexter, *Seymour Dexter*, 11–12.

21. John D. Billings, *Hardtack and Coffee: Or, The Unwritten Story of Army Life* (1887; reprint, Lincoln: University of Nebraska Press, 1993), 65–66.

22. Thomas Boatright Papers, SHC.

23. Dietrich C. Smith to Carrie Pieper, no date [April 1861], Dietrich C. Smith Papers, ISHL.

24. Alfred Tyler Fielder, *The Civil War Diaries of Capt. Alfred Tyler Fielder, 12th Tennessee Regiment Infantry, Company B, 1861–1865*, ed. Ann York Franklin (Louisville, Ky.: privately published, 1996), 1–8.

25. Alfred Bellard, *Gone for a Soldier: The Civil War Memoirs of Private Alfred Bellard*, ed. David H. Donald (Boston: Little, Brown, 1975), 17.

26. William Garrett Piston and Richard W. Hatcher III, *Wilson's Creek: The Second Battle of the Civil War and the Men Who Fought It* (Chapel Hill: University of North Carolina Press, 2000), 56.

27. Bellard, *Gone for a Soldier*, 17.

28. Fielder, *Civil War Diaries*, 8–21, 24.

29. Boyd, *Civil War Diary*, 56.

30. Recollections of James Iredell Hall, James Iredell Hall Papers, SHC.

31. James C. Bates, *A Texas Cavalry Officer's Civil War: The Diary and Letters of James C. Bates*, ed. Richard Lowe (Baton Rouge: Louisiana State University Press, 1999), 2–3. A similar case is found in Clifford Anderson to "My Dear Wife," November 16, 1862, Clifford Anderson Papers, SHC. See also Daniel, *Soldiering*, 116–17.

32. Bennett, *Narrative of the Great Revival*, 140.

33. Clifford Anderson to "My Dear Wife," November 16, 1862, Clifford Anderson Papers, SHC.

34. Henry G. Ankeny, *Kiss Josey for Me*, ed. Florence Marie Ankeny Cox (Santa Ana, Calif.: Friss-Pioneer Press, 1974), 25. Other examples are found in Joshua K. Callaway, *The Civil War Letters of Joshua K. Callaway*, ed. Judith Lee Hallock (Athens: University of Georgia Press, 1997), 33; and Philip Daingerfield Stephenson, *The Civil War Memoir of Philip Daingerfield Stephenson, D.D.*, ed. Nathaniel Cheairs Hughes, Jr. (Baton Rouge: Louisiana State University Press, 1995), 41.

35. Samuel Kirkpatrick to "Dear Father," October 13 and November 6, 1861, Samuel Cotter Kirkpatrick Letters, SHSW; Boyd, *Civil War Diary*, 15; Gasherie Decker to Gertrude Decker, October 10 and November 27, 1861, Gasherie Decker Papers, SHSW; Aurelius Lyman Voorhis Diary, October 13, 1861, IHS; John J. McKee Diary, May 13, 1862, Civil War Miscellaneous Collection, USAMHI; Frank R. Young Diary, May 25, 1862, Civil War Miscellaneous Collection, USAMHI; William Henry Walling to "My Dear Sisters, June 25, 1862, William Henry Walling Letters, Civil War Miscellaneous Collection, USAMHI; Diary of anonymous soldier of the 34th Illinois, July 13, 1862 (entries for other Sundays in July and August of that year are similar), ISHL; James Wren, *From New Bern to Fredericksburg: Captain James Wren's Diary*, ed. John Michael Priest (Shippensburg, Pa.: White Mane, 1990), 2; James Henry Harris Diary, August 1862–August 1863, IHS.

36. John Hampden Chamberlayne, *Ham Chamberlayne, Virginian: Letters and Papers of an Artillery Officer in the War for Southern Independence, 1861–1865* (Richmond, Va.: Dietz, 1932; reprint, Wilmington, N.C.: Broadfoot, 1992), 34.

37. Dexter, *Seymour Dexter*, 46.

38. Jeffrey D. Marshall, ed., *A War of the People: Vermont Civil War Letters* (Hanover, N.H.: University Press of New England, 1997), 29.

39. N. H. R. Dawson to Elodie Todd, May 20, 1861, N. H. R. Dawson Papers, SHC.

40. Elisha Hunt Rhodes, *All for the Union: The Civil War Diary and Letters of Elisha Hunt Rhodes*, ed. Robert Hunt Rhodes (New York: Orion Books, 1985), 20.

41. Allen Morgan Geer, *The Civil War Diary of Allen Morgan Geer: Twentieth Regiment, Illinois Volunteers*, ed. Mary Ann Andersen (Denver: Robert C. Appleman, 1977), 3.

42. John Beatty, *Memoirs of a Volunteer, 1861–1863* (New York: W. W. Norton, 1946), 66–67.

43. Bennett, *Narrative of the Great Revival*, 142.

44. Charles B. Haydon, *For Country, Cause and Leader: The Civil War Journal of Charles B. Haydon*, ed. Stephen W. Sears (New York: Ticknor and Fields, 1993), 157.

45. George W. Bicknell, *History of the Fifth Maine Volunteers* (Portland, Me.: K. I. Davis, 1871), 72–73.

46. Haydon, *For Country, Cause and Leader*, 5.

47. John William De Forest, *A Volunteer's Adventures: A Union Captain's Record of the Civil War*, ed. James H. Croushore (New Haven, Conn.: Yale University Press, 1946), 43, 79–80.

48. Boyd, *Civil War Diary*, 42.

49. Bennett, *Narrative of the Great Revival*, 31.

50. Beatty, *Memoirs of a Volunteer,* 20.

51. Haydon, *For Country, Cause and Leader,* 138.

52. Robertson, *Soldiers Blue and Gray,* 120.

53. Lucius W. Barber, *Army Memoirs of Lucius W. Barber, Company "D," 15th Illinois Volunteer Infantry* (Chicago: J. M. W. Jones Stationery and Printing Co., 1894), 77.

54. Stephen V. Ash, *When the Yankees Came: Conflict and Chaos in the Occupied South, 1861–1865* (Chapel Hill: University of North Carolina Press, 1995), 79.

55. Boyd, *Civil War Diary,* 57.

56. Mark Grimsley, *The Hard Hand of War* (New York: Cambridge University Press, 1995), 40.

57. Barber, *Army Memoirs,* 26.

58. Elliott B. McKeever recollections, Elliott B. McKeever Papers, Civil War Miscellaneous Collection, USAMHI.

59. Quoted in Grimsley, *Hard Hand of War,* 41.

60. Lydia Minturn Post, ed., *Soldiers' Letters from Camp, Battlefield and Prison* (New York: Bunce and Huntington, 1865), 218–22.

61. Haydon, *For Country, Cause and Leader,* 64.

62. Stephenson, *Civil War Memoir,* 39–40.

63. Fielder, *Civil War Diaries,* 24.

64. James Iredell Hall Papers, SHC.

65. Geer, *Civil War Diary,* 3–5; Haydon, *For Country, Cause and Leader,* 14, 26, 64.

66. Boyd, *Civil War Diary,* 24.

67. Fielder, *Civil War Diaries,* 41.

68. Nina Silber and Mary Beth Sievens, eds., *Yankee Correspondence: Civil War Letters Between New England Soldiers and the Home Front* (Charlottesville: University Press of Virginia, 1996), 89–90.

69. Rhodes, *All for the Union,* 60.

70. James Iredell Hall Papers, SHC.

71. Bennett, *Narrative of the Great Revival,* 81–82, 100–101.

72. Ibid., 133–36.

73. Fielder, *Civil War Diaries,* 43–44; the words of the hymn are from *The Free Methodist Hymnal,* ed. William B. Olmstead et al. (Chicago: Free Methodist Publishing House, 1910), 318.

74. Quoted in James M. McPherson, *For Cause and Comrades: Why Men Fought in the Civil War* (New York: Oxford University Press, 1997), 64.

75. Bennett, *Narrative of the Great Revival,* 77.

76. Ibid., 172–74.

77. Ibid., 177–79.

78. Thomas W. Cutrer and T. Michael Parrish, eds., *Brothers in Gray: The Civil War Letter of the Pierson Family* (Baton Rouge: Louisiana State University Press, 1997), 121.

79. Thomas M. Stevenson, *History of the 78th Regiment O.V.V.I. from Its "Muster-in" to its "Muster-out"* (Zanesville, Ohio: Hugh Dunne, 1865), 116–17.

80. John Henry Wilburn Stuckenberg, *I'm Surrounded by Methodists: Diary of John H. W. Stuckenberg, Chaplain of the 145th Pennsylvania Volunteer Infantry*, ed. David T. Hedrick and Gordon Barry Davis, Jr. (Gettysburg, Pa.: Thomas Publications, 1995), 25–26.

81. Marshall, *War of the People*, 45.

82. William Henry Walling to "My Dear Sister," July 9, 1862, William Henry Walling Letters, Civil War Miscellaneous Collection, USAMHI.

83. Peter Welsh, *Irish Green and Union Blue: The Civil War Letters of Peter Welsh, Color Sergeant, 28th Regiment Massachusetts Volunteers*, ed. Lawrence Frederick Kohl and Margaret Cosse Richard (New York: Fordham University Press, 1986), 42. Another similar expression is in Rhodes, *All for the Union*, 93.

84. Reid Mitchell, *The Vacant Chair: The Northern Soldier Leaves Home* (New York: Oxford University Press, 1993), 138.

85. Quoted in McPherson, *For Cause and Comrades*, 63.

86. Beatty, *Memoirs of a Volunteer*, 26.

87. Bennett, *Narrative of the Great Revival*, 176–77.

88. J. T. Armstrong to "My dearest Cousin," January 26, 1862, J. T. Armstrong Papers, SHC.

89. Bennett, *Narrative of the Great Revival*, 179–80.

90. Ibid., 182–83.

91. Ibid., 174–76.

92. Dexter, *Seymour Dexter*, 74.

93. Gaff, *On Many a Bloody Field*, 145.

94. Bennett, *Narrative of the Great Revival*, 176–77.

95. Fielder, *Civil War Diaries*, 71, 78–79.

96. Julius Birney Work Diary, August–December 1862, Civil War Miscellaneous Collection, USAMHI.

97. Melvin Dwinell, August 14, 1862, in *Rome Courier*, August 22, 1862.

98. Bennett, *Narrative of the Great Revival*, 172–74, 176.

99. S. J. G. Brewer, *My Dear Wife from Your Devoted Husband S. J. G. Brewer: Letters from a Rebel Soldier to His Wife*, ed. H. Candler Thaxton (Warrington, Fla.: privately printed, 1968), 68.

100. Bennett, *Narrative of the Great Revival*, 178–79.

101. James M. Simpson to "My Dear Mother," October 14, 1862, Allen-Simpson Papers, SHC.

Chapter 11. "A Great Revolution Has Been Wrought"

1. Chesley A. Mosman, *The Rough Side of War: The Civil War Journal of Chesley A. Mosman, 1st Lieutenant, Company D, 59th Illinois Volunteer Infantry Regiment*, ed. Arnold Gates (Garden City, N.Y.: Basin Publishing, 1987), 93.

2. Ira Blanchard, *I Marched with Sherman: Civil War Memoirs of the 20th Illinois Volunteer Infantry* (San Francisco: J. D. Huff, 1992), 107.

3. Elisha Hunt Rhodes, *All for the Union: The Civil War Diary and Letters of Elisha Hunt Rhodes*, ed. Robert Hunt Rhodes (New York: Orion Books, 1985), 122–23.

4. Aurelius Lyman Voorhis Diary, December 18, 1863, IHS.

5. Blanchard, *I Marched with Sherman*, 59–60.

6. Stephen V. Ash, *When the Yankees Came: Conflict and Chaos in the Occupied South, 1861–1865* (Chapel Hill: University of North Carolina Press, 1995), 220.

7. Mosman, *Rough Side of War*, 91.

8. Emilie Quiner Diary, September 16, 1863, SHSW.

9. Ash, *When the Yankees Came*, 57.

10. Rhodes, *All for the Union*, 128.

11. Flavel C. Barber, *Holding the Line: The Third Tennessee Infantry, 1861–1864*, ed. Robert H. Ferrell (Kent, Ohio: Kent State University Press, 1994), 46.

12. Melvin L. Clark to "Dear Sarah," March 22, 1863, Melvin L. Clark Papers, Civil War Miscellaneous Collection, USAMHI.

13. Quoted in Reid Mitchell, *Civil War Soldiers* (New York: Viking, 1988), 119–20.

14. Ralph Ely, *With the Wandering Regiment: The Diary of Captain Ralph Ely of the Eighth Michigan Infantry*, ed. George M. Blackburn (Mt. Pleasant: Central Michigan University Press, 1965), 24–25.

15. Blanchard, *I Marched with Sherman*, 59–60.

16. Edwin W. Keen Letter, Civil War Miscellaneous Collection, USAMHI.

17. Mitchell, *Civil War Soldiers*, 119–20.

18. Blanchard, *I Marched with Sherman*, 68.

19. James Wren, *From New Bern to Fredericksburg: Captain James Wren's Diary*, ed. John Michael Priest (Shippensburg, Pa.: White Mane, 1990), 76. For examples of the numerous reports of Sunday services every week, see Diary, unidentified author, Mss5:1, Un3:5, September 21, 1862, VHS; Ely, *With the Wandering Regiment*, 41; Berea M. Willsey, *The Civil War Diary of Berea M. Willsey: The Intimate Daily Observations of a Massachusetts Volunteer in the Union Army, 1862–1864*, ed. Jessica H. DeMay (Bowie, Md.: Heritage Books, 1995), 49; Daniel Hughes Diary, May–July 1863, IHS; Samuel P. Lockhart to "Dear Sister," May 6, 1863, Hugh Conway Browning Papers, PLDU; James G. Theaker, *Through One Man's Eyes: The Civil War Experiences of a Belmont County Volunteer*, ed. Paul E. Rieger (Mt. Vernon, Ohio: Printing Arts Press, 1974), 19; Theodore F. Upson, *With Sherman to the Sea: The Civil War Letters, Diaries and Reminiscences of Theodore F. Upson*, ed. Oscar Osburn Winther (Bloomington: Indiana University Press, 1977), 56–57.

20. Blanchard, *I Marched with Sherman*, 72–73; Philip Daingerfield Stephenson, *The Civil War Memoir of Philip Daingerfield Stephenson, D.D.*, ed. Nathaniel Cheairs Hughes, Jr. (Baton Rouge: Louisiana State University Press, 1995), 42.

21. Charles A. McCutchan to "Dear Friend Mattie," March 10, 1863, Charles A. McCutchan Papers, IHS.

22. John J. Warbinton to "Dear Aunt," October 4, 1863, John J. Warbinton Letters, Civil War Miscellaneous Collection, USAMHI.

23. James Iredell Hall Papers, SHC.

24. Mosman, *Rough Side of War*, 25.

25. Aurelius Lyman Voorhis Diary, November 23, 1862, IHS. Another example is found in Samuel P. Lockhart to "Dear Sister," May 6, 1863, Hugh Conway Browning Papers, PLDU.

26. Theodore W. Skinner to "My Dear Parents," February 15, 1863, Theodore W. Skinner Letters, Civil War Miscellaneous Collection, USAMHI.

27. Isaac Jackson, *Some of the Boys: The Civil War Letters of Isaac Jackson, 1862–1865* (Carbondale: Southern Illinois University Press, 1960), 26–27. An almost identical statement appears in Alburtus A. Dunham and Charles LaForest Dunham, *Through the South with a Union Soldier*, ed. Arthur H. DeRosier, Jr. (Johnson City: East Tennessee State University Research Advisory Council, 1969), 89–90. That Confederates had the same problem is demonstrated in Charles H. Andrews to "Dear Mother," February 28, 1862, C. H. Andrews Papers, SHC.

28. Aurelius Lyman Voorhis Diary, December 16, 1863, IHS.

29. Willsey, *Civil War Diary*, 49.

30. Dunham and Dunham, *Through the South*, 36.

31. Alfred Tyler Fielder, *The Civil War Diaries of Capt. Alfred Tyler Fielder, 12th Tennessee Regiment Infantry, Company B, 1861–1865*, ed. Ann York Franklin (Louisville, Ky.: privately published, 1996), 102–15, 131, 133–36.

32. William W. Bennett, *A Narrative of the Great Revival in the Southern Armies During the Late Civil War Between the States of the Federal Union* (Philadelphia: Claxton, Remsen and Haffelfinger, 1877), 268.

33. Aurelius Lyman Voorhis Diary, December 8–13, 1863, IHS.

34. Bennett, *Narrative of the Great Revival*, 254–55.

35. Samuel P. Lockhart to "Dear Sister," March 28, 1863, Hugh Conway Browning Papers, PLDU.

36. Rhodes, *All for the Union*, 125–26.

37. Bennett, *Narrative of the Great Revival*, 259–60, 262–63.

38. David Holt, *A Mississippi Rebel in the Army of Northern Virginia*, ed. Thomas D. Cockrell and Michael B. Ballard (Baton Rouge: Louisiana State University Press, 1995), 231–32.

39. Jeffrey D. Marshall, ed., *A War of the People: Vermont Civil War Letters* (Hanover, N.H.: University Press of New England, 1999), 119–20; Thomas Boatright, March 9, 1863, Boatright Papers, SHC.

40. N. G. Collins, "The Prospect—The Speech of Rev. N. G. Collins, Chaplain of the 57th Illinois, at Corinth, Miss., on the Day of National Thanksgiving, August 3d, 1863, to the Officers and Men of Col. Bane's Brigade. Published by Special Request," 11–13, PLDU.

41. Cyrus F. Boyd, *The Civil War Diary of Cyrus F. Boyd, Fifteenth Iowa Infantry, 1861–1863*, ed. Mildred Thorne (Millwood, N.Y.: Kraus, 1977), 125.

42. Bennett, *Narrative of the Great Revival*, 212–13.

43. Boyd, *Civil War Diary*, 67.

44. Dick Simpson and Tally Simpson, *"Far, Far from Home": The Wartime Letters of Dick and Tally Simpson, Third South Carolina Volunteers*, ed. Guy R. Everson and Edward H. Simpson, Jr. (New York: Oxford University Press, 1994), 293.

45. Ibid., 273–74.

46. Thomas Boatright to "My own dear one," April 22, 1863, Boatright to "My Dearest Cosin," April 26, 1863, and Boatright to "My own Dear E.," June 1, 1863, Boatright Papers, SHC.

47. Bennett, *Narrative of the Great Revival*, 207–11.

48. Ibid., 204; James I. Robertson, Jr., *Soldiers Blue and Gray* (Columbia: University of South Carolina Press, 1988), 187.

49. Bennett, *Narrative of the Great Revival*, 204, 206–7; Fielder, *Civil War Diaries*, 118, 120–21, 133.

50. Bennett, *Narrative of the Great Revival*, 207–9, 262–63, 281–83.

51. Fielder, *Civil War Diaries*, 120–21.

52. Bennett, *Narrative of the Great Revival*, 207–10, 315.

53. Gary W. Gallagher, *The Confederate War* (Cambridge, Mass.: Harvard University Press, 1997), 51–52.

54. Fielder, *Civil War Diaries*, 118, 120–21.

55. Gallagher, *The Confederate War*, 51–52.

56. Fielder, *Civil War Diaries*, 138.

57. Ibid., 114.

58. Bennett, *Narrative of the Great Revival*, 251–52.

59. Ibid., 324; Robertson gives a considerably lower estimate in *Soldiers Blue and Gray* (188): 1,000 men in September 1863 and a total of about 15,000 for all the revivals in the Confederate armies from 1862 to 1864.

60. Stephenson, *Civil War Memoir*, 113.

61. Bennett, *Narrative of the Great Revival*, 274–77, 281.

62. Albert M. Childs to "Dear Brother," April 21, 1863, Albert M. Childs Papers, SHSW.

63. Aurelius Lyman Voorhis Diary, December 8, 1863, IHS.

64. Marshall, *War of the People*, 119–20.

65. John Henry Wilburn Stuckenberg, *I'm Surrounded by Methodists: Diary of John H. W. Stuckenberg, Chaplain of the 145th Pennsylvania Volunteer Infantry*, ed. David T. Hedrik and Gordon Barry Davis, Jr. (Gettysburg, Pa.: Thomas Publications, 1995), 83.

66. Bennett, *Narrative of the Great Revival*, 337–39.

67. Wiley Sword, *Mountains Touched with Fire: Chattanooga Besieged, 1863* (New York: St. Martin's, 1995), 345–46.

68. Val C. Giles, *Rags and Hope: The Recollections of Val C. Giles, Four Years with Hood's Brigade, Fourth Texas Infantry, 1861–1865*, ed. Mary Lasswell (New York: Coward-McCann, 1961), 208.

69. John J. Hennessy, *Return to Bull Run: The Campaign and Battle of Second Manassas* (New York: Simon and Schuster, 1993), 416.

70. Bennett, *Narrative of the Great Revival*, 324.

71. Rhodes, *All for the Union*, 128–29.

72. Aurelius Lyman Voorhis Diary, October 28, 1862, IHS.

73. Bennett, *Narrative of the Great Revival*, 256.

74. Thomas W. Cutrer and T. Michael Parrish, eds., *Brothers in Gray: The Civil War Letters of the Pierson Family* (Baton Rouge: Louisiana State University Press, 1997), 198.

75. Bennett, *Narrative of the Great Revival*, 206–7.

76. Ibid., 209–10.

77. Joseph Whitney, *Kiss Clara for Me: The Story of Joseph Whitney and His Family, Early Days in the Midwest, and Soldiering in the American Civil War*, ed. Robert J. Snetsinger (State College, Pa.: Carnation Press, 1969), 96.

78. Fielder, *Civil War Diaries*, 120–21.

79. Stuckenberg, *I'm Surrounded by Methodists*, 56.

80. Bennett, *Narrative of the Great Revival*, 211–12, 262–64, 276, 330–31.

81. Ibid., 313.

82. Blanchard, *I Marched with Sherman*, 82; James K. Newton, *A Wisconsin Boy in Dixie: The Selected Letters of James K. Newton*, ed. Stephen E. Ambrose (Madison: University of Wisconsin Press, 1961), 77; Mosman, *Rough Side of War*, 65–66; Thomas Francis Gallwey, *The Valiant Hours*, ed. W. S. Nye (Harrisburg, Pa.: Stackpole, 1961), 93.

83. Larry J. Daniel, *Soldiering in the Army of Tennessee: A Portrait of Life in a Confederate Army* (Chapel Hill: University of North Carolina Press, 1991), 123. Robertson takes a different interpretation: "However, subsequent court-martial findings, statements of chaplains, and similar sources make it fairly clear that the consequences of revivals were short-lived" (*Soldiers Blue and Gray*, 188). It seems more apt to say that the consequences were not at all short-lived—for those who were in earnest.

84. Aurelius Lyman Voorhis Diary, March 5, 1863, IHS.

85. William H. Nugen to "Sister Mary," March 3, 1863, William H. Nugen Papers, PLDU.

86. Jackson, *Some of the Boys*, 69.

87. Samuel Ensminger, *Letters to Lanah: A Civil War Soldier Writes Home*, ed. Clarence M. Swinn, Jr. (Gettysburg, Pa.: privately published, 1986), 26.

88. Daniel Hughes Diary, July 19–August 6, 1863, IHS; I. C. Hall to Mr. and Mrs. Owen Sturtevant, April 12, 1863, Anne Sturtevant Letters, Civil War Miscellaneous Collection, USAMHI; George B. Carter to "Dear Brother Bill," March 1, 1863, George B. Carter Letters, SHSW.

89. Joshua K. Callaway, *The Civil War Letters of Joshua K. Callaway*, ed. Judith Lee Hallock (Athens: University of Georgia Press, 1997), 97–98.

90. Bennett, *Narrative of the Great Revival*, 324.

91. Ibid., 252–54, 261, 311, 325, 330–31.

92. Fielder, *Civil War Diaries*, 114, 138.

93. Bennett, *Narrative of the Great Revival*, 358.

94. Rhodes, *All for the Union*, 139.

95. Fielder, *Civil War Diaries*, 103–13.

96. Ibid., 104.

97. Ibid., 116–18.

98. Bennett, *Narrative of the Great Revival*, 279; see also Kurt O. Berends, "'Wholesome Reading Purifies and Elevates the Man': The Religious Military Press in the Confederacy," in *Religion and the American Civil War*, ed. Randall M. Miller, Harry S. Stout, and Charles Reagan Wilson (New York: Oxford University Press, 1998), 131–66.

99. Bennett, *Narrative of the Great Revival*, 269, 314–15.

100. Wilbur Fisk, *Hard Marching Every Day: The Civil War Letters of Private Wilbur Fisk, 1861–1865*, ed. Emil Rosenblatt and Ruth Rosenblatt (Lawrence: University Press of Kansas, 1992), 211–12.

101. Gardiner H. Shattuck, Jr., *A Shield and Hiding Place: The Religious Life of the Civil War Armies* (Macon, Ga.: Mercer University Press, 1987), 29–31.

102. Aurelius Lyman Voorhis Diary, September 22, 1863, IHS.

103. Rhodes, *All for the Union*, 123, 133.

104. J. P. Cannon, *Bloody Banners and Barefoot Boys: A History of the 27th Regiment Alabama Infantry CSA, the Civil War Memoirs and Diary Entries of J. P. Cannon, M.D.*, ed. Noel Crowson and John V. Brogden (Shippensburg, Pa.: Burd Street Press, 1997), 41–42.

105. Stuckenberg, *I'm Surrounded by Methodists*, 112.

106. Austin C. Stearns, *Three Years with Company K*, ed. Arthur A. Kent (Rutherford, N.J.: Fairleigh Dickinson University Press, 1976), 214–17.

107. Blanchard, *I Marched with Sherman*, 110–11; Allen Morgan Geer, *The Civil War Diary of Allen Morgan Geer, Twentieth Regiment, Illinois Volunteers*, ed. Maary Ann Andersen (Denver: Robert C. Appleman, 1977), 140–42.

108. Rhodes, *All for the Union*, 139.

109. Abner R. Small, *The Road to Richmond: The Civil War Memoirs of Maj. Abner R. Small of the 16th Maine Vols.: With His Diary as a Prisoner of War*, ed. Harold Adams Small (Berkeley: University of California Press, 1959), 125.

110. R. B. Scott, *The History of the 67th Regiment, Indiana Infantry Volunteers* (Bedford, Ind.: Herald Book and Job Printing, 1892), 66.

111. Mosman, *Rough Side of War*, 158–59.

112. William Pettis Buck, "Headquarter's Staff: Cleburne's Division, Hardee's Corps," in *A Meteor Shining Brightly: Essays on Maj. Gen. Patrick R. Cleburne*, ed. Mauriel Phillips Joslyn (Milledgeville, Ga.: Terrell House, 1997), 107–8.

113. Robertson, *Soldiers Blue and Gray*, 187–88.

114. Samuel P. Lockhart to Ellen Lockhart, March 14, 1864, Hugh Conway Browning Papers, PLDU.

Chapter 12. "If We Fall on the Field of Strife"

1. James M. McPherson, *For Cause and Comrades: Why Men Fought in the Civil War* (New York: Oxford University Press, 1997), 64.

2. Jeffrey D. Marshall, ed., *A War of the People: Vermont Civil War Letters* (Hanover, N.H.: University Press of New England, 1999), 208–11.

3. Wilbur Fisk, *Hard Marching Every Day: The Civil War Letters of Private Wilbur Fisk, 1861–1865,* ed. Emil Rosenblatt and Ruth Rosenblatt (Lawrence: University Press of Kansas, 1992), 200.

4. Marshall, *War of the People,* 208–11.

5. Fisk, *Hard Marching Every Day,* 200.

6. Charles W. Bardeen, *A Little Fifer's War Diary* (Syracuse, N.Y.: author, 1910), 293.

7. Elisha Hunt Rhodes, *All for the Union: The Civil War Diary and Letters of Elisha Hunt Rhodes,* ed. Robert Hunt Rhodes (New York: Orion Books, 1985), 140.

8. Marshall, *War of the People,* 208–11.

9. Rhodes, *All for the Union,* 141.

10. Chesley A. Mosman, *The Rough Side of War: The Civil War Journal of Chesley A. Mosman, 1st Lieutenant, Company D, 59th Illinois Volunteer Infantry Regiment,* ed. Arnold Gates (Garden City, N.Y.: Basin Publishing, 1987), 159–60.

11. Jacob S. Gantz, *Such Are the Trials: The Civil War Diaries of Jacob Gantz,* ed. Kathleen Davis (Ames: Iowa State University Press, 1991), 53.

12. Alburtus A. Dunham and Charles LaForest Dunham, *Through the South with a Union Soldier,* ed. Arthur H. DeRosier, Jr. (Johnson City: East Tennessee State University Research Advisory Council, 1969), 126.

13. George S. Marks Diary, July 23 and 24, 1864, George S. Marks Papers, Civil War Miscellaneous Collection, USAMHI.

14. Aurelius Lyman Voorhis Diary, February 14–26, 1864, IHS.

15. R. B. Scott, *The History of the 67th Regiment, Indiana Infantry Volunteers* (Bedford, Ind.: Herald Book and Job Printing, 1892), 68.

16. John Black to "My Dear Wife," March 24, 1864, John Black Letters, SHSW.

17. David Coon letter, headed "Camp Randall" and probably written in spring 1864, David Coon Papers, SHSW.

18. Cullen Andrews Battle, *Third Alabama! The Civil War Memoir of Brigadier General Cullen Andrews Battle, C.S.A.,* ed. Brandon H. Beck (Tuscaloosa: University of Alabama Press, 2000), 95.

19. Samuel P. Lockhart to Ellen Lockhart, March 14, 1864, Hugh Conway Browning Papers, PLDU; William W. Bennett, *A Narrative of the Great Revival in the Southern Armies During the Late Civil War Between the States of the Federal Union* (Philadelphia: Claxton, Remsen and Haffelfinger, 1877), 361.

20. David Holt, *A Mississippi Rebel in the Army of Northern Virginia,* ed. Thomas D. Cockrell and Michael B. Ballard (Baton Rouge: Louisiana State University, 1995), 232–33.

21. Bennett, *Narrative of the Great Revival*, 245–47.

22. Flavel C. Barber, *Holding the Line: The Third Tennessee Infantry, 1861–1864*, ed. Robert H. Ferrell (Kent, Ohio: Kent State University Press, 1994), 167–68, 173–75.

23. Bennett, *Narrative of the Great Revival*, 359–60.

24. John A. Simpson, *S. A. Cunningham and the Confederate Heritage* (Athens: University of Georgia Press, 1994), 35–36.

25. Larry J. Daniel, *Soldiering in the Army of Tennessee: A Portrait of Life in a Confederate Army* (Chapel Hill: University of North Carolina Press, 1991), 122–23.

26. Fisk, *Hard Marching Every Day*, 211–12.

27. Bennett, *Narrative of the Great Revival*, 365.

28. Rhodes, *All for the Union*, 142–43.

29. Mosman, *Rough Side of War*, 186–87.

30. Dunham and Dunham, *Through the South*, 116–17.

31. Tracy J. Power, *Lee's Miserables: Life in the Army of Northern Virginia from the Wilderness to Appomattox* (Chapel Hill: University of North Carolina Press, 1998), 17.

32. Bardeen, *Little Fifer's War Diary*, 300–301.

33. Holt, *Mississippi Rebel*, 233–34.

34. James Iredell Hall letter, June 13, 1864, James Iredell Hall Papers, SHC.

35. J. P. Cannon, *Bloody Banners and Barefoot Boys: A History of the 27th Regiment Alabama Infantry CSA, the Civil War Memoirs and Diary Entries of J. P. Cannon M.D.*, ed. Noel Crowson and John V. Brogden (Shippensburg, Pa.: Burd Street Press, 1997), 82–83.

36. Quoted in Gerald F. Linderman, *Embattled Courage: The Experience of Combat in the American Civil War* (New York: Free Press, 1987), 103–4.

37. J. W. Beckwith to "My dear Grully," June 26, 1864, and Beckwith to his wife, n.d., Beckwith Family Papers, SHC.

38. Bennett, *Narrative of the Great Revival*, 378–79, 384–85, 391–92.

39. Dunham and Dunham, *Through the South*, 140.

40. Ibid., 132.

41. Mosman, *Rough Side of War*, 259–60.

42. Charles B. Loop to "My Dear Wife," August 12, 1864, Charles B. Loop Papers, Civil War Miscellaneous Collection, USAMHI.

43. David C. Dutcher Diary, August 9 and 21, 1864, David C. Dutcher Papers, PLDU.

44. Alfred Tyler Fielder, *The Civil War Diaries of Capt. Alfred Tyler Fielder, 12th Tennessee Regiment Infantry, Company B, 1861–1865*, ed. Ann York Franklin (Louisville, Ky.: privately published, 1996), 188–89. Notwithstanding this and many other cases, Linderman (*Embattled Courage*, 254–55) makes the bizarre claim that the soldiers in the final year of the war actually turned away from Christianity and "lost or at least suspended a significant measure of their early-war piety." This they did, Linderman claims, because "combat could no longer be fitted easily within Christian precepts." The latter statement would have amazed the soldiers themselves. The former is flatly false. Indeed, quite the contrary is true, as soldiers turned increasingly to Christianity as the war continued and grew more terrible.

45. Bennett, *Narrative of the Great Revival*, 388, 416.

46. Ibid., 383.

47. Ibid., 369–70.

48. Cannon, *Bloody Banners*, 95.

49. Mosman, *Rough Side of War*, 275–85.

50. Dunham and Dunham, *Through the South*, 154.

51. William Russell Diary, September 18 and 25, 1864, PLDU.

52. Power, *Lee's Miserables*, 125–26.

53. Daniel Sober Diary, September 4, 1864, Civil War Miscellaneous Collection, USAMHI.

54. Albert M. Childs letter, Albert M. Childs Papers, SHSW.

55. Rhodes, *All for the Union*, 177; Daniel Chisholm, *The Civil War Notebook of Daniel Chisholm: A Chronicle of Daily Life in the Union Army, 1864–1865*, ed. W. Springer Menge and J. August Shimrak (New York: Orion, 1989), 31.

56. Bennett, *Narrative of the Great Revival*, 414.

57. Ibid., 413.

58. Gardiner H. Shattuck, Jr., "Revivals in the Camp," *Christian History* 11 (1992): 28–31.

59. Fisk, *Hard Marching Every Day*, 213–14.

60. David C. Dutcher Diary, November 21 and 23, 1864, David C. Dutcher Papers, PLDU.

61. Rhodes, *All for the Union*, 188–93.

62. Fisk, *Hard Marching Every Day*, 271.

63. Robert Hale Strong, *A Yankee Private's Civil War*, ed. Ashley Halsey (Chicago: H. Regnery, 1961), 151–52.

64. Henry Hitchcock, *Marching with Sherman: Passages from the Letters and Campaign Diaries of Henry Hitchcock*, ed. M. A. de Wolfe Howe (New Haven, Conn.: Yale University Press, 1927; reprint, Lincoln: University of Nebraska Press, 1995), 199.

65. Theodore F. Upson, *With Sherman to the Sea: The Civil War Letters, Diaries and Reminiscences of Theodore J. Upson*, ed. Oscar Osburn Winther (Bloomington: Indiana University Press, 1977), 156.

66. Peter S. Carmichael, "Christian Warriors," *Columbiad* 3 (summer 1999): 92; McPherson, *For Cause and Comrades*, 76.

67. John D. Billings, *Hardtack and Coffee: Or, The Unwritten Story of Army Life* (Lincoln: University of Nebraska Press, 1993), 232.

68. Elisha Stockwell, Jr., *Private Elisha Stockwell, Jr., Sees the Civil War*, ed. Byron R. Abernethy (Norman: University of Oklahoma Press, 1958), 54.

69. Benjamin Franklin Cooling, *Fort Donelson's Legacy: War and Society in Kentucky and Tennessee, 1862–1863* (Knoxville: University of Tennessee Press, 1997), 233.

70. William Henry Walling to "My Very Dear Sister," March 27, 1865, William Henry Walling Letters, Civil War Miscellaneous Collection, USAMHI.

71. Reid Mitchell, *Civil War Soldiers* (New York: Viking, 1988), 154–55.

72. See Mark Grimsley, *The Hard Hand of War* (New York: Cambridge University Press, 1995).

73. Charles W. Wills, *Army Life of an Illinois Soldier* (Carbondale: Southern Illinois University Press, 1996), 374–75.

74. Aurelius Lyman Voorhis Diary, March 22 and 26, 1865, IHS.

75. Mosman, *Rough Side of War*, 344.

76. Daniel G. Crotty, *Four Years Campaigning in the Army of the Potomac* (Kearny, N.J.: Belle Grove, 1995), 171.

77. Fisk, *Hard Marching Every Day*, 315–16.

78. Mosman, *Rough Side of War*, 258, 334.

79. Richard Robert Crowe letter, May 19, 1864, Richard Robert Crowe Papers, SHSW.

80. Fisk, *Hard Marching Every Day*, 212–13.

81. Nina Silber and Mary Beth Sievens, eds., *Yankee Correspondence: Civil War Letters Between New England Soldiers and the Home Front* (Charlottesville: University Press of Virginia, 1996), 147–48.

82. Isaac Jackson, *Some of the Boys: The Civil War Letters of Isaac Jackson, 1862–1865* (Carbondale: Southern Illinois University Press, 1960), 227.

83. William Henry Walling to "My Dear Sister," March 14, 1865, William Henry Walling Letters, Civil War Miscellaneous Collection, USAMHI.

84. James G. Theaker, *Through One Man's Eyes: The Civil War Experiences of a Belmont County Volunteer*, ed. Paul E. Rieger (Mt. Vernon, Ohio: Printing Arts Press, 1974), 88.

85. Lewis Chase to "My Friend Mr. Mitchell," February 13, 1865, Lewis Chase Papers, SHSW.

86. McPherson, *For Cause and Comrades*, 75–76.

87. Rhodes, *All for the Union*, 224.

88. Fisk, *Hard Marching Every Day*, 320–21.

89. Rhodes, *All for the Union*, 226.

90. Fielder, *Civil War Diaries*, 225.

91. Mosman, *Rough Side of War*, 351–52.

92. Fielder, *Civil War Diaries*, 230.

Chapter 13. "God Has Chastened Us"

1. N. G. Collins, "The Prospect—The Speech of Rev. N. G. Collins, Chaplain of the 57th Illinois, at Corinth, Miss., on the Day of National Thanksgiving, August 3d, 1863, to the Officers and Men of Col. Bane's Brigade. Published by Special Request," PLDU.

2. James A. Connolly, *Three Years in the Army of the Cumberland: The Letters and Diary of Major James A. Connolly*, ed. Paul M. Angle (Bloomington: Indiana University Press, 1959), 107.

3. Alfred Lacey Hough, *Soldier in the West: The Civil War Letters of Alfred Lacey Hough,* ed. Robert G. Athearn (Philadelphia: University of Pennsylvania Press, 1957), 178.

4. Wilbur Fisk, *Hard Marching Every Day: The Civil War Letters of Private Wilbur Fisk, 1861–1865,* ed. Emil Rosenblatt and Ruth Rosenblatt (Lawrence: University Press of Kansas, 1992), 207–8.

5. R. B. Scott, *The History of the 67th Regiment, Indiana Infantry Volunteers* (Bedford, Ind.: Herald Book and Job Printing, 1892), 66.

6. George W. Shingle to "Dear Sir," April 2, 1864, George W. Shingle Letters, Evans Family Papers, Civil War Miscellaneous Collection, USAMHI.

7. William Henry Walling to "My Dear Sister," May 25, 1864, William Henry Walling Letters, Civil War Miscellaneous Collection, USAMHI.

8. Quoted in James M. McPherson, *For Cause and Comrades: Why Men Fought in the Civil War* (New York: Oxford University Press, 1997), 174.

9. Connolly, *Three Years in the Army of the Cumberland,* 245. Another example of the same belief is found in Fisk, *Hard Marching Every Day,* 239.

10. Henry Kauffman, *The Civil War Letters of Private Henry Kauffman: The Harmony Boys Are All Well,* ed. David McCordick (Lewiston, N.Y.: Edwin Mellen Press, 1991), 68.

11. John M. Roberts, "A Pioneer's Story," John M. Roberts Reminiscences, IHS.

12. David Cornwell Memoir, Civil War Miscellaneous Collection, USAMHI.

13. See the Theodore W. Skinner Letters, Civil War Miscellaneous Collection, USAMHI.

14. John T. McMahon, *John T. McMahon's Diary of the 136th New York, 1861–1864,* ed. John Michael Priest (Shippensburg, Pa.: White Mane, 1993), 54; Jack K. Overmyer, *A Stupendous Effort: The 87th Indiana in the War of the Rebellion* (Bloomington: Indiana University Press, 1997), 95.

15. Elisha Hunt Rhodes, *All for the Union: The Civil War Diary and Letters of Elisha Hunt Rhodes,* ed. Robert Hunt Rhodes (New York: Orion Books, 1985), 161.

16. Fisk, *Hard Marching Every Day,* 239.

17. James K. Newton, *A Wisconsin Boy in Dixie: The Selected Letters of James K. Newton,* ed. Stephen E. Ambrose (Madison: University of Wisconsin Press, 1961), 153.

18. Letter to Sylvanus T. Harrison from his mother, March 12, 1864, Harrison Family Papers, SHSW.

19. P. J. Arndt to his parents, February 7, 1864, P. J. Arndt Letter, SHSW.

20. J. N. DeForest to J. H. Delavan, February 14, 1864, DeForest Family Letters, Civil War Miscellaneous Collection, USAMHI.

21. Jeffrey D. Marshall, ed., *A War of the People: Vermont Civil War Letters* (Hanover, N.H.: University Press of New England, 1999), 266.

22. William Henry Walling to "My Dear Sister," April 25, 1865, William Henry Walling Letters, Civil War Miscellaneous Collection, USAMHI.

23. Harold Holzer, ed., *Dear Mr. Lincoln: Letters to the President* (Reading, Mass.: Addison-Wesley, 1993), 139.

24. Gardiner H. Shattuck, Jr., *A Shield and Hiding Place: The Religious Life of the Civil War Armies* (Macon, Ga.: Mercer University Press, 1987), 18.

25. Nina Silber and Mary Beth Sievens, eds., *Yankee Correspondence: Civil War Letters Between New England Soldiers and the Home Front* (Charlottesville: University Press of Virginia, 1996), 79.

26. Quoted in Reid Mitchell, *Civil War Soldiers* (New York: Viking, 1988), 186.

27. David Humphrey Blair to "Dear Sister Lib," June 5, 1864, David Humphrey Blair Papers, Civil War Miscellaneous Collection, USAMHI.

28. Joseph Whitney, *Kiss Clara for Me: The Story of Joseph Whitney and His Family, Early Days in the Midwest, and Soldiering in the American Civil War*, ed. Robert J. Snetsinger (State College, Pa.: Carnation Press, 1969), 149–50.

29. Richard Robert Crowe to "Dear Mammy," March 4, 1865, Richard Robert Crowe Papers, SHSW.

30. James G. Theaker, *Through One Man's Eyes: The Civil War Experiences of a Belmont County Volunteer*, ed. Paul E. Rieger (Mt. Vernon, Ohio: Printing Arts Press, 1974), 93.

31. Fisk, *Hard Marching Every Day*, 298–99.

32. Marshall, *War of the People*, 307.

33. Mitchell, *Civil War Soldiers*, 187.

34. Quoted in McPherson, *For Cause and Comrades*, 175.

35. William Henry Church to "Dear Ella," September 3, 1864, William Henry Church Letters, SHSW.

36. William Henry Walling to "My Dear Sister," September 28, 1864, William Henry Walling Letters, Civil War Miscellaneous Collection, USAMHI.

37. Kauffman, *Civil War Letters*, 84.

38. Whitney, *Kiss Clara for Me*, 149–50.

39. Connolly, *Three Years in the Army of the Cumberland*, 282.

40. Warren Wilkinson, *Mother, May You Never See the Sights I Have Seen: The Fifty-seventh Massachusetts Veteran Volunteers in the Army of the Potomac, 1864–1865* (New York: Harper and Row, 1990), 345.

41. Rhodes, *All for the Union*, 229.

42. Chesley A. Mosman, *The Rough Side of War: The Civil War Journal of Chesley A. Mosman, 1st Lieutenant, Company D, 59th Illinois Volunteer Infantry Regiment*, ed. Arnold Gates (Garden City, N.Y.: Basin Publishing, 1987), 351–52.

43. Fisk, *Hard Marching Every Day*, 323–25.

44. Marshall, *War of the People*, 306.

45. Reid Mitchell, *The Vacant Chair: The Northern Soldier Leaves Home* (New York: Oxford University Press, 1993), 120.

46. George H. Allen, *Forty-six Months with the Fourth R.I. Volunteers, in the War of 1861 to 1865* (Providence, R.I.: J. A. and R. A. Reid, 1887), 353.

47. Daniel G. Crotty, *Four Years Campaigning in the Army of the Potomac* (Kearny, N.J.: Belle Grove, 1995), 186.

48. Allen C. Guelzo, *Abraham Lincoln: Redeemer President* (Grand Rapids, Mich.: Eerdmans, 1999).

49. George Wells Sermon, SHSW.

Chapter 14. "The Lord Has Forsaken His People"

1. Alfred Tyler Fielder, *The Civil War Diaries of Capt. Alfred Tyler Fielder, 12th Tennessee Regiment Infantry, Company B, 1861–1865,* ed. Ann York Franklin (Louisville, Ky.: privately published, 1996), 127.

2. Peter S. Carmichael, "Christian Warriors," *Columbiad* 3 (summer 1999): 102, 105.

3. Tracy J. Power, *Lee's Miserables: Life in the Army of Northern Virginia from the Wilderness to Appomattox* (Chapel Hill: University of North Carolina Press, 1998), 5–6; Christopher H. Owen, *The Sacred Flame of Love: Methodism and Society in Nineteenth-Century Georgia* (Athens: University of Georgia Press, 1998), 94–95.

4. Flavel C. Barber, *Holding the Line: The Third Tennessee Infantry, 1861–1864,* ed. Robert H. Ferrell (Kent, Ohio: Kent State University Press, 1994), 141.

5. Joshua K. Callaway, *The Civil War Letters of Joshua K. Callaway,* ed. Judith Lee Hallock (Athens: University of Georgia Press, 1997), 110–11.

6. Quoted in Gary W. Gallagher, *Lee and His Generals in War and Memory* (Baton Rouge: Louisiana State University Press, 1998), 48.

7. Johnny Green, *Johnny Green of the Orphan Brigade: The Journal of a Confederate Soldier,* ed. A. D. Kirwan (Lexington: University of Kentucky Press, 1956), 84–85.

8. Thomas W. Cutrer and T. Michael Parrish, eds., *Brothers in Gray: The Civil War Letters of the Pierson Family* (Baton Rouge: Louisiana State University Press, 1997), 204.

9. Dick Simpson and Tally Simpson, *"Far, Far from Home": The Wartime Letters of Dick and Tally Simpson, Third South Carolina Volunteers,* ed. Guy R. Everson and Edward H. Simpson, Jr. (New York: Oxford University Press, 1994), 258.

10. William W. Bennett, *A Narrative of the Great Revival in the Southern Armies During the Late Civil War Between the States of the Federal Union* (Philadelphia: Claxton, Remsen and Haffelfinger, 1877), 316–17.

11. *Rome Courier,* September 1, 1863.

12. *Richmond Christian Advocate,* September 24, 1863, Burke Family Papers, VHS.

13. Bennett, *Narrative of the Great Revival,* 41–42.

14. *Richmond Christian Advocate,* September 24, 1863, Burke Family Papers, VHS.

15. Bennett, *Narrative of the Great Revival,* 41–42, 226.

16. *Richmond Christian Advocate,* September 24, 1863, Burke Family Papers, VHS.

17. Carmichael, "Christian Warriors," 98.

18. *Richmond Christian Advocate,* September 24, 1863, Burke Family Papers, VHS.

19. J. Trooper Armstrong to "My Dear Wife," May 19, 1864, J. T. Armstrong Papers, SHC.

20. *Rome Courier,* July 21, 1863.

21. *Richmond Christian Advocate*, September 24, 1863, Burke Family Papers, VHS.

22. Fielder, *Civil War Diaries*, 135, 153.

23. Bennett, *Narrative of the Great Revival*, 345–46.

24. Callaway, *Civil War Letters*, 155.

25. Cutrer and Parrish, *Brothers in Gray*, 224.

26. Reid Mitchell, *Civil War Soldiers* (New York: Viking, 1988), 187–88.

27. Philip Daingerfield Stephenson, *The Civil War Memoir of Philip Daingerfield Stephenson, D.D.*, ed. Nathaniel Cheairs Hughs, Jr. (Baton Rouge: Louisiana State University Press, 1995), 160.

28. Barber, *Holding the Line*, 175.

29. Carmichael, "Christian Warriors," 101.

30. Barber, *Holding the Line*, 175.

31. Bennett, *Narrative of the Great Revival*, 372.

32. Gary W. Gallagher, *The Confederate War* (Cambridge, Mass.: Harvard University Press, 1997), 49–51; Cutrer and Parrish, *Brothers in Gray*, 229; Isaac Alexander to "Dear Sister," April 18, 1863, Isaac Alexander Letters, SHC.

33. George Phifer Erwin to "My dear Father," April 29, 1864, George Phifer Erwin Papers, SHC.

34. Bennett, *Narrative of the Great Revival*, 373–74.

35. Power, *Lee's Miserables*, 5.

36. J. Trooper Armstrong to his wife, August 28, 1864, J. T. Armstrong Papers, SHC.

37. Cutrer and Parrish, *Brothers in Gray*, 204.

38. Cullen A. Battle, *Third Alabama! The Civil War Memoir of Brigadier General Cullen Andrews Battle, C.S.A.*, ed. Brandon H. Beck (Tuscaloosa: University of Alabama Press, 2000), 142.

39. Carmichael, "Christian Warriors," 96–97, 100.

40. Edward A. Miller, Jr., *The Black Civil War Soldiers of Illinois: The Story of the Twenty-ninth U.S. Colored Infantry* (Columbia: University of South Carolina Press, 1998), 78.

41. Stephenson, *Civil War Memoir*, 320–21.

42. William Blair, *Virginia's Private War: Feeding Body and Soul in the Confederacy, 1861–1865* (New York: Oxford University Press, 1998), 144.

43. Mitchell, *Civil War Soldiers*, 173.

44. Eugene D. Genovese, *A Consuming Fire: The Fall of the Confederacy in the Mind of the White Christian South* (Athens: University of Georgia Press, 1998), 61.

45. Ignatius W. Brock to "My Dear Sister," November 18, 1864, Ignatius W. Brock Papers, PLDU.

46. Fielder, *Civil War Diaries*, 214.

47. Green, *Johnny Green of the Orphan Brigade*, 185.

48. George Phifer Erwin to "My dear Sister," January 25, 1865, George Phifer Erwin Papers, SHC.

49. Green, *Johnny Green of the Orphan Brigade*, 184.

50. Owen, *Sacred Flame of Love*, 105.

51. Carmichael, "Christian Warriors," 102, 105; Owen, *Sacred Flame of Love*, 94–95.

52. Quoted in Bennett, *Narrative of the Great Revival*, 416.

53. Fielder, *Civil War Diaries*, 220.

54. Carmichael, "Christian Warriors," 98, 100–101.

55. Power, *Lee's Miserables*, 263.

56. Bennett, *Narrative of the Great Revival*, 420.

57. Gallagher, *The Confederate War*, 50–51.

58. Thomas Conolly, *An Irishman in Dixie: Thomas Conolly's Diary of the Fall of the Confederacy*, ed. Nelson D. Lankford (Columbia: University of South Carolina Press, 1988), 83.

59. Edwin H. Fay, *"This Infernal War": The Confederate Letters of Sgt. Edwin H. Fay*, ed. Bell Irvin Wiley (Austin: University of Texas Press, 1958), 442, 447.

60. Stephenson, *Civil War Memoir*, 386–87.

Chapter 15. "We Shall Not Easily Forget"

1. Tracy J. Power, *Lee's Miserables: Life in the Army of Northern Virginia from the Wilderness to Appomattox* (Chapel Hill: University of North Carolina Press, 1998), 321.

2. Gardiner H. Shattuck, Jr., *A Shield and Hiding Place: The Religious Life of the Civil War Armies* (Macon, Ga.: Mercer University Press, 1987), 43.

3. Christopher H. Owen, *The Sacred Flame of Love: Methodism and Society in Nineteenth-Century Georgia* (Athens: University of Georgia Press, 1998), 94, 113, 131.

4. Ibid., 117.

5. William A. Clebsch, *Christian Interpretations of the Civil War* (Philadelphia: Fortress Press, 1969), 5.

6. Gary W. Gallagher, *The Confederate War* (Cambridge, Mass.: Harvard University Press, 1997), 163–64.

7. Shattuck, *Shield and Hiding Place*, 116.

8. Alfred Tyler Fielder, *The Civil War Diaries of Capt. Alfred Tyler Fielder, 12th Tennessee Regiment Infantry, Company B, 1861–1865*, ed. Ann York Franklin (Louisville, Ky.: privately published, 1996), 230.

9. Owen, *Sacred Flame of Love*, 137–38, 180.

10. J. William Jones, *Christ in the Camp: Or, Religion in the Confederate Army* (1904; reprint, Harrisonburg, Va.: Sprinkle Publications, 1986).

11. William W. Bennett, *A Narrative of the Great Revival in the Confederate Armies During the Late Civil War Between the States of the Federal Union* (Philadelphia: Claxton, Remsen and Haffelfinger, 1877), 23–30.

12. Shattuck, *Shield and Hiding Place*, 129.

13. Bell Irvin Wiley, *The Life of Billy Yank: The Common Soldier of the Union* (Indianapolis: Bobbs-Merrill, 1952).

14. Reid Mitchell, "Christian Soldiers? Perfecting the Confederacy," in *Religion and the American Civil War*, ed. Randall M. Miller, Harry S. Stout, and Charles Reagan Wil-

son (New York: Oxford University Press, 1998), 297–309. See also Charles Reagan Wilson, *Baptized in Blood: The Religion of the Lost Cause, 1865–1920* (Athens: University of Georgia Press, 1980).

15. John J. McKee Diary, April 18, 1866 [1865], Civil War Miscellaneous Collection, USAMHI.

16. William Henry Walling to "My Dear Sister," April 19, 1865, William Henry Walling Letters, Civil War Miscellaneous Collection, USAMHI.

17. Shattuck, *Shield and Hiding Place*, 130–31.

18. Elisha Hunt Rhodes, *All for the Union: The Civil War Diary and Letters of Elisha Hunt Rhodes*, ed. Robert Hunt Rhodes (New York: Orion Books, 1985), 246.

19. In *Embattled Courage: The Experience of Combat in the American Civil War* (New York: Free Press, 1987), 2, Gerald Linderman writes, "The experience of combat frustrated their attempts to fight the war as an expression of their values and generated in them a harsh disillusionment." He states later, "Few soldiers returned home professed skeptics, but neither had the war permitted its participants any easy retention of their prewar certainties. . . . It was indeed difficult to see God's hand in combat and remain convinced that it was driving the war forward in order that good might ensue" (257). In fact, what is hard to see is how Linderman ever came to this conclusion—clearly not by reading soldiers' own writings.

20. Reid Mitchell, *The Vacant Chair: The Northern Soldier Leaves Home* (New York: Oxford University Press, 1993), 137.

21. Francis A. Schaeffer, *How Should We Then Live* (Westchester, Ill.: Crossway Books, 1976); reprinted in *The Complete Works of Francis A. Schaeffer: A Christian Worldview*, 5 vols. (Westchester, Ill.: Crossway Books, 1982), 5:83.

22. Henry Hoyt to "Brother Edward," May 7, 1865, Henry Hoyt Letters, Civil War Miscellaneous Collection, USAMHI.

BIBLIOGRAPHY

Unpublished Primary Sources

Alabama Department of Archives and History, Montgomery
John Calvin Reed Memoirs
Atlanta History Center
Dwight Allen Letter
John Barnett Letter
Hugh Black Letters
R. M. Campbell Diary
Chicago Historical Society
Henry Asbury Papers
Eliza Brooks Bragg Letter
Charles Bartlett Diaries
Napoleon B. Bartlett Letters
Emory University, Atlanta, Georgia
William G. Baugh Letters
Illinois State Historical Library, Springfield
William Anderson Allen Papers
Austin S. Andrews Letters
William H. Austin Letters
Civil War letters written by Indiana soldiers
Edward and Mary Ann Craig Papers

Diary, anonymous, SC 771-26
Diary, anonymous, SC 771-34E
Joseph Forrest Papers
Douglas Hapeman Diary
William McCready Papers
John Sargent Letters
Dietrich C. Smith Papers
E. H. Stoddard Letter
William H. Tebbets Letters
Wallace-Dickey Family Papers
Indiana Historical Society, Indianapolis
Richard Emerson Blair Papers
Ezra Bowlus Letters
J. N. Collicutt Papers
Jesse B. Connelly Diary
Gilbert H. Denny Letters
John H. Ferree Letter
William Fifer Letter
Nathan T. Fuller Diary
James Watts Hamilton Papers
John J. Hardin Papers
Francis M. Harmon Papers
James Henry Harris Diary
Timothy L. Himes Letter
Daniel Hughes Diary
James Ireland Family Correspondence
George S. Johnson Papers
Charles A. McCutchan Papers
Willard Mendell Letter
Petition of 83rd Indiana
John William Prentiss Papers
Robert J. Price Papers
Thomas Prickett Papers
John M. Roberts Reminiscences
Noah Beecher Sharp Papers
Benjamin F. Sibert Letter
Benjamin J. Spooner Papers
Edward P. Stanfield Papers
Henry R. Strong Papers
Augustus M. Van Dyke Papers
Aurelius Lyman Voorhis Diary

Library of Congress, Washington, D.C.
   Samuel J. Baird Papers
   Jasper N. Barritt Papers
   Chauncey E. Barton Letter
   Francis Marion Bateman Letter
   Richard Beard Letter
   Wimer Bedford Papers
   George Darius Downey Diary
   Lincoln Papers
Licking County (Ohio) Historical Society
   Levi P. Coman Letters
Ohio Historical Society, Columbus
   S. C. Mendenhall Letter
   John J. Metzgar Letters
Perkins Library, Duke University, Durham, North Carolina
   Granville W. Belcher Papers
   Ignatius W. Brock Papers
   Hugh Conway Browning Papers
   David C. Dutcher Papers
   Benjamin Franklin McIntrye Diaries
   William H. Nugen Papers
   William Russell Diary
   Townsend Family Papers
   Henry B. Whitney Diary
Southern Historical Collection, University of North Carolina, Chapel Hill
   Isaac Alexander Letters
   Edward W. Allen Papers
   Allen-Simpson Papers
   Clifford Anderson Papers
   C. H. Andrews Papers
   J. T. Armstrong Papers
   Barkley Family Papers
   Beckwith Family Papers
   Thomas F. Boatright Papers
   R. H. Browne Papers
   N. H. R. Dawson Papers
   George Phifer Erwin Papers
   James Iredell Hall Papers
State Historical Society of Wisconsin, Madison
   P. J. Arndt Letter
   Autobiographical Notes by Wisconsin Veterans of the War of Secession

Charles L. Ballard Letters
John J. Barney Papers
William K. Barney Papers
Caleb Beal and Joseph James Clark Papers
Sidney A. Bean Papers
Charles E. Beecham Letters
Henry W. Beecham Letters
Elon G. Beers Diary
Ferdinand Bennett Diary
Sara Billings Letters
Bird Family Papers
John Black Letters
Oliva A. Brown Letters
Daniel Buck Letter
George B. Carter Letters
Richard E. Carter Letters
Robert Caystile Letter
George W. Chandler Letter
Hamlin L. Chapman Reminiscences
Lewis Chase Papers
Albert M. Childs Papers
William Henry Church Letters
George C. Clapp Letters
Henry Clemons Letters
Eugene E. Comstock Papers
George A. Cooley Diary
David Coon Papers
Wilson S. Covill Letters
Luther H. Cowan Papers
Richard Robert Crowe Papers
Henry Miller Culbertson Letters
Michael Cunningham Letters
Horace Currier Papers
Gasherie Decker Papers
George Dewey Letter
Eliza Wilcox Graves Letter
Harrison Family Papers
Samuel Cotter Kirkpatrick Letters
Ladies Union League Papers
Abraham Lincoln Letter
William C. Mefert Diary
Miscellaneous Confederate Letters

Emilie Quiner Diary
George Wells Sermon
United States Army Military History Institute, Carlisle Barracks, Pennsylvania
Civil War Miscellaneous Collection
   Amos S. Abbott Papers
   Alonzo Alden Letter
   Alvin H. Alexander Papers
   Anderson-Capehart-McCowan Family Papers
   Ashley Family Papers
   Jabez Banbury Papers
   John W. Bates Papers
   Rufus Bates Papers
   A. F. Beard Papers
   Jonathan Beaty Letters
   Simon Bennage Diary
   Wesley W. Bierly Diary
   Matthew Bracken Black Papers
   David Humphrey Blair Diary and Letters
   George H. Blakeslee Papers
   John H. Boyer Letters
   Jonathan W. W. Boynton Reminiscences
   William F. Boynton Letters
   Charles S. Bullard Papers
   William N. Bullard Papers
   William Burge Papers
   Gideon W. Burtch Papers
   John Howes Burton Letter
   Henry C. Campbell Recollections
   Henry T. Card Letter
   Robert H. Carnahan Papers
   George C. Chandler Letters
   Melvin L. Clark Papers
   Collier Family Papers
   John W. Compton Letters
   S. P. Conrad Letters
   David Cornwell Memoir
   Oscar Cram Letters
   Henry and Seth Crowhurst Papers
   Martin Davis Papers
   Thomas M. Davis Letters
   DeForest Family Letters
   Thomas B. Douglas Papers

Henry O. Dwight Papers
John M. Eaton Letter
Reese H. Egbert Letters
Jonas Denton Elliott Papers
Evans Family Papers
Thomas Lewis Evans Papers
Henry Fical Papers
Andrew Wellington Fink Papers
Thomas Y. Finley Papers
Lucian A. Foote Letter
Brigham Foster Letters
William Frink Papers
Ichabod Frisbie Papers
Abram Fulkerson Papers
Joseph B. Fuson Papers
John Garing Papers
Jasper P. George Papers
James H. Gillam Papers
Abijah F. Gore Papers
U. S. Grant Papers
Alpheus Harding Papers
Joseph W. Hawley Letters
David Helmick Papers
William Homan Diary
Henry Hoyt Letters
Simon Hubler Papers
Andrew Hug Papers
A. K. Humphrey Papers
Bezeleel Parker Hunt Papers
William Issard Papers
George W. Johnson Letter
Francis M. Johnson Papers
William H. Jones Papers
Royal N. Joy Papers
Edwin W. Keen Letter
George Keever Papers
Orrin Albert Kellam Papers
Kelly Family Papers
Charles Abbot Kennedy Papers
Ezra Kidder Papers
Ensign H. King Papers
Jacob Klein Letters

Dexter B. Ladd Diary
John W. Latimer Letter
Reynolds Laughlin Papers
Jacob Lester Papers
John Levy Letter
Camden Lewis Papers
John B. Linn Papers
Charles B. Loop Papers
Levi Losier Papers
Mark P. Lowrey Autobiography
Peter S. Ludwig Diary
Charles H. Lutz Papers
James Magill Papers
Isaac Mann Letters
George S. Marks Papers
Samuel J. Marks Papers
Massachusetts Infantry—16th
Charles Maxim Letters
William W. McCarty Papers
John J. McKee Diary
Elliott B. McKeever Papers
Luther B. Mesnard Papers
Frank Metcalf Letters
William A. Miller Reminiscences
William A. Moore Memoirs
Henry T. Morgan Letters
Charles C. Morrey Papers
Annesley N. Morton Letters
John Morton Letters
William C. Murray Papers
George Muzzey Letters
New York Infantry—81st
New York Infantry—126th
Oliver Norton Papers
John O'Connell Papers
William W. Osborn Papers
Aaron Overstreet Papers
Richard Packard Letter
Byron D. Paddock Letters
W. W. Parker Papers
Parks-Towle-Ferguson Family Papers
James H. Patton Papers

James Williams Letter
Julius Birney Work Diary
Marvin Wright Letter
Sydney T. Wygant Papers
Arthur B. Wyman Papers
Frank R. Young Diary
Christian Zook Papers
Civil War Times Illustrated Collection
  Francis A. Dawes Papers
  William B. Hazen Papers
  Andrew Hickenlooper Papers
  David McKinney Papers
  Frederick Pell Papers
  Edward Schweitzer Papers
  Adolphus P. Wolf Papers
Harrisburg Civil War Round Table Collection
  John Carr Papers
  James W. Denver Papers
  W. R. Eddington Papers
  Edgar Embley Papers
  Thomas P. LaRue Papers
  Valentine Rau Papers
  Charles C. Wilson Papers
  Enoch Weiss Papers
  Gregory A. Coco Collection
    Charles H. Kibler Papers
    Roswell L. Root Papers
    Howard and Victor H. Stevens Papers
    Joseph Stockton Papers
  William Margold Collection
    Charles C. Wilson Papers
  William T. Sherman Papers
  Joseph A. Sladen Papers
Vicksburg National Military Park
  R. W. Burt Letters
Virginia Historical Society, Richmond
  Jim A. Letters
  Charles Jefferies Anderson Letter
  William Roane Aylett Letter
  William Gaines Baldwin Papers
  Charles Edward Bates Papers
  John Yates Beall Papers

Bernard Family Papers
Burke Family Papers
Diary, unidentified author, Mss5:1 Un3:5
Fourteen Months in Prison, unidentified author
Western Historical Manuscript Collection, Ellis Library, University of Missouri, Columbia
  Richard W. Burt Letters
Western Reserve Historical Society, Cleveland, Ohio
  Franklin Augustus Wise Diary

                        Published Primary Sources

Allen, George H. *Forty-six Months with the Fourth R.I. Volunteers, in the War of 1861 to 1865.*
  Providence, R.I.: J. A. and R. A. Reid, 1887.
Andrus, Onley. *The Civil War Letters of Sergeant Onley Andrus.* Edited by Fred Albert
  Shannon. Urbana: University of Illinois Press, 1947.
Ankeny, Henry G. *Kiss Josey For Me.* Edited by Florence Marie Ankeny Cox. Santa Ana,
  Calif.: Friss-Pioneer Press, 1974.
Barber, Flavel C. *Holding the Line: The Third Tennessee Infantry, 1861–1864.* Edited by
  Robert H. Ferrell. Kent, Ohio: Kent State University Press, 1994.
Barber, Lucius W. *Army Memoirs of Lucius W. Barber, Company "D," 15th Illinois Volunteer
  Infantry.* Chicago: J. M. W. Jones Stationery and Printing Co., 1894.
Bardeen, Charles W. *A Little Fifer's War Diary.* Syracuse, N.Y.: author, 1910.
Barker, Lorenzo A. *With the Western Sharpshooters: Michigan Boys of Company D, 66th Illi-
  nois.* 1905. Reprint, Huntington, W.V.: Blue Acorn Press, 1994.
Barrett, Orvey S. *Reminiscences, Incidents, Battles, Marches and Camp Life of the Old 4th Michi-
  gan Infantry in the War of Rebellion, 1861 to 1864.* Detroit: W. S. Ostler, 1888.
Bates, James C. *A Texas Cavalry Officer's Civil War: The Diary and Letters of James C. Bates.*
  Edited by Richard Lowe. Baton Rouge: Louisiana State University Press, 1999.
Battle, Cullen Andrews. *Third Alabama! The Civil War Memoir of Brigadier General Cullen
  Andrews Battle, C.S.A.* Edited by Brandon H. Beck. Tuscaloosa: University of Alabama
  Press, 2000.
Beatty, John. *Memoirs of a Volunteer, 1861–1863.* New York: W. W. Norton, 1946.
Bellard, Alfred. *Gone for a Soldier: The Civil War Memoirs of Private Alfred Bellard.* Edited
  by David H. Donald. Boston: Little, Brown, 1975.
Bennett, William W. *A Narrative of the Great Revival in the Southern Armies During the Late
  Civil War Between the States of the Federal Union.* Philadelphia: Claxton, Remsen and
  Haffelfinger, 1877.
Bicknell, George W. *History of the Fifth Maine Volunteers.* Portland, Me.: K. I. Davis, 1871.
Billings, John D. *Hardtack and Coffee: Or, The Unwritten Story of Army Life.* 1887. Reprint,
  Lincoln: University of Nebraska Press, 1993.

Blackford, Susan Leigh, and Charles Minor Blackford. *Letters from Lee's Army: Memoirs of Life in and out of the Army in Virginia During the War Between the States.* New York: A. S. Barnes, 1947.

Blanchard, Ira. *I Marched with Sherman: Civil War Memoirs of the 20th Illinois Volunteer Infantry.* San Francisco: J. D. Huff, 1992.

Boyd, Cyrus F. *The Civil War Diary of Cyrus F. Boyd, Fifteenth Iowa Infantry, 1861–1863.* Edited by Mildred Thorne. Millwood, N.Y.: Kraus, 1977.

Brett, David. *"My Dear Wife": The Civil War Letters of David Bragg, 9th Massachusetts Battery, Union Cannoneer.* Edited by Frank Putnam Dean. Privately printed, 1964.

Brewer, S. J. G. *My Dear Wife from Your Devoted Husband S J. G. Brewer: Letters from a Rebel Soldier to His Wife.* Edited by H. Candler Thaxton. Warrington, Fla.: privately printed, 1968.

Bright, Adam S., and Michael S. Bright. *"Respects to All": Letters of Two Pennsylvania Boys in the War of the Rebellion.* Edited by Aida Craig Truxall. Pittsburgh: University of Pittsburgh Press, 1962.

Bull, Rice C. *Soldiering: The Civil War Diary of Rice C. Bull, 123rd New York Volunteer Infantry.* Edited by K. Jack Bauer. San Rafael, Calif.: Presidio Press, 1977.

Burgwyn, William H. S. *A Captain's War: The Letters and Diaries of William H. S. Burgwyn, 1861–1865.* Edited by Herbert M. Schiller. Shippensburg, Pa.: White Mane, 1994.

Buxton, Rufus B. "The Buxton Journal." *Licking Countian* 7, no. 35 (March 13, 1986).

Callaway, Joshua K. *The Civil War Letters of Joshua K. Callaway.* Edited by Judith Lee Hallock. Athens: University of Georgia Press, 1997.

Campbell, John Quincy Adams. *The Union Must Stand: The Civil War Diary of John Quincy Adams Campbell, Fifth Iowa Volunteer Infantry.* Edited by Mark Grimsley and Todd D. Miller. Knoxville: University of Tennessee Press, 2000.

Cannon, J. P. *Bloody Banners and Barefoot Boys: A History of the 27th Regiment Alabama Infantry CSA, the Civil War Memoirs and Diary Entries of J. P. Cannon, M.D.* Edited by Noel Crowson and John V. Brogden. Shippensburg, Pa.: Burd Street Press, 1997.

Cannon, Le Grand B. *Reminiscences of the Rebellion, 1861–1866.* Freeport, N.Y.: Books for Libraries Press, 1971.

Chamberlayne, John Hampden. *Ham Chamberlayne, Virginian: Letters and Papers of an Artillery Officer in the War for Southern Independence, 1861–1865.* Richmond, Va.: Dietz, 1932. Reprint, Wilimington, N.C.: Broadfoot, 1992.

Chipman, Albert. "'We Must Do the Best We Can': The Civil War Letters of Albert Chipman 76th Illinois Infantry." Edited by Daniel E. Sutherland. *Military History of the West* 28 (1998): 49–94, 185–224.

Chisholm, Daniel. *The Civil War Notebook of Daniel Chisholm: A Chronicle of Daily Life in the Union Army, 1864–1865.* Edited by W. Springer Menge and J. August Shimrak. New York: Orion, 1989.

Coe, Hamlin Alexander. *Mine Eyes Have Seen the Glory: Combat Diaries of Union Sergeant Hamlin Alexander Coe.* Rutherford, N.J.: Fairleigh Dickinson University Press, 1975.

Coles, Robert T. *From Huntsville to Appomattox: R. T. Coles's History of the 4th Regiment, Alabama Volunteer Infantry, C.S.A., Army of Northern Virginia.* Edited by Jeffrey D. Stocker. Knoxville: University of Tennessee Press, 1996.

Collins, George K. *Memoirs of the 149th Regiment New York Volunteer Infantry.* Syracuse, N.Y.: author, 1891.

Connelly, Thomas W. *History of the Seventieth Ohio Regiment from Its Organization to Its Mustering Out.* Cincinnati: Peak Brothers, 1894.

Connolly, James A. *Three Years in the Army of the Cumberland: The Letters and Diary of Major James A. Connolly.* Edited by Paul M. Angle. Bloomington: Indiana University Press, 1959.

Conolly, Thomas. *An Irishman in Dixie: Thomas Conolly's Diary of the Fall of the Confederacy.* Edited by Nelson D. Lankford. Columbia: University of South Carolina Press, 1988.

Crotty, Daniel G. *Four Years Campaigning in the Army of the Potomac.* Kearny, N.J.: Belle Grove, 1995.

Cunningham, Sumner A. *Reminiscences of the Forty-first Tennessee Regiment.* Edited by John A. Simpson. Nashville: Vanderbilt University Press, 1997.

Cutrer, Thomas W., and T. Michael Parrish, eds. *Brothers in Gray: The Civil War Letters of the Pierson Family.* Baton Rouge: Louisiana State University Press, 1997.

Daniels, Nathan W. *Thank God My Regiment an African One: The Civil War Diary of Colonel Nathan W. Daniels.* Edited by C. P. Weaver. Baton Rouge: Louisiana State University Press, 1998.

Dawson, Francis W. *Reminiscences of Confederate Service, 1861–1865.* Edited by Bell I. Wiley. Baton Rouge: Louisiana State University Press, 1980.

De Forest, John William. *A Volunteer's Adventures: A Union Captain's Record of the Civil War.* Edited by James H. Croushore. New Haven, Conn.: Yale University Press, 1946.

Dexter, Seymour. *Seymour Dexter, Union Army: Journal and Letters of Civil War Service in Company K, 23rd New York Volunteer Regiment of Elmira.* Edited by Carl A. Morrell. Jefferson, N.C.: McFarland, 1996.

Dunham, Alburtus A., and Charles LaForest Dunham. *Through the South with a Union Soldier.* Edited by Arthur R. DeRosier, Jr. Johnson City: East Tennessee State University Reserach Advisory Council, 1969.

Ely, Ralph. *With the Wandering Regiment: The Diary of Captain Ralph Ely of the Eighth Michigan Infantry.* Edited by George M. Blackburn. Mt. Pleasant: Central Michigan University Press, 1965.

Ensminger, Samuel. *Letters to Lanah: A Civil War Soldier Writes Home.* Edited by Clarence M. Swinn, Jr. Gettysburg, Pa.: privately published, 1986.

Fay, Edwin H. *"This Infernal War": The Confederate Letters of Sgt. Edwin H. Fay.* Edited by Bell Irvin Wiley. Austin: University of Texas Press, 1958.

Fielder, Alfred Tyler. *The Civil War Diaries of Capt. Alfred Tyler Fielder, 12th Tennessee Regiment Infantry, Company B, 1861–1865.* Edited by Ann York Franklin. Louisville, Ky.: privately published, 1996.

Finney, Charles G. *Revival Lectures.* Reprint, Old Tappan, N.J.: Fleming Revell, 1970.

Fisk, Wilbur. *Hard Marching Every Day: The Civil War Letters of Private Wilbur Fisk, 1861–1865.* Edited by Emil Rosenblatt and Ruth Rosenblatt. Lawrence: University Press of Kansas, 1992.

Gaff, Alan D. *On Many a Bloody Field: Four Years in the Iron Brigade.* Bloomington: Indiana University Press, 1996.

Gallwey, Thomas Francis. *The Valiant Hours.* Edited by W. S. Nye. Harrisburg, Pa.: Stackpole, 1961.

Gantz, Jacob S. *Such Are the Trials: The Civil War Diaries of Jacob Gantz.* Edited by Kathleen Davis. Ames: Iowa State University Press, 1991.

Geer, Allen Morgan. *The Civil War Diary of Allen Morgan Geer: Twentieth Regiment, Illinois Volunteers.* Edited by Mary Ann Andersen. Denver: Robert C. Appleman, 1977.

Giles, Val C. *Rags and Hope: The Recollections of Val C. Giles, Four Years with Hood's Brigade, Fourth Texas Infantry, 1861–1865.* Edited by Mary Lasswell. New York: Coward-McCann, 1961.

Gooding, James Henry. *On the Altar of Freedom: A Black Soldier's Civil War Letters from the Front.* Edited by Virginia Matzke Adams. Amherst: University of Massachusetts Press, 1991.

Green, Johnny. *Johnny Green of the Orphan Brigade: The Journal of a Confederate Soldier.* Edited by A. D. Kirwan. Lexington: University of Kentucky Press, 1956.

Grisamore, Silas T. *The Civil War Reminiscences of Major Silas T. Grisamore.* Edited by Arthur W. Bergeron, Jr. Baton Rouge: Louisiana State University Press, 1993.

Haskell, Franklin Aretas. *Haskell of Gettysburg: His Life and Civil War Papers.* Edited by Frank L. Byrne and Andrew T. Weaver. Madison: State Historical Society of Wisconsin, 1970.

Haydon, Charles B. *For Country, Cause and Leader: The Civil War Journal of Charles B. Haydon.* Edited by Stephen W. Sears. New York: Ticknor and Fields, 1993.

Heller, J. Roderick III, and Carolynn Ayres Heller, eds. *The Confederacy Is on Her Way up the Spout: Letters to South Carolina, 1861–1864.* Athens: University of Georgia Press, 1992.

Higginson, Thomas Wentworth. *The Complete Civil War Journal and Selected Letters of Thomas Wentworth Higginson.* Edited by Christopher Looby. Chicago: University of Chicago Press, 2000.

Hitchcock, Henry. *Marching with Sherman: Passages from the Letters and Campaign Diaries of Henry Hitchcock.* Edited by M. A. de Wolfe Howe. New Haven, Conn.: Yale University Press, 1927. Reprint, Lincoln: University of Nebraska Press, 1995.

Holmes, Oliver Wendell, Jr. *Touched with Fire: Civil War Letters and Diary of Oliver Wendell Holmes, Jr., 1861–1864.* Edited by Mark de Wolfe Howe. Cambridge, Mass.: Harvard University Press, 1947.

Holmes, Robert Masten. *Kemper County Rebel: The Civil War Diary of Robert Masten Holmes, C.S.A.* Edited by Frank Allen Dennis. Jackson: University and College Press of Mississippi, 1973.

Holt, David. *A Mississippi Rebel in the Army of Northern Virginia.* Edited by Thomas D. Cockrell and Michael B. Ballard. Baton Rouge: Louisiana State University, 1995.

Holzer, Harold, ed. *Dear Mr. Lincoln: Letters to the President.* Reading, Mass.: Addison-Wesley, 1993.

Hough, Alfred Lacey. *Soldier in the West: The Civil War Letters of Alfred Lacey Hough.* Edited by Robert G. Athearn. Philadelphia: University of Pennsylvania Press, 1957.

Jackson, Isaac. *Some of the Boys: The Civil War Letters of Isaac Jackson, 1862–1865.* Carbondale: Southern Illinois University Press, 1960.

Johnson, Hannibal Augustus. *The Sword of Honor: A Story of the Civil War.* Worcester, Mass.: Blanchard Press, 1906.

Jones, J. William. *Christ in the Camp: Or, Religion in the Confederate Army.* 1904. Reprint, Harrisonburg, Va.: Sprinkle Publications, 1986.

Kauffman, Henry. *The Civil War Letters of Private Henry Kauffman: The Harmony Boys Are All Well.* Edited by David McCordick. Lewiston, N.Y.: Edwin Mellen Press, 1991.

Kircher, Henry A. *A German in the Yankee Fatherland: The Civil War Letters of Henry A. Kircher.* Edited by Earl J. Hess. Kent, Ohio: Kent State University Press, 1983.

Leeke, Jim. *A Hundred Days to Richmond: Ohio's "Hundred Days" Men in the Civil War.* Bloomington: Indiana University Press, 1999.

Livermore, Mary. *My Story of the War.* Hartford, Conn.: A. D. Worthington, 1890.

Marshall, Jeffrey D.. *A War of the People: Vermont Civil War Letters.* Hanover, N.H.: University Press of New England, 1999.

Matrau, Henry. *Letters Home: Henry Matrau of the Iron Brigade.* Edited by Marcia Reid-Green. Lincoln: University of Nebraska Press, 1993.

McCarter, William. *My Life in the Irish Brigade: The Civil War Memoirs of Private William McCarter, 116th Pennsylvania Infantry.* Edited by Kevin E. O'Brien. Campbell, Calif.: Savas, 1996.

McIlvaine, Samuel. *By the Dim and Flaring Lamps: The Civil War Diaries of Samuel McIlvaine.* Edited by Clayton E. Cramer. Monroe, N.Y.: Library Research Associates, 1990.

McMahon, John T. *John T. McMahon's Diary of the 136th New York, 1861–1864.* Edited by John Michael Priest. Shippensburg, Pa.: White Mane, 1993.

Montgomery, William Rhadamanthus. *Georgia Sharpshooter: The Civil War Diary and Letters of William Rhadamanthus Montgomery.* Edited by George Montgomery, Jr. Macon, Ga.: Mercer University Press, 1997.

Mosman, Chesley A. *The Rough Side of War: The Civil War Journal of Chesley A. Mosman, 1st Lieutenant, Company D, 59th Illinois Volunteer Infantry Regiment.* Edited by Arnold Gates. Garden City, N.Y.: Basin Publishing, 1987.

Musser, Charles O. *Soldier Boy: The Civil War Letters of Charles O. Musser, 29th Iowa.* Iowa City: University of Iowa Press, 1995.

Newton, James K. *A Wisconsin Boy in Dixie: The Selected Letters of James K. Newton.* Edited by Stephen E. Ambrose. Madison: University of Wisconsin Press, 1961.

Olmstead, William B., John M. Critchlow, A. T. Jennings, and Thoro Harris, eds. *The Free Methodist Hymnal.* Chicago: Free Methodist Publishing House, 1910.

Pettit, Ira S. *The Diary of a Dead Man: Letters and Diary of Private Ira S. Pettit.* Edited by Jean P. Ray. N.p.: Acorn Press, 1979.

Poriss, Gerry Harder, and Ralph G. Poriss. *While My Country Is in Danger: The Life and Letters of Lieutenant Colonel Richard S. Thompson, Twelfth New Jersey Volunteers.* Hamilton, N.Y.: Edmonston Publishing, 1994.

Post, Lydia Minturn, ed. *Soldiers' Letters from Camp, Battlefield and Prison.* New York: Bunce and Huntington, 1865.

Rhodes, Elisha Hunt. *All for the Union: The Civil War Diary and Letters of Elisha Hunt Rhodes.* Edited by Robert Hunt Rhodes. New York: Orion Books, 1985.

Rogers, George. "My Dear Friend." *In Camp on the Rappahannock: The Newsletter of the Blue & Gray Education Society* 4, no. 2 (fall 1998).

Roy, Andrew. *Fallen Soldier: Memoir of a Civil War Casualty.* Edited by William J. Miller. Birmingham, Ala.: Elliott and Clark, 1996.

Scott, R. B. *The History of the 67th Regiment, Indiana Infantry Volunteers.* Bedford, Ind.: Herald Book and Job Printing, 1892.

Seymour, William J. *The Civil War Memoirs of Captain William J. Seymour: Reminiscences of a Louisiana Tiger.* Edited by Terry L. Jones. Baton Rouge: Louisiana State University Press, 1991.

Shanklin, James Maynard. *Dearest Lizzie: The Civil War Letters of Lt. Col. James Maynard Shanklin.* Edited by Kenneth P. McCutchan. Evansville, Ind.: Friends of Willard Library Press, 1988.

Silber, Nina, and Mary Beth Sievens, eds. *Yankee Correspondence: Civil War Letters Between New England Soldiers and the Home Front.* Charlottesville: University Press of Virginia, 1996.

Simpson, Dick, and Tally Simpson. *"Far, Far from Home": The Wartime Letters of Dick and Tally Simpson, Third South Carolina Volunteers.* Edited by Guy R. Everson and Edward H. Simpson, Jr. New York: Oxford University Press, 1994.

Small, Abner R. *The Road to Richmond: The Civil War Memoirs of Maj. Abner R. Small of the 16th Maine Vols.: With His Diary as a Prisoner of War.* Edited by Harold Adams Small. Berkeley: University of California Press, 1959.

Smith, Benjamin T. *Private Smith's Journal: Recollections of the Late War.* Edited by Clyde C. Walton. Chicago: Lakeside Press, 1963.

Stearns, Austin C. *Three Years with Company K.* Edited by Arthur A. Kent. Rutherford, N.J.: Fairleigh Dickinson University Press, 1976.

Stephenson, Philip Daingerfield. *The Civil War Memoir of Philip Daingerfield Stephenson, D.D.* Edited by Nathaniel Cheairs Hughes, Jr. Baton Rouge: Louisiana State University Press, 1995.

Stevenson, Thomas M. *History of the 78th Regiment O.V.V.I. from Its "Muster-in" to Its "Muster-out."* Zanesville, Ohio: Hugh Dunne, 1865.

Stillwell, William Ross. "My Dear Molly." *In Camp on the Rappahannock: The Newsletter of the Blue & Gray Education Society* 4, no. 3 (spring 1999).

Stockwell, Elisha, Jr. *Private Elisha Stockwell, Jr., Sees the Civil War.* Edited by Byron R. Abernethy. Norman: University of Oklahoma Press, 1958.

Stuber, Johann. *Mein Tagebuch über die Erlebnisse im Revolutions-Kriege.* Cincinnati: S. Rosenthal, 1896.

Stuckenberg, John Henry Wilburn. *I'm Surrounded by Methodists: Diary of John H. W. Stuckenberg, Chaplain of the 145th Pennsylvania Volunteer Infantry.* Edited by David T. Hedrik and Gordon Barry Davis, Jr. Gettysburg, Pa.: Thomas Publications, 1995.

Theaker, James G. *Through One Man's Eyes: The Civil War Experiences of a Belmont County Volunteer.* Edited by Paul E. Rieger. Mt. Vernon, Ohio: Printing Arts Press, 1974.

Tyler, William N. *The Dispatch Carrier.* Bernalillo, N.M.: Joel Beer and Gwendy MacMaster, 1992.

———. *Memoirs of Andersonville.* Bernalillo, N.M.: Joel Beer and Gwendy MacMaster, 1992.

United States War Department. *The War of the Rebellion: Official Records of the Union and Confederate Armies.* 128 vols. Washington, D.C.: Government Printing Office, 1881–1901.

Upson, Theodore F. *With Sherman to the Sea: The Civil War Letters, Diaries and Reminiscences of Theodore F. Upson.* Edited by Oscar Osburn Winther. Bloomington: Indiana University Press, 1977.

Watkins, Samuel R. *"Co. Aytch," Maury Grays, First Tennessee Regiment; or, A Side Show of the Big Show.* Wilmington, N.C.: Broadfoot, 1987.

Welsh, Peter. *Irish Green and Union Blue: The Civil War Letters of Peter Welsh, Color Sergeant, 28th Regiment Massachusetts Volunteers.* Edited by Lawrence Frederick Kohl and Margaret Cosse Richard. New York: Fordham University Press, 1986.

Whitney, Joseph. *Kiss Clara for Me: The Story of Joseph Whitney and His Family, Early Days in the Midwest, and Soldiering in the American Civil War.* Edited by Robert J. Snetsinger. State College, Pa.: Carnation Press, 1969.

Wilkeson, Frank. *Recollections of a Private Soldier in the Army of the Potomac.* 1886. Reprint, Freeport, N.Y.: Books for Libraries Press, 1972.

Williams, Alpheus S. *From the Cannon's Mouth: The Civil War Letters of General Alpheus S. Williams.* Edited by Milo M. Quaife. Detroit: Wayne State University Press and the Detroit Historical Society, 1959.

Williams, John Melvin. *The Eagle Regiment.* Belleville, Wis.: Recorder Print, 1890.

Willison, Charles A. *Reminiscences of a Boy's Service with the 76th Ohio.* 1908. Reprint, Huntington, W.V.: Blue Acorn Press, 1995.

Wills, Charles W. *Army Life of an Illinois Soldier.* Carbondale: Southern Illinois University Press, 1996.

Willsey, Bera M. *The Civil War Diary of Berea M. Willsey: The Intimate Daily Obersvations of a Massachusetts Volunteer in the Union Army, 1862–1864.* Edited by Jessica H. DeMay. Bowie, Md.: Heritage Books, 1995.

Wilson, Suzanne Colton. *Column South: With the 15th Pennsylvania Cavalry.* Flagstaff, Ariz.: J. F. Colton, 1960.

Winters, William. *The Musick of the Mocking Birds, the Roar of the Cannon: The Civil War Diary and Letters of William Winters.* Edited by Steven E. Woodworth. Lincoln: University of Nebraska Press, 1998.

Woodward, Evan Morrison. *Our Campaigns: The Second Regiment Pennsylvania Reserve Volunteers, 1861–1864.* Edited by Stanley W. Zamonski. Shippensburg, Pa.: Burd Street Press, 1995.

Wren, James. *From New Bern to Fredericksburg: Captain James Wren's Diary.* Edited by John Michael Priest. Shippensburg, Pa.: White Mane, 1990.

Secondary Works

Abernethy, Thomas P. *The South in the New Nation, 1789–1819.* Baton Rouge: Louisiana State University, 1961.

Armstrong, Warren B. *For Courageous Fighting and Confident Dying: Union Chaplains in the Civil War.* Lawrence: University Press of Kansas, 1998.

Arnold, James R. *Grant Wins the War: Decision at Vicksburg.* New York: John Wiley and Sons, 1997.

Ash, Stephen V. *When the Yankees Came: Conflict and Chaos in the Occupied South, 1861–1865.* Chapel Hill: University of North Carolina Press, 1995.

Barton, David. *The Myth of Separation.* Aledo, Tex.: WallBuilder Press, 1991.

Barton, Michael. *Goodmen: The Character of Civil War Soldiers.* University Park: Penn State University Press, 1981.

Blair, William. *Virginia's Private War: Feeding Body and Soul in the Confederacy, 1861–1865.* New York: Oxford University Press, 1998.

Boles, John B. *The Great Revival, 1787–1805.* Lexington: University Press of Kentucky, 1972.

Carmichael, Peter S. "Christian Warriors." *Columbiad* 3 (summer 1999): 88–106.

Clebsch, William A. *Christian Interpretations of the Civil War.* Philadelphia: Fortress Press, 1969.

Clinton, Catherine. *Civil War Stories.* Athens: University of Georgia Press, 1998.

Cooling, Benjamin Franklin. *Fort Donelson's Legacy: War and Society in Kentucky and Tennessee, 1861–1863.* Knoxville: University of Tennessee Press, 1997.

Craven, Avery O. *The Growth of Southern Nationalism, 1848–1861.* Baton Rouge: Louisiana State University Press, 1953.

Daniel, Larry J. *Soldiering in the Army of Tennessee: A Portrait of Life in a Confederate Army.* Chapel Hill: University of North Carolina Press, 1991.

Davis, William C. *A Government of Our Own: The Making of the Confederacy.* New York: Free Press, 1994.

Eidsmoe, John. *Christianity and the Constitution: The Faith of Our Founding Fathers.* Grand Rapids, Mich.: Baker, 1987.

Farmer, James Oscar, Jr. *The Metaphysical Confederacy: James Henley Thornwell and the Synthesis of Southern Values.* Macon, Ga.: Mercer University Press, 1986.

Gallagher, Gary W. *The Confederate War.* Cambridge, Mass.: Harvard University Press, 1997.

————. *Lee and His Generals in War and Memory*. Baton Rouge: Louisiana State University Press, 1998.

————, ed. *The Wilderness Campaign*. Chapel Hill: University of North Carolina Press, 1997.

Genovese, Eugene D. *A Consuming Fire: The Fall of the Confederacy in the Mind of the White Christian South*. Athens: University of Georgia Press, 1998.

Gordon, Lesley J. *General George E. Picket in Life and Legend*. Chapel Hill: University of North Carolina Press, 1998.

Grimsley, Mark. *The Hard Hand of War*. New York: Cambridge University Press, 1995.

Guelzo, Allen. *Abraham Lincoln: Redeemer President*. Grand Rapids, Mich.: Eerdmans, 1999.

Guth, James L., et al. *The Bully Pulpit: The Politics of Protestant Clergy*. Lawrence: University Press of Kansas, 1997.

Hattaway, Herman. *Shades of Blue and Gray: An Introductory Military History of the Civil War*. Columbia: University of Missouri Press, 1997.

Hennessy, John J. *Return to Bull Run: The Campaign and Battle of Second Manassas*. New York: Simon and Schuster, 1993.

Hughes, Nathaniel Cheairs, Jr. *The Battle of Belmont: Grant Strikes South*. Chapel Hill: University of North Carolina Press, 1995.

Joslyn, Mauriel Phillips, ed. *A Meteor Shining Brightly: Essays on Maj. Gen. Patrick R. Cleburne*. Milledgeville, Ga.: Terrell House, 1997.

Linderman, Gerald F. *Embattled Courage: The Experience of Combat in the American Civil War*. New York: Free Press, 1987.

Marten, James. *Texas Divided: Loyalty and Dissent in the Lone Star State, 1856–1874*. Lexington: University of Kentucky Press, 1990.

McPherson, James M. *For Cause and Comrades: Why Men Fought in the Civil War*. New York: Oxford University Press, 1997.

Miller, Edward A., Jr. *The Black Civil War Soldiers of Illinois: The Story of the Twenty-ninth U.S. Colored Infantry*. Columbia: University of South Carolina Press, 1998.

Miller, Randall M., Harry S. Stout, and Charles Reagan Wilson, eds. *Religion and the American Civil War*. New York: Oxford University Press, 1998.

Mitchell, Reid. *Civil War Soldiers*. New York: Viking, 1988.

————. *The Vacant Chair: The Northern Soldier Leaves Home*. New York: Oxford University Press, 1993.

Myers, Robert Manson, ed. *The Children of Pride: A True Story of Georgia and the Civil War*. New Haven, Conn.: Yale University Press, 1972.

Noll, Mark. "The Puzzling Faith of Abraham Lincoln." *Christian History* 11 (1992): 10–15.

Oates, Stephen B. *With Malice Toward None: The Life of Abraham Lincoln*. New York: Harper and Row, 1977.

Olasky, Marvin. *Abortion Rites: A Social History of Abortion in America*. Washington, D.C.: Regnery, 1995.

————. *The Tragedy of American Compassion*. Washington, D.C.: Regnery, 1992.

Overmyer, Jack K. *A Stupendous Effort: The 87th Indiana in the War of the Rebellion.* Bloomington: Indiana University Press, 1997.

Owen, Christopher H. *The Sacred Flame of Love: Methodism and Society in Nineteenth-Century Georgia.* Athens: University of Georgia Press, 1998.

Paludan, Phillip Shaw. *The Presidency of Abraham Lincoln.* Lawrence: University Press of Kansas, 1994.

Piston, William Garrett, and Richard W. Hatcher III. *Wilson's Creek: The Second Battle of the Civil War and the Men Who Fought It.* Chapel Hill: University of North Carolina Press, 2000.

Power, Tracy J. *Lee's Miserables: Life in the Army of Northern Virginia from the Wilderness to Appomattox.* Chapel Hill: University of North Carolina Press, 1998.

Rable, George. *The Confederate Republic: A Revolution Against Politics.* Chapel Hill: University of North Carolina Press, 1994.

Robertson, James I., Jr. *Soldiers Blue and Gray.* Columbia: University of South Carolina Press, 1988.

———. *Stonewall Jackson.* New York: Macmillan, 1998.

Schaeffer, Francis A. *How Should We Then Live.* Westchester, Ill.: Crossway Books, 1976. Reprinted in *The Complete Works of Francis A. Schaeffer.* 5 vols. Westchester, Ill.: Crossway Books, 1982.

Shattuck, Gardiner H., Jr. "Revivals in the Camp." *Christian History* 11 (1992): 28–31.

———. *A Shield and Hiding Place: The Religious Life of the Civil War Armies.* Macon, Ga.: Mercer University Press, 1987.

Sheldon, Henry C. *History of the Christian Church.* 5 vols. 1895. Reprint, Peabody, Mass.: Hendrickson Publishers, 1988.

Sifakis, Stewart. *Who Was Who in the Civil War.* New York: Facts on File, 1988.

Simpson, John A. *S. A. Cunningham and the Confederate Heritage.* Athens: University of Georgia Press, 1994.

Smith, Timothy L. *Revivalism and Social Reform: American Protestantism on the Eve of the Civil War.* Baltimore: Johns Hopkins University Press, 1980.

Stafford, Tim. "The Abolitionists." *Christian History* 11 (1992): 21–25.

Strong, Robert Hale. *A Yankee Private's Civil War.* Edited by Ashley Halsey. Chicago: H. Regnery, 1961.

Sword, Wiley. *Mountains Touched with Fire: Chattanooga Besieged, 1863.* New York: St. Martin's, 1995.

Tanner, Robert G. *Stonewall in the Valley: Thomas J. "Stonewall" Jackson's Shenandoah Valley Campaign, Spring 1862.* Mechanicsburg, Pa.: Stackpole, 1996.

Tucker, Spencer. *Andrew Hull Foote.* Annapolis, Md.: Naval Institute Press, 2000.

Wiley, Bell Irvin. *The Life of Billy Yank: The Common Soldier of the Union.* Indianapolis: Bobbs-Merrill, 1952.

Wilkinson, Warren. *Mother, May You Never See the Sights that I Have Seen: The Fifty-seventh Massachusetts Veteran Volunteers in the Army of the Potomac, 1864–1865.* New York: Harper and Row, 1990.

Wilkinson, Warren, and Steven E. Woodworth. *A Scythe of Fire: The Civil War Story of the Eighth Georgia Regiment.* New York: HarperCollins, in press.

Williams, David. *Rich Man's War: Class, Caste, and Confederate Defeat in the Lower Chatta-hoochee Valley.* Athens: University of Georgia Press, 1998.

Wilson, Charles Reagan. *Baptized in Blood: The Religion of the Lost Cause, 1865–1920.* Athens: University of Georgia Press, 1980.

Woodworth, Steven E. *Cultures in Conflict: The American Civil War.* Westport, Conn.: Greenwood Press, 2000.

INDEX